PENGUIN C

T0368791

THE RAPE OF T.
AND OTHER MAJOR WRITINGS

LEXANDER POPE was born in London in 1688, the son of a
ell-to-do cloth merchant who thought it prudent soon after-
rd to retire from trade in order to avoid penalties against
nan Catholics. Though never especially religious himself, the
emained loyal to the family faith, even when conversion to
urch of England would have brought social and political

showed very early an extraordinary gift for language,
e age of eight became enraptured with poetry through an
translation of Homer. In childhood he contracted
s of the spine, which left him hunchbacked and
nd reinforced a conviction that his best hope for
vas as a writer. When he was twelve his family
ld, near Windsor, where a number of distinguished
uraged his poetic development, and in 1709 he
eer with a set of four pastorals. Soon afterward
icism' (1711) gained fame, and 'Windsor Forest'
liar scenes from his youth to develop an impres-
d political view of England. By the time the
of the Lock' was published (1712, with an aug-
1714), Pope stood unchallenged as the greatest

f Queen Anne in 1714, the writers and states-
e was allied found themselves in permanent
literary rivalries surfaced as well, he found
ticize a culture that he regarded as artistic-
ically corrupt. Meanwhile he settled in a
nham, where he cultivated extensive gar-
lf to the arduous labour of translating
(the latter with the help of others),
independent. After a period of with-
e-emerged in 1728 as a trenchant
Dunciad' (1728) was followed in
ms in a mode of conversational
liantly adapting 'Epistles' and

'Satires' by Horace. Pope's views on psychology and culture were further expressed in a set of four 'Epistles to Several Persons' and in the ambitious 'Essay on Man'. His final major work was an enlarged and revised 'Dunciad' in 1743; he died the following year.

LEO DAMROSCH, Research Professor of Literature at Harvard University, was educated at Yale, Cambridge and Princeton, has taught at the universities of Virginia and Maryland, and is the author of eight books on seventeenth- and eighteenth-century literature and culture, including *The Imaginative World of Alexander Pope*, *God's Plot and Man's Stories: Studies in the Fictional Imagination from Milton to Fielding*, and *Jean-Jacques Rousseau: Restless Genius*.

ALEXANDER POPE

The Rape of the Lock and Other Major Writings

Edited with an Introduction and Notes by
LEO DAMROSCH

PENGUIN BOOKS

PENGUIN CLASSICS

Published by the Penguin Group
Penguin Books Ltd, 80 Strand, London WC2R ORL, England
Penguin Group (USA) Inc., 375 Hudson Street, New York, New York 10014, USA
Penguin Group (Canada), 90 Eglinton Avenue East, Suite 700, Toronto, Ontario,
Canada M4P 2Y3 (a division of Pearson Penguin Canada Inc.)
Penguin Ireland, 25 St Stephen's Green, Dublin 2, Ireland (a division of Penguin Books Ltd)
Penguin Group (Australia), 250 Camberwell Road, Camberwell, Victoria 3124, Australia
(a division of Pearson Australia Group Pty Ltd)
Penguin Books India Pvt Ltd, 11 Community Centre, Panchsheel Park, New Delhi – 110 017, India
Penguin Group (NZ), 67 Apollo Drive, Rosedale, Auckland 0632, New Zealand
(a division of Pearson New Zealand Ltd)
Penguin Books (South Africa) (Pty) Ltd, 24 Sturdee Avenue, Rosebank, Johannesburg 2196, South Africa

Penguin Books Ltd, Registered Offices: 80 Strand, London WC2R ORL, England

www.penguin.com

This collection first published in Penguin Classics 2011

022

Introduction and notes © Leo Damrosch, 2011
All rights reserved

The moral right of the editor has been asserted

Set in 10.25/12.25pt PostScript Adobe Sabon
Typeset by Jouve (UK), Milton Keynes
Printed in Great Britain by Clays Ltd, Elcograf S.p.A.

ISBN: 978-0-140-42350-1

www.greenpenguin.co.uk

MIX
Paper | Supporting
responsible forestry
FSC
www.fsc.org   FSC® C018179

Penguin Books is committed to a sustainable
future for our business, our readers and our planet.
This book is made from Forest Stewardship
Council™ certified paper.

Contents

EARLY POEMS

LATER POEMS

PROSE WRITINGS

Chronology

1688 21 May Born, son of Alexander Pope, linen merchant, and his second wife Edith Turner Pope. In December, in the Glorious Revolution, the Catholic James II is forced to abdicate in favour of his daughter Mary and her husband, William of Orange.

1692 Reacting to restrictions on Catholics in trade, Pope's father moves his family to Hammersmith, outside London.

1700 The family retires to Binfield in Windsor Forest and near Windsor Castle, where the boy's poetic talent is recognized and encouraged by his family and by distinguished friends of advanced years. Contracts tuberculosis of the spine, stunting growth and causing agonizing headaches.

1702 Queen Anne succeeds to the throne. Start of the War of the Spanish Succession.

1704 Jonathan Swift, *A Tale of a Tub* and *The Battle of the Books*. Famous victory by Marlborough at Blenheim, for which the nation will later reward him with Blenheim Palace.

1705 Begins writing *Pastorals*.

1707 Meets Martha and Teresa Blount and forms lifelong friendship, especially with Martha.

1708 St Paul's Cathedral completed, thirty-five years after construction began.

1709 First publication of Pope's poems, in a London miscellany.

1710 Tory ministry formed under Robert Harley and Henry St John (later Lords Oxford and Bolingbroke).

1711 'An Essay on Criticism' immensely successful. Occasional contributions to the new periodical *Spectator*, and short-lived friendship with its co-editor Joseph Addison.

1712 First version of 'The Rape of the Lock', in two cantos.

1713 Forms Scriblerus Club with Swift, John Arbuthnot, John Gay, and Thomas Parnell. Treaty of Utrecht ends the War of the Spanish Succession; the peace is celebrated in 'Windsor Forest'. Addison's tragedy *Cato*, with a prologue by Pope, a great success.

1714 Expanded five-canto 'Rape of the Lock'. Death of Queen Anne and accession of George I ends the Tory ministry, forcing Bolingbroke into exile. Swift reluctantly accepts position as Dean of St Patrick's Cathedral in his native Dublin.

1715 First volume of *Iliad* translation, funded by subscriptions paid by wealthy purchasers (further instalments in each of the next three years). Infatuation with Lady Mary Wortley Montagu, soon to become an enemy. After failure of a Jacobite rebellion intended to restore the Stuart monarchy, legislation further restricts Catholic rights.

1716 In response to the anti-Catholic measures the Pope family moves to Chiswick, close to London.

1717 Pope publishes a volume of *Works*, including some new poems, notably 'Eloisa to Abelard' and 'Elegy to the Memory of an Unfortunate Lady'. Collaborates with Gay and Arbuthnot on a farce, *Three Hours after Marriage*. Death of Pope's father.

1718 Pope leases villa and garden of five acres at Twickenham, where he will spend the rest of his life, and moves there with his mother. Death of Parnell.

1719 Daniel Defoe, *Robinson Crusoe*. Death of Addison.

1720 Final instalment of *Iliad*. South Sea Bubble financial crash, in which Pope is less affected than many of his friends.

1721 Robert Walpole comes to power at the head of a Whig coalition; Pope's political friends will remain in opposition for the rest of his life.

1723 Pope's friend Bishop Francis Atterbury on trial for involvement in a new Jacobite plot; Pope testifies on his behalf. After conviction, Atterbury goes into permanent exile in France. Bolingbroke is pardoned and returns to England, devoting himself henceforth to writing.

1724 Swift's *Drapier's Letters*, exposing a British scheme to enrich profiteers by debasing Irish coinage, makes him a national hero there.

1725 First volumes of translation of the *Odyssey*, with assistance from two collaborators. Six-volume edition of Shakespeare, with preface and notes by Pope.

1726 Final instalment of *Odyssey*. Lewis Theobald's *Shakespeare Restored* attacks Pope's edition. Swift visits Pope, and publishes *Gulliver's Travels*.

1727 In collaboration with Swift, two volumes of *Miscellanies*. Swift's final visit to England. Death of George I, succeeded by George II.

1728 Final volume of *Miscellanies*, including *Peri Bathous*. First edition of 'Dunciad' in three books, with Theobald as anti-hero. Gay's play *The Beggar's Opera* an unprecedented hit.

1729 'Dunciad Variorum', expanded with pseudo-scholarly prefaces and notes. Swift, 'A Modest Proposal'.

1730 The actor Colley Cibber appointed Poet Laureate.

1731 Epistle IV 'To Burlington', first of four poems later collected as *Moral Essays*.

1732 Fourth volume of *Miscellanies*. Death of Gay.

1733 Epistle III 'To Bathurst'. First three books of 'An Essay on Man'. First poems in a series of 'Imitations of Horace'. Death of Pope's mother.

1734 Epistle I 'To Cobham'. Final book of 'Essay on Man'. More Horatian imitations.

1735 'An Epistle to Dr Arbuthnot' (Arbuthnot dies shortly after publication). Epistle II 'To a Lady'. Second volume of *Works*. Pope's letters published by Edmund Curll in an 'unauthorized' edition at which he secretly connives.

1737 More Horatian imitations. 'Authorized' edition of letters. Death of Queen Caroline.

1738 Final imitations of Horace, concluding with 'Epilogue to the Satires'.

1740 Samuel Richardson, *Pamela, or, Virtue Rewarded*.

1741 *Memoirs of Scriblerus*, compiled by Pope from contributions by the now-disbanded Scriblerus Club.

1742 'The New Dunciad' (Book IV). Henry Fielding, *Joseph Andrews*. Swift, succumbing to dementia, officially declared of unsound mind. Handel, *Messiah*. Walpole driven from office and elevated to the House of Lords.

1743 Final four-book 'Dunciad', with Cibber replacing Theobald as the anti-hero.

1744 30 May Death of Pope.

1745 Deaths of Swift and Walpole.

Introduction

Alexander Pope was the greatest British poet for over a century, from the death of Milton in 1674 to the advent of Blake and Wordsworth in the 1790s, yet of all our great poets he is perhaps the least read today. In part this neglect is due to his own choices, especially the inclusion of hundreds of topical references in his later poems that became dated as quickly as they were inserted. But his mastery of sounds, rhythms, and images is nothing short of brilliant, and his insights into human nature are often crystallized so memorably that they have taken root in our common language. 'Hope springs eternal' sounds like a proverb, but it began as an iambic pentameter line by Pope, 'Hope springs eternal in the human breast.'[1] In 'An Essay on Criticism', published in 1711 when he was only twenty-three, familiar expressions repeatedly startle by turning up in their original contexts: 'To err is human, to forgive, divine'; 'For fools rush in where angels fear to tread'; 'A little learning is a dang'rous thing'; 'What oft was thought, but ne'er so well expressed.'[2] Few people are likely to have realized, until the poem was quoted partway through the 2004 film *Eternal Sunshine of the Spotless Mind*, that the title is a line from Pope's 'Eloisa to Abelard', expressing Eloisa's grief at the peace her broken and guilty heart can never know; or as another of his poems has it, 'The soul's calm sunshine, and the heartfelt joy'.[3]

Pope aspired to be a poet of wisdom, and lines like these fulfil that aspiration. Byron called him 'the great moral poet of all times, of all climes, of all feelings, and of all stages of existence . . . His poetry is the Book of Life.'[4] Samuel Johnson, still one of his most insightful critics, declared admiringly that he had 'a mind active, ambitious, and adventurous, always investigating, always aspiring; in its widest searches still longing to go forward, in its highest flights still wishing to be higher; always imagining something greater than it knows, always endeavouring more than it can do'.[5] Yet the story of Pope's career is also one of frustration and lowered aspirations. His extraordinary talent was recognized very early, and by his mid-twenties he had published several masterpieces, including 'The Rape of the Lock'. For the next decade he toiled at translations of the *Iliad* and the *Odyssey* that won him financial independence and would remain standard for nearly a century. But he originally intended to build a career in the manner of Virgil, Spenser, and Milton: after beginning with pastoral and georgic verse, he would assume in due course the mantle of the great epic poet of his age. It was not to be. He could translate epics, and he could write witty mock-epics, but readers didn't care for the elevated grandeur of epic itself. Its scope and narrative energy were being domesticated in a new form, the realist novel, and Pope found himself playing the role that many poets after him have had to play: an eloquent outsider critiquing a culture that no longer pays much attention.

From the beginning, Pope had painful handicaps as well as great abilities. He was born in London into a well-to-do and loving family that warmly encouraged his literary aspirations, but in an era of anti-Catholic repression he was debarred from most careers and even from owning property. In childhood he contracted Pott disease, in which a tubercular infection spreads to the spine. The usual consequences of this condition are progressive bone loss, nerve pain, and deformity, and he experienced all of them. As an adult he was weak, hunchbacked, and four and a half feet tall, condemned to continuous discomfort in what he wryly called 'this long disease, my life'.[6] Amorous by temperament, he formed close friendships with several women, but seems never to have had a sexual relationship, bitterly aware that he was 'that little Alexander the women laugh at'.[7] As his poetic talent matured, he understood that it was not only his best claim to recognition, but offered an imaginative realm that could provide relief from too much actuality. 'Let me tell you,' he wrote to a friend, 'my life in thought and imagination is as much superior to my life in action and reality as the best soul can be to the vilest body.'[8]

Pope's emotional yearnings and sense of exclusion came together unforgettably in 1712, when he was just twenty-four, in the mock-epic 'Rape of the Lock', which dramatizes an incident in which a wilful young aristocrat publicly embarrassed a young belle by snipping off a lock of her hair. Flirtation and seduction are described with an unmistakable note of poignant yearning, which became still more apparent two years later, when Pope unexpectedly brought out an enlarged version. Now female attractions were represented by lovely aerial spirits called 'sylphs', in playful imitation of the gods who watch over mortals in classical epic:

> Some to the sun their insect-wings unfold,
> Waft on the breeze, or sink in clouds of gold;
> Transparent forms too fine for mortal sight,
> Their fluid bodies half dissolved in light . . .
> Some in the fields of purest ether play,
> And bask and whiten in the blaze of day . . .

The sylphs' chief function is to protect the chastity of their young charges, but they are no match for the social game in which rakish 'sparks' pursue women who have every intention of 'melting':

> What guards the purity of melting maids
> In courtly balls, and midnight masquerades,
> Safe from the treach'rous friend, the daring spark,
> The glance by day, the whisper in the dark;
> When kind occasion prompts their warm desires,
> When music softens, and when dancing fires?

The whole point of the game is consummation, and Pope makes

brilliant use of the whalebone braces that undergirded the voluminous gowns of the time:

> To fifty chosen sylphs, of special note,
> We trust th' important charge, the petticoat;
> Oft have we known that sev'n-fold fence to fail,
> Though stiff with hoops, and armed with ribs of whale.

There are hints in the poem, too, of larger concerns that the self-indulgent patrician culture chooses to ignore. Homer indicates seasons and times of day by referring to rural tasks, and Pope gives the epic convention a chilling twist:

> Meanwhile, declining from the noon of day,
> The sun obliquely shoots his burning ray;
> The hungry judges soon the sentence sign,
> And wretches hang that jurymen may dine . . .[9]

A world of political and social implications is crystallized in those lines.

Johnson once declared in conversation, 'Sir, a thousand years may elapse before there shall appear another man with a power of versification equal to that of Pope.'[10] By 'versification' Johnson meant complex effects of rhythm, melody, vowel sounds, alliteration, and rhyme to which his contemporaries were far more attuned than modern readers are likely to be. From this perspective it is poets who have best appreciated Pope; Coleridge admired his 'almost faultless position and the choice of words'.[11] Above all, Pope sought to fill his lines with energy, and he was a tireless reviser. 'He examined lines and words,' Johnson commented, 'with minute and punctilious observation, and retouched every part with indefatigable diligence, till he had nothing left to be forgiven.'[12] The term 'forgiven' is notable: a reader like Johnson was offended by careless writing, such as he thought Dryden often got away with. But the ultimate purpose was to make hard-won harmony seem effortless and inevitable. As Pope himself put it,

> True ease in writing comes from art, not chance,
> As those move easiest who have learned to dance.[13]

He knew how to make language dance, and he was always alert to add force and sharpness to lines that were already excellent.

These skills are apparent in the description of Belinda waking up, at the beginning of 'The Rape of the Lock'. In the original 1712 version it runs like this:

> Sol through white curtains did his beams display,
> And oped those eyes which brighter shine than they;
> Shock had just given himself the rousing shake,
> And nymphs prepared their chocolate to take;
> Thrice the wrought slipper knocked against the ground,
> And striking watches the tenth hour resound.[14]

Contemporary readers appreciated the allusions to everyday experience; in an era when it was difficult to get a light in the night-time, watches would chime the hour when a button was pressed, and 'Shock' was a common name for pet lapdogs. At other points elevated diction rises to the level of romance, though always with an amused sense of incongruity: 'Sol' is a pompous name for the sun, and London ladies are not exactly 'nymphs'.

Other poets of the time might well have been satisfied with these lines, but despite the poem's success, Pope was not. Two years later the passage reappeared (with the principal changes highlighted):

> Sol through white curtains **shot a tim'rous ray,**
> And oped those eyes **that must eclipse the day,**
> **Now lapdogs give themselves the rousing shake,**
> **And sleepless lovers, just at twelve, awake;**
> Thrice **rung the bell,** the slipper knocked the ground,
> And the pressed watch **returned a silver sound.**[15]

The sequence of ideas and even the rhyme-sounds remain the same, but everything is sharper and more energetic. Belinda's eyes don't just shine brighter than the sun – a conventional

hyperbole – but will eclipse the sun altogether, while the bell
and the 'silver sound' of the watch add aural richness to visual.
New verbs contribute punch, as 'did his beams display' becomes
'*shot* a tim'rous ray'. Most tellingly, with teasing irony, lovers
who are conventionally sleepless have in fact slept soundly
until noon, and they share a couplet with the lapdogs, fore-
shadowing the brilliant line later in the poem, 'When husbands,
or when lapdogs breathe their last' (III, 158). No wonder Swift
declared, with affectionate envy,

> In Pope, I cannot read a line
> But with a sigh, I wish it mine:
> When he can in one couplet fix
> More sense than I can do in six,
> It gives me such a jealous fit
> I cry, 'Pox take him, and his wit!'[16]

Pope was a great poet at an earlier age than any English poet
except Keats, and his range seemed limitless. In between the
two versions of 'The Rape of the Lock' he published 'Windsor
Forest', invoking historical associations and the landscape sur-
rounding Windsor Castle, near which he had spent his childhood,
to reflect on the Peace of Utrecht that was finally concluding the
bloody War of the Spanish Succession. The poem's theme is that
violence and cruelty are all too human, and its fantasy is that the
passions of war might be sublimated in the cruel but at least not
homicidal game of hunting. Pope's sympathies are entirely with
the victims in both arenas. Other poets had celebrated Britain's
triumphs in war with complacent generalizations like these:

> Rivers of blood I see, and hills of slain,
> An Iliad rising out of one campaign.[17]

Pope, very differently, imagines the fate of a town besieged by
Britain's 'eager sons':

> Some thoughtless town, with ease and plenty blest,
> Near, and more near, the closing lines invest;

> Sudden they seize th' amazed, defenceless prize,
> And high in air Britannia's standard flies.

Closer to home, the deaths even of small birds are poignantly immediate:

> Oft, as in airy rings they skim the heath,
> The clam'rous lapwings feel the leaden death;
> Oft, as the mounting larks their notes prepare,
> They fall, and leave their little lives in air.[18]

Quoted out of context, 'leaden death' might seem poetic diction at its most artificial. Read in its place, it brings home the shock and weight of the pellets of lead, and the phrase 'leave their little lives in air' tenderly catches the last echo of the larks that sing no more.

Pope nearly always wrote in rhymed couplets (known at the time as heroic couplets), not just because they were then in fashion, but because they embodied his artistic ideal, distilling order and harmony out of the welter of experience. In classical theory the function of art was to hold a mirror up to nature, but Pope knew well that an image must always transform what it represents. In a lovely passage in 'Windsor Forest', when an imagined nymph called Lodona metamorphoses into the rural river Loddon, she becomes literally the mirror of art, with a virtuoso range of colours, textures, and movement:

> Oft in her glass the musing shepherd spies
> The headlong mountains and the downward skies,
> The wat'ry landscape of the pendent woods,
> And absent trees that tremble in the floods;
> In the clear azure gleam the flocks are seen,
> And floating forests paint the waves with green.[19]

Modern literary theory has had much to say about the evocation of presence in absence, and Pope does have 'absent trees' in the inverted watery landscape, but he also has the immediacy of pleasure in the presence of beauty. And as always in his writing, the lines are filled with movement and life: the reflected mountains seem to have fallen 'headlong' into the stream, the reflected trees 'tremble' with shimmering mobility, and they 'paint' their watery reflections even as Pope (who became an accomplished amateur painter) seeks to paint with words.

In 1717, when he was not yet thirty, Pope brought out a volume of *Works*. By this point in his career he had engaged with many of the traditional themes of poetry: love in 'Eloisa to Abelard' and 'The Rape of the Lock', death in 'Elegy to the Memory of an Unfortunate Lady', religion in 'Messiah' (not included in this edition) and in 'Eloisa', art in 'An Essay on Criticism', and nature and war in 'Windsor Forest'. By then he had also published the first instalments of his *Iliad*, which Johnson, half a century later, would call 'the noblest version of poetry which the world has ever seen'.[20] But his career now took an unexpected turn. After completing the translation of Homer, which occupied most of the next decade, he astonished his public in 1728 by issuing an altogether different kind of poem, the mock-epic 'Dunciad', in which scores of contemporary writers were derided as venal and incompetent 'dunces'.

One final flight of high seriousness did remain, 'An Essay on Man', but in his other writings Pope abandoned the mode of elevated, urbane art to explore a different imaginative realm, one that was embedded in – or even dragged down by – the complexity of contemporary politics and culture. As he himself put it, he 'stooped to truth, and moralized his song'.[21] Scholars gloss this as alluding to the fierce 'stoop' or plunge of a hunting falcon upon its prey, and Pope may well have intended that, but in any case it was a descent. In earlier days the elderly playwright William Wycherley had predicted that Pope's career would mirror Virgil's:

> Whose muse did once, like thine, in plains delight;
> Thine shall, like his, soon take a higher flight;
> So larks, which first from lowly fields arise,
> Mount by degrees, and reach at last the skies.[22]

Larks are singers, falcons are killers, and Pope transformed himself into a trenchant and sometimes furious satirist. If he had once sought 'truth' as an ideal realm of eternal verities, now it was just a modest standard of integrity against which to measure a world that was 'mean' in the eighteenth-century sense of 'low':

> Truth guards the poet, sanctifies the line,
> And makes immortal, verse as mean as mine.[23]

In this diminished context, the very notion of truth was compromised by the myriad ways in which people invoked, manipulated, and dissembled it. In a pregnant aphorism Pope acknowledged, 'In the cunning, truth itself's a lie.'[24]

'The Dunciad' is filled with anger at individuals who irritated Pope, and the project became an obsession, reappearing in three expanded editions over the next fifteen years. From the very beginning of his career, in fact, he had been wounded by personal attacks by jealous rivals. His mildly sarcastic reference to the older critic John Dennis in 'An Essay on Criticism' provoked Dennis to publish a cruel description of Pope's physical deformity. More insidiously, Joseph Addison, eminent poet and essayist – it was he who celebrated 'rivers of blood' in battle – seemed at first inclined to assist Pope's career but then turned against him by promoting a rival translation of Homer. Addison's covert malice is immortalized in the portrait of 'Atticus', published after Addison's death and given final burnishing in the 1735 'Epistle to Dr Arbuthnot'. To give him the name of an ancient Roman called 'Atticus' was a deliberately transparent disguise, not just because 'Atticus' and 'Addison' sound much alike, but because the portrait is immediately preceded by actual mention of Addison's name. After a brief compliment to his 'genius', his behaviour as the dominant writer of the age comes into focus:

> Should such a man, too fond to rule alone,
> Bear, like the Turk, no brother near the throne;
> View him with scornful, yet with jealous eyes,
> And hate for arts that caused himself to rise;
> Damn with faint praise, assent with civil leer,

> And without sneering, teach the rest to sneer;
> Willing to wound, and yet afraid to strike,
> Just hint a fault, and hesitate dislike ...
> Who but must laugh if such a man there be?
> Who would not weep, if Atticus were he?[25]

Still more powerful in 'Arbuthnot' is another counterattack, this time on a sly and worldly courtier called Lord John Hervey. Hervey was a close friend of Lady Mary Wortley Montagu, with whom Pope had once been infatuated, and the friends had collaborated to satirize Pope mercilessly. His response this time was a masterpiece of eloquent disgust, wickedly casting Hervey as 'Sporus', the name of a handsome youth whom Nero caused to be castrated and then married. With elegantly balanced antitheses Pope skewers his enemy:

> Amphibious thing! that acting either part,
> The trifling head, or the corrupted heart,
> Fop at the toilet, flatt'rer at the board,
> Now trips a lady, and now struts a lord.
> Eve's tempter thus the rabbins have expressed:
> A cherub's face, a reptile all the rest;
> Beauty that shocks you, parts that none will trust,
> Wit that can creep, and pride that licks the dust.[26]

The description shrewdly acknowledges Hervey's genuine gifts – he does have wit, in the sense then current of 'intelligence', and he is a man of 'parts' – but the gifts are spoiled by sycophancy and self-display, so that he resembles the rabbinical image of the tempter in Eden with a lovely face above and reptilian coils below. There was indeed something equivocal about Hervey – Lady Mary herself remarked that there were 'three sexes: men, women, and Herveys'[27] – but the way Pope exploited it quickly got him a reputation of being thin-skinned and vindictive. Satire, he said proudly in another poem, was 'my weapon', adding that he was 'armed for virtue when I point the pen'; but when he derided Hervey's use of milk to treat a skin condition – 'Sporus, that mere white curd of asses' milk' – or when he hinted that contact with Lady Mary might result in venereal infection, it was not obvious that he was – in a claim he borrowed from Horace – 'to VIRTUE ONLY and HER FRIENDS, A FRIEND'.[28]

More sympathetically, one can say that Pope never felt really at home in a culture that was turning literature into commercial speculation and that honoured the absurd actor-playwright Colley Cibber as Poet Laureate (as a Catholic, Pope was in any case ineligible). 'Windsor Forest' had been published when Queen Anne, last of the Stuart line, was on the throne and when traditionalist Tories whom Pope admired controlled her government. A year later she was dead, the Tory ministry had collapsed, and a German who spoke no English had arrived as George I. The politics of the ensuing decades – the final thirty years of Pope's life – were repugnant to him, as were the larger social and economic changes of that era.

For years Pope dreamed of creating an immense *Opus Magnum*, a systematic cycle of 'moral' poems in which the 'Essay on Man' would be just one of many parts. In the early 1730s he did compose four major poems in a newly developed conversational style, addressed to individual friends – three noblemen, and his closest female friend, Martha Blount – that were meant to form part of this grand design. The topics are at first sight rather miscellaneous: they are subtitled '*Of the* Knowledge *and Characters of* MEN', '*Of the* Characters *of* WOMEN', and '*Of the* Use *of* RICHES' (two). But the latter emphasis was not at all eccentric, for Britain was being shaken by the tectonic tremors of what has become known as the financial revolution, which Pope and other Tory sympathizers saw as the deplorable ascendancy of an acquisitive middle-class culture that was amassing fortunes from colonial exploitation and risky financial speculation, encouraged by Sir Robert Walpole's Whig coalition that held power through bribery and patronage for twenty years. The frightening collapse in 1720 of the investment scheme that became known as the South Sea Bubble, which took down many of Pope's friends (he himself got out in

time to save most of his money), convinced him that the imper-
sonal operation of the modern capitalist marketplace was little
short of criminal:

> While with the silent growth of ten per cent
> In dirt and darkness hundreds stink content.[29]

More and more, the *Opus Magnum* project seemed unattain-
able, and when it became evident that the group of four poems
was unlikely to expand, Pope collected them under the modest
title 'Epistles to Several Persons' (after his death his executor Wil-
liam Warburton gave them the grander name of *Moral Essays*).

For the rest of his career, Pope was firmly committed to the
conversational mode, and in a series of superb adaptations of
the Epistles and Satires of Horace, he invoked his classical fore-
bear as a kindred spirit, seeking to rise above a vulgar culture
but constantly dragged back into it. Pope's poetic gifts were in
no way diminished. 'In dirt and darkness hundreds stink con-
tent' enacts an almost physical disgust, with the jammed-together
'k' sounds in 'stink content'. But he deliberately relinquished
the grace and loveliness that he had deployed with such mas-
tery in his early work; he was now 'Verse-man or prose-man,
term me which you will'.[30] And although his poems continued
to sparkle with ironic wit, there was seldom much of the
amused humour that made 'The Rape of the Lock' so buoyant.
Johnson thought it telling that according to people who knew
Pope, 'he sometimes condescended to be jocular with servants
or inferiors, but by no merriment, either of others or his own,
was he ever seen excited to laughter'.[31]

Traditional Pope scholarship used to be anxious to clean up his
image, exalting him as a high-minded spokesman for Western
civilization who was righteously indignant at the unjust prom-
inence of bad writers, but many of the so-called 'dunces' were
actually very intelligent, and some were even good writers.
What really baffled and frustrated Pope was that the traditional
hierarchy of aesthetic value was in a state of collapse, yet as his
critics were quick to point out, he himself was hardly above

exploiting publication for gain. He sold his Homer, in an opulent edition, by advance subscription to highly placed admirers, and when he tried to capitalize on that success with an edition of Shakespeare's plays, a pompous but competent scholar named Lewis Theobald detailed its faults and followed with an edition of his own that greatly outsold Pope's. Theobald's reward was to become the ignoble hero of the 'Dunciad', where even his name was made ludicrous as 'piddling Tibbalds',[32] and Pope found himself embroiled in a permanent war against commercial publishing in which a horde of badly paid hack writers inhabited the maze of alleys and garrets that was known in those days as Grub Street. In Pope's conception, a soporific goddess of Dullness presides over a sick civilization in which literary incompetence mirrors social disorder:

> There motley images her fancy strike,
> Figures ill paired, and similes unlike.
> She sees a mob of metaphors advance,
> Pleased with the madness of the mazy dance:
> How Tragedy and Comedy embrace,
> How Farce and Epic get a jumbled race . . .[33]

In the hands of the hacks, all that was beautiful becomes gross. In 'Windsor Forest' Pope had written,

> Through the fair scene roll slow the ling'ring streams,
> Then foaming pour along, and rush into the Thames.[34]

In those days he loved to make sound echo sense, as *roll slow* and *ling'ring* enact the hesitation before *pour along* and *rush*. Now, in the gutters of urban streets, everything is choked and degraded:

> To where Fleet Ditch with disemboguing streams
> Rolls the large tribute of dead dogs to Thames . . .[35]

The 'Dunciad' turned out to be more process than product, with successive editions in which some names dropped out – often because their owners interceded with Pope for mercy – while new offenders found themselves included. Pope's own bland explanation was that the whole lot of them were merely symptoms of a larger disease: 'There may arise some obscurity in chronology from the names in the poem, by the inevitable removal of some authors, and insertion of others in their niches. For whoever will consider the unity of the whole design will be sensible that the poem was not made for these authors, but these authors for the poem; and I should judge they were clapped in as they rose, fresh and fresh, and changed from day to day, in like manner as when the old boughs wither, we thrust new ones into a chimney.'[36] Even the hero of the poem got changed, as Theobald was replaced by Cibber. A fourth and final book was added to the 'Dunciad' in 1742, fourteen years after the original version, incorporating reflections on education and intellectual fads that had once been intended for the unrealized *Opus Magnum*, and it rose to an apocalyptic vision of the triumph of Dullness:

> Thy hand, great Anarch! lets the curtain fall,
> And universal darkness buries all.[37]

But Pope's mood was not always this bleak, and the ironies could be playfully tolerant rather than corrosive. Consider the two-line poem entitled 'Epigram. Engraved on the Collar of a Dog which I gave to his Royal Highness':

> I am his Highness' dog at Kew;
> Pray tell me sir, whose dog are you?

On the face of it, this challenging couplet is calculated to embarrass whoever bends down to read it, since only a person of very high standing would be in a position to examine the collar of the Prince of Wales's pet. But eighteenth-century society was profoundly hierarchical, and to say that a courtier needs to obey and flatter those still higher than himself was a simple fact, not an insult. In a genial commentary William Empson brings out further layers of implication: 'The joke carries a certain praise for the underdog; the point is not that men are slaves but that they find it suits them and remain good-humoured. The dog is proud of being the prince's dog and expects no one to take offence at the question. There is also a hearty independence in its lack of respect for the inquirer.'[38]

A man of his age who longed to separate himself from his age, a caustic satirist who claimed to be a satirist against his will, Pope was above all a poet from start to finish. Art brought him fame and wealth, but most of all it gave shape and meaning to a life that was filled with frustration and pain. In one of his Horatian imitations, admitting that there was something compulsive about his tireless composition, he acknowledges that it defines who he is and gives meaning to his life. In sad, meditative lines he catalogues the irreplaceable losses of each successive year:

> Years foll'wing years steal something ev'ry day;
> At last they steal us from ourselves away.
> In one our frolics, one amusements end,
> In one a mistress drops, in one a friend.
> This subtle thief of life, this paltry time,
> What will it leave me, if it snatch my rhyme?
> If ev'ry wheel of that unwearied mill
> That turned ten thousand verses, now stands still?[39]

In that heavy final line nearly every syllable receives a stress, as the turning wheels of a lifelong vocation slow down, and at last cease to turn. But the poems have lived on, and two and a half centuries after Pope's death, their energy and freshness continue to astonish.

NOTES

1. 'An Essay on Man', I, 95.
2. 'An Essay on Criticism', 525, 625, 215, 298.
3. 'Essay on Man', IV, 168.
4. 'Observations on "Observation": A Second Letter to John

Murray, Esq. (1821)', *The Works of Lord Byron: Letters and Journals*, ed. Rowland E. Prothero (London: John Murray, 1901), V, p. 591.

5. Samuel Johnson, *Life of Pope*, in *Lives of the English Poets*, ed. G. B. Hill (Oxford: Clarendon Press, 1905), III, p. 217.

6. 'An Epistle to Dr Arbuthnot', 132.

7. Pope to John Caryll, 25 January 1711, *The Correspondence of Alexander Pope*, ed. George Sherburn (Oxford: Clarendon Press, 1956), I, p. 113.

8. Pope to Lord Bathurst, 18 December 1730, *Correspondence*, ed. Sherburn, III, p. 156.

9. 'The Rape of the Lock', II, 59–62, 77–8; I, 71–6; II, 117–20; III, 19–22.

10. James Boswell, *Life of Johnson*, ed. G. B. Hill, rev. L. F. Powell (Oxford: Clarendon Press, 1934–50), IV, 46.

11. Samuel Taylor Coleridge, *Biographia Literaria*, ed. J. Shawcross (Oxford: Clarendon Press, 1907), ch. 2, I, p. 26n.

12. *Life of Pope*, pp. 220–21.

13. 'Essay on Criticism', 362–3.

14. 'Rape of the Lock', (1712 version), in *The Rape of the Lock and Other Poems*, vol. II of the Twickenham edition, ed. Geoffrey Tillotson (London: Methuen, 1962), I, pp. 13–18.

15. 'Rape of the Lock' (1714 version), I, pp. 13–18. My comments are indebted to those of John Sitter, 'Pope's Versification of Voice', in *The Cambridge Companion to Alexander Pope*, ed. Pat Rogers (Cambridge: Cambridge University Press, 2007), pp. 45–6.

16. 'Verses on the Death of Dr Swift', 47–52, in Jonathan Swift, *The Complete Poems*, ed. Pat Rogers (London: Penguin, 1983), p. 486.

17. Joseph Addison, 'The Campaign', in Addison, *Works* (1721), I, p. 65.

18. 'Windsor Forest', 107–10, 131–4.

19. Ibid., 211–16.

20. *Life of Pope*, p. 119.

21. 'Arbuthnot', 341.

22. Wycherley, introductory poem in Pope's *Works* (1717).

23. 'Epilogue to the Satires', II, 246–7.

24. 'Epistle I To Cobham', 68.

25. 'Arbuthnot', 197–204, 213–14.

26. Ibid., 326–33.

27. Horace Walpole, *Commonplace Book of Verses*, quoted in Walpole, *Correspondence*, ed. W. S. Lewis (New Haven: Yale University Press, 1954), XVII, p. 274n.

28. [Imitations of Horace], Satire, II, i, 69, 105; 'Arbuthnot', 306; Satire, II, i, 121.
29. Epistle, I, i, 132–3.
30. Satire, II, i, 64.
31. *Life of Pope*, p. 202.
32. 'Arbuthnot', 164.
33. 'Dunciad', I, 65–70.
34. 'Windsor Forest', 217–18.
35. 'Dunciad', II, 271–2.
36. 'Dunciad Variorum', Appendix I, in the Twickenham edition, V, pp. 205–6.
37. 'Dunciad', IV, 655–6.
38. William Empson, *Some Versions of Pastoral* (New York: New Directions, 1960), p. 247.
39. Horace, Epistle, II, ii, 72–9.

Further Reading

EDITIONS

Ault, Norman, and Rosemary Cowler, *The Prose Works of Alexander Pope*, 2 vols. (Oxford: Blackwell, 1936, and Hamden, CT: Archon, 1986)

Butt, John, et al. (eds.), *The Twickenham Edition of the Works of Alexander Pope*, 11 vols. (London: Methuen, 1938–68). The standard edition, and the basis for the single-volume *The Poems of Alexander Pope*, ed. Butt (London: Methuen, 1963)

Davis, Herbert (ed.), *Poetical Works* (Oxford: Oxford University Press, 1966)

Erskine-Hill, Howard (ed.), *Alexander Pope: Selected Letters* (Oxford: Oxford University Press, 2000)

Goldgar, Bernard A., *Literary Criticism of Alexander Pope* (Lincoln: University of Nebraska Press, 1965)

Kerby-Miller, Charles (ed.), *Memoirs of the Life of Martinus Scriblerus* (New Haven: Yale University Press, 1950; repr. Oxford University Press, 1989). The collaborative writings of Pope and his 'Scriblerian' friends

Mack, Maynard (ed.), *The Last and Greatest Art: Some Unpublished Poetical Manuscripts of Alexander Pope* (Newark: University of Delaware Press, 1984)

Rumbold, Valerie (ed.), *The Dunciad in Four Books*, rev. edn. (Harlow: Longman, 2009)

Shankman, Steven (ed.), *The Iliad* (London: Penguin, 1996)

Sherburn, George (ed.), *The Correspondence of Alexander Pope*, 5 vols. (Oxford: Clarendon Press, 1965)

Wall, Cynthia (ed.), *The Rape of the Lock* (Boston: Bedford Books, 1998)

BIOGRAPHICAL AND HISTORICAL

Erskine-Hill, Howard, *The Social Milieu of Alexander Pope: Lives, Example, and the Poetic Response* (New Haven: Yale University Press, 1975)

Johnson, Samuel, *Life of Pope*, in *Lives of the English Poets*, ed. G. B. Hill, 3 vols. (Oxford: Clarendon, 1905), III, pp. 82–276. Classic study by a younger contemporary of Pope (available in many modern editions)

Mack, Maynard, *Alexander Pope: A Life* (New Haven: Yale University Press, 1985). The standard biography

—, *The Garden and the City: Retirement and Politics in the Later Poetry of Pope, 1731–1743* (Toronto: University of Toronto Press, 1969)

McLaverty, James, *Pope, Print, and Meaning* (Oxford: Oxford University Press, 2001)

Nicolson, Marjorie Hope, and G. S. Rousseau, '*This Long Disease, My Life*': *Alexander Pope and the Sciences* (Princeton: Princeton University Press, 1968)

Sherburn, George, *The Early Career of Alexander Pope* (Oxford: Clarendon Press, 1934)

Spence, Joseph, *Anecdotes, Observations, and Characters of Books and Men*, ed. J. M. Osborn, 2 vols. (Oxford: Clarendon Press, 1966). Important record of conversations with Pope

BIBLIOGRAPHIC RESOURCES

Baines, Paul, *The Complete Critical Guide to Alexander Pope* (London: Routledge, 2000)

Barnard, John, *Pope: The Critical Heritage* (London: Routledge, 1973)

Bedford, E. G., and R. J. Dilligan (eds.)., *A Concordance to the Poems of Alexander Pope*, 2 vols. (Detroit: Gale, 1974)

Rogers, Pat, *The Alexander Pope Encyclopedia* (Westport, CT: Greenwood, 2004)

CRITICAL STUDIES

Brower, Reuben A., *Alexander Pope: The Poetry of Allusion* (Oxford: Clarendon Press, 1959)

Damrosch, Leo: *The Imaginative World of Alexander Pope* (Berkeley: University of California Press, 1987)

Deutsch, Helen, *Resemblance and Disgrace: Alexander Pope and the Deformation of Culture* (Cambridge: Harvard University Press, 1996)

Fairer, David, *Pope's Imagination* (Manchester: Manchester University Press, 1984)

Griffin, Dustin H., *Alexander Pope: The Poet in the Poems* (Princeton: Princeton University Press, 1978)

Hammond, Brean S. (ed.), *Pope* (London: Longman, 1996). Collection of essays

King, Christa Knellwolf, *A Contradiction Still: Representations of Women in the Poetry of Alexander Pope* (Manchester: Manchester University Press, 1998)

Leranbaum, Miriam, *Alexander Pope's 'Opus Magnum,' 1729–1744* (Oxford: Clarendon Press, 1977)

Mack, Maynard (ed.), *Essential Articles for the Study of Alexander Pope* (Hamden, CT: Archon, rev. edn., 1968). Includes many studies that have been widely influential

Morris, David B., *Alexander Pope: The Genius of Sense* (Cambridge: Harvard University Press, 1984)

Nuttall, A. D., *Pope's 'Essay on Man'* (London: Allen & Unwin, 1984)

Rogers, Pat, *Essays on Pope* (Cambridge: Cambridge University Press, 2006)

— (ed.), *The Cambridge Companion to Alexander Pope* (Cambridge: Cambridge University Press, 2007)

Rumbold, Valerie, *Women's Place in Pope's World* (Cambridge: Cambridge University Press, 1989)

Spacks, Patricia M., *An Argument of Images: The Poetry of*

Alexander Pope (Cambridge: Harvard University Press, 1971)

Stack, Frank, *Pope and Horace: Studies in Imitation* (Cambridge: Cambridge University Press, 1985)

Williams, Aubrey, *Pope's 'Dunciad': A Study of Its Meaning* (London: Methuen, 1955)

Winn, James A., *A Window in the Bosom: The Letters of Alexander Pope* (Hamden, CT: Archon, 1977)

A Note on the Texts

The poems and prose writings in this volume are presented in order of publication, with the exception that the Imitations of Horace are grouped in logical order, rather than in the rather confusing sequence in which they originally appeared over a five-year period. All of Pope's major poems are here, and nothing is abridged except the *Iliad* excerpts and the prose writings. The texts given in this edition follow three sources: (1) for the majority of poems, the 1751 edition of Pope's executor William Warburton, which is the one used in the *Twickenham Edition of the Works of Alexander Pope*, 11 vols. (London: Methuen, 1938–68); (2) for the 'Dunciad' of 1743 and the 'Epistles to Several Persons' of 1744, the first editions are used, as they are by Herbert Davis in his edition of *Poetical Works* (Oxford: Oxford University Press, 1966); Warburton chose to publish these in rearrangements of his own devising – possibly having obtained Pope's approval at the very end of his life, but certainly not under his direct supervision; (3) for works in prose, the first editions, as used likewise in *Literary Criticism of Alexander Pope*, ed. Bertrand A. Goldgar (Lincoln: University of Nebraska Press, 1965). The letters are taken from *The Correspondence of Alexander Pope*, ed. George Sherburn, 5 vols. (Oxford: Clarendon Press, 1965).

In order to present Pope's writings in their full freshness, the text is modernized throughout, eliminating typographical conventions that confer an inappropriately antiquarian flavour. In particular these are the capitalization of ordinary nouns; italics when they indicate names or quotations rather than emphasis; oddities of punctuation, especially colons where semicolons would be used today; and unnecessary apostrophes (thus, 'produc'd' is replaced by 'produced', and 'seem'd by 'seemed'). Pope himself, it should be noted, used all of these devices much less in his later works than in earlier ones, and soon after his death printers began dropping them altogether. Moreover, Warburton himself frequently altered Pope's punctuation to suit his own taste.

Apostrophes do appear, however, whenever they indicate elisions that support the metre, for example 'gen'rous' and 'wand'ring'; otherwise the reader would be likely to hear both as three syllables rather than two. When Pope writes 'disposing Pow'r', he intends an exact rhyme with 'mortal hour' ('Essay on Man', I, 287–8). (The ubiquitous 'ev'ry' is more ambiguous, but has been retained to confirm its disyllabic status.)

Pope used commas much more heavily than is normal today, which may seem at times to slow the verse down unnecessarily, but his pauses are important, with constant weighing and balancing of phrases, and for the most part these have therefore been retained. In other subjective editorial decisions, capitals are retained when they seem integral to the meaning, e.g. 'Man' is capitalized in 'An Essay on Man', 'Nature' when personification is evident, and 'Heaven' when the religious term is clearly intended (but not in casual expressions such as 'heaven forbid').

Spellings, too, are modernized when neither meaning nor pronunciation is affected. 'Money' replaces 'mony' and 'bias' replaces 'byas'; but 'corse' and 'gripe' are retained (for 'corpse' and 'grip').

The occasional triplet – a sequence of three lines with the same rhyme – is indicated in the margin as it was in the original, allowing the eye to anticipate what the ear will hear.

The notes are necessarily extensive, since Pope names hundreds of contemporaries and frequently incorporates literary allusions, most of which need to be identified for modern readers. The notes also give help in two additional ways: by sorting out syntax at times when Pope's condensed style makes it hard to grasp his meaning, and by defining words whose usage has changed from his day to ours. For these Samuel Johnson's great 1755 *Dictionary* is an invaluable guide, especially since many of its illustrative quotations are taken from Pope himself, and Johnson's definitions are frequently quoted here.

In addition, there are interpretive headnotes, preceding the notes on individual lines, that provide contexts and perspectives for each major poem or group of poems.

I owe especial thanks to Melissa Pino for her painstaking care in helping to prepare the text.

EARLY POEMS

EARLY POEMS

An Essay on Criticism

Si quid novisti rectius istis,
Candidus imperti; si non, his utere mecum.
HORACE

Part I

Introduction. That 'tis as great a fault to judge ill as to write ill, and a more dangerous one to the public. That a true taste is as rare to be found as a true genius. That most men are born with some taste, but spoiled by false education. The multitude of critics, and causes of them. That we are to study our own taste, and know the limits of it. Nature the best guide of judgement. Improved by art and rules, which are but methodized Nature. Rules derived from the practice of the ancient poets. That therefore the ancients are necessary to be studied by a critic, particularly Homer and Virgil. Of licences, and the use of them by the ancients. Reverence due to the ancients, and praise of them.

'Tis hard to say if greater want of skill
Appear in writing or in judging ill;
But of the two, less dang'rous is th' offence
To tire our patience than mislead our sense:
Some few in that, but numbers err in this,
Ten censure wrong for one who writes amiss;
A fool might once himself alone expose,
Now one in verse makes many more in prose.
    'Tis with our judgements as our watches, none
Go just alike, yet each believes his own.   10
In poets as true genius is but rare,
True taste as seldom is the critic's share;
Both must alike from Heav'n derive their light,
These born to judge, as well as those to write.

Let such teach others who themselves excel,
And censure freely who have written well.
Authors are partial to their wit, 'tis true,
But are not critics to their judgement too?
    Yet if we look more closely, we shall find
20 Most have the seeds of judgement in their mind:
Nature affords at least a glimm'ring light;
The lines, though touched but faintly, are drawn right.
But as the slightest sketch, if justly traced, ⎫
Is by ill colouring but the more disgraced, ⎬
So by false learning is good sense defaced: ⎭
Some are bewildered in the maze of schools,
And some made coxcombs Nature meant but fools.
In search of wit these lose their common sense,
And then turn critics in their own defence;
30 Each burns alike, who can or cannot write,
Or with a rival's or an eunuch's spite.
All fools have still an itching to deride,
And fain would be upon the laughing side.
If Maevius scribble in Apollo's spite,
There are who judge still worse than he can write.
    Some have at first for wits, then poets passed;
Turned critics next, and proved plain fools at last.
Some neither can for wits nor critics pass,
As heavy mules are neither horse nor ass.
40 Those half-learn'd witlings, numerous in our isle,
As half-formed insects on the banks of Nile,
Unfinished things, one knows not what to call,
Their generation's so equivocal;
To tell 'em would a hundred tongues require,
Or one vain wit's, that might a hundred tire.
    But you who seek to give and merit fame,
And justly bear a critic's noble name,
Be sure yourself and your own reach to know,
How far your genius, taste, and learning go;
50 Launch not beyond your depth, but be discreet,
And mark that point where sense and dullness meet.
    Nature to all things fixed the limits fit,

And wisely curbed proud man's pretending wit.
  As on the land while here the ocean gains,
  In other parts it leaves wide sandy plains,
  Thus in the soul while memory prevails,
  The solid pow'r of understanding fails;
  Where beams of warm imagination play,
  The memory's soft figures melt away.
  One science only will one genius fit;   60
  So vast is art, so narrow human wit:
  Not only bounded to peculiar arts,
  But oft in those confined to single parts.
  Like kings we lose the conquests gained before,
  By vain ambition still to make them more;
  Each might his several province well command,
  Would all but stoop to what they understand.
    First follow Nature, and your judgement frame
  By her just standard, which is still the same:
  Unerring Nature, still divinely bright,   70
  One clear, unchanged, and universal light,
  Life, force, and beauty must to all impart,
  At once the source, and end, and test of art.
  Art from that fund each just supply provides,
  Works without show, and without pomp presides.
  In some fair body thus th' informing soul
  With spirits feeds, with vigour fills the whole;
  Each motion guides, and every nerve sustains,
  Itself unseen, but in th' effects remains.
  Some, to whom Heav'n in wit has been profuse,   80
  Want as much more to turn it to its use,
  For wit and judgement often are at strife,
  Though meant each other's aid, like man and wife.
  'Tis more to guide than spur the Muse's steed;
  Restrain his fury than provoke his speed:
  The wingèd courser, like a gen'rous horse,
  Shows most true mettle when you check his course.
    Those rules of old discovered, not devised,
  Are nature still, but nature methodized;
  Nature, like liberty, is but restrained   90

By the same laws which first herself ordained.
    Hear how learn'd Greece her useful rules indites,
When to repress and when indulge our flights:
High on Parnassus' top her sons she showed,
And pointed out those arduous paths they trod;
Held from afar, aloft, th' immortal prize,
And urged the rest by equal steps to rise.
Just precepts thus from great examples giv'n,
She drew from them what they derived from Heav'n.
The gen'rous critic fanned the poet's fire,
And taught the world with reason to admire.
Then Criticism the Muse's handmaid proved,
To dress her charms, and make her more belov'd,
But foll'wing wits from that intention strayed:
Who could not win the mistress, wooed the maid;
Against the poets their own arms they turned,
Sure to hate most the men from whom they learned.
So modern 'pothecaries, taught the art
By doctors' bills to play the doctor's part,
Bold in the practice of mistaken rules
Prescribe, apply, and call their masters fools.
Some on the leaves of ancient authors prey,
Nor time nor moths e'er spoiled so much as they;
Some drily plain, without invention's aid,
Write dull receipts how poems may be made.
These leave the sense their learning to display,
And those explain the meaning quite away.
    You then whose judgement the right course would
        steer,
Know well each ancient's proper character;
His fable, subject, scope in every page,
Religion, country, genius of his age;
Without all these at once before your eyes,
Cavil you may, but never criticize.
Be Homer's works your study and delight,
Read them by day, and meditate by night;
Thence form your judgement, thence your maxims
        bring,

And trace the Muses upward to their spring.
Still with itself compared, his text peruse;
And let your comment be the Mantuan Muse.
   When first young Maro in his boundless mind   130
A work t' outlast immortal Rome designed,
Perhaps he seemed above the critic's law,
And but from Nature's fountains scorned to draw;
But when t' examine ev'ry part he came,
Nature and Homer were, he found, the same.
Convinced, amazed, he checks the bold design, ⎫
And rules as strict his laboured work confine ⎬
As if the Stagyrite o'erlooked each line.   ⎭
Learn hence for ancient rules a just esteem;
To copy Nature is to copy them.   140
   Some beauties yet no precepts can declare,
For there's a happiness as well as care.
Music resembles poetry, in each   ⎫
Are nameless graces which no methods teach, ⎬
And which a master-hand alone can reach.   ⎭
If, where the rules not far enough extend
(Since rules were made but to promote their end),
Some lucky licence answers to the full
Th' intent proposed, that licence is a rule.
Thus Pegasus, a nearer way to take,   150
May boldly deviate from the common track.
Great wits sometimes may gloriously offend,
And rise to faults true critics dare not mend;
From vulgar bounds with brave disorder part,
And snatch a grace beyond the reach of art,
Which, without passing through the judgement, gains
The heart, and all its end at once attains.
In prospects thus, some objects please our eyes, ⎫
Which out of Nature's common order rise,   ⎬
The shapeless rock, or hanging precipice.   ⎭   160
But though the ancients thus their rules invade
(As kings dispense with laws themselves have made),
Moderns, beware! or if you must offend
Against the precept, ne'er transgress its end;

Let it be seldom, and compelled by need,
And have at least their precedent to plead;
The critic else proceeds without remorse,
Seizes your fame, and puts his laws in force.

    I know there are, to whose presumptuous thoughts
170 Those freer beauties, e'en in them, seem faults.
Some figures monstrous and misshaped appear,
Considered singly, or beheld too near,
Which, but proportioned to their light, or place,
Due distance reconciles to form and grace.
A prudent chief not always must display
His pow'rs in equal ranks and fair array,
But with th' occasion and the place comply,
Conceal his force, nay, seem sometimes to fly.
Those oft are stratagems which errors seem,
180 Nor is it Homer nods, but we that dream.

    Still green with bays each ancient altar stands,
Above the reach of sacrilegious hands,
Secure from flames, from envy's fiercer rage,
Destructive war, and all-involving age.
See, from each clime the learn'd their incense bring!
Hear, in all tongues consenting paeans ring!
In praise so just let ev'ry voice be joined,
And fill the gen'ral chorus of mankind.
Hail, bards triumphant! born in happier days,
190 Immortal heirs of universal praise!
Whose honours with increase of ages grow,
As streams roll down, enlarging as they flow;
Nations unborn your mighty names shall sound,
And worlds applaud that must not yet be found!
O may some spark of your celestial fire
The last, the meanest of your sons inspire
(That on weak wings, from far, pursues your flights,
Glows while he reads, but trembles as he writes),
To teach vain wits a science little known,
200 T' admire superior sense, and doubt their own.

Part II

Causes hindering a true judgement. Pride. Imperfect learning. Judging by parts, and not by the whole. Critics in wit, language, versification only. Being too hard to please, or too apt to admire. Partiality – too much love to a sect – to the ancients or moderns. Prejudice or prevention. Singularity. Inconstancy. Party spirit. Envy. Against envy, and in praise of good nature. When severity is chiefly to be used by critics.

Of all the causes which conspire to blind
Man's erring judgement, and misguide the mind,
What the weak head with strongest bias rules,
Is pride, the never-failing vice of fools.
Whatever nature has in worth denied
She gives in large recruits of needful pride;
For as in bodies, thus in souls we find
What wants in blood and spirits swelled with wind;
Pride, where wit fails, steps in to our defence,
And fills up all the mighty void of sense: 210
If once right reason drives that cloud away,
Truth breaks upon us with resistless day.
Trust not yourself; but your defects to know,
Make use of every friend – and ev'ry foe.
A little learning is a dang'rous thing;
Drink deep, or taste not the Pierian spring:
There shallow draughts intoxicate the brain,
And drinking largely sobers us again.
Fired at first sight with what the Muse imparts,
In fearless youth we tempt the heights of arts,   220
While from the bounded level of our mind
Short views we take, nor see the lengths behind;
But more advanced, behold with strange surprise
New distant scenes of endless science rise!
So pleased at first the towering Alps we try,
Mount o'er the vales, and seem to tread the sky;

Th' eternal snows appear already passed,
And the first clouds and mountains seem the last:
But those attained, we tremble to survey
230   The growing labours of the lengthened way;
Th' increasing prospect tires our wand'ring eyes,
Hills peep o'er hills, and Alps on Alps arise!
    A perfect judge will read each work of wit
With the same spirit that its author writ;
Survey the whole, nor seek slight faults to find
Where Nature moves, and rapture warms the mind;
Nor lose, for that malignant dull delight,
The gen'rous pleasure to be charmed with wit.
But in such lays as neither ebb nor flow,
240   Correctly cold, and regularly low,
That shunning faults one quiet tenor keep,
We cannot blame indeed – but we may sleep.
In wit, as nature, what affects our hearts
Is not th' exactness of peculiar parts;
'Tis not a lip or eye we beauty call,
But the joint force and full result of all.
Thus when we view some well proportioned dome
(The world's just wonder, and ev'n thine, O Rome),
No single parts unequally surprise;
250   All comes united to th' admiring eyes;
No monstrous height, or breadth, or length appear;
The whole at once is bold and regular.
    Whoever thinks a faultless piece to see,
Thinks what ne'er was, nor is, nor e'er shall be.
In ev'ry work regard the writer's end,
Since none can compass more than they intend,
And if the means be just, the conduct true,
Applause, in spite of trivial faults, is due.
As men of breeding, sometimes men of wit,
260   T' avoid great errors must the less commit;
Neglect the rules each verbal critic lays,
For not to know some trifles is a praise.
Most critics, fond of some subservient art,
Still make the whole depend upon a part:

They talk of principles, but notions prize,
And all to one lov'd folly sacrifice.
  Once on a time La Mancha's Knight, they say,
A certain bard encountering on the way,
Discoursed in terms as just, with looks as sage,
As e'er could Dennis of the Grecian stage,   270
Concluding all were desp'rate sots and fools
Who durst depart from Aristotle's rules.
Our author, happy in a judge so nice,
Produced his play, and begged the knight's advice;
Made him observe the subject and the plot,
The manners, passions, unities, what not?
All which exact to rule were brought about,
Were but a combat in the lists left out.
'What! leave the combat out?' exclaims the knight;
'Yes, or we must renounce the Stagyrite.'   280
'Not so, by Heaven! (he answers in a rage)
Knights, squires, and steeds must enter on the stage.'
'So vast a throng the stage can ne'er contain.'
'Then build a new, or act it on a plain.'
  Thus critics, of less judgement than caprice,
Curious, not knowing, not exact, but nice,
Form short ideas, and offend in arts
(As most in manners) by a love to parts.
  Some to conceit alone their taste confine,
And glitt'ring thoughts struck out at ev'ry line,   290
Pleased with a work where nothing's just or fit,
One glaring chaos and wild heap of wit.
Poets, like painters, thus unskilled to trace
The naked nature and the living grace,
With gold and jewels cover ev'ry part,
And hide with ornaments their want of art.
True wit is Nature to advantage dressed,
What oft was thought, but ne'er so well expressed;
Something whose truth convinced at sight we find,
That gives us back the image of our mind.   300
As shades more sweetly recommend the light,
So modest plainness sets off sprightly wit:

For works may have more wit than does 'em good,
As bodies perish through excess of blood.
   Others for language all their care express,
And value books, as women men, for dress:
Their praise is still – 'the style is excellent';
The sense they humbly take upon content.
Words are like leaves; and where they most abound,
310   Much fruit of sense beneath is rarely found.
False eloquence, like the prismatic glass,
Its gaudy colours spreads on ev'ry place;
The face of nature we no more survey,
All glares alike, without distinction gay.
But true expression, like th' unchanging sun, ⎫
Clears and improves whate'er it shines upon; ⎬
It gilds all objects, but it alters none. ⎭
Expression is the dress of thought, and still
Appears more decent as more suitable.
320   A vile conceit in pompous words expressed
Is like a clown in regal purple dressed:
For diff'rent styles with diff'rent subjects sort,
As sev'ral garbs with country, town, and court.
Some by old words to fame have made pretence,
Ancients in phrase, mere moderns in their sense;
Such labour'd nothings, in so strange a style,
Amaze th' unlearn'd, and make the learnèd smile.
Unlucky as Fungoso in the play, ⎫
These sparks with awkward vanity display ⎬
330   What the fine gentleman wore yesterday; ⎭
And but so mimic ancient wits at best,
As apes our grandsires in their doublets dressed.
In words as fashions the same rule will hold,
Alike fantastic if too new or old:
Be not the first by whom the new are tried,
Nor yet the last to lay the old aside.
   But most by numbers judge a poet's song,
And smooth or rough with them is right or wrong.
In the bright Muse though thousand charms conspire,
340   Her voice is all these tuneful fools admire,

Who haunt Parnassus but to please their ear,
Not mend their minds; as some to church repair,
Not for the doctrine, but the music there.
These equal syllables alone require,
Though oft the ear the open vowels tire,
While expletives their feeble aid do join,
And ten low words oft creep in one dull line,
While they ring round the same unvaried chimes
With sure returns of still expected rhymes;
Where'er you find 'the cooling western breeze',   350
In the next line, it 'whispers through the trees';
If crystal streams 'with pleasing murmurs creep',
The reader's threatened (not in vain) with 'sleep'.
Then, at the last and only couplet fraught
With some unmeaning thing they call a thought,
A needless Alexandrine ends the song,
That like a wounded snake drags its slow length along.
Leave such to tune their own dull rhymes, and know
What's roundly smooth, or languishingly slow,
And praise the easy vigour of a line   360
Where Denham's strength and Waller's sweetness join.
True ease in writing comes from art, not chance,
As those move easiest who have learned to dance.
'Tis not enough no harshness gives offence;
The sound must seem an echo to the sense.
Soft is the strain when zephyr gently blows,
And the smooth stream in smoother numbers flows;
But when loud surges lash the sounding shore,
The hoarse rough verse should like the torrent roar.
When Ajax strives some rock's vast weight to throw,   370
The line too labours, and the words move slow;
Not so when swift Camilla scours the plain,
Flies o'er th' unbending corn, and skims along
          the main.
Hear how Timotheus' varied lays surprise,
And bid alternate passions fall and rise!
While at each change the son of Libyan Jove
Now burns with glory, and then melts with love;

Now his fierce eyes with sparkling fury glow,
Now sighs steal out, and tears begin to flow:
380   Persians and Greeks like turns of nature found,
And the world's victor stood subdued by sound!
The power of music all our hearts allow,
And what Timotheus was is Dryden now.

Avoid extremes, and shun the fault of such
Who still are pleased too little or too much,
At ev'ry trifle scorn to take offence;
That always shows great pride or little sense.
Those heads, as stomachs, are not sure the best
Which nauseate all, and nothing can digest.
390   Yet let not each gay turn thy rapture move,
For fools admire, but men of sense approve:
As things seem large which we through mist descry,
Dullness is ever apt to magnify.

Some foreign writers, some our own despise;
The ancients only, or the moderns prize:
Thus wit, like faith, by each man is applied
To one small sect, and all are damned beside.
Meanly they seek the blessing to confine,
And force that sun but on a part to shine,
400   Which not alone the southern wit sublimes,
But ripens spirits in cold northern climes;
Which from the first has shone on ages past,
Enlights the present, and shall warm the last;
Though each may feel increases and decays,
And see now clearer and now darker days.
Regard not then if wit be old or new,
But blame the false, and value still the true.

Some ne'er advance a judgement of their own,
But catch the spreading notion of the town;
410   They reason and conclude by precedent,
And own stale nonsense which they ne'er invent.
Some judge of authors' names, not works, and then
Nor praise nor blame the writings, but the men.
Of all this servile herd, the worst is he
That in proud dullness joins with quality,

A constant critic at the great man's board,
To fetch and carry nonsense for my lord.
What woeful stuff this madrigal would be
In some starved hackney sonneteer, or me!
But let a lord once own the happy lines,   420
How the wit brightens! how the style refines!
Before his sacred name flies ev'ry fault,
And each exalted stanza teems with thought!
    The vulgar thus through imitation err,
As oft the learn'd by being singular;
So much they scorn the crowd, that if the throng
By chance go right, they purposely go wrong.
So schismatics the plain believers quit,
And are but damned for having too much wit.
Some praise at morning what they blame at night,   430
But always think the last opinion right.
A Muse by these is like a mistress used,
This hour she's idolized, the next abused;
While their weak heads, like towns unfortified,
'Twixt sense and nonsense daily change their side.
Ask them the cause: they're wiser still, they say;
And still tomorrow's wiser than today.
We think our fathers fools, so wise we grow;
Our wiser sons no doubt will think us so.
Once school-divines this zealous isle o'erspread;   440
Who knew most sentences was deepest read;
Faith, gospel, all seemed made to be disputed,
And none had sense enough to be confuted.
Scotists and Thomists now in peace remain
Amidst their kindred cobwebs in Duck Lane.
If faith itself has diff'rent dresses worn,
What wonder modes in wit should take their turn?
Oft, leaving what is natural and fit,
The current folly proves the ready wit;
And authors think their reputation safe,   450
Which lives as long as fools are pleased to laugh.
    Some, valuing those of their own side or mind,
Still make themselves the measure of mankind:

Fondly we think we honour merit then,
When we but praise ourselves in other men.
Parties in wit attend on those of state,
And public faction doubles private hate.
Pride, malice, folly, against Dryden rose,
In various shapes of parsons, critics, beaus:
But sense survived when merry jests were past,
For rising merit will buoy up at last.
Might he return and bless once more our eyes,
New Blackmores and new Milbournes must arise;
Nay, should great Homer lift his awful head,
Zoilus again would start up from the dead.
Envy will merit as its shade pursue,
But like a shadow, proves the substance true;
For envied wit, like Sol eclipsed, makes known
Th' opposing body's grossness, not its own.
When first that sun too powerful beams displays,
It draws up vapours which obscure its rays;
But e'en those clouds at last adorn its way,
Reflect new glories, and augment the day.

Be thou the first true merit to befriend;
His praise is lost who stays till all commend.
Short is the date, alas! of modern rhymes,
And 'tis but just to let them live betimes.
No longer now that golden age appears,
When patriarch wits survived a thousand years;
Now length of fame (our second life) is lost,
And bare threescore is all ev'n that can boast:
Our sons their fathers' failing language see,
And such as Chaucer is, shall Dryden be.
So when the faithful pencil has designed
Some bright idea of the master's mind,
Where a new world leaps out at his command,
And ready nature waits upon his hand;
When the ripe colours soften and unite,
And sweetly melt into just shade and light;
When mell'wing years their full perfection give,
And each bold figure just begins to live;

The treach'rous colours the fair art betray,
And all the bright creation fades away!
　　Unhappy wit, like most mistaken things,
Atones not for that envy which it brings:
In youth alone its empty praise we boast,
But soon the short-lived vanity is lost;
Like some fair flower the early spring supplies,
That gaily blooms, but ev'n in blooming dies.
What is this wit, which must our cares employ?　　　500
The owner's wife that other men enjoy;
Then most our trouble still when most admired,
And still the more we give, the more required;
Whose fame with pains we guard, but lose with ease,
Sure some to vex, but never all to please;
'Tis what the vicious fear, the virtuous shun;
By fools 'tis hated, and by knaves undone!
　　If wit so much from ign'rance undergo,
Ah, let not learning too commence its foe!
Of old those met rewards who could excel,　　　　　510
And such were praised who but endeavoured well:
Though triumphs were to gen'rals only due,
Crowns were reserved to grace the soldiers too.
Now they who reach Parnassus' lofty crown
Employ their pains to spurn some others down;
And while self-love each jealous writer rules,
Contending wits become the sport of fools;
But still the worst with most regret commend,
For each ill author is as bad a friend.
To what base ends, and by what abject ways,　　　520
Are mortals urged through sacred lust of praise!
Ah, ne'er so dire a thirst of glory boast,
Nor in the critic let the man be lost.
Good nature and good sense must ever join;
To err is human, to forgive, divine.
　　But if in noble minds some dregs remain,
Not yet purged off, of spleen and sour disdain,
Discharge that rage on more provoking crimes,
Nor fear a dearth in these flagitious times.

530 No pardon vile obscenity should find,
     Though wit and art conspire to move your mind;
     But dullness with obscenity must prove
     As shameful sure as impotence in love.
     In the fat age of pleasure, wealth, and ease,
     Sprung the rank weed, and thrived with large increase;
     When love was all an easy monarch's care;
     Seldom at council, never in a war;
     Jilts ruled the state, and statesmen farces writ;
     Nay wits had pensions, and young lords had wit;
540 The fair sat panting at a courtier's play,
     And not a mask went unimproved away;
     The modest fan was lifted up no more,
     And virgins smiled at what they blushed before.
     The following licence of a foreign reign
     Did all the dregs of bold Socinus drain;
     Then unbelieving priests reformed the nation,
     And taught more pleasant methods of salvation,
     Where Heav'n's free subjects might their rights dispute,
     Lest God himself should seem too absolute:
550 Pulpits their sacred satire learned to spare,
     And vice admired to find a flatt'rer there!
     Encouraged thus, wit's Titans braved the skies,
     And the press groaned with licensed blasphemies.
     These monsters, critics! with your darts engage,
     Here point your thunder, and exhaust your rage!
     Yet shun their fault, who, scandalously nice,
     Will needs mistake an author into vice:
     All seems infected that th' infected spy,
     As all looks yellow to the jaundiced eye.

Part III

Rules for the conduct and manners in a critic. Candour. Modesty. Good breeding. Sincerity and freedom of advice. When one's counsel is to be restrained. Character of an incorrigible poet. And of an impertinent critic. Character of a good critic.

The history of criticism, and characters of the best critics; Aristotle. Horace. Dionysius. Petronius. Quintilian. Longinus. Of the decay of Criticism, and its revival. Erasmus. Vida. Boileau. Lord Roscommon, etc. Conclusion.

Learn then what morals critics ought to show,   560
For 'tis but half a judge's task to know.
'Tis not enough taste, judgement, learning join;
In all you speak let truth and candour shine,
That not alone what to your sense is due
All may allow, but seek your friendship too.

Be silent always when you doubt your sense,
And speak, though sure, with seeming diffidence;
Some positive persisting fops we know,
Who, if once wrong, will needs be always so;
But you with pleasure own your errors past,   570
And make each day a critique on the last.

'Tis not enough your counsel still be true;
Blunt truths more mischief than nice falsehoods do;
Men must be taught as if you taught them not,
And things unknown proposed as things forgot.
Without good breeding, truth is disapproved;
That only makes superior sense belov'd.

Be niggards of advice on no pretence,
For the worst avarice is that of sense.
With mean complacence ne'er betray your trust,   580
Nor be so civil as to prove unjust.
Fear not the anger of the wise to raise;
Those best can bear reproof who merit praise.

'Twere well might critics still this freedom take,
But Appius reddens at each word you speak,
And stares, tremendous, with a threat'ning eye,
Like some fierce tyrant in old tapestry.
Fear most to tax an honourable fool,
Whose right it is, uncensured, to be dull:
Such, without wit, are poets when they please,   590
As without learning they can take degrees.

Leave dang'rous truths to unsuccessful satyrs,
And flattery to fulsome dedicators;
Whom, when they praise, the world believes no more
Than when they promise to give scribbling o'er.
'Tis best sometimes your censure to restrain,
And charitably let the dull be vain:
Your silence there is better than your spite,
For who can rail so long as they can write?
600   Still humming on, their drowsy course they keep,
And lashed so long, like tops, are lashed asleep.
False steps but help them to renew the race,
As after stumbling, jades will mend their pace.
What crowds of these, impenitently bold,
In sounds and jingling syllables grown old,
Still run on poets, in a raging vein,
Ev'n to the dregs and squeezings of the brain,
Strain out the last dull droppings of their sense,
And rhyme with all the rage of impotence.
610   Such shameless bards we have; and yet 'tis true,
There are as mad abandoned critics too.
The bookful blockhead, ignorantly read,
With loads of learnèd lumber in his head,
With his own tongue still edifies his ears,
And always list'ning to himself appears.
All books he reads, and all he reads assails,
From Dryden's *Fables* down to Durfey's *Tales*.
With him, most authors steal their works, or buy;
Garth did not write his own *Dispensary*.
620   Name a new play, and he's the poet's friend;
Nay, showed his faults – but when would poets mend?
No place so sacred from such fops is barred,
Nor is Paul's church more safe than Paul's churchyard:
Nay, fly to altars; there they'll talk you dead,
For fools rush in where angels fear to tread.
Distrustful sense with modest caution speaks;   ⎫
It still looks home, and short excursions makes;   ⎬
But rattling nonsense in full volleys breaks,   ⎭

And never shocked, and never turned aside,
Bursts out, resistless, with a thund'ring tide.   630
    But where's the man who counsel can bestow,
Still pleased to teach, and yet not proud to know?
Unbiased or by favour or by spite,
Not dully prepossessed nor blindly right;
Though learn'd, well bred, and though well bred, sincere;
Modestly bold, and humanly severe;
Who to a friend his faults can freely show,
And gladly praise the merit of a foe?
Blessed with a taste exact, yet unconfined;
A knowledge both of books and human kind;   640
Gen'rous converse; a soul exempt from pride;
And love to praise, with reason on his side?
    Such once were critics; such the happy few
Athens and Rome in better ages knew.
The mighty Stagyrite first left the shore,
Spread all his sails, and durst the deeps explore;
He steered securely, and discovered far,
Led by the light of the Maeonian star.
Poets, a race long unconfined and free,
Still fond and proud of savage liberty,   650
Received his laws, and stood convinced 'twas fit
Who conquered nature should preside o'er wit.
    Horace still charms with graceful negligence,
And without method talks us into sense;
Will, like a friend, familiarly convey
The truest notions in the easiest way.
He, who supreme in judgement, as in wit,
Might boldly censure as he boldly writ,
Yet judged with coolness, though he sung with fire;
His precepts teach but what his works inspire.   660
Our critics take a contrary extreme,
They judge with fury, but they write with phlegm:
Nor suffers Horace more in wrong translations
By wits, than critics in as wrong quotations.
    See Dionysius Homer's thoughts refine,
        And call new beauties forth from ev'ry line!

Fancy and art in gay Petronius please,
The scholar's learning, with the courtier's ease.
In grave Quintilian's copious work we find
670   The justest rules and clearest method joined.
Thus useful arms in magazines we place,
All ranged in order, and disposed with grace;
But less to please the eye than arm the hand,
Still fit for use, and ready at command.

Thee, bold Longinus! all the Nine inspire,
And bless their critic with a poet's fire:
An ardent judge, who zealous in his trust,
With warmth gives sentence, yet is always just;
Whose own example strengthens all his laws,
680   And is himself that great sublime he draws.

Thus long succeeding critics justly reigned,
Licence repressed, and useful laws ordained:
Learning and Rome alike in empire grew,
And arts still followed where her eagles flew;
From the same foes, at last, both felt their doom,
And the same age saw learning fall and Rome.
With tyranny, then superstition joined,
As that the body, this enslaved the mind;
Much was believed, but little understood,
690   And to be dull was construed to be good:
A second deluge learning thus o'errun,
And the monks finished what the Goths begun.

At length Erasmus, that great injured name
(The glory of the priesthood, and the shame!)
Stemmed the wild torrent of a barb'rous age,
And drove those holy Vandals off the stage.

But see! each Muse, in Leo's golden days,
Starts from her trance, and trims her withered bays;
Rome's ancient genius, o'er its ruins spread,
700   Shakes off the dust, and rears his rev'rend head.
Then sculpture and her sister arts revive;
Stones leaped to form, and rocks began to live;

With sweeter notes each rising temple rung;
A Raphael painted, and a Vida sung;
Immortal Vida! on whose honoured brow
The poet's bays and critic's ivy grow:
Cremona now shall ever boast thy name,
As next in place to Mantua, next in fame!
   But soon by impious arms from Latium chased,
Their ancient bounds the banish'd Muses passed;   710
Thence arts o'er all the northern world advance,
But critic learning flourished most in France;
The rules a nation born to serve obeys,
And Boileau still in right of Horace sways.
But we, brave Britons, foreign laws despised,
And kept unconquered, and uncivilized;
Fierce for the liberties of wit, and bold,
We still defied the Romans, as of old.
Yet some there were, among the sounder few
Of those who less presumed, and better knew,   720
Who durst assert the juster ancient cause,
And here restored wit's fundamental laws.
Such was the Muse, whose rules and practice tell,
'Nature's chief masterpiece is writing well.'
Such was Roscommon, not more learn'd than good,
With manners gen'rous as his noble blood;
To him the wit of Greece and Rome was known,
And ev'ry author's merit but his own.
Such late was Walsh – the Muse's judge and friend,
Who justly knew to blame or to commend;   730
To failings mild, but zealous for desert,
The clearest head, and the sincerest heart.
This humble praise, lamented shade! receive;
This praise at least a grateful Muse may give:
The Muse whose early voice you taught to sing,
Prescribed her heights, and pruned her tender wing,
(Her guide now lost) no more attempts to rise,
But in low numbers short excursions tries;
Content, if hence th' unlearn'd their wants may view,
The learn'd reflect on what before they knew: 740

Careless of censure, nor too fond of fame;
Still pleased to praise, yet not afraid to blame;
Averse alike to flatter or offend;
Not free from faults, nor yet too vain to mend.

Windsor Forest

Non injussa cano: Te nostrae, Vare, myricae,
Te Nemus omne canet; nec Phoebo gratior ulla est
Quam sibi quae Vari praescripsit pagina nomen.
                                        VIRGIL

Thy forests, Windsor! and thy green retreats,
At once the monarch's and the Muse's seats,
Invite my lays. Be present, sylvan maids!
Unlock your springs, and open all your shades.
Granville commands: your aid, O Muses, bring!
What muse for Granville can refuse to sing?
  The groves of Eden, vanished now so long,
Live in description, and look green in song:
These, were my breast inspired with equal flame,
Like them in beauty, should be like in fame.
Here hills and vales, the woodland and the plain,
Here earth and water seem to strive again,
Not chaos-like together crushed and bruised,
But as the world, harmoniously confused:
Where order in variety we see,
And where, though all things differ, all agree.
Here waving groves a chequered scene display,
And part admit, and part exclude the day,
As some coy nymph her lover's warm address
Nor quite indulges, nor can quite repress.
There, interspersed in lawns and opening glades,
Thin trees arise that shun each other's shades.
Here in full light the russet plains extend;
There wrapped in clouds the bluish hills ascend.

Ev'n the wild heath displays her purple dyes,
And 'midst the desert fruitful fields arise,
That crowned with tufted trees and springing corn
Like verdant isles the sable waste adorn.
Let India boast her plants, nor envy we
The weeping amber or the balmy tree,   30
While by our oaks the precious loads are borne,
And realms commanded which those trees adorn.
Not proud Olympus yields a nobler sight,
Though gods assembled grace his towering height,
Than what more humble mountains offer here,
Where, in their blessings, all those gods appear.
See Pan with flocks, with fruits Pomona crowned,
Here blushing Flora paints the enamelled ground,
Here Ceres' gifts in waving prospect stand,
And nodding tempt the joyful reaper's hand;   40
Rich Industry sits smiling on the plains,
And peace and plenty tell, a Stuart reigns.
     Not thus the land appeared in ages past,
A dreary desert, and a gloomy waste,
To savage beasts and savage laws a prey,
And kings more furious and severe than they,
Who claimed the skies, dispeopled air and floods,
The lonely lords of empty wilds and woods:
Cities laid waste, they stormed the dens and caves
(For wiser brutes were backward to be slaves).   50
What could be free, when lawless beasts obeyed,
And ev'n the elements a tyrant swayed?
In vain kind seasons swelled the teeming grain,
Soft showers distilled, and suns grew warm in vain;
The swain with tears his frustrate labour yields,
And famished dies amidst his ripened fields.
What wonder then, a beast or subject slain
Were equal crimes in a despotic reign?
Both doomed alike, for sportive tyrants bled,
But while the subject starved, the beast was fed.   60
Proud Nimrod first the bloody chase began,
A mighty hunter, and his prey was man;

Our haughty Norman boasts that barbarous name,
And makes his trembling slaves the royal game.
The fields are ravished from th' industrious swains,
From men their cities, and from gods their fanes;
The levelled towns with weeds lie covered o'er;
The hollow winds through naked temples roar;
Round broken columns clasping ivy twined;
70   O'er heaps of ruin stalked the stately hind;
The fox obscene to gaping tombs retires,
And savage howlings fill the sacred choirs.
Awed by his nobles, by his commons cursed,
Th' oppressor ruled tyrannic where he durst,
Stretch'd o'er the poor and church his iron rod,
And served alike his vassals and his God.
Whom ev'n the Saxon spared, and bloody Dane,
The wanton victims of his sport remain.
But see, the man who spacious regions gave
80   A waste for beasts, himself denied a grave!
Stretched on the lawn his second hope survey,
At once the chaser, and at once the prey!
Lo Rufus, tugging at the deadly dart,
Bleeds in the forest like a wounded hart!
Succeeding monarchs heard the subjects' cries,
Nor saw displeased the peaceful cottage rise;
Then gath'ring flocks on unknown mountains fed,
O'er sandy wilds were yellow harvests spread,
The forests wondered at th' unusual grain,
90   And secret transport touched the conscious swain.
Fair Liberty, Britannia's goddess, rears
Her cheerful head, and leads the golden years.
     Ye vigorous swains! while youth ferments your blood,
And purer spirits swell the sprightly flood,
Now range the hills, the gameful woods beset,
Wind the shrill horn, or spread the waving net.
When milder autumn summer's heat succeeds,
And in the new-shorn field the partridge feeds,
Before his lord the ready spaniel bounds,
100 Panting with hope, he tries the furrowed grounds;

But when the tainted gales the game betray,
Couched close he lies, and meditates the prey;
Secure they trust th' unfaithful field, beset,
Till hovering o'er 'em sweeps the swelling net.
Thus (if small things we may with great compare)
When Albion sends her eager sons to war,
Some thoughtless town, with ease and plenty blest,
Near, and more near, the closing lines invest;
Sudden they seize th' amazed, defenceless prize,
And high in air Britannia's standard flies.   110
  See! from the brake the whirring pheasant springs,
And mounts exulting on triumphant wings:
Short is his joy; he feels the fiery wound,
Flutters in blood, and panting beats the ground.
Ah! what avail his glossy, varying dyes,
His purple crest, and scarlet-circled eyes,
The vivid green his shining plumes unfold,
His painted wings, and breast that flames with gold?
  Nor yet, when moist Arcturus clouds the sky,
The woods and fields their pleasing toils deny.   120
To plains with well breathed beagles we repair,
And trace the mazes of the circling hare
(Beasts, urged by us, their fellow beasts pursue,
And learn of man each other to undo).
With slaught'ring guns th' unwearied fowler roves,
When frosts have whitened all the naked groves,
Where doves in flocks the leafless trees o'ershade,
And lonely woodcocks haunt the wat'ry glade.
He lifts the tube, and levels with his eye;
Straight a short thunder breaks the frozen sky.   130
Oft, as in airy rings they skim the heath,
The clam'rous lapwings feel the leaden death;
Oft, as the mounting larks their notes prepare,
They fall, and leave their little lives in air.
  In genial spring, beneath the quivering shade,
Where cooling vapours breathe along the mead,
The patient fisher takes his silent stand,
Intent, his angle trembling in his hand;

With looks unmoved, he hopes the scaly breed,
140 And eyes the dancing cork and bending reed.
Our plenteous streams a various race supply,
The bright-eyed perch with fins of Tyrian dye,
The silver eel, in shining volumes rolled,
The yellow carp, in scales bedropped with gold,
Swift trouts, diversified with crimson stains,
And pikes, the tyrants of the watery plains.
    Now Cancer glows with Phoebus' fiery car:
The youth rush eager to the sylvan war,
Swarm o'er the lawns, the forest walks surround,
150 Rouse the fleet hart, and cheer the opening hound.
Th' impatient courser pants in every vein,
And, pawing, seems to beat the distant plain:
Hills, vales, and floods appear already crossed,
And ere he starts, a thousand steps are lost.
See the bold youth strain up the threat'ning steep,
Rush through the thickets, down the valleys sweep,
Hang o'er their coursers' heads with eager speed,
And earth rolls back beneath the flying steed.
Let old Arcadia boast her ample plain,
160 Th' immortal huntress, and her virgin train;
Nor envy, Windsor! since thy shades have seen
As bright a goddess, and as chaste a queen;
Whose care, like hers, protects the sylvan reign,
The earth's fair light, and empress of the main.
    Here too, 'tis sung, of old Diana strayed,
And Cynthus' top forsook for Windsor shade;
Here was she seen o'er airy wastes to rove,
Seek the clear spring, or haunt the pathless grove;
Here armed with silver bows, in early dawn,
170 Her buskined virgins traced the dewy lawn.
    Above the rest a rural nymph was famed,
Thy offspring, Thames! the fair Lodona named.
(Lodona's fate, in long oblivion cast,
The Muse shall sing, and what she sings shall last.)
Scarce could the goddess from her nymph be known,
But by the crescent and the golden zone.

She scorned the praise of beauty, and the care;
A belt her waist, a fillet binds her hair;
A painted quiver on her shoulder sounds,
And with her dart the flying deer she wounds.   180
It chanced, as eager of the chase, the maid
Beyond the forest's verdant limits strayed,
Pan saw and loved, and, burning with desire
Pursued her flight; her flight increased his fire.
Not half so swift the trembling doves can fly,
When the fierce eagle cleaves the liquid sky;
Not half so swiftly the fierce eagle moves,
When through the clouds he drives the trembling doves,
As from the god she flew with furious pace,
Or as the god, more furious, urged the chase.   190
Now fainting, sinking, pale, the nymph appears;
Now close behind, his sounding steps she hears;
And now his shadow reached her as she run
(His shadow lengthened by the setting sun),
And now his shorter breath, with sultry air
Pants on her neck, and fans her parting hair.
In vain on father Thames she calls for aid,
Nor could Diana help her injured maid.
Faint, breathless, thus she prayed, nor prayed in vain;
'Ah, Cynthia! ah – though banished from thy train,   200
Let me, O let me, to the shades repair,
My native shades – there weep, and murmur there.'
She said, and melting as in tears she lay,
In a soft, silver stream dissolved away.
The silver stream her virgin coldness keeps,
For ever murmurs, and for ever weeps;
Still bears the name the hapless virgin bore,
And bathes the forest where she ranged before.
In her chaste current oft the goddess laves,
And with celestial tears augments the waves.   210
Oft in her glass the musing shepherd spies
The headlong mountains and the downward skies,
The wat'ry landscape of the pendent woods,
And absent trees that tremble in the floods;

In the clear azure gleam the flocks are seen,
And floating forests paint the waves with green.
Through the fair scene roll slow the ling'ring streams,
Then foaming pour along, and rush into the Thames.
   Thou, too, great father of the British floods!
220 With joyful pride survey'st our lofty woods,
Where towering oaks their growing honours rear,
And future navies on thy shores appear.
Not Neptune's self from all his streams receives
A wealthier tribute, than to thine he gives.
No seas so rich, so gay no banks appear,
No lake so gentle, and no spring so clear.
Nor Po so swells the fabling poet's lays,
While led along the skies his current strays,
As thine, which visits Windsor's famed abodes,
230 To grace the mansion of our earthly gods;
Nor all his stars above a lustre show
Like the bright beauties on thy banks below;
Where Jove, subdued by mortal passion still,
Might change Olympus for a nobler hill.
   Happy the man whom this bright court approves,
His sovereign favours, and his country loves:
Happy next him, who to these shades retires,
Whom Nature charms, and whom the Muse inspires:
Whom humbler joys of home-felt quiet please,
240 Successive study, exercise, and ease.
He gathers health from herbs the forest yields,
And of their fragrant physic spoils the fields:
With chemic art exalts the mineral powers,
And draws the aromatic souls of flowers;
Now marks the course of rolling orbs on high;
O'er figured worlds now travels with his eye;
Of ancient writ unlocks the learnèd store,
Consults the dead, and lives past ages o'er:
Or wand'ring thoughtful in the silent wood,
250 Attends the duties of the wise and good,

T' observe a mean, be to himself a friend,
To follow Nature, and regard his end;
Or looks on Heaven with more than mortal eyes,
Bids his free soul expatiate in the skies,
Amid her kindred stars familiar roam,
Survey the region, and confess her home!
Such was the life great Scipio once admired;
Thus Atticus, and Trumbull thus retired.

    Ye sacred Nine! that all my soul possess,
Whose raptures fire me, and whose visions bless,   260
Bear me, O bear me to sequestered scenes,
The bow'ry mazes, and surrounding greens;
To Thames's banks, which fragrant breezes fill,
Or where ye Muses sport on Cooper's Hill.
(On Cooper's Hill eternal wreaths shall grow,
While lasts the mountain, or while Thames shall flow.)
I seem through consecrated walks to rove,
I hear soft music die along the grove;
Led by the sound, I roam from shade to shade,
By godlike poets venerable made: 270
Here his first lays majestic Denham sung;
There the last numbers flowed from Cowley's tongue.
Oh early lost! what tears the river shed
When the sad pomp along his banks was led!
His drooping swans on every note expire,
And on his willows hung each Muse's lyre.

    Since fate relentless stopped their heavenly voice,
No more the forests ring, or groves rejoice;
Who now shall charm the shades where Cowley strung
His living harp, and lofty Denham sung?   280
But hark! the groves rejoice, the forest rings!
Are these revived, or is it Granville sings?
'Tis yours, my Lord, to bless our soft retreats,
And call the Muses to their ancient seats;
To paint anew the flowery sylvan scenes,
To crown the forests with immortal greens,
Make Windsor hills in lofty numbers rise,
And lift her turrets nearer to the skies;

To sing those honours you deserve to wear,
290   And add new lustre to her silver star!
      Here noble Surrey felt the sacred rage,
Surrey, the Granville of a former age:
Matchless his pen, victorious was his lance,
Bold in the lists, and graceful in the dance;
In the same shades the Cupids tuned his lyre
To the same notes, of love, and soft desire:
Fair Geraldine, bright object of his vow,
Then filled the groves, as heavenly Myra now.
      Oh wouldst thou sing what heroes Windsor bore,
300   What kings first breathed upon her winding shore,
Or raise old warriors, whose adored remains
In weeping vaults her hallowed earth contains!
With Edward's acts adorn the shining page,
Stretch his long triumphs down through every age,
Draw monarchs chained, and Cressi's glorious field,
The lilies blazing on the regal shield;
Then, from her roofs when Verrio's colours fall,
And leave inanimate the naked wall,
Still in thy song should vanquished France appear,
310   And bleed for ever under Britain's spear.
      Let softer strains ill-fated Henry mourn,
And palms eternal flourish round his urn.
Here o'er the martyr-king the marble weeps,
And, fast beside him, once-feared Edward sleeps:
Whom not th' extended Albion could contain,
From old Belerium to the northern main,
The grave unites; where ev'n the great find rest,
And blended lie th' oppressor and th' oppressed!
      Make sacred Charles's tomb for ever known
320   (Obscure the place, and uninscribed the stone);
Oh fact accurst! what tears has Albion shed,
Heavens! what new wounds! and how her old have bled!
She saw her sons with purple death expire,
Her sacred domes involved in rolling fire,

A dreadful series of intestine wars,
Inglorious triumphs, and dishonest scars.
At length great Anna said, 'Let discord cease!'
She said! the world obeyed, and all was peace!
    In that blest moment from his oozy bed
Old father Thames advanced his reverend head;   330
His tresses dropped with dews, and o'er the stream
His shining horns diffused a golden gleam:
Graved on his urn appeared the moon, that guides
His swelling waters and alternate tides;
The figured streams in waves of silver rolled,
And on their banks Augusta rose in gold.
Around his throne the sea-born brothers stood,
Who swell with tributary urns his flood.
First the famed authors of his ancient name,
The winding Isis, and the fruitful Thame;   340
The Kennet swift, for silver eels renowned;
The Lodden slow, with verdant alders crowned;
Cole, whose dark streams his flow'ry islands lave;
And chalky Wey, that rolls a milky wave;
The blue, transparent Vandalis appears;
The gulfy Lee his sedgy tresses rears;
And sullen Mole, that hides his diving flood;
And silent Darent, stained with Danish blood.
    High in the midst, upon his urn reclined
(His sea-green mantle waving with the wind),   350
The god appeared: he turned his azure eyes
Where Windsor domes and pompous turrets rise;
Then bowed and spoke; the winds forget to roar,
And the hushed waves glide softly to the shore.
    'Hail, sacred peace! hail, long-expected days,
That Thames's glory to the stars shall raise!
Though Tiber's streams immortal Rome behold,
Though foaming Hermus swells with tides of gold,
From Heaven itself though sev'nfold Nilus flows,
And harvests on a hundred realms bestows;   360
These now no more shall be the Muse's themes,
Lost in my fame, as in the sea their streams.

Let Volga's banks with iron squadrons shine,
And groves of lances glitter on the Rhine;
Let barb'rous Ganges arm a servile train,
Be mine the blessings of a peaceful reign.
No more my sons shall dye with British blood
Red Iber's sands, or Ister's foaming flood;
Safe on my shore each unmolested swain
370   Shall tend the flocks, or reap the bearded grain;
The shady empire shall retain no trace
Of war or blood, but in the sylvan chase;
The trumpets sleep while cheerful horns are blown,
And arms employed on birds and beasts alone.
Behold! th' ascending villas on my side
Project long shadows o'er the crystal tide;
Behold! Augusta's glittering spires increase,
And temples rise, the beauteous works of Peace.
I see, I see, where two fair cities bend
380   Their ample bow, a new Whitehall ascend!
There mighty nations shall inquire their doom,
The world's great oracle in times to come;
There kings shall sue, and suppliant states be seen
Once more to bend before a British queen.
     'Thy trees, fair Windsor! now shall leave their woods,
And half thy forests rush into my floods,
Bear Britain's thunder, and her cross display
To the bright regions of the rising day;
Tempt icy seas, where scarce the waters roll,
390   Where clearer flames glow round the frozen pole;
Or under southern skies exalt their sails,
Led by new stars, and borne by spicy gales!
For me the balm shall bleed, and amber flow,
The coral redden, and the ruby glow,
The pearly shell its lucid globe infold,
And Phoebus warm the ripening ore to gold.
The time shall come, when free as seas or wind,
Unbounded Thames shall flow for all mankind,

Whole nations enter with each swelling tide,
And seas but join the regions they divide;   400
Earth's distant ends our glory shall behold,
And the new world launch forth to seek the old.
Then ships of uncouth form shall stem the tide,
And feathered people crowd my wealthy side,
And naked youths and painted chiefs admire
Our speech, our colour, and our strange attire!
O stretch thy reign, fair Peace! from shore to shore,
Till conquest cease, and slavery be no more;
Till the freed Indians in their native groves
Reap their own fruits, and woo their sable loves;   410
Peru once more a race of kings behold,
And other Mexicos be roofed with gold.
Exiled by thee from earth to deepest Hell,
In brazen bonds shall barb'rous Discord dwell;
Gigantic Pride, pale Terror, gloomy Care,
And mad Ambition shall attend her there;
There purple Vengeance, bathed in gore, retires,
Her weapons blunted, and extinct her fires;
There hated Envy her own snakes shall feel,
And Persecution mourn her broken wheel;   420
There Faction roar, Rebellion bite her chain,
And gasping Furies thirst for blood in vain.'

    Here cease thy flight, nor with unhallowed lays
Touch the fair fame of Albion's golden days:
The thoughts of gods let Granville's verse recite,
And bring the scenes of opening fate to light.
My humble Muse, in unambitious strains,
Paints the green forests and the flowery plains,
Where Peace descending bids her olives spring,
And scatters blessings from her dovelike wing.   430
Ev'n I more sweetly pass my careless days,
Pleased in the silent shade with empty praise;
Enough for me, that to the list'ning swains
First in these fields I sung the sylvan strains.

Prologue to Mr Addison's Tragedy of Cato

To wake the soul by tender strokes of art,
To raise the genius, and to mend the heart;
To make mankind, in conscious virtue bold,
Live o'er each scene, and be what they behold:
For this the tragic Muse first trod the stage,
Commanding tears to stream through ev'ry age;
Tyrants no more their savage nature kept,
And foes to virtue wondered how they wept.
Our author shuns by vulgar springs to move
10   The hero's glory, or the virgin's love;
In pitying love, we but our weakness show,
And wild ambition well deserves its woe.
Here tears shall flow from a more gen'rous cause,
Such tears as patriots shed for dying laws;
He bids your breasts with ancient ardour rise,
And calls forth Roman drops from British eyes.
Virtue confessed in human shape he draws,
What Plato thought, and godlike Cato was:
No common object to your sight displays,
20   But what with pleasure Heav'n itself surveys,
A brave man struggling in the storms of fate,
And greatly falling with a falling state.
While Cato gives his little senate laws,
What bosom beats not in his country's cause?
Who sees him act, but envies ev'ry deed?
Who hears him groan, and does not wish to bleed?
Ev'n when proud Caesar, midst triumphal cars,
The spoils of nations, and the pomp of wars,
Ignobly vain, and impotently great,
30   Showed Rome her Cato's figure drawn in state;
As her dead father's rev'rend image passed,
The pomp was darkened, and the day o'ercast;
The triumph ceased, tears gushed from ev'ry eye;
The world's great victor passed unheeded by;

Her last good man dejected Rome adored,
And honoured Caesar's less than Cato's sword.
  Britons, attend: be worth like this approved,
And show you have the virtue to be moved.
With honest scorn the first famed Cato viewed
Rome learning arts from Greece, whom she subdued;   40
Your scene precariously subsists too long
On French translation, and Italian song.
Dare to have sense yourselves; assert the stage,
Be justly warmed with your own native rage:
Such plays alone should please a British ear,
As Cato's self had not disdained to hear.

The Rape of the Lock
An Heroi-Comical Poem

To Mrs Arabella Fermor

Madam,
  It will be in vain to deny that I have some regard for this
piece, since I dedicate it to you. Yet you may bear me witness,
it was intended only to divert a few young ladies, who have
good sense and good humour enough to laugh not only at their
sex's little unguarded follies, but at their own. But as it was
communicated with the air of a secret, it soon found its way
into the world. An imperfect copy having been offered to a
bookseller, you had the good nature, for my sake, to consent to
the publication of one more correct: this I was forced to, before
I had executed half my design, for the machinery was entirely
wanting to complete it.
  The machinery, Madam, is a term invented by the critics, to
signify that part which the deities, angels, or demons are made
to act in a poem: for the ancient poets are in one respect like
many modern ladies; let an action be never so trivial in itself,
they always make it appear of the utmost importance. These
machines I determined to raise on a very new and odd founda-
tion, the Rosicrucian doctrine of spirits.

I know how disagreeable it is to make use of hard words before a lady; but 'tis so much the concern of a poet to have his works understood, and particularly by your sex, that you must give me leave to explain two or three difficult terms.

The Rosicrucians are a people I must bring you acquainted with. The best account I know of them is in a French book called *Le Comte de Gabalis*, which, both in its title and size, is so like a novel that many of the fair sex have read it for one by mistake. According to these gentlemen, the four elements are inhabited by spirits, which they call sylphs, gnomes, nymphs, and salamanders. The gnomes, or demons of earth, delight in mischief; but the sylphs, whose habitation is in the air, are the best-conditioned creatures imaginable; for, they say, any mortal may enjoy the most intimate familiarities with these gentle spirits, upon a condition very easy to all true adepts, an inviolate preservation of chastity.

As to the following cantos, all the passages of them are as fabulous as the vision at the beginning, or the transformation at the end (except the loss of your hair, which I always mention with reverence). The human persons are as fictitious as the airy ones; and the character of Belinda, as it is now managed, resembles you in nothing but in beauty.

If this poem had as many graces as there are in your person, or in your mind, yet I could never hope it should pass through the world half so uncensured as you have done. But let its fortune be what it will, mine is happy enough, to have given me this occasion of assuring you that I am, with the truest esteem, Madam,

Your most obedient, humble servant,

A. Pope

The Rape of the Lock

Nolueram, Belinda, tuos violare capillos;
Sed juvat, hoc precibus me tribuisse tuis.

Canto I

What dire offence from am'rous causes springs,
What mighty contests rise from trivial things,
I sing – This verse to Caryll, Muse! is due:
This, ev'n Belinda may vouchsafe to view:
Slight is the subject, but not so the praise,
If she inspire, and he approve my lays.
　　Say what strange motive, Goddess! could compel
A well-bred lord t' assault a gentle belle?
O say what stranger cause, yet unexplored,
Could make a gentle belle reject a lord?　　　　　　　10
In tasks so bold can little men engage,
And in soft bosoms dwells such mighty rage?
　　Sol through white curtains shot a tim'rous ray,
And oped those eyes that must eclipse the day.
Now lapdogs give themselves the rousing shake,
And sleepless lovers, just at twelve, awake;
Thrice rung the bell, the slipper knocked the ground,
And the pressed watch returned a silver sound.
Belinda still her downy pillow pressed,
Her guardian sylph prolonged the balmy rest:　　　　20
'Twas he had summoned to her silent bed
The morning-dream that hovered o'er her head.
A youth more glittering than a birthnight beau
(That ev'n in slumber caused her cheek to glow)
Seemed to her ear his winning lips to lay,
And thus in whispers said, or seemed to say:
　　'Fairest of mortals, thou distinguished care
Of thousand bright inhabitants of air!

If e'er one vision touched thy infant thought,
Of all the nurse and all the priest have taught;
Of airy elves by moonlight-shadows seen,
The silver token, and the circled green,
Or virgins visited by angel pow'rs,
With golden crowns and wreaths of heavenly flow'rs;
Hear and believe! thy own importance know,
Nor bound thy narrow views to things below.
Some secret truths, from learnèd pride concealed,
To maids alone and children are revealed.
What though no credit doubting wits may give?
The fair and innocent shall still believe.
Know then, unnumbered spirits round thee fly,
The light militia of the lower sky;
These, though unseen, are ever on the wing,
Hang o'er the box, and hover round the ring.
Think what an equipage thou hast in air,
And view with scorn two pages and a chair.
As now your own, our beings were of old,
And once enclosed in woman's beauteous mould;
Thence, by a soft transition, we repair
From earthly vehicles to these of air.
Think not, when woman's transient breath is fled,
That all her vanities at once are dead;
Succeeding vanities she still regards,
And, though she plays no more, o'erlooks the cards.
Her joy in gilded chariots, when alive,
And love of ombre, after death survive.
For when the fair in all their pride expire,
To their first elements their souls retire.
The sprites of fiery termagants in flame
Mount up, and take a salamander's name.
Soft yielding minds to water glide away,
And sip, with nymphs, their elemental tea.
The graver prude sinks downward to a gnome,
In search of mischief still on earth to roam.
The light coquettes in sylphs aloft repair,
And sport and flutter in the fields of air.

    'Know further yet; whoever fair and chaste
Rejects mankind, is by some sylph embraced:
For spirits, freed from mortal laws, with ease
Assume what sexes and what shapes they please.   70
What guards the purity of melting maids
In courtly balls, and midnight masquerades,
Safe from the treach'rous friend, the daring spark,
The glance by day, the whisper in the dark;
When kind occasion prompts their warm desires,
When music softens, and when dancing fires?
'Tis but their sylph, the wise celestials know,
Though honour is the word with men below.
    'Some nymphs there are, too conscious of their face,
For life predestined to the gnomes' embrace.   80
These swell their prospects and exalt their pride
When offers are disdained, and love denied;
Then gay ideas crowd the vacant brain,
While peers, and dukes, and all their sweeping train,
And garters, stars, and coronets appear,
And in soft sounds, "Your Grace" salutes their ear.
'Tis these that early taint the female soul,
Instruct the eyes of young coquettes to roll,
Teach infant-cheeks a bidden blush to know,
And little hearts to flutter at a beau.   90
    'Oft, when the world imagine women stray,
The sylphs through mystic mazes guide their way;
Through all the giddy circle they pursue,
And old impertinence expel by new.
What tender maid but must a victim fall
To one man's treat, but for another's ball?
When Florio speaks, what virgin could withstand,
If gentle Damon did not squeeze her hand?
With varying vanities, from every part,
They shift the moving toyshop of their heart;   100
Where wigs with wigs, with sword-knots
        sword-knots strive,
Beaus banish beaus, and coaches coaches drive.
This erring mortals levity may call;
Oh blind to truth! the sylphs contrive it all.

'Of these am I, who thy protection claim,
A watchful sprite, and Ariel is my name.
Late, as I ranged the crystal wilds of air,
In the clear mirror of thy ruling star
I saw, alas! some dread event impend,
110   Ere to the main this morning sun descend,
But Heav'n reveals not what, or how or where:
Warned by the sylph, O pious maid, beware!
This to disclose is all thy guardian can:
Beware of all, but most beware of man!'
    He said; when Shock, who thought she slept too long,
Leaped up, and waked his mistress with his tongue.
'Twas then, Belinda, if report say true,
Thy eyes first opened on a billet-doux;
'Wounds', 'charms', and 'ardours' were no sooner read,
120   But all the vision vanished from thy head.
    And now, unveiled, the toilet stands displayed,
Each silver vase in mystic order laid.
First, robed in white, the nymph intent adores,
With head uncovered, the cosmetic powers.
A heavenly image in the glass appears,
To that she bends, to that her eyes she rears;
Th' inferior priestess, at her altar's side,
Trembling begins the sacred rites of pride.
Unnumbered treasures ope at once, and here
130   The various offerings of the world appear;
From each she nicely culls with curious toil,
And decks the goddess with the glittering spoil.
This casket India's glowing gems unlocks,
And all Arabia breathes from yonder box.
The tortoise here and elephant unite,
Transformed to combs, the speckled and the white.
Here files of pins extend their shining rows,
Puffs, powders, patches, Bibles, billet-doux.
Now awful beauty puts on all its arms;
140   The fair each moment rises in her charms,
Repairs her smiles, awakens ev'ry grace,
And calls forth all the wonders of her face;

Sees by degrees a purer blush arise,
And keener lightnings quicken in her eyes.
The busy sylphs surround their darling care;
These set the head, and those divide the hair,
Some fold the sleeve, whilst others plait the gown;
And Betty's praised for labours not her own.

Canto II

Not with more glories, in th' ethereal plain,
The sun first rises o'er the purpled main,
Than, issuing forth, the rival of his beams
Launched on the bosom of the silver Thames.
Fair nymphs and well-dressed youths around her shone,
But every eye was fixed on her alone.
On her white breast a sparkling cross she wore,
Which Jews might kiss, and infidels adore.
Her lively looks a sprightly mind disclose,
Quick as her eyes, and as unfixed as those: 10
Favours to none, to all she smiles extends;
Oft she rejects, but never once offends.
Bright as the sun, her eyes the gazers strike,
And, like the sun, they shine on all alike.
Yet graceful ease, and sweetness void of pride,
Might hide her faults, if belles had faults to hide;
If to her share some female errors fall,
Look on her face, and you'll forget 'em all.
  This nymph, to the destruction of mankind,
Nourished two locks, which graceful hung behind   20
In equal curls, and well conspired to deck
With shining ringlets the smooth iv'ry neck.
Love in these labyrinths his slaves detains,
And mighty hearts are held in slender chains.
With hairy springes we the birds betray,
Slight lines of hair surprise the finny prey,
Fair tresses man's imperial race ensnare,
And beauty draws us with a single hair.

Th' adv'nturous Baron the bright locks admired;
He saw, he wished, and to the prize aspired.   30
Resolved to win, he meditates the way,
By force to ravish, or by fraud betray;
For when success a lover's toil attends,
Few ask if fraud or force attained his ends.

For this, ere Phoebus rose, he had implored
Propitious Heav'n, and ev'ry pow'r adored,
But chiefly Love – to Love an altar built,
Of twelve vast French romances, neatly gilt.
There lay three garters, half a pair of gloves,
And all the trophies of his former loves;   40
With tender billet-doux he lights the pyre,
And breathes three am'rous sighs to raise the fire.
Then prostrate falls, and begs with ardent eyes
Soon to obtain, and long possess the prize:
The pow'rs gave ear, and granted half his prayer,
The rest the winds dispersed in empty air.

But now secure the painted vessel glides,
The sunbeams trembling on the floating tides;
While melting music steals upon the sky,
And softened sounds along the waters die.   50
Smooth flow the waves, the zephyrs gently play,
Belinda smiled, and all the world was gay.
All but the sylph – with careful thoughts oppressed,
Th' impending woe sat heavy on his breast.
He summons straight his denizens of air;
The lucid squadrons round the sails repair:
Soft o'er the shrouds aerial whispers breathe,
That seemed but zephyrs to the train beneath.
Some to the sun their insect-wings unfold,
Waft on the breeze, or sink in clouds of gold;   60
Transparent forms too fine for mortal sight,
Their fluid bodies half dissolved in light,
Loose to the wind their airy garments flew,
Thin glittering textures of the filmy dew,
Dipped in the richest tincture of the skies,
Where light disports in ever-mingling dyes,

While ev'ry beam new transient colours flings,
Colours that change whene'er they wave their wings.
Amid the circle, on the gilded mast,
Superior by the head, was Ariel placed;   70
His purple pinions opening to the sun,
He raised his azure wand, and thus begun:
    'Ye sylphs and sylphids, to your chief give ear!
Fays, fairies, genii, elves, and demons, hear!
Ye know the spheres, and various tasks assigned
By laws eternal to th' aerial kind.
Some in the fields of purest aether play,
And bask and whiten in the blaze of day;
Some guide the course of wand'ring orbs on high,
Or roll the planets through the boundless sky;   80
Some, less refined, beneath the moon's pale light
Pursue the stars that shoot athwart the night,
Or suck the mists in grosser air below,
Or dip their pinions in the painted bow,
Or brew fierce tempests on the wintry main,
Or o'er the glebe distil the kindly rain.
Others, on earth, o'er human race preside,
Watch all their ways, and all their actions guide:
Of these the chief the care of nations own,
And guard with arms divine the British throne.   90
    'Our humbler province is to tend the fair,
Not a less pleasing, though less glorious care;
To save the powder from too rude a gale,
Nor let th' imprisoned essences exhale;
To draw fresh colours from the vernal flow'rs;
To steal from rainbows ere they drop in show'rs
A brighter wash; to curl their waving hairs,
Assist their blushes, and inspire their airs;
Nay oft, in dreams, invention we bestow,
To change a flounce, or add a furbelow.   100
    'This day black omens threat the brightest fair
That e'er deserved a watchful spirit's care,
Some dire disaster, or by force or slight;
But what, or where, the fates have wrapped in night.

Whether the nymph shall break Diana's law,
Or some frail china jar receive a flaw;
Or stain her honour, or her new brocade;
Forget her prayers, or miss a masquerade;
Or lose her heart, or necklace, at a ball;
110 Or whether heaven has doomed that Shock must fall.
Haste, then, ye spirits! to your charge repair:
The flutt'ring fan be Zephyretta's care;
The drops to thee, Brillante, we consign;
And, Momentilla, let the watch be thine;
Do thou, Crispissa, tend her favourite lock;
Ariel himself shall be the guard of Shock.
    'To fifty chosen sylphs, of special note,
We trust th' important charge, the petticoat;
Oft have we known that sev'n-fold fence to fail,
120 Though stiff with hoops, and armed with ribs of whale.
Form a strong line about the silver bound,
And guard the wide circumference around.
    'Whatever spirit, careless of his charge,
His post neglects, or leaves the fair at large,
Shall feel sharp vengeance soon o'ertake his sins,
Be stopped in vials, or transfixed with pins;
Or plunged in lakes of bitter washes lie,
Or wedged whole ages in a bodkin's eye;
Gums and pomatums shall his flight restrain,
130 While clogged he beats his silken wings in vain;
Or alum styptics with contracting pow'r
Shrink his thin essence like a rivelled flow'r:
Or, as Ixion fixed, the wretch shall feel
The giddy motion of the whirling mill,
In fumes of burning chocolate shall glow,
And tremble at the sea that froths below!'
    He spoke; the spirits from the sails descend;
Some, orb in orb, around the nymph extend;
Some thread the mazy ringlets of her hair;
140 Some hang upon the pendants of her ear;
With beating hearts the dire event they wait,
Anxious, and trembling for the birth of fate.

Canto III

Close by those meads, for ever crowned with flow'rs,
Where Thames with pride surveys his rising tow'rs,
There stands a structure of majestic frame,
Which from the neighbouring Hampton takes its name.
Here Britain's statesmen oft the fall foredoom
Of foreign tyrants, and of nymphs at home;
Here thou, great Anna! whom three realms obey,
Dost sometimes counsel take – and sometimes tea.
   Hither the heroes and the nymphs resort,
To taste awhile the pleasures of a court;   10
In various talk th' instructive hours they passed,
Who gave the ball, or paid the visit last;
One speaks the glory of the British queen,
And one describes a charming Indian screen;
A third interprets motions, looks, and eyes;
At ev'ry word a reputation dies.
Snuff, or the fan, supply each pause of chat,
With singing, laughing, ogling, and all that.
   Meanwhile, declining from the noon of day,
The sun obliquely shoots his burning ray;   20
The hungry judges soon the sentence sign,
And wretches hang that jurymen may dine;
The merchant from th' Exchange returns in peace,
And the long labours of the toilet cease.
Belinda now, whom thirst of fame invites,
Burns to encounter two advent'rous knights,
At ombre singly to decide their doom,
And swells her breast with conquests yet to come.
Straight the three bands prepare in arms to join,
Each band the number of the sacred Nine.   30
Soon as she spreads her hand, th' aerial guard
Descend, and sit on each important card:
First Ariel perched upon a matadore,
Then each according to the rank they bore;

For sylphs, yet mindful of their ancient race,
Are, as when women, wondrous fond of place.
　　Behold, four kings in majesty revered,
With hoary whiskers and a forky beard;
And four fair queens, whose hands sustain a flow'r,
40　Th' expressive emblem of their softer pow'r;
Four knaves, in garbs succinct, a trusty band,
Caps on their heads, and halberts in their hand;
And particoloured troops, a shining train,
Draw forth to combat on the velvet plain.
　　The skilful nymph reviews her force with care;
'Let spades be trumps!' she said, and trumps they were.
　　Now move to war her sable matadores,
In show like leaders of the swarthy Moors.
Spadillio first, unconquerable lord!
50　Led off two captive trumps, and swept the board.
As many more Manillio forced to yield,
And marched a victor from the verdant field.
Him Basto followed, but his fate more hard
Gained but one trump and one plebeian card.
With his broad sabre next, a chief in years,
The hoary majesty of spades appears,
Puts forth one manly leg, to sight revealed,
The rest his many-coloured robe concealed.
The rebel knave, who dares his prince engage,
60　Proves the just victim of his royal rage.
Ev'n mighty Pam, that kings and queens o'erthrew,
And mowed down armies in the fights of Lu,
Sad chance of war! now destitute of aid,
Falls undistinguished by the victor spade!
　　Thus far both armies to Belinda yield;
Now to the Baron fate inclines the field.
His warlike Amazon her host invades,
Th' imperial consort of the crown of spades.
The club's black tyrant first her victim died,
70　Spite of his haughty mien and barbarous pride:
What boots the regal circle on his head,
His giant limbs, in state unwieldy spread;

That long behind he trails his pompous robe,
And, of all monarchs, only grasps the globe?
   The Baron now his diamonds pours apace;
Th' embroidered king who shows but half his face,
And his refulgent queen, with powers combined,
Of broken troops an easy conquest find.
Clubs, diamonds, hearts, in wild disorder seen,
With throngs promiscuous strew the level green.   80
Thus when dispersed a routed army runs
Of Asia's troops, and Afric's sable sons,
With like confusion different nations fly,
Of various habit, and of various dye,
The pierced battalions disunited fall
In heaps on heaps; one fate o'erwhelms them all.
The knave of diamonds tries his wily arts,
And wins (oh shameful chance!) the queen of hearts.
At this, the blood the virgin's cheek forsook,
A livid paleness spreads o'er all her look;   90
She sees, and trembles at th' approaching ill,
Just in the jaws of ruin, and codille.
And now (as oft in some distempered state)
On one nice trick depends the gen'ral fate:
An ace of hearts steps forth: the king unseen
Lurked in her hand, and mourned his captive queen.
He springs to vengeance with an eager pace,
And falls like thunder on the prostrate ace.
The nymph exulting fills with shouts the sky;
The walls, the woods, and long canals reply.   100
   O thoughtless mortals! ever blind to fate,
Too soon dejected, and too soon elate:
Sudden these honours shall be snatched away,
And cursed for ever this victorious day.
   For lo! the board with cups and spoons is crowned,
The berries crackle, and the mill turns round;
On shining altars of Japan they raise
The silver lamp; the fiery spirits blaze:
From silver spouts the grateful liquors glide,
While China's earth receives the smoking tide.   110

At once they gratify their scent and taste,
And frequent cups prolong the rich repast.
Straight hover round the fair her airy band;
Some, as she sipped the fuming liquor fanned,
Some o'er her lap their careful plumes displayed,
Trembling, and conscious of the rich brocade.
Coffee (which makes the politician wise,
And see through all things with his half-shut eyes)
Sent up in vapours to the Baron's brain
120   New stratagems, the radiant lock to gain.
Ah cease, rash youth! desist ere 'tis too late,
Fear the just gods, and think of Scylla's fate!
Changed to a bird, and sent to flit in air,
She dearly pays for Nisus' injured hair!

But when to mischief mortals bend their will,
How soon they find fit instruments of ill!
Just then, Clarissa drew with tempting grace
A two-edged weapon from her shining case:
So ladies in romance assist their knight,
130   Present the spear, and arm him for the fight.
He takes the gift with rev'rence, and extends
The little engine on his fingers' ends;
This just behind Belinda's neck he spread,
As o'er the fragrant steams she bends her head.
Swift to the lock a thousand sprites repair,
A thousand wings, by turns, blow back the hair,
And thrice they twitched the diamond in her ear;
Thrice she looked back, and thrice the foe drew near.
Just in that instant, anxious Ariel sought
140   The close recesses of the virgin's thought,
As on the nosegay in her breast reclined,
He watched th' ideas rising in her mind,
Sudden he viewed, in spite of all her art,
An earthly lover lurking at her heart.
Amazed, confused, he found his power expired,
Resigned to fate, and with a sigh retired.

The peer now spreads the glittering forfex wide
T' enclose the lock; now joins it, to divide.

Ev'n then, before the fatal engine closed,
A wretched sylph too fondly interposed;   150
Fate urged the shears, and cut the sylph in twain
(But airy substance soon unites again),
The meeting points the sacred hair dissever
From the fair head, for ever, and for ever!
  Then flashed the living lightning from her eyes,
And screams of horror rend th' affrighted skies.
Not louder shrieks to pitying Heaven are cast,
When husbands, or when lapdogs breathe their last,
Or when rich China vessels, fall'n from high,
In glittering dust and painted fragments lie!   160
  'Let wreaths of triumph now my temples twine,'
The victor cried, 'the glorious prize is mine!
While fish in streams, or birds delight in air,
Or in a coach and six the British fair,
As long as *Atalantis* shall be read,
Or the small pillow grace a lady's bed;
While visits shall be paid on solemn days,
When num'rous wax-lights in bright order blaze;
While nymphs take treats, or assignations give,
So long my honour, name, and praise shall live!   170
What Time would spare, from steel receives its date,
And monuments, like men, submit to fate!
Steel could the labour of the gods destroy,
And strike to dust th' imperial tow'rs of Troy;
Steel could the works of mortal pride confound,
And hew triumphal arches to the ground.
What wonder then, fair nymph! thy hairs should feel
The conqu'ring force of unresisted steel?'

Canto IV

But anxious cares the pensive nymph oppressed,
And secret passions laboured in her breast.
Not youthful kings in battle seized alive,
Not scornful virgins who their charms survive,

Not ardent lovers robbed of all their bliss,
Not ancient ladies when refused a kiss,
Not tyrants fierce that unrepenting die,
Not Cynthia when her manteau's pinned awry,
E'er felt such rage, resentment, and despair,
10   As thou, sad virgin! for thy ravished hair.

For that sad moment, when the sylphs withdrew,
And Ariel weeping from Belinda flew,
Umbriel, a dusky, melancholy sprite
As ever sullied the fair face of light,
Down to the central earth, his proper scene,
Repaired to search the gloomy cave of Spleen.

Swift on his sooty pinions flits the gnome,
And in a vapour reached the dismal dome.
No cheerful breeze this sullen region knows,
20   The dreaded east is all the wind that blows.
Here in a grotto sheltered close from air,
And screened in shades from day's detested glare,
She sighs for ever on her pensive bed,
Pain at her side, and Megrim at her head.

Two handmaids wait the throne: alike in place,
But diff'ring far in figure and in face.
Here stood Ill-nature, like an ancient maid,
Her wrinkled form in black and white arrayed!
With store of prayers for mornings, nights, and noons,
30   Her hand is filled; her bosom with lampoons.
There Affectation, with a sickly mien,
Shows in her cheek the roses of eighteen,
Practised to lisp, and hang the head aside,
Faints into airs, and languishes with pride;
On the rich quilt sinks with becoming woe,
Wrapped in a gown, for sickness, and for show.
The fair ones feel such maladies as these
When each new night-dress gives a new disease.

A constant vapour o'er the palace flies;
40   Strange phantoms rising as the mists arise;
Dreadful, as hermits' dreams in haunted shades,
Or bright, as visions of expiring maids.

Now glaring fiends, and snakes on rolling spires,
Pale spectres, gaping tombs, and purple fires;
Now lakes of liquid gold, Elysian scenes,
And crystal domes, and angels in machines.
    Unnumbered throngs on ev'ry side are seen
Of bodies changed to various forms by Spleen.
Here living teapots stand, one arm held out,
One bent; the handle this, and that the spout;   50
A pipkin there like Homer's tripod walks;
Here sighs a jar, and there a goose-pie talks;
Men prove with child, as powerful fancy works,
And maids, turned bottles, call aloud for corks.
    Safe passed the gnome through this fantastic band,
A branch of healing spleenwort in his hand.
Then thus addressed the Pow'r: 'Hail, wayward queen!
Who rule the sex to fifty from fifteen:
Parent of vapours and of female wit,
Who give th' hysteric or poetic fit,   60
On various tempers act by various ways,
Make some take physic, others scribble plays;
Who cause the proud their visits to delay,
And send the godly in a pet to pray.
A nymph there is that all your pow'r disdains,
And thousands more in equal mirth maintains.
But oh! if e'er thy gnome could spoil a grace,
Or raise a pimple on a beauteous face,
Like citron-waters matrons' cheeks inflame,
Or change complexions at a losing game;   70
If e'er with airy horns I planted heads,
Or rumpled petticoats, or tumbled beds,
Or caused suspicion when no soul was rude,
Or discomposed the headdress of a prude,
Or e'er to costive lapdog gave disease,
Which not the tears of brightest eyes could ease:
Hear me, and touch Belinda with chagrin;
That single act gives half the world the spleen.'
    The goddess, with a discontented air,
Seems to reject him, though she grants his pray'r.   80

A wondrous bag with both her hands she binds,
Like that where once Ulysses held the winds;
There she collects the force of female lungs,
Sighs, sobs, and passions, and the war of tongues.
A vial next she fills with fainting fears,
Soft sorrows, melting griefs, and flowing tears.
The gnome rejoicing bears her gifts away,
Spreads his black wings, and slowly mounts to day.
    Sunk in Thalestris' arms the nymph he found,
90   Her eyes dejected, and her hair unbound.
Full o'er their heads the swelling bag he rent,
And all the furies issued at the vent.
Belinda burns with more than mortal ire,
And fierce Thalestris fans the rising fire.
'O wretched maid!' she spread her hands, and cried
(While Hampton's echoes, 'Wretched maid,' replied),
'Was it for this you took such constant care
The bodkin, comb, and essence to prepare?
For this your locks in paper-durance bound?
100 For this with torturing irons wreathed around?
For this with fillets strained your tender head,
And bravely bore the double loads of lead?
Gods! shall the ravisher display your hair
While the fops envy, and the ladies stare!
Honour forbid! at whose unrivalled shrine
Ease, pleasure, virtue, all, our sex resign.
Methinks already I your tears survey,
Already hear the horrid things they say,
Already see you a degraded toast,
110 And all your honour in a whisper lost!
How shall I, then, your hapless fame defend?
'Twill then be infamy to seem your friend!
And shall this prize, th' inestimable prize,
Exposed through crystal to the gazing eyes,
And heightened by the diamond's circling rays,
On that rapacious hand for ever blaze?
Sooner shall grass in Hyde Park Circus grow,
And wits take lodgings in the sound of Bow;

Sooner let earth, air, sea, to chaos fall,
Men, monkeys, lapdogs, parrots, perish all!'   120
    She said; then raging to Sir Plume repairs,
And bids her beau demand the precious hairs
(Sir Plume, of amber snuff-box justly vain,
And the nice conduct of a clouded cane).
With earnest eyes, and round unthinking face,
He first the snuff-box opened, then the case,
And thus broke out – 'My Lord, why, what the devil!
Z—ds! damn the lock! 'fore Gad, you must be civil!
Plague on't! 'tis past a jest – nay prithee, pox!
Give her the hair' – he spoke, and rapped his box.   130
    'It grieves me much (replied the peer again)
Who speaks so well should ever speak in vain.
But by this lock, this sacred lock, I swear
(Which never more shall join its parted hair;
Which never more its honours shall renew,
Clipped from the lovely head where late it grew)
That while my nostrils draw the vital air,
This hand, which won it, shall for ever wear.'
He spoke, and speaking, in proud triumph spread
The long-contended honours of her head.   140
    But Umbriel, hateful gnome! forbears not so;
He breaks the vial whence the sorrows flow.
Then see! the nymph in beauteous grief appears,
Her eyes half-languishing, half-drowned in tears;
On her heaved bosom hung her drooping head,
Which with a sigh she raised, and thus she said:
    'For ever curs'd be this detested day,
Which snatched my best, my fav'rite curl away;
Happy! ah ten times happy had I been
If Hampton Court these eyes had never seen!   150
Yet am not I the first mistaken maid
By love of courts to num'rous ills betrayed.
Oh had I rather unadmired remained
In some lone isle, or distant northern land,
Where the gilt chariot never marks the way,
Where none learn ombre, none e'er taste bohea!

There kept my charms concealed from mortal eye,
Like roses, that in deserts bloom and die.
What moved my mind with youthful lords to roam?
160   Oh had I stayed, and said my pray'rs at home!
'Twas this, the morning omens seemed to tell:
Thrice from my trembling hand the patch-box fell;
The tott'ring china shook without a wind,
Nay, Poll sat mute, and Shock was most unkind!
A sylph too warned me of the threats of fate,
In mystic visions, now believed too late!
See the poor remnants of these slighted hairs!
My hands shall rend what ev'n thy rapine spares:
These in two sable ringlets taught to break,
170   Once gave new beauties to the snowy neck.
The sister-lock now sits uncouth, alone,
And in its fellow's fate foresees its own;
Uncurled it hangs, the fatal shears demands,
And tempts once more thy sacrilegious hands.
Oh hadst thou, cruel! been content to seize
Hairs less in sight, or any hairs but these!'

Canto V

She said: the pitying audience melt in tears,
But fate and Jove had stopped the Baron's ears.
In vain Thalestris with reproach assails,
For who can move when fair Belinda fails?
Not half so fixed the Trojan could remain,
While Anna begged and Dido raged in vain.
Then grave Clarissa graceful waved her fan;
Silence ensued, and thus the nymph began:
        'Say, why are beauties praised and honoured most,
10   The wise man's passion, and the vain man's toast?
Why decked with all that land and sea afford,
Why angels called, and angel-like adored?
Why round our coaches crowd the white-gloved beaus?
Why bows the side-box from its inmost rows?

How vain are all these glories, all our pains,
Unless good sense preserve what beauty gains;
That men may say, when we the front-box grace,
Behold the first in virtue, as in face!
Oh! if to dance all night, and dress all day,
Charmed the smallpox, or chased old age away;   20
Who would not scorn what housewife's cares produce,
Or who would learn one earthly thing of use?
To patch, nay ogle, might become a saint,
Nor could it sure be such a sin to paint.
But since, alas! frail beauty must decay,
Curled or uncurled, since locks will turn to grey;
Since painted, or not painted, all shall fade,
And she who scorns a man must die a maid;
What then remains, but well our pow'r to use,
And keep good humour still whate'er we lose?   30
And trust me, dear! good humour can prevail,
When airs, and flights, and screams, and scolding fail.
Beauties in vain their pretty eyes may roll;
Charms strike the sight, but merit wins the soul.'
  So spoke the dame, but no applause ensued;
Belinda frowned, Thalestris called her prude.
'To arms, to arms!' the fierce virago cries,
And swift as lightning to the combat flies.
All side in parties, and begin th' attack;
Fans clap, silks rustle, and tough whalebones crack;   40
Heroes' and heroines' shouts confus'dly rise,
And bass and treble voices strike the skies.
No common weapons in their hands are found,
Like gods they fight, nor dread a mortal wound.
  So when bold Homer makes the gods engage,
And heav'nly breasts with human passions rage;
'Gainst Pallas, Mars; Latona, Hermes arms;
And all Olympus rings with loud alarms;
Jove's thunder roars, heav'n trembles all around,
Blue Neptune storms, the bellowing deeps resound;   50
Earth shakes her nodding tow'rs, the ground gives way,
And the pale ghosts start at the flash of day!

Triumphant Umbriel, on a sconce's height,
Clapped his glad wings, and sat to view the fight;
Propped on their bodkin-spears, the sprites survey
The growing combat, or assist the fray.
    While through the press enraged Thalestris flies,
And scatters death around from both her eyes,
A beau and witling perished in the throng,
One died in metaphor, and one in song:
'O cruel nymph! a living death I bear,'
Cried Dapperwit, and sunk beside his chair.
A mournful glance Sir Fopling upwards cast,
'Those eyes are made so killing' – was his last.
Thus on Meander's flow'ry margin lies
Th' expiring swan, and as he sings he dies.
    When bold Sir Plume had drawn Clarissa down,
Chloe stepped in, and killed him with a frown;
She smiled to see the doughty hero slain,
But at her smile the beau revived again.
    Now Jove suspends his golden scales in air,
Weighs the men's wits against the lady's hair;
The doubtful beam long nods from side to side;
At length the wits mount up, the hairs subside.
    See fierce Belinda on the Baron flies,
With more than usual lightning in her eyes;
Nor feared the chief th' unequal fight to try,
Who sought no more than on his foe to die.
But this bold lord, with manly strength endued,
She with one finger and a thumb subdued:
Just where the breath of life his nostrils drew,
A charge of snuff the wily virgin threw;
The gnomes direct, to ev'ry atom just,
The pungent grains of titillating dust.
Sudden, with starting tears each eye o'erflows,
And the high dome re-echoes to his nose.
    'Now meet thy fate,' incensed Belinda cried,
And drew a deadly bodkin from her side.
(The same, his ancient personage to deck,
Her great-great-grandsire wore about his neck

60

70

80

90

In three seal-rings; which after, melted down,
Formed a vast buckle for his widow's gown;
Her infant grandame's whistle next it grew,
The bells she jingled, and the whistle blew;
Then in a bodkin graced her mother's hairs,
Which long she wore, and now Belinda wears.)
  'Boast not my fall (he cried), insulting foe!
Thou by some other shalt be laid as low.
Nor think to die dejects my lofty mind;
All that I dread is leaving you behind!   100
Rather than so, ah let me still survive,
And burn in Cupid's flames – but burn alive.'
  'Restore the lock!' she cries; and all around
'Restore the lock!' the vaulted roofs rebound.
Not fierce Othello in so loud a strain
Roared for the handkerchief that caused his pain.
But see how oft ambitious aims are crossed,
And chiefs contend till all the prize is lost!
The lock, obtained with guilt, and kept with pain,
In ev'ry place is sought, but sought in vain: 110
With such a prize no mortal must be blest,
So heav'n decrees! with heav'n who can contest?
  Some thought it mounted to the lunar sphere,
Since all things lost on earth are treasured there.
There heroes' wits are kept in pond'rous vases,
And beaus' in snuff-boxes and tweezer-cases.
There broken vows, and death-bed alms are found,
And lovers' hearts with ends of ribbon bound,
The courtier's promises, and sick man's pray'rs,
The smiles of harlots, and the tears of heirs,   120
Cages for gnats, and chains to yoke a flea,
Dried butterflies, and tomes of casuistry.
  But trust the Muse – she saw it upward rise,
Though marked by none but quick poetic eyes:
(So Rome's great founder to the heav'ns withdrew,
To Proculus alone confessed in view)

A sudden star, it shot through liquid air,
And drew behind a radiant trail of hair.
Not Berenice's locks first rose so bright,
130   The heav'ns bespangling with dishevelled light.
The sylphs behold it kindling as it flies,
And pleased pursue its progress through the skies.

    This the beau monde shall from the Mall survey,
And hail with music its propitious ray.
This the blest lover shall for Venus take,
And send up vows from Rosamonda's lake;
This Partridge soon shall view in cloudless skies,
When next he looks through Galileo's eyes;
And hence th' egregious wizard shall foredoom
140   The fate of Louis, and the fall of Rome.

    Then cease, bright nymph! to mourn thy ravished hair,
Which adds new glory to the shining sphere!
Not all the tresses that fair head can boast
Shall draw such envy as the lock you lost.
For, after all the murders of your eye,
When, after millions slain, yourself shall die;
When those fair suns shall set, as set they must,
And all those tresses shall be laid in dust,
This lock, the Muse shall consecrate to fame,
150   And 'midst the stars inscribe Belinda's name.

Epistle to Mrs Teresa Blount,
on her Leaving the Town, after the Coronation

As some fond virgin, whom her mother's care
Drags from the town to wholesome country air,
Just when she learns to roll a melting eye,
And hear a spark, yet think no danger nigh;
From the dear man unwilling she must sever,
Yet takes one kiss before she parts for ever:
Thus from the world fair Zephalinda flew,
Saw others happy, and with sighs withdrew;

Not that their pleasures caused her discontent;
She sighed not that they stayed, but that she went.   10
    She went to plain-work, and to purling brooks,
Old-fashioned halls, dull aunts, and croaking rooks;
She went from op'ra, park, assembly, play,
To morning walks, and pray'rs three hours a day;
To part her time 'twixt reading and bohea,
To muse, and spill her solitary tea,
Or o'er cold coffee trifle with the spoon,
Count the slow clock, and dine exact at noon;
Divert her eyes with pictures in the fire,
Hum half a tune, tell stories to the squire;   20
Up to her godly garret after sev'n,
There starve and pray, for that's the way to heav'n.
    Some squire, perhaps, you take delight to rack,
Whose game is whisk, whose treat a toast in sack;
Who visits with a gun, presents you birds,
Then gives a smacking buss, and cries – 'No words';
Or with his hounds comes hallooing from the stable,
Makes love with nods, and knees beneath a table;
Whose laughs are hearty, though his jests are coarse,
And loves you best of all things – but his horse.   30
    In some fair evening, on your elbow laid,
You dream of triumphs in the rural shade;
In pensive thought recall the fancied scene,
See coronations rise on ev'ry green:
Before you pass th' imaginary sights
Of lords, and earls, and dukes, and gartered knights,
While the spread fan o'ershades your closing eyes;
Then give one flirt, and all the vision flies.
Thus vanish sceptres, coronets, and balls,
And leave you in lone woods, or empty walls.   40
    So when your slave, at some dear idle time
(Not plagued with headaches or the want of rhyme),
Stands in the streets, abstracted from the crew,
And while he seems to study, thinks of you;
Just when his fancy points your sprightly eyes,
Or sees the blush of soft Parthenia rise,

Gay pats my shoulder, and you vanish quite;
Streets, chairs, and coxcombs rush upon my sight.
Vexed to be still in town, I knit my brow,
50   Look sour, and hum a tune, as you may now.

Eloisa to Abelard

ARGUMENT

Abelard and Eloisa flourished in the twelfth century; they were
two of the most distinguished persons of their age in learning
and beauty, but for nothing more famous than for their unfor-
tunate passion. After a long course of calamities, they retired
each to a several convent, and consecrated the remainder of
their days to religion. It was many years after this separation
that a letter of Abelard's to a friend, which contained the his-
tory of his misfortune, fell into the hands of Eloisa. This
awakening all her tenderness, occasioned those celebrated let-
ters (out of which the following is partly extracted), which give
so lively a picture of the struggles of grace and nature, virtue
and passion.

In these deep solitudes and awful cells,
Where heav'nly-pensive contemplation dwells,
And ever-musing melancholy reigns,
What means this tumult in a vestal's veins?
Why rove my thoughts beyond this last retreat?
Why feels my heart its long-forgotten heat?
Yet, yet I love! – From Abelard it came,
And Eloisa yet must kiss the name.
        Dear fatal name! rest ever unrevealed,
10   Nor pass these lips, in holy silence sealed.
Hide it, my heart, within that close disguise,
Where mixed with God's, his loved idea lies;
O write it not, my hand – the name appears
Already written – wash it out, my tears!

In vain lost Eloisa weeps and prays,
Her heart still dictates, and her hand obeys.
   Relentless walls! whose darksome round contains
Repentant sighs, and voluntary pains;
Ye rugged rocks! which holy knees have worn,
Ye grots and caverns shagged with horrid thorn!   20
Shrines! where their vigils pale-eyed virgins keep,
And pitying saints, whose statues learn to weep!
Though cold like you, unmoved and silent grown,
I have not yet forgot myself to stone.
All is not Heav'n's while Abelard has part,
Still rebel nature holds out half my heart;
Nor pray'rs nor fasts its stubborn pulse restrain,
Nor tears, for ages taught to flow in vain.
   Soon as thy letters trembling I unclose,
That well-known name awakens all my woes.   30
Oh name for ever sad! for ever dear!
Still breathed in sighs, still ushered with a tear.
I tremble too, where'er my own I find,
Some dire misfortune follows close behind.
Line after line my gushing eyes o'erflow,
Led through a sad variety of woe:
Now warm in love, now with'ring in my bloom,
Lost in a convent's solitary gloom!
There stern religion quenched th' unwilling flame,
There died the best of passions, love and fame.   40
   Yet write, oh write me all, that I may join
Griefs to thy griefs, and echo sighs to thine.
Nor foes nor fortune take this pow'r away;
And is my Abelard less kind than they?
Tears still are mine, and those I need not spare;
Love but demands what else were shed in prayer;
No happier task these faded eyes pursue;
To read and weep is all they now can do.
   Then share thy pain, allow that sad relief;
Ah, more than share it! give me all thy grief.   50
Heav'n first taught letters for some wretch's aid,
Some banished lover, or some captive maid;

They live, they speak, they breathe what love inspires,
Warm from the soul, and faithful to its fires.
The virgin's wish without her fears impart,
Excuse the blush, and pour out all the heart,
Speed the soft intercourse from soul to soul,
And waft a sigh from Indus to the Pole.

   Thou know'st how guiltless first I met thy flame,
60   When Love approached me under Friendship's name;
My fancy formed thee of angelic kind,
Some emanation of th' all-beauteous Mind.
Those smiling eyes, attemp'ring every ray,
Shone sweetly lambent with celestial day.
Guiltless I gazed; Heav'n listened while you sung;
And truths divine came mended from that tongue.
From lips like those what precept failed to move?
Too soon they taught me 'twas no sin to love.
Back through the paths of pleasing sense I ran,
70   Nor wished an angel whom I loved a man.
Dim and remote the joys of saints I see;
Nor envy them, that Heav'n I lose for thee.

   How oft, when pressed to marriage, have I said,
Curse on all laws but those which love has made?
Love, free as air, at sight of human ties
Spreads his light wings, and in a moment flies.
Let wealth, let honour, wait the wedded dame,
August her deed, and sacred be her fame;
Before true passion all those views remove;
80   Fame, wealth, and honour! what are you to love?
The jealous god, when we profane his fires,
Those restless passions in revenge inspires,
And bids them make mistaken mortals groan
Who seek in love for aught but love alone.
Should at my feet the world's great master fall,
Himself, his throne, his world, I'd scorn 'em all:
Not Caesar's empress would I deign to prove;
No, make me mistress to the man I love;
If there be yet another name more free,
90   More fond than mistress, make me that to thee!

Oh happy state! when souls each other draw,
When love is liberty, and nature law:
All then is full, possessing and possessed,
No craving void left aching in the breast;
Ev'n thought meets thought, ere from the lips it part,
And each warm wish springs mutual from the heart.
This sure is bliss (if bliss on earth there be),
And once the lot of Abelard and me.

    Alas, how changed! what sudden horrors rise!
A naked lover bound and bleeding lies!   100
Where, where was Eloise? her voice, her hand,
Her poniard had opposed the dire command.
Barbarian, stay! that bloody stroke restrain;
The crime was common, common be the pain.
I can no more; by shame, by rage suppressed,
Let tears and burning blushes speak the rest.

    Canst thou forget that sad, that solemn day,
When victims at yon altar's foot we lay?
Canst thou forget what tears that moment fell,
When, warm in youth, I bade the world farewell?   110
As with cold lips I kissed the sacred veil,
The shrines all trembled, and the lamps grew pale:
Heav'n scarce believed the conquest it surveyed,
And saints with wonder heard the vows I made.
Yet then, to those dread altars as I drew,
Not on the cross my eyes were fixed, but you;
Not grace or zeal, love only was my call,
And if I lose thy love, I lose my all.
Come! with thy looks, thy words, relieve my woe;
Those still at least are left thee to bestow.   120
Still on that breast enamoured let me lie,
Still drink delicious poison from thy eye,
Pant on thy lip, and to thy heart be pressed;
Give all thou canst – and let me dream the rest.
Ah no! instruct me other joys to prize,
With other beauties charm my partial eyes!
Full in my view set all the bright abode,
And make my soul quit Abelard for God.

Ah, think at least thy flock deserves thy care,
130   Plants of thy hand, and children of thy prayer.
From the false world in early youth they fled,
By thee to mountains, wilds, and deserts led.
You raised these hallowed walls; the desert smiled,
And Paradise was opened in the wild.
No weeping orphan saw his father's stores
Our shrines irradiate, or emblaze the floors;
No silver saints, by dying misers giv'n,
Here bribed the rage of ill-requited Heav'n:
But such plain roofs as piety could raise,
140   And only vocal with the Maker's praise.
In these lone walls (their day's eternal bound),
These moss-grown domes with spiry turrets crowned,
Where awful arches make a noonday night,
And the dim windows shed a solemn light;
Thy eyes diffused a reconciling ray,
And gleams of glory brightened all the day.
But now no face divine contentment wears,
'Tis all blank sadness, or continual tears.
See how the force of others' prayers I try
150   (O pious fraud of amorous charity!).
But why should I on others' prayers depend?
Come thou, my father, brother, husband, friend!
Ah, let thy handmaid, sister, daughter, move,
And all those tender names in one, thy love!
The darksome pines that o'er yon rocks reclined
Wave high, and murmur to the hollow wind,
The wandering streams that shine between the hills,
The grots that echo to the tinkling rills,
The dying gales that pant upon the trees,
160   The lakes that quiver to the curling breeze;
No more these scenes my meditation aid,
Or lull to rest the visionary maid.
But o'er the twilight groves and dusky caves,
Long-sounding aisles and intermingled graves,
Black Melancholy sits, and round her throws
A death-like silence, and a dread repose.

Her gloomy presence saddens all the scene,
Shades ev'ry flower, and darkens ev'ry green,
Deepens the murmur of the falling floods,
And breathes a browner horror on the woods.   170
   Yet here for ever, ever must I stay;
Sad proof how well a lover can obey!
Death, only death can break the lasting chain,
And here, ev'n then shall my cold dust remain;
Here all its frailties, all its flames resign,
And wait till 'tis no sin to mix with thine.
   Ah wretch! believed the spouse of God in vain,
Confessed within the slave of love and man.
Assist me, Heav'n! but whence arose that prayer?
Sprung it from piety, or from despair?   180
Ev'n here, where frozen chastity retires,
Love finds an altar for forbidden fires.
I ought to grieve, but cannot what I ought;
I mourn the lover, not lament the fault;
I view my crime, but kindle at the view,
Repent old pleasures, and solicit new;
Now turned to Heav'n, I weep my past offence,
Now think of thee, and curse my innocence.
Of all affliction taught a lover yet,
'Tis sure the hardest science to forget!   190
How shall I lose the sin, yet keep the sense,
And love th' offender, yet detest th' offence?
How the dear object from the crime remove,
Or how distinguish penitence from love?
Unequal task! a passion to resign,
For hearts so touched, so pierced, so lost as mine.
Ere such a soul regains its peaceful state,
How often must it love, how often hate!
How often hope, despair, resent, regret,
Conceal, disdain – do all things but forget!   200
But let Heav'n seize it, all at once 'tis fired;
Not touched, but rapt; not wakened, but inspired!
O come! O teach me Nature to subdue,
Renounce my love, my life, my self – and you.

Fill my fond heart with God alone, for he
Alone can rival, can succeed to thee.
    How happy is the blameless vestal's lot!
The world forgetting, by the world forgot:
Eternal sunshine of the spotless mind!
210 Each prayer accepted, and each wish resigned;
Labour and rest, that equal periods keep;
Obedient slumbers that can wake and weep;
Desires composed, affections ever ev'n;
Tears that delight, and sighs that waft to Heav'n.
Grace shines around her with serenest beams,
And whisp'ring angels prompt her golden dreams.
For her th' unfading rose of Eden blooms,
And wings of seraphs shed divine perfumes;
For her the Spouse prepares the bridal ring;
220 For her white virgins hymeneals sing;
To sounds of heav'nly harps she dies away,
And melts in visions of eternal day.
    Far other dreams my erring soul employ,
Far other raptures of unholy joy.
When at the close of each sad, sorrowing day
Fancy restores what vengeance snatched away,
Then conscience sleeps, and leaving nature free,
All my loose soul unbounded springs to thee.
Oh curs'd dear horrors of all-conscious night!
230 How glowing guilt exalts the keen delight!
Provoking demons all restraint remove,
And stir within me ev'ry source of love.
I hear thee, view thee, gaze o'er all thy charms,
And round thy phantom glue my clasping arms.
I wake – no more I hear, no more I view,
The phantom flies me, as unkind as you.
I call aloud; it hears not what I say;
I stretch my empty arms; it glides away.
To dream once more I close my willing eyes;
240 Ye soft illusions, dear deceits, arise!
Alas, no more! methinks we wand'ring go
Through dreary wastes, and weep each other's woe,

Where round some mould'ring tow'r pale ivy creeps,
And low-browed rocks hang nodding o'er the deeps.
Sudden you mount! you beckon from the skies;
Clouds interpose, waves roar, and winds arise.
I shriek, start up, the same sad prospect find,
And wake to all the griefs I left behind.

For thee the fates, severely kind, ordain
A cool suspense from pleasure and from pain;   250
Thy life a long, dead calm of fixed repose;
No pulse that riots, and no blood that glows.
Still as the sea, ere winds were taught to blow,
Or moving Spirit bade the waters flow;
Soft as the slumbers of a saint forgiv'n,
And mild as op'ning gleams of promised Heav'n.

Come, Abelard! for what hast thou to dread?
The torch of Venus burns not for the dead.
Nature stands checked; Religion disapproves;
Ev'n thou art cold – yet Eloisa loves.   260
Ah hopeless, lasting flames! like those that burn
To light the dead, and warm th' unfruitful urn.

What scenes appear where'er I turn my view?
The dear ideas, where I fly, pursue;
Rise in the grove, before the altar rise,
Stain all my soul, and wanton in my eyes.
I waste the matin lamp in sighs for thee,
Thy image steals between my God and me;
Thy voice I seem in ev'ry hymn to hear,
With ev'ry bead I drop too soft a tear.   270
When from the censer clouds of fragrance roll,
And swelling organs lift the rising soul,
One thought of thee puts all the pomp to flight,
Priests, tapers, temples, swim before my sight:
In seas of flame my plunging soul is drowned,
While altars blaze, and angels tremble round.

While prostrate here in humble grief I lie,
Kind, virtuous drops just gathering in my eye,
While praying, trembling, in the dust I roll,
And dawning grace is opening on my soul: 280

Come, if thou dar'st, all charming as thou art!
Oppose thyself to Heav'n; dispute my heart;
Come, with one glance of those deluding eyes
Blot out each bright idea of the skies;
Take back that grace, those sorrows and those tears,
Take back my fruitless penitence and prayers;
Snatch me, just mounting, from the blest abode;
Assist the fiends, and tear me from my God!
No, fly me, fly me, far as pole from pole;
290   Rise Alps between us! and whole oceans roll!
Ah, come not, write not, think not once of me,
Nor share one pang of all I felt for thee.
Thy oaths I quit, thy memory resign;
Forget, renounce me, hate whate'er was mine.
Fair eyes, and tempting looks (which yet I view),
Long loved, adored ideas, all adieu!
O Grace serene! O Virtue heav'nly fair!
Divine oblivion of low-thoughted care!
Fresh blooming Hope, gay daughter of the sky!
300   And Faith, our early immortality!
Enter each mild, each amicable guest;
Receive, and wrap me in eternal rest!
   See in her cell sad Eloisa spread,
Propped on some tomb, a neighbour of the dead.
In each low wind methinks a spirit calls,
And more than echoes talk along the walls.
Here, as I watched the dying lamps around,
From yonder shrine I heard a hollow sound:
'Come, sister, come! (it said, or seemed to say)
310   Thy place is here, sad sister, come away!
Once, like thyself, I trembled, wept, and prayed,
Love's victim then, though now a sainted maid.
But all is calm in this eternal sleep;
Here grief forgets to groan, and love to weep;
Ev'n superstition loses ev'ry fear:
For God, not man, absolves our frailties here.'
   I come, I come! prepare your roseate bow'rs,
Celestial palms, and ever-blooming flow'rs.

Thither, where sinners may have rest, I go,
Where flames refined in breasts seraphic glow.						320
Thou, Abelard! the last sad office pay,
And smooth my passage to the realms of day:
See my lips tremble, and my eyeballs roll,
Suck my last breath, and catch my flying soul!
Ah, no – in sacred vestments mayst thou stand,
The hallowed taper trembling in thy hand,
Present the cross before my lifted eye,
Teach me at once, and learn of me to die.
Ah then, thy once-loved Eloisa see!
It will be then no crime to gaze on me.							330
See from my cheek the transient roses fly!
See the last sparkle languish in my eye!
Till ev'ry motion, pulse, and breath be o'er;
And ev'n my Abelard be loved no more.
O Death, all-eloquent! you only prove
What dust we dote on, when 'tis man we love.

   Then too, when fate shall thy fair frame destroy
(That cause of all my guilt, and all my joy),
In trance ecstatic may thy pangs be drowned,
Bright clouds descend, and angels watch thee round;					340
From op'ning skies may streaming glories shine,
And saints embrace thee with a love like mine.

   May one kind grave unite each hapless name,
And graft my love immortal on thy fame!
Then, ages hence, when all my woes are o'er,
When this rebellious heart shall beat no more,
If ever chance two wand'ring lovers brings,
To Paraclete's white walls and silver springs,
O'er the pale marble shall they join their heads,
And drink the falling tears each other sheds;						350
Then sadly say, with mutual pity moved,
'O may we never love as these have loved!'
From the full choir, when loud hosannas rise,
And swell the pomp of dreadful sacrifice,
Amid that scene if some relenting eye
Glance on the stone where our cold relics lie,

Devotion's self shall steal a thought from Heav'n,
One human tear shall drop, and be forgiv'n.
And sure if fate some future bard shall join
360   In sad similitude of griefs to mine,
Condemned whole years in absence to deplore,
And image charms he must behold no more;
Such if there be, who loves so long, so well,
Let him our sad, our tender story tell;
The well-sung woes will soothe my pensive ghost;
He best can paint 'em who shall feel 'em most.

Elegy to the Memory of an Unfortunate Lady

What beck'ning ghost along the moonlight shade
Invites my step, and points to yonder glade?
'Tis she! – but why that bleeding bosom gored?
Why dimly gleams the visionary sword?
Oh ever beauteous, ever friendly! tell,
Is it, in Heav'n, a crime to love too well?
To bear too tender or too firm a heart,
To act a lover's or a Roman's part?
Is there no bright reversion in the sky
10   For those who greatly think, or bravely die?
    Why bade ye else, ye Pow'rs! her soul aspire
Above the vulgar flight of low desire?
Ambition first sprung from your blest abodes,
The glorious fault of angels and of gods:
Thence to their images on earth it flows,
And in the breasts of kings and heroes glows.
Most souls, 'tis true, but peep out once an age,
Dull sullen pris'ners in the body's cage:
Dim lights of life, that burn a length of years
20   Useless, unseen, as lamps in sepulchres;
Like eastern kings a lazy state they keep,
And close confined to their own palace sleep.

From these, perhaps (ere Nature bade her die),
Fate snatched her early to the pitying sky.
As into air the purer spirits flow,
And sep'rate from their kindred dregs below,
So flew the soul to its congenial place,
Nor left one virtue to redeem her race.
  But thou, false guardian of a charge too good,
Thou, mean deserter of thy brother's blood!   30
See on these ruby lips the trembling breath,
These cheeks, now fading at the blast of death;
Cold is that breast which warmed the world before,
And those love-darting eyes must roll no more.
Thus, if eternal justice rules the ball,
Thus shall your wives, and thus your children fall:
On all the line a sudden vengeance waits,
And frequent hearses shall besiege your gates;
There passengers shall stand, and pointing say
(While the long fun'rals blacken all the way),   40
Lo, these were they whose souls the Furies steeled,
And cursed with hearts unknowing how to yield.
Thus unlamented pass the proud away,
The gaze of fools, and pageant of a day!
So perish all whose breast ne'er learned to glow
For others' good, or melt at others' woe.
  What can atone (oh, ever-injured shade!)
Thy fate unpitied, and thy rites unpaid?
No friend's complaint, no kind domestic tear
Pleased thy pale ghost, or graced thy mournful bier.   50
By foreign hands thy dying eyes were closed,
By foreign hands thy decent limbs composed,
By foreign hands thy humble grave adorned,
By strangers honoured, and by strangers mourned!
What though no friends in sable weeds appear,
Grieve for an hour, perhaps, then mourn a year,
And bear about the mockery of woe
To midnight dances, and the public show?
What though no weeping loves thy ashes grace,
Nor polished marble emulate thy face?   60

What though no sacred earth allow thee room,
Nor hallowed dirge be muttered o'er thy tomb?
Yet shall thy grave with rising flow'rs be dressed,
And the green turf lie lightly on thy breast:
There shall the morn her earliest tears bestow,
There the first roses of the year shall blow;
While angels with their silver wings o'ershade
The ground, now sacred by thy relics made.

So peaceful rests, without a stone, a name,
70   What once had beauty, titles, wealth, and fame.
How loved, how honoured once, avails thee not,
To whom related, or by whom begot;
A heap of dust alone remains of thee;
'Tis all thou art, and all the proud shall be!

Poets themselves must fall like those they sung;
Deaf the praised ear, and mute the tuneful tongue.
Ev'n he, whose soul now melts in mournful lays,
Shall shortly want the gen'rous tear he pays;
Then from his closing eyes thy form shall part,
80   And the last pang shall tear thee from his heart;
Life's idle business at one gasp be o'er,
The Muse forgot, and thou beloved no more!

From the Iliad

[From the description of the first battle, Book IV]

Dire was the clang, and dreadful from afar,
Of armed Tydides rushing to the war.
As when the winds, ascending by degrees,
First move the whit'ning surface of the seas,
480   The billows float in order to the shore,
The wave behind rolls on the wave before;
Till, with the growing storm, the deeps arise,
Foam o'er the rocks, and thunder to the skies.

So to the fight the thick battalions throng,
Shields urged on shields, and men drove men along.
Sedate and silent move the num'rous bands;
No sound, no whisper, but the chief's commands,
Those only heard; with awe the rest obey
As if some god had snatched their voice away.
Not so the Trojans; from their host ascends   490
A general shout that all the region rends.
As when the fleecy flocks unnumbered stand
In wealthy folds, and wait the milker's hand,
The hollow vales incessant bleating fills,
The lambs reply from all the neighb'ring hills:
Such clamours rose from various nations round,
Mixed was the murmur, and confused the sound.
Each host now joins, and each a god inspires:
These Mars incites, and those Minerva fires.
Pale Flight around, and dreadful Terror reign;   500
And Discord raging bathes the purple plain:
Discord! dire sister of the slaught'ring pow'r,
Small at her birth, but rising ev'ry hour,
While scarce the skies her horrid head can bound,
She stalks on earth, and shakes the world around;
The nations bleed where'er her steps she turns,
The groan still deepens, and the combat burns.
    Now shield with shield, with helmet helmet closed,
To armour armour, lance to lance opposed,
Host against host with shadowy squadrons drew,   510
The sounding darts in iron tempests slew,
Victors and vanquished join promiscuous cries,
And shrilling shouts and dying groans arise;
With streaming blood the slipp'ry fields are dyed,
And slaughtered heroes swell the dreadful tide.
    As torrents roll, increased by numerous rills,
With rage impetuous down their echoing hills
Rush to the vales, and poured along the plain
Roar through a thousand channels to the main;
The distant shepherd trembling hears the sound: 520
So mix both hosts, and so their cries rebound.

The bold Antilochus the slaughter led,
The first who struck a valiant Trojan dead;
At great Echepolus the lance arrives,
Razed his high crest, and through his helmet drives.
Warmed in the brain the brazen weapon lies,
And shades eternal settle o'er his eyes;
So sinks a tow'r, that long assaults had stood
Of force and fire, its walls besmeared with blood.
530 Him, the bold leader of the Abantian throng
Seized to despoil, and dragged the corpse along,
But while he strove to tug th' inserted dart,
Agenor's jav'lin reached the hero's heart.
His flank, unguarded by his ample shield,
Admits the lance: he falls, and spurns the field;
The nerves unbraced support his limbs no more;
The soul comes floating in a tide of gore.
Trojans and Greeks now gather round the slain;
The war renews, the warriors bleed again;
540 As o'er their prey rapacious wolves engage,
Man dies on man, and all is blood and rage.
    In blooming youth fair Simoïsius fell,
Sent by great Ajax to the shades of hell;
Fair Simoïsius, whom his mother bore
Amid the flocks on silver Simois' shore:
The nymph descending from the hills of Ide,
To seek her parents on his flow'ry side,
Brought forth the babe, their common care and joy,
And thence from Simois named the lovely boy.
550 Short was his date! by dreadful Ajax slain
He falls, and renders all their cares in vain!
So falls a poplar, that in wat'ry ground
Raised high the head, with stately branches crowned
(Felled by some artist with his shining steel,
To shape the circle of the bending wheel),
Cut down it lies, tall, smooth, and largely spread,
With all its beauteous honours on its head;
There, left a subject to the wind and rain
And scorched by suns, it withers on the plain.

Thus pierced by Ajax, Simoïsius lies   560
Stretched on the shore, and thus neglected dies.
  At Ajax, Antiphus his jav'lin threw;
The pointed lance with erring fury flew,
And Leucus, loved by wise Ulysses, slew.
He drops the corse of Simoïsius slain,
And sinks a breathless carcass on the plain.
This saw Ulysses, and with grief enraged
Strode where the foremost of the foes engaged;
Armed with his spear, he meditates the wound,
In act to throw; but cautious, looked around.   570
Struck at his sight, the Trojans backward drew,
And trembling heard the jav'lin as it flew.
A chief stood nigh, who from Abydos came,
Old Priam's son, Democoön was his name.
The weapon entered close above his ear,
Cold through his temples glides the whizzing spear.
With piercing shrieks the youth resigns his breath;
His eyeballs darken with the shades of death;
Pond'rous he falls: his clanging arms resound,
And his broad buckler rings against the ground.   580

[The council of deities, Book VIII]

  Aurora now, fair daughter of the dawn,
Sprinkled with rosy light the dewy lawn,
When Jove convened the senate of the skies,
Where high Olympus' cloudy tops arise.
The sire of gods his awful silence broke;
The heav'ns attentive trembled as he spoke:
  'Celestial states, immortal gods! give ear,
Hear our decree, and rev'rence what ye hear,
The fixed decree which not all heav'n can move;
Thou fate! fulfil it! and ye powers! approve.   10
What god but enters yon forbidden field,
Who yields assistance, or but wills to yield,
Back to the skies with shame he shall be driv'n,

Gashed with dishonest wounds, the scorn of heav'n.
Or far, oh far from steep Olympus thrown,
Low in the dark Tartarean gulf shall groan,
With burning chains fixed to the brazen floors,
And locked by hell's inexorable doors;
As deep beneath th' infernal centre hurled,
20 As from that centre to th' ethereal world.
Let him who tempts me dread those dire abodes,
And know, th' Almighty is the god of gods.
League all your forces then, ye pow'rs above,
Join all, and try th' omnipotence of Jove.
Let down our golden everlasting chain
Whose strong embrace holds heav'n, and earth, and main;
Strive all, of mortal and immortal birth,
To drag, by this, the Thund'rer down to earth.
Ye strive in vain! if I but stretch this hand,
30 I heave the gods, the ocean, and the land;
I fix the chain to great Olympus' height,
And the vast world hangs trembling in my sight!
For such I reign, unbounded and above;
And such are men, and gods, compared to Jove.'
    Th' Almighty spoke, nor durst the pow'rs reply:
A rev'rend horror silenced all the sky;
Trembling they stood before their sov'reign's look.
At length his best-belov'd, the power of Wisdom, spoke:
    'O first and greatest! God by gods adored!
40 We own thy might, our father and our lord!
But ah! permit to pity human state:
If not to help, at least lament their fate.
From fields forbidden we submiss refrain,
With arms unaiding mourn our Argives slain;
Yet grant my counsels still their breasts may move,
Or all must perish in the wrath of Jove.'
    The cloud-compelling god her suit approved,
And smiled superior on his best belov'd;
Then called his coursers, and his chariot took;
50 The steadfast firmament beneath them shook.

Rapt by th' ethereal steeds the chariot rolled;
Brass were their hoofs, their curling manes of gold.
Of heav'n's undrossy gold, the god's array,
Refulgent, flashed intolerable day.
High on the throne he shines; his coursers fly
Between th' extended earth and starry sky.
But when to Ida's topmost height he came
(Fair nurse of fountains, and of savage game),
Where o'er her pointed summits proudly raised,
His fane breathed odours, and his altar blazed: 60
There, from his radiant car, the sacred sire
Of gods and men released the steeds of fire.
Blue ambient mists th' immortal steeds embraced;
High on the cloudy point his seat he placed.
Thence his broad eye the subject world surveys,
The town, and tents, and navigable seas.

[Sarpedon's speech, Book XII]

Thus godlike Hector and his troops contend
To force the ramparts, and the gates to rend,
Nor Troy could conquer, nor the Greeks would yield,
Till great Sarpedon towered amid the field;
For mighty Jove inspired with martial flame
His matchless son, and urged him on to fame.   350
In arms he shines, conspicuous from afar,
And bears aloft his ample shield in air,
Within whose orb the thick bull-hides were rolled,
Pond'rous with brass, and bound with ductile gold,
And while two pointed jav'lins arm his hands,
Majestic moves along, and leads his Lycian bands.
So pressed with hunger, from the mountain's brow
Descends a lion on the flocks below;
So stalks the lordly savage o'er the plain
In sullen majesty, and stern disdain.   360
In vain loud mastiffs bay him from afar,

And shepherds gall him with an iron war;
Regardless, furious, he pursues his way;
He foams, he roars, he rends the panting prey.
    Resolved alike, divine Sarpedon glows
With gen'rous rage that drives him on the foes.
He views the tow'rs, and meditates their fall,
To sure destruction dooms th' aspiring wall;
Then casting on his friend an ardent look,
370   Fired with the thirst of glory, thus he spoke:
    'Why boast we, Glaucus! our extended reign,
Where Xanthus' streams enrich the Lycian plain,
Our num'rous herds that range the fruitful field,
And hills where vines their purple harvest yield,
Our foaming bowls with purer nectar crowned,
Our feasts enhanced with music's sprightly sound?
Why on those shores are we with joy surveyed,
Admired as heroes, and as gods obeyed?
Unless great acts superior merit prove
380   And vindicate the bounteous pow'rs above.
'Tis ours, the dignity they give, to grace;
The first in valour, as the first in place;
That when with wond'ring eyes our martial bands
Behold our deeds transcending our commands,
"Such," they may cry, "deserve the sov'reign state,
Whom those that envy dare not imitate!"
Could all our care elude the gloomy grave,
Which claims no less the fearful than the brave,
For lust of fame I should not vainly dare
390   In fighting fields, nor urge thy soul to war.
But since, alas! ignoble age must come,
Disease, and death's inexorable doom,
The life which others pay, let us bestow,
And give to fame what we to nature owe;
Brave though we fall, and honoured if we live,
Or let us glory gain, or glory give!'
    He said; his words the list'ning chief inspire
With equal warmth, and rouse the warrior's fire;

The troops pursue their leaders with delight,
Rush to the foe, and claim the promised fight.   400

[Vulcan forges the shield of Achilles, Book XVIII]

 Then from his anvil the lame artist rose;
Wide with distorted legs, oblique he goes,   480
And stills the bellows, and (in order laid)
Locks in their chest his instruments of trade.
Then with a sponge the sooty workman dressed
His brawny arms embrowned, and hairy breast;
With his huge sceptre graced, and red attire,
Came halting forth the sov'reign of the fire.
The monarch's steps two female forms uphold,
That moved, and breathed, in animated gold;
To whom was voice, and sense, and science given
Of works divine (such wonders are in heav'n!).   490
On these supported, with unequal gait,
He reached the throne where pensive Thetis sate;
There, placed beside her on the shining frame,
He thus addressed the silver-footed dame:
 'Thee welcome, goddess! what occasion calls
(So long a stranger) to these honoured walls?
'Tis thine, fair Thetis, the command to lay,
And Vulcan's joy, and duty, to obey.'
 To whom the mournful mother thus replies
(The crystal drops stood trembling in her eyes),   500
'Oh Vulcan! say, was ever breast divine
So pierced with sorrows, so o'erwhelmed as mine?
Of all the goddesses, did Jove prepare
For Thetis only such a weight of care?
I, only I, of all the wat'ry race
By force subjected to a man's embrace,
Who, sinking now with age and sorrow, pays
The mighty fine imposed on length of days.
Sprung from my bed, a godlike hero came,

510 The bravest sure that ever bore the name;
     Like some fair plant beneath my careful hand
     He grew, he flourished, and he graced the land.
     To Troy I sent him! but his native shore
     Never, ah never, shall receive him more;
     (Ev'n while he lives, he wastes with secret woe)
     Nor I, a goddess, can retard the blow!
     Robbed of the prize the Grecian suffrage gave,
     The king of nations forced his royal slave;
     For this he grieved, and, till the Greeks oppressed
520 Required his arm, he sorrowed unredressed.
     Large gifts they promise, and their elders send;
     In vain – he arms not, but permits his friend
     His arms, his steeds, his forces to employ;
     He marches, combats, almost conquers Troy;
     Then slain by Phoebus (Hector had the name)
     At once resigns his armour, life, and fame.
     But thou, in pity, by my pray'r be won:
     Grace with immortal arms this short-lived son,
     And to the field in martial pomp restore,
530 To shine with glory, till he shines no more!'
         To her the artist-god: 'Thy griefs resign,
     Secure, what Vulcan can, is ever thine.
     O could I hide him from the Fates as well,
     Or with these hands the cruel stroke repel,
     As I shall forge most envied arms, the gaze
     Of wond'ring ages, and the world's amaze!'
         Thus having said, the father of the fires
     To the black labours of his forge retires.
     Soon as he bade them blow, the bellows turned
540 Their iron mouths, and where the furnace burned
     Resounding breathed: at once the blast expires,
     And twenty forges catch at once the fires;
     Just as the god directs, now loud, now low,
     They raise a tempest, or they gently blow.
     In hissing flames huge silver bars are rolled,
     And stubborn brass, and tin, and solid gold;

Before, deep fixed, th' eternal anvils stand,
The pond'rous hammer loads his better hand,
His left with tongs turns the vexed metal round,
And thick, strong strokes the doubling vaults rebound.   550

   Then first he formed th' immense and solid shield;
Rich, various artifice emblazed the field;
Its utmost verge a threefold circle bound;
A silver chain suspends the massy round;
Five ample plates the broad expanse compose,
And godlike labours on the surface rose.
There shone the image of the master-mind:
There earth, there heav'n, there ocean he designed;
Th' unwearied sun, the moon completely round;
The starry lights that heav'n's high convex crowned;   560
The Pleiads, Hyads, with the northern team,
And great Orion's more refulgent beam,
To which, around the axle of the sky,
The Bear revolving, points his golden eye,
Still shines exalted on th' ethereal plain,
Nor bathes his blazing forehead in the main.

   Two cities radiant on the shield appear,
The image one of peace, and one of war.
Here sacred pomp and genial feast delight,
And solemn dance, and hymeneal rite;   570
Along the street the new-made brides are led
With torches flaming, to the nuptial bed;
The youthful dancers in a circle bound
To the soft flute, and cithern's silver sound,
Through the fair streets, the matrons in a row
Stand in their porches, and enjoy the show.

   There in the forum swarm a numerous train;
The subject of debate, a townsman slain.
One pleads the fine discharged, which one denied,
And bade the public and the laws decide;   580
The witness is produced on either hand:
For this, or that, the partial people stand.
Th' appointed heralds still the noisy bands,
And form a ring, with sceptres in their hands,

On seats of stone, within the sacred place,
The rev'rend elders nodded o'er the case;
Alternate, each th' attesting sceptre took,
And rising solemn, each his sentence spoke.
Two golden talents lay amidst, in sight,
590   The prize of him who best adjudged the right.
        Another part (a prospect differing far)
Glowed with refulgent arms and horrid war.
Two mighty hosts a leaguered town embrace,
And one would pillage, one would burn the place.
Meantime the townsmen, armed with silent care,
A secret ambush on the foe prepare,
Their wives, their children, and the watchful band
Of trembling parents on the turrets stand.
They march, by Pallas and by Mars made bold;
600   Gold were the gods, their radiant garments gold,
And gold their armour: these the squadron led,
August, divine, superior by the head!
A place for ambush fit they found, and stood,
Covered with shields, beside a silver flood.
Two spies at distance lurk, and watchful seem
If sheep or oxen seek the winding stream.
Soon the white flocks proceeded o'er the plains,
And steers slow-moving, and two shepherd swains;
Behind them, piping on their reeds, they go,
610   Nor fear an ambush, nor suspect a foe.
In arms the glitt'ring squadron rising round
Rush sudden; hills of slaughter heap the ground;
Whole flocks and herds lie bleeding on the plains,
And, all amidst them, dead, the shepherd swains!
The bellowing oxen the besiegers hear;
They rise, take horse, approach, and meet the war;
They fight, they fall, beside the silver flood;
The waving silver seemed to blush with blood.
There Tumult, there Contention stood confessed:
620   One reared a dagger at a captive's breast;
One held a living foe, that freshly bled
With new-made wounds, another dragged a dead;

Now here, now there, the carcasses they tore.
Fate stalked amidst them, grim with human gore,
And the whole war came out, and met the eye,
And each bold figure seemed to live, or die.

A field deep furrowed next the god designed,
The third time laboured by the sweating hind;
The shining shares full many ploughmen guide,
And turn their crooked yokes on every side.   630
Still as at either end they wheel around,
The master meets 'em with his goblet crowned;
The hearty draught rewards, renews their toil,
Then back the turning ploughshares cleave the soil.
Behind, the rising earth in ridges rolled,
And sable looked, though formed of molten gold.

Another field rose high with waving grain;
With bended sickles stand the reaper train.
Here stretched in ranks the levelled swarths are found,
Sheaves heaped on sheaves here thicken up the ground.   640
With sweeping stroke the mowers strew the lands;
The gath'rers follow, and collect in bands;
And last the children, in whose arms are borne
(Too short to gripe them) the brown sheaves of corn.
The rustic monarch of the field descries
With silent glee, the heaps around him rise.
A ready banquet on the turf is laid,
Beneath an ample oak's expanded shade.
The victim ox the sturdy youth prepare:
The reaper's due repast, the woman's care.   650

Next, ripe in yellow gold, a vineyard shines,
Bent with the pond'rous harvest of its vines;
A deeper dye the dangling clusters show,
And curled on silver props, in order glow;
A darker metal mixed, intrenched the place,
And pales of glitt'ring tin th' enclosure grace.
To this, one pathway gently winding leads,
Where march a train with baskets on their heads,

(Fair maids, and blooming youths) that smiling bear
660   The purple product of th' autumnal year.
To these a youth awakes the warbling strings,
Whose tender lay the fate of Linus sings;
In measured dance behind him move the train,
Tune soft the voice, and answer to the strain.

Here, herds of oxen march, erect and bold,
Rear high their horns, and seem to low in gold,
And speed to meadows on whose sounding shores
A rapid torrent through the rushes roars:
Four golden herdsmen as their guardians stand,
670   And nine sour dogs complete the rustic band.
Two lions rushing from the wood appeared
And seized a bull, the master of the herd;
He roared: in vain the dogs, the men withstood;
They tore his flesh, and drank the sable blood.
The dogs (oft cheered in vain) desert the prey,
Dread the grim terrors, and at distance bay.

Next this, the eye the art of Vulcan leads
Deep through fair forests, and a length of meads,
And stalls, and folds, and scattered cots between;
680   And fleecy flocks, that whiten all the scene.
A figured dance succeeds: such once was seen
In lofty Gnossus for the Cretan queen,
Formed by Daedalean art. A comely band
Of youths and maidens, bounding hand in hand:
The maids in soft simars of linen dressed,
The youths all graceful in the glossy vest;
Of those the locks with flow'ry wreath inrolled,
Of these the sides adorned with swords of gold,
That glitt'ring gay, from silver belts depend.
690   Now all at once they rise, at once descend,
With well-taught feet: now shape, in oblique ways
Confus'dly regular, the moving maze;
Now forth at once, too swift for sight, they spring,
And undistinguished blend the flying ring:
So whirls a wheel, in giddy circle tossed,
And rapid as it runs, the single spokes are lost.

The gazing multitudes admire around;
Two active tumblers in the centre bound;
Now high, now low, their pliant limbs they bend,
And gen'ral songs the sprightly revel end.   700

    Thus the broad shield complete the artist crowned
With his last hand, and poured the ocean round:
In living silver seemed the waves to roll,
And beat the buckler's verge, and bound the whole.

    This done, whate'er a warrior's use requires
He forged; the cuirass that outshone the fires,
The greaves of ductile tin, the helm impressed
With various sculpture, and the golden crest.
At Thetis' feet the finished labour lay;
She, as a falcon cuts th' aerial way,   710
Swift from Olympus' snowy summit flies,
And bears the blazing present through the skies.

[The reception of Hector's body in Troy, Book XXIV]

    In thronging crowds they issue to the plains,
Nor man, nor woman, in the walls remains.
In ev'ry face the self-same grief is shown,
And Troy sends forth one universal groan.
At Scaea's gates they meet the mourning wain,
Hang on the wheels, and grovel round the slain.
The wife and mother, frantic with despair,
Kiss his pale cheek, and rend their scattered hair:
Thus wildly wailing, at the gates they lay,   890
And here had sighed and sorrowed out the day;
But godlike Priam from the chariot rose:
'Forbear (he cried) this violence of woes;
First to the palace let the car proceed,
Then pour your boundless sorrows o'er the dead.'

    The waves of people at his word divide;
Slow rolls the chariot through the foll'wing tide.
Ev'n to the palace the sad pomp they wait:
They weep, and place him on the bed of state.

900 A melancholy choir attend around
With plaintive sighs, and music's solemn sound:
Alternately they sing, alternate flow
Th' obedient tears, melodious in their woe,
While deeper sorrows groan from each full heart,
And nature speaks at ev'ry pause of art.
First to the corse the weeping consort flew;
Around his neck her milk-white arms she threw,
'And oh my Hector! Oh my lord! (she cries)
Snatched in thy bloom from these desiring eyes!
910 Thou to the dismal realms for ever gone!
And I abandoned, desolate, alone!
An only son, once comfort of our pains,
Sad product now of hapless love, remains!
Never to manly age that son shall rise,
Or with increasing graces glad my eyes:
For Ilion now (her great defender slain)
Shall sink, a smoking ruin on the plain.
Who now protects her wives with guardian care?
Who saves her infants from the rage of war?
920 Now hostile fleets must waft those infants o'er
(Those wives must wait them) to a foreign shore!
Thou too, my son! to barb'rous climes shalt go,
The sad companion of thy mother's woe,
Driv'n hence a slave before the victor's sword,
Condemned to toil for some inhuman lord,
Or else some Greek whose father pressed the plain,
Or son, or brother, by great Hector slain,
In Hector's blood his vengeance shall enjoy,
And hurl thee headlong from the tow'rs of Troy;
930 For thy stern father never spared a foe:
Thence all these tears, and all this scene of woe!
Thence many evils his sad parents bore,
His parents many, but his consort more.
Why gav'st thou not to me thy dying hand?
And why received not I thy last command?
Some word thou would'st have spoke, which sadly dear,
My soul might keep, or utter with a tear;

Which never, never could be lost in air,
Fixed in my heart, and oft repeated there!'
    Thus to her weeping maids she makes her moan;   940
Her weeping handmaids echo groan for groan.
    The mournful mother next sustains her part:
'O thou, the best, the dearest to my heart!
Of all my race thou most by heaven approved,
And by th' immortals ev'n in death belov'd!
While all my other sons in barb'rous bands
Achilles bound, and sold to foreign lands,
This felt no chains, but went a glorious ghost,
Free, and a hero, to the Stygian coast.
Sentenced, 'tis true, by his inhuman doom,   950
Thy noble corse was dragged around the tomb
(The tomb of him thy warlike arm had slain);
Ungen'rous insult, impotent and vain!
Yet glow'st thou fresh with ev'ry living grace;
No mark of pain, or violence of face:
Rosy and fair! as Phoebus' silver bow
Dismissed thee gently to the shades below.'
    Thus spoke the dame, and melted into tears.
Sad Helen next in pomp of grief appears;
Fast from the shining sluices of her eyes   960
Fall the round crystal drops, while thus she cries:
    'Ah, dearest friend! in whom the gods had joined
The mildest manners with the bravest mind!
Now twice ten years (unhappy years) are o'er
Since Paris brought me to the Trojan shore,
(O had I perished, ere that form divine
Seduced this soft, this easy heart of mine!)
Yet was it ne'er my fate, from thee to find
A deed ungentle, or a word unkind.
When others cursed the authoress of their woe,   970
Thy pity checked my sorrows in their flow.
If some proud brother eyed me with disdain,   ⎫
Or scornful sister with her sweeping train,   ⎬
Thy gentle accents softened all my pain.   ⎭

For thee I mourn, and mourn myself in thee,
The wretched source of all this misery.
The fate I caused, for ever I bemoan;
Sad Helen has no friend now thou art gone!
Through Troy's wide streets abandoned shall I roam,
980   In Troy deserted, as abhorred at home!'
      So spoke the fair, with sorrow-streaming eye;
Distressful beauty melts each stander-by.
On all around th' infectious sorrow grows,
But Priam checked the torrent as it rose:
'Perform, ye Trojans! what the rites require,
And fell the forests for a fun'ral pyre;
Twelve days, nor foes, nor secret ambush dread;
Achilles grants these honours to the dead.'
      He spoke; and at his word, the Trojan train
990   Their mules and oxen harness to the wain,
Pour through the gates, and felled from Ida's crown,
Roll back the gathered forests to the town.
These toils continue nine succeeding days,
And high in air a sylvan structure raise.
But when the tenth fair morn began to shine,
Forth to the pile was borne the man divine,
And placed aloft; while all, with streaming eyes,
Beheld the flames and rolling smokes arise.
Soon as Aurora, daughter of the dawn,
1000   With rosy lustre streaked the dewy lawn,
Again the mournful crowds surround the pyre,
And quench with wine the yet remaining fire.
The snowy bones his friends and brothers place
(With tears collected) in a golden vase;
The golden vase in purple palls they rolled
Of softest texture, and inwrought with gold.
Last o'er the urn the sacred earth they spread,
And raised the tomb, memorial of the dead.
(Strong guards and spies, till all the rites were done,
1010   Watched from the rising to the setting sun.)
All Troy then moves to Priam's court again,

A solemn, silent, melancholy train:
Assembled there, from pious toil they rest,
And sadly shared the last sepulchral feast.
Such honours Ilion to her hero paid,
And peaceful slept the mighty Hector's shade.

THE END OF THE *ILIAD*

LATER POEMS

[TWO EPIGRAMS]

Epigram. Engraved on the Collar of a Dog which I gave to his Royal Highness

I am his Highness' dog at Kew;
Pray tell me sir, whose dog are you?

Epitaph. Intended for Sir Isaac Newton, in Westminster Abbey

Nature and Nature's laws lay hid in night.
God said, 'Let Newton be!' and all was light.

An Essay on Man
in Four Epistles
to Henry St John Lord Bolingbroke

The Design

Having proposed to write some pieces on human life and manners, such as (to use my Lord Bacon's expression) 'come home to men's business and bosoms', I thought it more satisfactory to begin with considering *Man* in the abstract, his *Nature* and his *State*; since, to prove any moral duty, to enforce any moral precept, or to examine the perfection or imperfection of any creature whatsoever, it is necessary first to know what *condition* and *relation* it is placed in, and what is the proper *end* and *purpose* of its *being*.

The science of human nature is, like all other sciences,

reduced to a *few clear points*; there are not *many certain truths* in this world. It is therefore in the anatomy of the mind as in that of the body: more good will accrue to mankind by attending to the large, open, and perceptible parts, than by studying too much such finer nerves and vessels, the conformations and uses of which will for ever escape our observation. The *disputes* are all upon these last, and, I will venture to say, they have less sharpened the *wits* than the *hearts* of men against each other, and have diminished the practice, more than advanced the theory, of morality. If I could flatter myself that this Essay has any merit, it is in steering betwixt the extremes of doctrines seemingly opposite, in passing over terms utterly unintelligible, and in forming a *temperate* yet not *inconsistent*, and a *short* yet not *imperfect* system of ethics.

This I might have done in prose; but I chose verse, and even rhyme, for two reasons. The one will appear obvious; that principles, maxims, or precepts so written, both strike the reader more strongly at first, and are more easily retained by him afterwards. The other may seem odd, but it is true: I found I could express them more *shortly* this way than in prose itself; and nothing is more certain, than that much of the *force* as well as *grace* of arguments or instructions, depends on their *conciseness*. I was unable to treat this part of my subject more in *detail*, without becoming dry and tedious; or more *poetically*, without sacrificing perspicuity to ornament, without wandering from the precision, or breaking the chain of reasoning. If any man can unite all these without diminution of any of them, I freely confess he will compass a thing above my capacity.

What is now published, is only to be considered as a *general map* of MAN, marking out no more than the *greater parts*, their *extent*, their *limits*, and their *connection*, but leaving the particular to be more fully delineated in the charts which are to follow. Consequently, these Epistles in their progress (if I have health and leisure to make any progress) will be less dry, and more susceptible of poetical ornament. I am here only opening the *fountains*, and clearing the passage. To deduce the *rivers*, to follow them in their course, and to observe their effects, may be a task more agreeable.

Epistle I

ARGUMENT
Of the Nature and State of Man
with respect to the UNIVERSE

Of Man *in the abstract.* – I. *That we can judge only with regard to our* own system, *being ignorant of the relations of systems and things,* v. 17, etc. II. *That Man is not to be deemed* imperfect, *but a being suited to his* place *and* rank *in the creation, agreeable to the* general order *of things, and conformable to* ends *and* relations *to him unknown,* v. 35, etc. III. *That it is partly upon his* ignorance *of* future *events, and partly upon the* hope *of a* future *state, that all his happiness in the present depends,* v. 77, etc. IV. *The* pride *of aiming at more knowledge, and pretending to more perfection, the cause of Man's error and misery. The* impiety *of putting himself in the place of God, and judging of the fitness or unfitness, perfection or imperfection, justice or injustice of his dispensations,* v. 113, etc. V. *The* absurdity *of conceiting himself the* final cause *of the creation, or expecting that perfection in the* moral *world, which is not in the* natural, v. 131, etc. VI. *The* unreasonableness *of his complaints against* Providence, *while on the one hand he demands the perfections of the angels, and on the other the bodily qualifications of the brutes; though to possess any of the* sensitive *faculties in a higher degree, would render him miserable,* v. 173, etc. VII. *That throughout the whole visible world, an* universal order *and* gradation *in the sensual and mental faculties is observed, which causes a* subordination *of creature to creature, and of all creatures to Man. The* gradations *of* sense, instinct, thought, reflection, reason; *that reason alone countervails all the other faculties,* v. 207. VIII. *How much farther this* order *and* subordination *of living creatures may extend, above and below us; were any part of which broken, not that part only, but the whole connected* creation *must be destroyed*, v. 233. IX. *The* extravagance, madness, *and* pride *of such a* desire, v. 259. X. *The consequence of all, the* absolute submission *due to Providence, both as to our* present *and* future state, v. 281, etc. *to the end.*

Awake, my St John! leave all meaner things
To low ambition, and the pride of kings.
Let us (since life can little more supply
Than just to look about us and to die)
Expatiate free o'er all this scene of Man;
A mighty maze! but not without a plan;
A wild, where weeds and flow'rs promiscuous shoot,
Or garden, tempting with forbidden fruit.
Together let us beat this ample field,
10   Try what the open, what the covert yield;
The latent tracts, the giddy heights explore
Of all who blindly creep, or sightless soar;
Eye Nature's walks, shoot folly as it flies,
And catch the manners living as they rise;
Laugh where we must, be candid where we can,
But vindicate the ways of God to Man.
    I. Say first, of God above, or Man below
What can we reason, but from what we know?
Of man what see we, but his station here,
20   From which to reason, or to which refer?
Through worlds unnumbered though the God be known,
'Tis ours to trace him only in our own.
He, who through vast immensity can pierce,
See worlds on worlds compose one universe,
Observe how system into system runs,
What other planets circle other suns,
What varied being peoples ev'ry star,
May tell why Heav'n has made us as we are.
But of this frame, the bearings and the ties,
30   The strong connections, nice dependencies,

Gradations just, has thy pervading soul
Looked through, or can a part contain the whole?
    Is the great chain, that draws all to agree,
And drawn supports, upheld by God, or thee?
    II. Presumptuous Man! the reason wouldst thou find,
Why formed so weak, so little, and so blind!
First, if thou canst, the harder reason guess
Why formed no weaker, blinder, and no less?
Ask of thy mother earth, why oaks are made
Taller or stronger than the weeds they shade!   40
Or ask of yonder argent fields above
Why Jove's satellites are less than Jove!
    Of systems possible, if 'tis confessed
That wisdom infinite must form the best,
Where all must full or not coherent be,
And all that rises, rise in due degree;
Then, in the scale of reas'ning life, 'tis plain
There must be, somewhere, such a rank as Man;
And all the question (wrangle e'er so long)
Is only this, if God has placed him wrong?   50
    Respecting Man, whatever wrong we call,
May, must be right, as relative to all.
In human works, though laboured on with pain,
A thousand movements scarce one purpose gain;
In God's, one single can its end produce,
Yet serves to second too some other use.
So Man, who here seems principal alone,
Perhaps acts second to some sphere unknown,
Touches some wheel, or verges to some goal;
'Tis but a part we see, and not a whole.   60
    When the proud steed shall know why Man restrains
His fiery course, or drives him o'er the plains;
When the dull ox, why now he breaks the clod,
Is now a victim, and now Egypt's god;
Then shall Man's pride and dullness comprehend
His actions', passions', being's, use and end;
Why doing, suff'ring, checked, impelled; and why
This hour a slave, the next a deity.

Then say not Man's imperfect, Heav'n in fault;
70 Say rather, Man's as perfect as he ought:
His knowledge measured to his state and place,
His time a moment, and a point his space.
If to be perfect in a certain sphere,
What matter soon or late, or here or there?
The blest today is as completely so
As who began a thousand years ago.
      III. Heav'n from all creatures hides the book of fate,
All but the page prescribed, their present state:
From brutes what men, from men what spirits know;
80 Or who could suffer being here below?
The lamb thy riot dooms to bleed today,
Had he thy reason, would he skip and play?
Pleased to the last, he crops the flow'ry food,
And licks the hand just raised to shed his blood.
O blindness to the future! kindly giv'n,
That each may fill the circle marked by Heav'n;
Who sees with equal eye, as God of all,
A hero perish, or a sparrow fall,
Atoms or systems into ruin hurled,
90 And now a bubble burst, and now a world.
      Hope humbly then; with trembling pinions soar;
Wait the great teacher Death; and God adore!
What future bliss, he gives not thee to know,
But gives that hope to be thy blessing now.
Hope springs eternal in the human breast:
Man never is, but always to be blessed.
The soul, uneasy and confined from home,
Rests and expatiates in a life to come.
      Lo! the poor Indian, whose untutored mind
100 Sees God in clouds, or hears him in the wind;
His soul proud science never taught to stray
Far as the solar walk, or Milky Way;
Yet simple nature to his hope has giv'n
Behind the cloud topped hill, an humbler heav'n;
Some safer world in depth of woods embraced,
Some happier island in the wat'ry waste,

Where slaves once more their native land behold,
No fiends torment, no Christians thirst for gold!
To be, contents his natural desire;
He asks no angel's wing, no seraph's fire;   110
But thinks, admitted to that equal sky,
His faithful dog shall bear him company.

    IV. Go, wiser thou! and in thy scale of sense
Weigh thy opinion against Providence;
Call imperfection what thou fanciest such:
Say, here He gives too little, there too much;
Destroy all creatures for thy sport or gust,
Yet cry, if Man's unhappy, God's unjust;
If Man alone engross not Heav'n's high care,
Alone made perfect here, immortal there,   120
Snatch from his hand the balance and the rod,
Rejudge his justice, be the god of God!
In pride, in reas'ning pride our error lies;
All quit their sphere, and rush into the skies.
Pride still is aiming at the bless'd abodes,
Men would be angels, angels would be gods.
Aspiring to be gods, if angels fell,
Aspiring to be angels, men rebel;
And who but wishes to invert the laws
Of order, sins against th' eternal Cause.   130

    V. Ask for what end the heav'nly bodies shine,
Earth for whose use? Pride answers, ''Tis for mine:
For me kind Nature wakes her genial pow'r,
Suckles each herb, and spreads out ev'ry flower;
Annual for me the grape, the rose renew
The juice nectareous, and the balmy dew;
For me, the mine a thousand treasures brings;
For me, health gushes from a thousand springs;
Seas roll to waft me, suns to light me rise;
My footstool earth, my canopy the skies.'   140

    But errs not Nature from this gracious end,
From burning suns when livid deaths descend,
When earthquakes swallow, or when tempests sweep
Towns to one grave, whole nations to the deep?

'No, ('tis replied) the first Almighty Cause
Acts not by partial, but by gen'ral laws;
Th' exceptions few; some change since all began;
And what created perfect?' – Why then Man?
If the great end be human happiness,
Then Nature deviates; and can Man do less?
As much that end a constant course requires
Of show'rs and sunshine, as of Man's desires;
As much eternal springs and cloudless skies,
As men for ever temp'rate, calm, and wise.
If plagues or earthquakes break not Heav'n's design,
Why then a Borgia or a Catiline!
Who knows but He, whose hand the lightning forms,
Who heaves old ocean, and who wings the storms,
Pours fierce ambition in a Caesar's mind,
Or turns young Ammon loose to scourge mankind?
From pride, from pride, our very reas'ning springs;
Account for moral as for nat'ral things:
Why charge we Heav'n in those, in these acquit?
In both, to reason right is to submit.
    Better for us, perhaps, it might appear,
Were there all harmony, all virtue here;
That never air or ocean felt the wind,
That never passion discomposed the mind:
But all subsists by elemental strife;
And passions are the elements of life.
The gen'ral order, since the whole began,
Is kept in nature, and is kept in Man.
    VI. What would this Man? Now upward will he soar,
And little less than angel, would be more;
Now looking downwards, just as grieved appears
To want the strength of bulls, the fur of bears.
Made for his use all creatures if he call,
Say what their use, had he the pow'rs of all?
Nature to these, without profusion kind,
The proper organs, proper pow'rs assigned;
Each seeming want compensated of course,
Here with degrees of swiftness, there of force;

All in exact proportion to the state:
Nothing to add, and nothing to abate.
Each beast, each insect, happy in its own,
Is Heav'n unkind to Man, and Man alone?
Shall he alone, whom rational we call,
Be pleased with nothing if not blessed with all?
    The bliss of Man (could pride that blessing find)
Is not to act or think beyond Mankind;   190
No pow'rs of body or of soul to share,
But what his nature and his state can bear.
Why has not Man a microscopic eye?
For this plain reason, Man is not a fly.
Say what the use, were finer optics giv'n,
T' inspect a mite, not comprehend the heav'n?
Or touch, if tremblingly alive all o'er,
To smart and agonize at ev'ry pore?
Or quick effluvia darting through the brain,
Die of a rose in aromatic pain?   200
If nature thundered in his op'ning ears,
And stunned him with the music of the spheres,
How would he wish that Heav'n had left him still
The whisp'ring zephyr and the purling rill?
Who finds not Providence all good and wise,
Alike in what it gives, and what it denies?
    VII. Far as creation's ample range extends,
The scale of sensual, mental pow'rs ascends:
Mark how it mounts, to Man's imperial race,
From the green myriads in the peopled grass: 210
What modes of sight betwixt each wide extreme,
The mole's dim curtain and the lynx's beam!
Of smell, the headlong lioness between
And hound sagacious on the tainted green!
Of hearing, from the life that fills the flood
To that which warbles through the vernal wood!
The spider's touch, how exquisitely fine!
Feels at each thread, and lives along the line;
In the nice bee, what sense so subtly true
From pois'nous herbs extracts the healing dew;   220

How instinct varies in the grov'ling swine,
Compared, half-reas'ning elephant, with thine!
'Twixt that and reason, what a nice barrier!
For ever sep'rate, yet for ever near!
Remembrance and reflection how allied!
What thin partitions sense from thought divide!
And middle natures, how they long to join,
Yet never pass th' insuperable line!
Without this just gradation could they be
230   Subjected these to those, or all to thee?
The pow'rs of all subdued by thee alone,
Is not thy reason all these pow'rs in one?
    VIII. See, through this air, this ocean, and this earth,
All matter quick, and bursting into birth.
Above, how high progressive life may go!
Around, how wide! how deep extend below!
Vast chain of being, which from God began:
Natures ethereal, human, angel, man,
Beast, bird, fish, insect, what no eye can see,
240   No glass can reach! from infinite to thee,
From thee to nothing! – On superior pow'rs
Were we to press, inferior might on ours;
Or in the full creation leave a void,
Where, one step broken, the great scale's destroyed:
From Nature's chain whatever link you strike,
Tenth, or ten thousandth, breaks the chain alike.
    And if each system in gradation roll,
Alike essential to th' amazing whole,
The least confusion but in one, not all
250   That system only, but the whole must fall.
Let earth unbalanced from her orbit fly,
Planets and stars run lawless through the sky,
Let ruling angels from their spheres be hurled,
Being on being wrecked, and world on world,
Heav'n's whole foundations to their centre nod,
And Nature tremble to the throne of God:
All this dread order break – for whom? for thee?

Vile worm! – oh madness! pride! impiety!
　IX. What if the foot, ordained the dust to tread,
Or hand to toil, aspired to be the head?   260
What if the head, the eye, or ear repined
To serve mere engines to the ruling mind?
Just as absurd, for any part to claim
To be another in this gen'ral frame;
Just as absurd, to mourn the tasks or pains
The great directing Mind of All ordains.
　All are but parts of one stupendous whole,
Whose body Nature is, and God the soul;
That changed through all, and yet in all the same,
Great in the earth, as in th' ethereal frame,   270
Warms in the sun, refreshes in the breeze,
Glows in the stars, and blossoms in the trees;
Lives through all life, extends through all extent,
Spreads undivided, operates unspent;
Breathes in our soul, informs our mortal part,
As full, as perfect, in a hair as heart;
As full, as perfect, in vile man that mourns
As the rapt seraph that adores and burns:
To him no high, no low, no great, no small;
He fills, he bounds, connects, and equals all!   280
　X. Cease then, nor order imperfection name;
Our proper bliss depends on what we blame.
Know thy own point: this kind, this due degree
Of blindness, weakness, Heav'n bestows on thee.
Submit – In this or any other sphere,
Secure to be as bless'd as thou canst bear;
Safe in the hand of one disposing Pow'r,
Or in the natal, or the mortal hour.
All Nature is but art, unknown to thee;
All chance, direction, which thou canst not see;   290
All discord, harmony, not understood;
All partial evil, universal good:
And spite of pride, in erring reason's spite,
One truth is clear, 'Whatever IS, is RIGHT.'

Epistle II

ARGUMENT

Of the Nature and State of Man with respect to Himself, as an Individual

I. *The business of Man not to pry into* God, *but to study* himself. *His* Middle Nature; *his powers and frailties*, v. 1 to 18. *The limits of his* capacity, v. 19, etc. II. *The two principles of Man,* Self-love *and* Reason, *both necessary*, v. 53, etc. Self-love *the stronger, and why*, v. 67, etc. *Their end the same*, v. 81, etc. III. *The* PASSIONS, *and their use*, v. 93 to 130. *The* predominant passion, *and its force*, v. 131 to 160. *Its necessity, in directing men to different purposes*, v. 165, etc. *Its providential use, in fixing our principle, and ascertaining our virtue*, v. 177. IV. Virtue *and* Vice *joined in our* mixed nature; *the limits near, yet the things* separate *and* evident: *What is the office of* reason, v. 203 to 216. V. *How odious* vice *in itself, and how we deceive ourselves into it*, v. 217. VI. *That, however, the* ends *of* Providence *and* general good *are answered in our passions and imperfections*, v. 238, etc. *How usefully these are distributed to all* orders of Men, v. 241. *How useful they are to* Society, v. 249. *And to the* Individuals, v. 261. *In every* state, *and every* age *of* life, v. 271, etc.

     I. Know then thyself, presume not God to scan;
    The proper study of Mankind is Man.
    Placed on this isthmus of a middle state,
    A being darkly wise, and rudely great:
    With too much knowledge for the sceptic side,
    With too much weakness for the stoic's pride,
    He hangs between, in doubt to act, or rest;
    In doubt to deem himself a god, or beast;
    In doubt his mind or body to prefer;
10   Born but to die, and reas'ning but to err;
    Alike in ignorance, his reason such,
    Whether he thinks too little, or too much:

Chaos of thought and passion, all confused;
Still by himself abused or disabused;
Created half to rise, and half to fall;
Great lord of all things, yet a prey to all;
Sole judge of truth, in endless error hurled;
The glory, jest, and riddle of the world!

    Go, wondrous creature! mount where science guides;
Go, measure earth, weigh air, and state the tides;   20
Instruct the planets in what orbs to run,
Correct old Time, and regulate the sun;
Go, soar with Plato to th' empyreal sphere,
To the first good, first perfect, and first fair;
Or tread the mazy round his followers trod,
And quitting sense call imitating God;
As eastern priests in giddy circles run,
And turn their heads to imitate the sun.
Go, teach Eternal Wisdom how to rule –
Then drop into thyself, and be a fool!   30

    Superior beings, when of late they saw
A mortal Man unfold all Nature's law,
Admired such wisdom in an earthly shape,
And showed a Newton as we show an ape.

    Could he, whose rules the rapid comet bind,
Describe or fix one movement of his mind?
Who saw its fires here rise, and there descend,
Explain his own beginning, or his end?
Alas, what wonder! Man's superior part
Unchecked may rise, and climb from art to art;   40
But when his own great work is but begun,
What reason weaves, by passion is undone.

    Trace science then, with modesty thy guide:
First strip off all her equipage of pride,
Deduct what is but vanity, or dress,
Or learning's luxury, or idleness;
Or tricks to show the stretch of human brain,
Mere curious pleasure, or ingenious pain;
Expunge the whole, or lop th' excrescent parts
Of all, our vices have created arts;   50

Then see how little the remaining sum,
Which served the past, and must the times to come!
   II. Two principles in human nature reign,
Self-love, to urge, and reason, to restrain;
Nor this a good, nor that a bad we call;
Each works its end, to move or govern all,
And to their proper operation still
Ascribe all good; to their improper, ill.
   Self-love, the spring of motion, acts the soul;
60 Reason's comparing balance rules the whole.
Man, but for that, no action could attend,
And but for this, were active to no end;
Fixed like a plant on his peculiar spot,
To draw nutrition, propagate, and rot;
Or, meteor-like, flame lawless through the void,
Destroying others, by himself destroyed
   Most strength the moving principle requires;
Active its task, it prompts, impels, inspires.
Sedate and quiet the comparing lies,
70 Formed but to check, delib'rate, and advise.
Self-love still stronger, as its objects nigh;
Reason's at distance, and in prospect lie:
That sees immediate good by present sense;
Reason, the future and the consequence.
Thicker than arguments, temptations throng;
At best more watchful this, but that more strong.
The action of the stronger to suspend,
Reason still use, to reason still attend.
Attention, habit and experience gains;
80 Each strengthens reason, and self-love restrains.
   Let subtle schoolmen teach these friends to fight,
More studious to divide than to unite,
And grace and virtue, sense and reason split,
With all the rash dexterity of wit.
Wits, just like fools, at war about a name,
Have full as oft no meaning, or the same.
Self-love and reason to one end aspire,
Pain their aversion, pleasure their desire;

But greedy that, its object would devour;
This taste the honey, and not wound the flow'r.   90
Pleasure, or wrong or rightly understood,
Our greatest evil, or our greatest good.
    III. Modes of self-love the passions we may call;
'Tis real good, or seeming, moves them all:
But since not every good we can divide,
And reason bids us for our own provide,
Passions, though selfish, if their means be fair,
List under reason, and deserve her care;
Those that imparted, court a nobler aim,
Exalt their kind, and take some virtue's name.   100
    In lazy apathy let Stoics boast
Their virtue fixed; 'tis fixed as in a frost,
Contracted all, retiring to the breast;
But strength of mind is exercise, not rest;
The rising tempest puts in act the soul,
Parts it may ravage, but preserves the whole.
On life's vast ocean diversely we sail,
Reason the card, but passion is the gale;
Nor God alone in the still calm we find,
He mounts the storm, and walks upon the wind.   110
    Passions, like elements, though born to fight,
Yet, mixed and softened, in his work unite:
These 'tis enough to temper and employ;
But what composes Man, can Man destroy?
Suffice that reason keep to Nature's road;
Subject, compound them, follow her and God.
Love, hope, and joy, fair pleasure's smiling train,
Hate, fear, and grief, the family of pain,
These mixed with art, and to due bounds confined,
Make and maintain the balance of the mind: 120
The lights and shades, whose well-accorded strife
Gives all the strength and colour of our life.
    Pleasures are ever in our hands or eyes,
And when in act they cease, in prospect rise;
Present to grasp, and future still to find,
The whole employ of body and of mind.

All spread their charms, but charm not all alike;
On diff'rent senses diff'rent objects strike;
Hence diff'rent passions more or less inflame,
130 As strong or weak, the organs of the frame,
And hence one master-passion in the breast,
Like Aaron's serpent, swallows up the rest.

As Man, perhaps, the moment of his breath,
Receives the lurking principle of death,
The young disease, that must subdue at length,
Grows with his growth, and strengthens with his strength:
So, cast and mingled with his very frame,
The mind's disease, its ruling passion, came;
Each vital humour, which should feed the whole,
140 Soon flows to this in body and in soul;
Whatever warms the heart or fills the head,
As the mind opens and its functions spread,
Imagination plies her dang'rous art,
And pours it all upon the peccant part.

Nature its mother, habit is its nurse;
Wit, spirit, faculties, but make it worse;
Reason itself but gives it edge and pow'r,
As Heav'n's bless'd beam turns vinegar more sour.

We, wretched subjects, though to lawful sway,
150 In this weak queen some fav'rite still obey.
Ah! if she lend not arms, as well as rules,
What can she more than tell us we are fools?
Teach us to mourn our nature, not to mend,
A sharp accuser, but a helpless friend!
Or from a judge turn pleader, to persuade
The choice we make, or justify it made;
Proud of an easy conquest all along,
She but removes weak passions for the strong:
So when small humours gather to a gout,
160 The doctor fancies he has driv'n them out.

Yes, Nature's road must ever be preferred;
Reason is here no guide, but still a guard.
'Tis hers to rectify, not overthrow,
And treat this passion more as friend than foe;

A mightier Pow'r the strong direction sends,
And sev'ral men impels to sev'ral ends:
Like varying winds, by other passions tossed,
This drives them constant to a certain coast.
Let pow'r or knowledge, gold or glory, please,
Or (oft more strong than all) the love of ease;   170
Through life 'tis followed, ev'n at life's expense;
The merchant's toil, the sage's indolence,
The monk's humility, the hero's pride,
All, all alike, find reason on their side.

  Th' Eternal Art educing good from ill,
Grafts on this passion our best principle:
'Tis thus the mercury of man is fixed,
Strong grows the virtue with his nature mixed,
The dross cements what else were too refined,
And in one interest body acts with mind.   180

  As fruits ungrateful to the planter's care
On savage stocks inserted, learn to bear;
The surest virtues thus from passions shoot,
Wild Nature's vigour working at the root.
What crops of wit and honesty appear
From spleen, from obstinacy, hate, or fear!
See anger, zeal, and fortitude supply;
Ev'n av'rice, prudence; sloth, philosophy;
Lust, through some certain strainers well refined,
Is gentle love, and charms all womankind;   190
Envy, to which th' ignoble mind's a slave,
Is emulation in the learn'd or brave;
Nor virtue male or female can we name,
But what will grow on pride, or grow on shame.

  Thus nature gives us (let it check our pride)
The virtue nearest to our vice allied:
Reason the bias turns to good from ill,
And Nero reigns a Titus, if he will.
The fiery soul abhorred in Catiline,
In Decius charms, in Curtius is divine;   200
The same ambition can destroy or save,
And make a patriot as it makes a knave.

    IV. This light and darkness in our chaos joined,
What shall divide? – the God within the mind.
    Extremes in nature equal ends produce,
In man they join to some mysterious use;
Though each by turns the other's bounds invade,
As in some well-wrought picture, light and shade,
And oft so mix, the diff'rence is too nice
210 Where ends the virtue, or begins the vice.
    Fools! who from hence into the notion fall
That vice or virtue there is none at all.
If white and black blend, soften, and unite
A thousand ways, is there no black or white?
Ask your own heart, and nothing is so plain;
'Tis to mistake them costs the time and pain.
    V. Vice is a monster of so frightful mien,
As to be hated needs but to be seen;
Yet seen too oft, familiar with her face,
220 We first endure, then pity, then embrace.
But where th' extreme of vice, was ne'er agreed:
Ask where's the north? – at York 'tis on the Tweed;
In Scotland at the Orcades; and there
At Greenland, Zembla, or the Lord knows where.
No creature owns it in the first degree,
But thinks his neighbour further gone than he.
Ev'n those who dwell beneath its very zone,
Or never feel the rage, or never own;
What happier natures shrink at with affright,
230 The hard inhabitant contends is right.
    VI. Virtuous and vicious ev'ry man must be,
Few in th' extreme, but all in the degree:
The rogue and fool by fits is fair and wise,
And ev'n the best, by fits, what they despise.
'Tis but by parts we follow good or ill;
For vice or virtue, self directs it still;
Each individual seeks a sev'ral goal,
But Heav'n's great view is one, and that the whole:
That counterworks each folly and caprice;
240 That disappoints th' effect of ev'ry vice;

That happy frailties to all ranks applied,
Shame to the virgin, to the matron pride,
Fear to the statesman, rashness to the chief,
To kings presumption, and to crowds belief;
That, virtue's ends from vanity can raise,
Which seeks no int'rest, no reward but praise;
And build on wants, and on defects of mind,
The joy, the peace, the glory of mankind!
  Heav'n forming each on other to depend,
A master, or a servant, or a friend,   250
Bids each on other for assistance call
Till one man's weakness grows the strength of all.
Wants, frailties, passions, closer still ally
The common int'rest, or endear the tie:
To these we owe true friendship, love sincere,
Each home-felt joy, that life inherits here;
Yet from the same we learn, in its decline,
Those joys, those loves, those int'rests to resign;
Taught, half by reason, half by mere decay,
To welcome death, and calmly pass away.   260
  Whate'er the passion, knowledge, fame, or pelf,
Not one will change his neighbour with himself.
The learn'd is happy nature to explore,
The fool is happy that he knows no more;
The rich is happy in the plenty giv'n,
The poor contents him with the care of Heav'n.
See the blind beggar dance, the cripple sing,
The sot a hero, lunatic a king;
The starving chemist in his golden views
Supremely blest, the poet in his muse.   270
  See some strange comfort ev'ry state attend,
And pride bestowed on all, a common friend:
See some fit passion ev'ry age supply;
Hope travels through, nor quits us when we die.
  Behold the child, by Nature's kindly law,
Pleased with a rattle, tickled with a straw;
Some livelier plaything gives his youth delight,

A little louder, but as empty quite;
Scarfs, garters, gold, amuse his riper stage,
280   And beads and pray'r-books are the toys of age;
Pleased with this bauble still, as that before,
Till tired he sleeps, and life's poor play is o'er.
　　Meanwhile opinion gilds with varying rays
Those painted clouds that beautify our days:
Each want of happiness by hope supplied,
And each vacuity of sense by pride;
These build as fast as knowledge can destroy;
In folly's cup still laughs the bubble, joy;
One prospect lost, another still we gain,
290   And not a vanity is giv'n in vain:
Ev'n mean self-love becomes, by force divine,
The scale to measure others' wants by thine.
See! and confess one comfort still must rise;
'Tis this, though Man's a fool, yet God is wise.

Epistle III

ARGUMENT
Of the Nature and State of Man
with respect to Society

I. *The whole universe one system of society*, v. 7, etc. *Nothing
made wholly for* itself, *nor yet wholly for* another, v. 27. *The hap-
piness of* animals *mutual*, v. 49. II. Reason *or* instinct *operate
alike to the good of each individual*, v. 79. Reason *or* instinct *oper-
ate also to Society, in all animals*, v. 109. III. *How far* Society
carried by instinct, v. 115. *How much farther by reason*, v. 131.
IV. *Of that which is called the* State of Nature, v. 147. *Reason
instructed by instinct in the invention of* Arts, v. 171, *and in the
forms of* Society, v. 179. V. *Origin of political societies*, v. 199. *Ori-
gin of monarchy*, v. 209. *Patriarchal government*, v. 215. VI. *Origin
of true religion and government, from the same principle, of love,*

v. 231, etc. *Origin of superstition and tyranny, from the same prin-ciple, of fear*, v. 241, etc. *The influence of self-love operating to the* social *and* public *good*, v. 269. *Restoration of true religion and government on their first principle*, v. 283. *Mixed government*, v. 294. *Various forms of each, and the true end of all*, v. 303, etc.

Here then we rest: 'the Universal Cause
Acts to one end, but acts by various laws.'
In all the madness of superfluous health,
The trim of pride, the impudence of wealth,
Let this great truth be present night and day,
But most be present, if we preach or pray.
   I. Look round our world; behold the chain of love
Combining all below and all above.
See plastic Nature working to this end,
The single atoms each to other tend,   10
Attract, attracted to, the next in place
Formed and impelled its neighbour to embrace.
See matter next, with various life endued,
Press to one centre still, the gen'ral good:
See dying vegetables life sustain,
See life dissolving vegetate again:
All forms that perish other forms supply
(By turns we catch the vital breath, and die);
Like bubbles on the sea of matter borne,
They rise, they break, and to that sea return.   20
Nothing is foreign; parts relate to whole;
One all-extending, all-preserving soul
Connects each being, greatest with the least,
Made beast in aid of Man, and Man of beast;
All served, all serving! nothing stands alone;
The chain holds on, and where it ends unknown.
   Has God, thou fool! worked solely for thy good,
Thy joy, thy pastime, thy attire, thy food?
Who for thy table feeds the wanton fawn,
For him as kindly spreads the flow'ry lawn.   30
Is it for thee the lark ascends and sings?
Joy tunes his voice, joy elevates his wings.

Is it for thee the linnet pours his throat?
Loves of his own and raptures swell the note.
The bounding steed you pompously bestride
Shares with his lord the pleasure and the pride.
Is thine alone the seed that strews the plain?
The birds of heav'n shall vindicate their grain.
Thine the full harvest of the golden year?
40   Part pays, and justly, the deserving steer.
The hog that ploughs not, nor obeys thy call,
Lives on the labours of this lord of all.
        Know, Nature's children all divide her care;
The fur that warms a monarch, warmed a bear.
While man exclaims, 'See all things for my use!'
'See man for mine!' replies a pampered goose:
And just as short of reason he must fall,
Who thinks all made for one, not one for all.
        Grant that the pow'rful still the weak control;
50   Be Man the wit and tyrant of the whole:
Nature that tyrant checks; he only knows,
And helps, another creature's wants and woes.
Say, will the falcon, stooping from above,
Smit with her varying plumage, spare the dove?
Admires the jay the insect's gilded wings?
Or hears the hawk when Philomela sings?
Man cares for all: to birds he gives his woods,
To beasts his pastures, and to fish his floods;
For some his int'rest prompts him to provide,
60   For more his pleasure, yet for more his pride:
All feed on one vain patron, and enjoy
Th' extensive blessing of his luxury.
That very life his learnèd hunger craves
He saves from famine, from the savage saves;
Nay, feasts the animal he dooms his feast,
And till he ends the being, makes it blest;
Which sees no more the stroke, or feels the pain,
Than favoured Man by touch ethereal slain.
The creature had his feast of life before;
70   Thou too must perish, when thy feast is o'er!

To each unthinking being, Heav'n, a friend,
Gives not the useless knowledge of its end;
To man imparts it, but with such a view
As while he dreads it, makes him hope it too:
The hour concealed, and so remote the fear,
Death still draws nearer, never seeming near.
Great standing miracle! that Heav'n assigned
Its only thinking thing, this turn of mind.
    II. Whether with reason, or with instinct blest,
Know, all enjoy that pow'r which suits them best;   80
To bliss alike by that direction tend,
And find the means proportioned to their end.
Say, where full instinct is th' unerring guide,
What pope or council can they need beside?
Reason, however able, cool at best,
Cares not for service, or but serves when pressed,
Stays till we call, and then not often near,
But honest instinct comes a volunteer,
Sure never to o'ershoot, but just to hit,
While still too wide or short is human wit;   90
Sure by quick Nature happiness to gain,
Which heavier reason labours at in vain.
This too serves always; reason, never long;
One must go right, the other may go wrong.
See then the acting and comparing pow'rs
One in their nature, which are two in ours;
And reason raise o'er instinct as you can,
In this 'tis God directs, in that 'tis Man.
    Who taught the nations of the field and wood
To shun their poison, and to choose their food?   100
Prescient, the tides or tempests to withstand,
Build on the wave, or arch beneath the sand?
Who made the spider parallels design,
Sure as De Moivre, without rule or line?
Who bade the stork, Columbus-like, explore
Heav'ns not his own, and worlds unknown before?
Who calls the council, states the certain day,
Who forms the phalanx, and who points the way?

III. God, in the nature of each being, founds
110 Its proper bliss, and sets its proper bounds;
But as he framed a whole, the whole to bless,
On mutual wants built mutual happiness:
So from the first eternal order ran,
And creature linked to creature, Man to Man.
Whate'er of life all-quick'ning ether keeps,
Or breathes through air, or shoots beneath the deeps,
Or pours profuse on earth, one nature feeds
The vital flame, and swells the genial seeds.
Not Man alone, but all that roam the wood,
120 Or wing the sky, or roll along the flood,
Each loves itself, but not itself alone,
Each sex desires alike, till two are one.
Nor ends the pleasure with the fierce embrace:
They love themselves, a third time, in their race.
Thus beast and bird their common charge attend,
The mothers nurse it, and the sires defend;
The young dismissed to wander earth or air,
There stops the instinct, and there ends the care;
The link dissolves, each seeks a fresh embrace,
130 Another love succeeds, another race.
A longer care Man's helpless kind demands;
That longer care contracts more lasting bands:
Reflection, reason, still the ties improve,
At once extend the int'rest and the love;
With choice we fix, with sympathy we burn;
Each virtue in each passion takes its turn;
And still new needs, new helps, new habits rise,
That graft benevolence on charities.
Still as one brood, and as another rose,
140 These nat'ral love maintained, habitual those:
The last, scarce ripened into perfect man,
Saw helpless him from whom their life began:
Mem'ry and forecast just returns engage,
That pointed back to youth, this on to age;
While pleasure, gratitude, and hope, combined,
Still spread the int'rest, and preserved the kind.

IV. Nor think in Nature's state they blindly trod;
The state of Nature was the reign of God.
Self-love and social at her birth began,
Union the bond of all things, and of Man.   150
Pride then was not, nor arts that pride to aid;
Man walked with beast, joint tenant of the shade;
The same his table, and the same his bed;
No murder clothed him, and no murder fed.
In the same temple, the resounding wood,
All vocal beings hymned their equal God:
The shrine with gore unstained, with gold undressed,
Unbribed, unbloody, stood the blameless priest:
Heav'n's attribute was universal care,
And Man's prerogative to rule, but spare.   160
Ah! how unlike the Man of times to come!
Of half that live, the butcher and the tomb;
Who, foe to Nature, hears the gen'ral groan,
Murders their species, and betrays his own.
But just disease to luxury succeeds,
And ev'ry death its own avenger breeds;
The fury passions from that blood began,
And turned on Man a fiercer savage, Man.
   See him from Nature rising slow to art!
To copy instinct then was reason's part;   170
Thus then to Man the voice of Nature spake –
'Go, from the creatures thy instructions take:
Learn from the birds what food the thickets yield;
Learn from the beasts the physic of the field;
Thy arts of building from the bee receive;
Learn of the mole to plough, the worm to weave;
Learn of the little nautilus to sail,
Spread the thin oar, and catch the driving gale.
Here too all forms of social union find,
And hence let reason, late, instruct mankind: 180
Here subterranean works and cities see;
There towns aerial on the waving tree.
Learn each small people's genius, policies,
The ant's republic, and the realm of bees;

How those in common all their wealth bestow,
And anarchy without confusion know;
And these for ever, though a monarch reign,
Their sep'rate cells and properties maintain.
Mark what unvaried laws preserve each state,
190 Laws wise as nature, and as fixed as fate.
In vain thy reason finer webs shall draw,
Entangle justice in her net of law,
And right, too rigid, harden into wrong;
Still for the strong too weak, the weak too strong.
Yet go! and thus o'er all the creatures sway,
Thus let the wiser make the rest obey;
And for those arts mere instinct could afford,
Be crowned as monarchs, or as gods adored.'
        V. Great Nature spoke; observant Man obeyed;
200 Cities were built, societies were made:
Here rose one little state; another near
Grew by like means, and joined, through love or fear.
Did here the trees with ruddier burdens bend,
And there the streams in purer rills descend?
What war could ravish, commerce could bestow,
And he returned a friend, who came a foe.
Converse and love mankind might strongly draw,
When love was liberty, and Nature law.
Thus states were formed, the name of king unknown,
210 Till common int'rest placed the sway in one.
'Twas virtue only (or in arts or arms,
Diffusing blessings, or averting harms)
The same which in a sire the sons obeyed,
A prince the father of a people made.
        VI. Till then, by Nature crowned, each patriarch sate,
King, priest, and parent of his growing state;
On him, their second Providence, they hung,
Their law his eye, their oracle his tongue.
He from the wond'ring furrow called the food,
220 Taught to command the fire, control the flood,
Draw forth the monsters of th' abyss profound,
Or fetch th' aerial eagle to the ground;

Till drooping, sick'ning, dying, they began
Whom they revered as God to mourn as man:
Then, looking up from sire to sire, explored
One great first Father, and that first adored.
Or plain tradition that this all begun,
Conveyed unbroken faith from sire to son;
The Worker from the work distinct was known,
And simple reason never sought but one.   230
Ere wit oblique had broke that steady light,
Man, like his Maker, saw that all was right;
To virtue in the paths of pleasure trod,
And owned a father when he owned a God.
Love all the faith, and all th' allegiance then,
For Nature knew no right divine in men;
No ill could fear in God, and understood
A sov'reign being but a sov'reign good,
True faith, true policy, united ran;
That was but love of God, and this of Man.   240
  Who first taught souls enslaved, and realms undone,
Th' enormous faith of many made for one;
That proud exception to all Nature's laws,
T' invert the world, and counterwork its cause?
Force first made conquest, and that conquest law;
Till superstition taught the tyrant awe,
Then shared the tyranny, then lent it aid,
And gods of conqu'rors, slaves of subjects made:
She, midst the lightning's blaze and thunder's sound,
When rocked the mountains, and when groaned   250
      the ground,
She taught the weak to bend, the proud to pray,
To pow'r unseen, and mightier far than they:
She, from the rending earth and bursting skies,
Saw gods descend, and fiends infernal rise;
Here fixed the dreadful, there the bless'd abodes;
Fear made her devils, and weak hope her gods:
Gods partial, changeful, passionate, unjust,
Whose attributes were rage, revenge, or lust;

Such as the souls of cowards might conceive,
260   And, formed like tyrants, tyrants would believe.
Zeal then, not charity, became the guide,
And Hell was built on spite, and Heaven on pride.
Then sacred seemed th' ethereal vault no more;
Altars grew marble then, and reeked with gore:
Then first the flamen tasted living food,
Next his grim idol smeared with human blood;
With Heav'n's own thunders shook the world below,
And play'd the god an engine on his foe.

        So drives self-love, through just and through unjust,
270   To one man's pow'r, ambition, lucre, lust:
The same self-love, in all, becomes the cause
Of what restrains him, government and laws.
For, what one likes, if others like as well,
What serves one will, when many wills rebel?
How shall he keep what, sleeping or awake,
A weaker may surprise, a stronger take?
His safety must his liberty restrain:
All join to guard what each desires to gain.
Forced into virtue thus by self-defence,
280   Ev'n kings learned justice and benevolence:
Self-love forsook the path it first pursued,
And found the private in the public good.

        'Twas then, the studious head or generous mind,
Follow'r of God, or friend of human kind,
Poet or patriot, rose but to restore
The faith and moral Nature gave before;
Relumed her ancient light, not kindled new;
If not God's image, yet his shadow drew;
Taught pow'r's due use to people and to kings,
290   Taught nor to slack, nor strain its tender strings;
The less or greater set so justly true
That touching one must strike the other too;
Till jarring int'rests of themselves create
Th' according music of a well-mixed state.
Such is the world's great harmony, that springs
From order, union, full consent of things!

Where small and great, where weak and mighty, made
To serve, not suffer, strengthen, not invade;
More pow'rful each as needful to the rest,
And, in proportion as it blesses, blest;   300
Draw to one point, and to one centre bring
Beast, man, or angel, servant, lord, or king.
For forms of government let fools contest:
Whate'er is best administered is best.
For modes of faith let graceless zealots fight;
His can't be wrong whose life is in the right:
In faith and hope the world will disagree,
But all mankind's concern is charity.
All must be false that thwart this one great end,
And all of God, that bless mankind or mend.   310
 Man, like the gen'rous vine, supported lives;
The strength he gains is from th' embrace he gives.
On their own axis as the planets run,
Yet make at once their circle round the sun,
So two consistent motions act the soul,
And one regards itself, and one the whole.
 Thus God and Nature linked the gen'ral frame,
And bade self-love and social be the same.

Epistle IV

ARGUMENT
Of the Nature and State of Man
with respect to Happiness

I. *False notions of happiness, philosophical and popular,
answered from* v. 19 to 76. II. *It is the end of all men, and
attainable by all,* v. 29. *God intends happiness to be* equal; *and
to be so, it must be* social, *since all particular happiness depends
on general, and since he governs by* general, *not particular
laws,* v. 35. *As it is necessary for* order, *and the peace and wel-
fare of* society, *that* external goods *should be* unequal, *happiness*

*is not made to consist in these, v. 49. But, notwithstanding
that inequality, the* balance of *happiness among mankind is
kept even by Providence, by the two passions of* Hope *and*
Fear, v. 67. III. *What the happiness of* Individuals *is, as far as
is consistent with the constitution of this world; and that
the* good Man *has here the advantage,* v. 77. *The error of
imputing to* Virtue *what are only the calamities of* Nature,
or of Fortune, v. 93. IV. *The folly of expecting that God should
alter his general laws in favour of particulars,* v. 111. V. *That
we are not judges who are good; but that, whoever they are,
they must be happiest,* v. 131, *etc.* VI. *That* external goods *are
not the proper rewards, but often inconsistent with, or destruc-
tive of virtue,* v. 167. *That even these can make no man happy
without virtue: instanced in* Riches, v. 185. Honours, v. 193.
Nobility, v. 205. Greatness, v. 217. Fame, v. 237. Superior
Talents, v. 259, *etc. With pictures of human infelicity in men
possessed of them all,* v. 269, *etc.* VII. *That* Virtue *only consti-
tutes a happiness, whose object is* universal, *and whose
prospect* eternal, v. 309, *etc. That the* perfection *of* Virtue
and Happiness *consists in a* conformity *to the* ORDER *of*
PROVIDENCE *here, and a* Resignation *to it here and hereafter,*
v. 327, *etc.*

    I. O happiness! our being's end and aim!
    Good, pleasure, ease, content! whate'er thy name:
    That something still which prompts th' eternal sigh,
    For which we bear to live, or dare to die;
    Which still so near us, yet beyond us lies,
    O'erlooked, seen double, by the fool and wise.
    Plant of celestial seed! if dropped below,
    Say in what mortal soil thou deign'st to grow?
    Fair op'ning to some court's propitious shine,
10   Or deep with diamonds in the flaming mine?
    Twined with the wreaths Parnassian laurels yield,
    Or reaped in iron harvests of the field?
    Where grows? – where grows it not? If vain our toil,
    We ought to blame the culture, not the soil.

Fixed to no spot is happiness sincere;
'Tis nowhere to be found, or ev'rywhere:
'Tis never to be bought, but always free,
And fled from monarchs, ST JOHN! dwells with thee.

   Ask of the learn'd the way? the learn'd are blind;
This bids to serve, and that to shun mankind;   20
Some place the bliss in action, some in ease,
Those call it pleasure, and contentment these;
Some sunk to beasts, find pleasure end in pain;
Some swelled to gods, confess ev'n virtue vain!
Or indolent, to each extreme they fall,
To trust in ev'rything, or doubt of all.

   Who thus define it, say they more or less
Than this, that happiness is happiness?

   II. Take Nature's path, and mad Opinion's leave;
All states can reach it, and all heads conceive;   30
Obvious her goods, in no extreme they dwell;
There needs but thinking right, and meaning well;
And mourn our various portions as we please,
Equal is common sense and common ease.

   Remember, Man: 'the Universal Cause
Acts not by partial but by gen'ral laws',
And makes what happiness we justly call
Subsist not in the good of one, but all.
There's not a blessing individuals find,
But some way leans and hearkens to the kind.   40
No bandit fierce, no tyrant mad with pride,
No caverned hermit, rests self-satisfied;
Who most to shun or hate mankind pretend,
Seek an admirer, or would fix a friend.
Abstract what others feel, what others think,
All pleasures sicken, and all glories sink:
Each has his share, and who would more obtain,
Shall find the pleasure pays not half the pain.

   Order is Heav'n's first law; and, this confessed,
Some are, and must be, greater than the rest,   50
More rich, more wise; but who infers from hence
That such are happier, shocks all common sense.

Heav'n to mankind impartial we confess,
If all are equal in their happiness;
But mutual wants this happiness increase;
All nature's diff'rence keeps all nature's peace.
Condition, circumstance is not the thing;
Bliss is the same in subject or in king,
In who obtain defence, or who defend,
60   In him who is, or him who finds a friend:
Heav'n breathes through ev'ry member of the whole
One common blessing, as one common soul.
But fortune's gifts, if each alike possessed,
And each were equal, must not all contest?
If then to all men happiness was meant,
God in externals could not place content.
      Fortune her gifts may variously dispose,
And these be happy called, unhappy those;
But Heav'n's just balance equal will appear
70   While those are placed in hope, and these in fear:
Not present good or ill, the joy or curse,
But future views of better, or of worse.
      O sons of earth! attempt ye still to rise
By mountains piled on mountains, to the skies?
Heav'n still with laughter the vain toil surveys,
And buries madmen in the heaps they raise.
      III. Know, all the good that individuals find,
Or God and Nature meant to mere mankind,
Reason's whole pleasure, all the joys of sense,
80   Lie in three words: health, peace, and competence.
But health consists with temperance alone,
And peace, O virtue! peace is all thy own.
The good or bad the gifts of fortune gain;
But these less taste them, as they worse obtain.
Say, in pursuit of profit or delight,
Who risk the most, that take wrong means, or right?
Of vice or virtue, whether blest or cursed,
Which meets contempt, or which compassion first?
Count all th' advantage prosp'rous vice attains,
90   'Tis but what virtue flies from and disdains;

And grant the bad what happiness they would,
One they must want, which is, to pass for good.
  O blind to truth, and God's whole scheme below,
Who fancy bliss to vice, to virtue woe!
Who sees and follows that great scheme the best,
Best knows the blessing, and will most be blest.
But fools the good alone unhappy call,
For ills or accidents that chance to all.
See Falkland dies, the virtuous and the just!
See godlike Turenne prostrate on the dust!   100
See Sidney bleeds amid the martial strife!
Was this their virtue or contempt of life?
Say, was it virtue, more though Heav'n ne'er gave,
Lamented Digby! sunk thee to the grave?
Tell me, if virtue made the son expire,
Why full of days and honour lives the sire?
Why drew Marseilles' good bishop purer breath
When Nature sickened, and each gale was death?
Or why so long (in life if long can be)
Lent Heav'n a parent to the poor and me?   110
  IV. What makes all physical or moral ill?
There deviates Nature, and here wanders will.
God sends not ill; if rightly understood,
Or partial ill is universal good,
Or change admits, or Nature lets it fall,
Short and but rare, till Man improved it all.
We just as wisely might of Heav'n complain
That righteous Abel was destroyed by Cain,
As that the virtuous son is ill at ease
When his lewd father gave the dire disease.   120
Think we, like some weak prince, th' Eternal Cause
Prone for his fav'rites to reverse his laws?
  Shall burning Aetna, if a sage requires,
Forget to thunder, and recall her fires?
On air or sea new motions be impressed,
O blameless Bethel! to relieve thy breast?
When the loose mountain trembles from on high,
Shall gravitation cease, if you go by?

Or some old temple, nodding to its fall,
130 For Chartres' head reserve the hanging wall?
    V. But still this world (so fitted for the knave)
Contents us not. A better shall we have?
A kingdom of the just then let it be;
But first consider how those just agree.
The good must merit God's peculiar care;
But who but God can tell us who they are?
One thinks on Calvin Heav'n's own spirit fell,
Another deems him instrument of Hell;
If Calvin feel Heav'n's blessing or its rod,
140 This cries there is, and that, there is no God.
What shocks one part will edify the rest,
Nor with one system can they all be blest.
The very best will variously incline,
And what rewards your virtue, punish mine.
Whatever IS, is RIGHT. – This world, 'tis true,
Was made for Caesar – but for Titus too:
And which more bless'd? who chained his country, say,
Or he whose virtue sighed to lose a day?
    'But sometimes virtue starves while vice is fed.'
150 What then? is the reward of virtue bread?
That, vice may merit; 'tis the price of toil;
The knave deserves it, when he tills the soil,
The knave deserves it, when he tempts the main,
Where folly fights for kings, or dives for gain.
The good man may be weak, be indolent;
Nor is his claim to plenty, but content.
But grant him riches, your demand is o'er?
'No – shall the good want health, the good want pow'r?'
Add health and pow'r, and ev'ry earthly thing.
160 'Why bounded pow'r? why private? why no king?
Nay, why external for internal giv'n?
Why is not Man a god, and earth a heav'n?'
Who ask and reason thus, will scarce conceive
God gives enough, while he has more to give:
Immense the pow'r, immense were the demand;
Say, at what part of Nature will they stand?

VI. What nothing earthly gives, or can destroy,
The soul's calm sunshine and the heartfelt joy,
Is virtue's prize: a better would you fix?
Then give humility a coach and six,   170
Justice a conqu'ror's sword, or truth a gown,
Or public spirit its great cure, a crown.
Weak, foolish man! will Heav'n reward us there
With the same trash mad mortals wish for here?
The boy and man an individual makes,
Yet sigh'st thou now for apples and for cakes?
Go, like the Indian, in another life
Expect thy dog, thy bottle, and thy wife;
As well as dream such trifles are assigned,
As toys and empires, for a godlike mind.   180
Rewards, that either would to virtue bring
No joy, or be destructive of the thing:
How oft by these at sixty are undone
The virtues of a saint at twenty-one!
To whom can riches give repute, or trust,
Content, or pleasure, but the good and just?
Judges and senates have been bought for gold;
Esteem and love were never to be sold.
O fool! to think God hates the worthy mind,
The lover and the love of humankind,   190
Whose life is healthful, and whose conscience clear,
Because he wants a thousand pounds a year.
   Honour and shame from no condition rise;
Act well your part, there all the honour lies.
Fortune in men has some small diff'rence made:
One flaunts in rags, one flutters in brocade;
The cobbler aproned, and the parson gowned,
The friar hooded, and the monarch crowned.
'What differ more (you cry) than crown and cowl?'
I'll tell you, friend, a wise man and a fool.   200
You'll find, if once the monarch acts the monk,
Or, cobbler-like, the parson will be drunk,
Worth makes the man, and want of it, the fellow:
The rest is all but leather or prunello.

Stuck o'er with titles, and hung round with strings,
That, thou mayst be by kings, or whores of kings;
Boast the pure blood of an illustrious race,
In quiet flow from Lucrece to Lucrece;
But by your fathers' worth if yours you rate,
Count me those only who were good and great.
Go! if your ancient, but ignoble blood
Has crept through scoundrels ever since the Flood,
Go! and pretend your family is young,
Nor own, your fathers have been fools so long.
What can ennoble sots, or slaves, or cowards?
Alas! not all the blood of all the Howards.

Look next on greatness; say where greatness lies?
'Where, but among the heroes and the wise?'
Heroes are much the same, the point's agreed,
From Macedonia's madman to the Swede;
The whole strange purpose of their lives, to find
Or make, an enemy of all mankind!
Not one looks backward, onward still he goes,
Yet ne'er looks forward further than his nose.
No less alike the politic and wise;
All sly slow things, with circumspective eyes:
Men in their loose unguarded hours they take,
Not that themselves are wise, but others weak.
But grant that those can conquer, these can cheat,
'Tis phrase absurd to call a villain great:
Who wickedly is wise, or madly brave,
Is but the more a fool, the more a knave.
Who noble ends by noble means obtains,
Or failing, smiles in exile or in chains,
Like good Aurelius let him reign, or bleed
Like Socrates, that man is great indeed.

What's fame? a fancied life in others' breath;
A thing beyond us, ev'n before our death:
Just what you hear, you have; and what's unknown
The same (my lord) if Tully's or your own.
All that we feel of it begins and ends
In the small circle of our foes or friends;

210

220

230

240

To all beside as much an empty shade,
An Eugene living, as a Caesar dead,
Alike or when or where, they shone or shine,
Or on the Rubicon, or on the Rhine.
A wit's a feather, and a chief a rod;
An honest man's the noblest work of God.
Fame but from death a villain's name can save,
As justice tears his body from the grave;   250
When what t' oblivion better were resigned
Is hung on high, to poison half mankind.
All fame is foreign, but of true desert,
Plays round the head, but comes not to the heart:
One self-approving hour whole years outweighs
Of stupid starers, and of loud huzzas,
And more true joy Marcellus exiled feels
Than Caesar with a senate at his heels.
      In parts superior what advantage lies?
Tell (for you can) what is it to be wise?   260
'Tis but to know how little can be known,
To see all others' faults, and feel our own.
Condemned in business or in arts to drudge,
Without a second, or without a judge:
Truths would you teach, or save a sinking land?
All fear, none aid you, and few understand.
Painful pre-eminence! yourself to view
Above life's weakness, and its comforts too.
      Bring then these blessings to a strict account,
Make fair deductions, see to what they 'mount;   270
How much of other each is sure to cost;
How each for other oft is wholly lost;
How inconsistent greater goods with these;
How sometimes life is risked, and always ease:
Think, and if still the things thy envy call,
Say, wouldst thou be the man to whom they fall?
To sigh for ribbons if thou art so silly,
Mark how they grace Lord Umbra, or Sir Billy.
Is yellow dirt the passion of thy life?
Look but on Gripus, or on Gripus' wife.   280

If parts allure thee, think how Bacon shined,
The wisest, brightest, meanest of mankind!
Or ravished with the whistling of a name,
See Cromwell, damned to everlasting fame!
If all, united, thy ambition call,
From ancient story learn to scorn them all:
There, in the rich, the honoured, famed, and great,
See the false scale of happiness complete!
In hearts of kings, or arms of queens who lay,
290 How happy! those to ruin, these betray.
Mark by what wretched steps their glory grows,
From dirt and seaweed as proud Venice rose;
In each how guilt and greatness equal ran,
And all that raised the hero sunk the man:
Now Europe's laurels on their brows behold,
But stained with blood, or ill exchanged for gold;
Then see them broke with toils, or sunk in ease,
Or infamous for plundered provinces.
O wealth ill fated! which no act of fame
300 E'er taught to shine, or sanctified from shame!
What greater bliss attends their close of life?
Some greedy minion, or imperious wife
The trophied arches, storied halls invade,
And haunt their slumbers in the pompous shade.
Alas! not dazzled with their noontide ray,
Compute the morn and evening to the day;
The whole amount of that enormous fame,
A tale that blends their glory with their shame!
         VII. Know then this truth (enough for Man to know),
310 'Virtue alone is happiness below.'
The only point where human bliss stands still,
And tastes the good without the fall to ill;
Where only merit constant pay receives,
Is blest in what it takes and what it gives;
The joy unequalled if its end it gain,
And, if it lose, attended with no pain;
Without satiety, though e'er so blessed,
And but more relished as the more distress'd:

The broadest mirth unfeeling folly wears,
Less pleasing far than virtue's very tears;   320
Good, from each object, from each place acquired,
For ever exercised, yet never tired;
Never elated, while one man's oppressed;
Never dejected, while another's blessed:
And where no wants, no wishes can remain,
Since but to wish more virtue, is to gain.

    See the sole bliss Heav'n could on all bestow!
Which who but feels can taste, but thinks can know;
Yet poor with fortune, and with learning blind,
The bad must miss, the good, untaught, will find: 330
Slave to no sect, who takes no private road,
But looks through Nature, up to Nature's God;
Pursues that chain which links th' immense design,
Joins Heav'n and earth, and mortal and divine;
Sees, that no being any bliss can know,
But touches some above, and some below;
Learns, from this union of the rising whole,
The first, last purpose of the human soul;
And knows where faith, law, morals, all began,
All end, in love of God and love of Man.   340

    For him alone, hope leads from goal to goal,
And opens still, and opens on his soul,
Till lengthened on to faith, and unconfined
It pours the bliss that fills up all the mind.
He sees, why Nature plants in man alone
Hope of known bliss, and faith in bliss unknown
(Nature, whose dictates to no other kind
Are giv'n in vain, but what they seek they find).
Wise is her present: she connects in this
His greatest virtue with his greatest bliss;   350
At once his own bright prospect to be blest,
And strongest motive to assist the rest.

    Self-love thus pushed to social, to divine,
Gives thee to make thy neighbour's blessing thine.
Is this too little for the boundless heart?
Extend it, let thy enemies have part.

Grasp the whole world of reason, life, and sense,
In one close system of benevolence:
Happier as kinder, in whate'er degree,
And height of bliss but height of charity.
360

God loves from whole to parts, but human soul
Must rise from individual to the whole.
Self-love but serves the virtuous mind to wake,
As the small pebble stirs the peaceful lake;
The centre moved, a circle straight succeeds,
Another still, and still another spreads;
Friend, parent, neighbour, first it will embrace;
His country next, and next all human race;
Wide and more wide, th' o'erflowings of the mind
370
Take ev'ry creature in of ev'ry kind;
Earth smiles around, with boundless bounty blest,
And Heav'n beholds its image in his breast.

Come then, my friend, my genius, come along;
O master of the poet, and the song!
And while the Muse now stoops, or now ascends.
To Man's low passions, or their glorious ends,
Teach me, like thee, in various Nature wise,
To fall with dignity, with temper rise;
Formed by thy converse, happily to steer
380
From grave to gay, from lively to severe;
Correct with spirit, eloquent with ease,
Intent to reason, or polite to please.
Oh! while along the stream of time thy name
Expanded flies, and gathers all its fame,
Say, shall my little bark attendant sail,
Pursue the triumph, and partake the gale?
When statesmen, heroes, kings, in dust repose,
Whose sons shall blush their fathers were thy foes,
Shall then this verse to future age pretend
390
Thou wert my guide, philosopher, and friend?
That, urged by thee, I turned the tuneful art
From sounds to things, from fancy to the heart;
For wit's false mirror held up Nature's light,
Showed erring pride, 'WHATEVER IS, IS RIGHT';

That REASON, PASSION, answer one great aim;
That true SELF-LOVE and SOCIAL are the same;
That VIRTUE only makes our bliss below;
And all our knowledge is, OURSELVES TO KNOW.

Epistles to Several Persons

Est brevitate opus, ut currat sententia, neu se
Impediat verbis lassas onerantibus aures:
Et sermone opus est modo tristi, sæpe jocoso,
Defendente vicem modo Rhetoris atque Poetæ,
Interdum urbani, parcentis viribus, atque
Extenuantis eas consultô.

Epistle I

TO
Sir Richard Temple, Lord Cobham

ARGUMENT
Of the Knowledge and Characters of MEN

That it is not sufficient for this knowledge to consider Man in the abstract: books *will not serve the purpose, nor yet our own* experience *singly,* v. 1. *General maxims, unless they be formed upon* both, *will be but notional,* v. 10. *Some Peculiarity in every man, characteristic to himself, yet varying from himself,* v. 15. *Difficulties arising from our own Passions, Fancies, Faculties,* etc. v. 31. *The shortness of life, to observe in, and the uncertainty of the* principles of action *in men, to observe by,* v. 37, etc. *Our own Principle of action often hid from ourselves,* v. 41. *Some few Characters plain, but in general confounded, dissembled, or inconsistent,* v. 51. *The same man utterly different in different places and seasons,* v. 71. *Unimaginable weaknesses in the greatest,* v. 70, etc. *Nothing constant*

and certain but God *and* Nature, v. 95. No *judging of the*
Motives *from the actions; the same actions proceeding from
contrary motives, and the same motives influencing contrary
actions,* v. 100. II. *Yet to form* Characters, *we can only take the*
strongest actions *of a man's life, and try to make them* agree;
the utter uncertainty of this, from Nature *itself, and from* pol-
icy, v. 120. Characters *given according to the* rank *of men of
the world,* v. 135. *And some reason for it,* v. 140. Education
alters the nature, *or at least* character *of many,* v. 149. Actions,
Passions, Opinions, Manners, Humours, *or* Principles *all sub-
ject to change. No judging by* Nature, *from* v. 158 to 178. III.
It only remains to find (if we can) his RULING PASSION: *that
will certainly influence all the rest, and can reconcile the seem-
ing or real inconsistency of all his actions,* v. 175. *Instanced in
the extraordinary character of* Clodio, v. 179. *A caution against
mistaking* second qualities *for* first, *which will destroy all pos-
sibility of the knowledge of mankind,* v. 210. *Examples of the
strength of the* Ruling Passion, *and its continuation to the last
breath,* v. 222, etc.

Yes, you despise the man to books confined,
Who from his study rails at human kind;
Though what he learns, he speaks, and may advance
Some gen'ral maxims, or be right by chance.
The coxcomb bird, so talkative and grave,
That from his cage cries Cuckold, Whore, and Knave,
Though many a passenger he rightly call,
You hold him no philosopher at all.
    And yet the fate of all extremes is such,
10 Men may be read, as well as books, too much.
To observations which ourselves we make,
We grow more partial for th'observer's sake;
To written wisdom, as another's, less:
Maxims are drawn from notions, these from guess.
There's some peculiar in each leaf and grain,
Some unmarked fibre, or some varying vein;
Shall only Man be taken in the gross?
Grant but as many sorts of mind, as moss.

That each from other differs, first confess;
Next, that he varies from himself no less;   20
Add Nature's, Custom's, Reason's, Passion's strife,
And all Opinion's colours cast on life.
  Our depths who fathoms, or our shallows finds,
Quick whirls, and shifting eddies, of our minds?
On human actions reason though you can,
It may be reason, but it is not Man:
His principle of action once explore,
That instant 'tis his principle no more.
Like foll'wing life through creatures you dissect,
You lose it in the moment you detect.   30
  Yet more: the diff'rence is as great between
The optics seeing, as the objects seen.
All manners take a tincture from our own,
Or come discoloured through our Passions shown.
Or Fancy's beam enlarges, multiplies,
Contracts, inverts, and gives ten thousand dyes.
  Nor will life's stream for observation stay,
It hurries all too fast to mark their way:
In vain sedate reflections we would make
When half our knowledge we must snatch, not take.   40
Oft, in the passions' wild rotation tossed,
Our spring of action to ourselves is lost:
Tired, not determined, to the last we yield,
And what comes then is master of the field.
As the last image of that troubled heap,
When sense subsides, and fancy sports in sleep
(Though past the recollection of the thought),
Becomes the stuff of which our dream is wrought;
Something, as dim to our internal view,
Is thus perhaps the cause of most we do.   50
  True, some are open, and to all men known;
Others so very close, they're hid from none
(So darkness strikes the sense no less than light);
Thus gracious CHANDOS is belov'ed at sight;
And ev'ry child hates Shylock, though his soul
Still sits at squat, and peeps not from its hole.

At half mankind when gen'rous Manly raves,
All know 'tis virtue, for he thinks them knaves:
When universal homage Umbra pays,
60   All see 'tis vice, and itch of vulgar praise.
When flatt'ry glares, all hate it in a queen,
While one there is who charms us with his spleen.

   But these plain Characters we rarely find;
Though strong the bent, yet quick the turns of mind;
Or puzzling contraries confound the whole,
Or affectations quite reverse the soul.
The dull, flat falsehood serves for policy,
And in the cunning, truth itself's a lie.
Unthought-of frailties cheat us in the wise;
70   The fool lies hid in inconsistencies.

   See the same man, in vigour, in the gout;
Alone, in company; in place, or out;
Early at bus'ness, and at hazard late;
Mad at a fox-chase, wise at a debate;
Drunk at a borough, civil at a ball;
Friendly at Hackney, faithless at Whitehall.

   Catius is ever moral, ever grave,
Thinks who endures a knave, is next a knave,
Save just at dinner – then prefers, no doubt,
80   A rogue with ven'son to a saint without.

   Who would not praise Patritio's high desert,
His hand unstained, his uncorrupted heart,
His comprehensive head? all int'rests weighed,
All Europe saved, yet Britain not betrayed.
He thanks you not, his pride is in picquette,
Newmarket fame, and judgement at a bet.

   What made (say Montaigne, or more sage Charron!)
Otho a warrior, Cromwell a buffoon?
A perjured prince a leaden saint revere?
90   A godless regent tremble at a star?
The throne a bigot keep, a genius quit,
Faithless through piety, and duped through wit?
Europe a woman, child, or dotard rule,
And just her ablest monarch made a fool?

Know, GOD and NATURE only are the same:
In Man, the judgement shoots at flying game,
A bird of passage! gone as soon as found,
Now in the moon perhaps, now under ground.
    In vain the sage, with retrospective eye,
Would from th'apparent What conclude the Why,   100
Infer the motive from the deed, and show
That what we chanced, was what we meant to do.
Behold! If Fortune or a mistress frowns,
Some plunge in bus'ness, others shave their crowns.
To ease the soul of one oppressive weight,
This quits an empire, that embroils a state:
The same adust complexion has impelled
Charles to the convent, Philip to the field.
    Not always actions show the man: we find
Who does a kindness, is not therefore kind;   110
Perhaps prosperity becalmed his breast,
Perhaps the wind just shifted from the east.
Not therefore humble he who seeks retreat,
Pride guides his steps, and bids him shun the great.
Who combats bravely is not therefore brave,
He dreads a deathbed like the meanest slave;
Who reasons wisely is not therefore wise,
His pride in reas'ning, not in acting lies.
    But grant that actions best discover man:
Take the most strong, and sort them as you can.   120
The few that glare, each character must mark,
You balance not the many in the dark.
What will you do with such as disagree?
Suppress them, or miscall them policy?
Must then at once (the character to save)
The plain rough hero turn a crafty knave?
Alas! in truth the man but changed his mind,
Perhaps was sick, in love, or had not dined.
Ask why from Britain Caesar would retreat?
Caesar himself might whisper he was beat.   130
Why risk the world's great empire for a punk?
Caesar perhaps might answer he was drunk.

But, sage historians! 'tis your task to prove
One action, Conduct; one, heroic Love.
    'Tis from high life high characters are drawn;
A saint in crape is twice a saint in lawn;
A judge is just, a chanc'lor juster still;
A gownman, learn'd; a bishop, what you will;
Wise, if a minister; but, if a king,
140 More wise, more learn'd, more just, more ev'rything.
Court-virtues bear, like gems, the highest rate,
Born where Heav'n's influence scarce can penetrate:
In life's low vale, the soil the virtues like,
They please as beauties, here as wonders strike.
Though the same sun with all-diffusive rays
Blush in the rose, and in the diamond blaze,
We prize the stronger effort of his pow'r,
And justly set the gem above the flow'r.
    'Tis education forms the common mind,
150 Just as the twig is bent, the tree's inclined.
Boastful and rough, your first son is a squire;
The next a tradesman, meek, and much a liar;
Tom struts a soldier, open, bold, and brave;
Will sneaks a scriv'ner, an exceeding knave:
Is he a churchman? then he's fond of pow'r; ⎫
A Quaker? sly; A Presbyterian? sour;   ⎬
A smart freethinker? all things in an hour. ⎭
    Ask men's opinions: Scoto now shall tell
How trade increases, and the world goes well;
160 Strike off his pension by the setting sun,
And Britain, if not Europe, is undone.
    That gay freethinker, a fine talker once,
What turns him now a stupid silent dunce?
Some god or spirit he has lately found;
Or chanced to meet a minister that frowned.
    Judge we by Nature? Habit can efface,
Int'rest o'ercome, or policy take place.
By actions? those uncertainty divides;
By passions? these dissimulation hides;

Opinions? they still take a wider range: 170
Find, if you can, in what you cannot change.
    Manners with fortunes, humours turn with climes.
Tenets with books, and principles with times.
    Search then the RULING PASSION: there, alone,
The wild are constant, and the cunning known;
The fool consistent, and the false sincere;
Priests, princes, women, no dissemblers here.
This clue once found unravels all the rest,
The prospect clears, and Wharton stands confessed.
Wharton, the scorn and wonder of our days,   180
Whose ruling passion was the lust of praise;
Born with whate'er could win it from the wise,
Women and fools must like him or he dies;
Though wond'ring senates hung on all he spoke,
The club must hail him master of the joke.
Shall parts so various aim at nothing new?
He'll shine a Tully and a Wilmot too.
Then turns repentant, and his God adores
With the same spirit that he drinks and whores;
Enough if all around him but admire,   190
And now the punk applaud, and now the friar.
Thus, with each gift of nature and of art,
And wanting nothing but an honest heart;
Grown all to all, from no one vice exempt,
And most contemptible, to shun contempt;
His passion still, to covet gen'ral praise,
His life, to forfeit it a thousand ways;
A constant bounty, which no friend has made;
An angel tongue, which no man can persuade;
A fool, with more of wit than half mankind,   200
Too rash for thought, for action too refined;
A tyrant to the wife his heart approves;
A rebel to the very king he loves;
He dies, sad outcast of each church and state,
And, harder still! flagitious, yet not great.
Ask you why Wharton broke through ev'ry rule?
'Twas all for fear the knaves should call him fool.

Nature well known, no prodigies remain,
Comets are regular and Wharton plain.
210   Yet, in this search, the wisest may mistake,
If second qualities for first they take.
When Catiline by rapine swelled his store;
When Caesar made a noble dame a whore;
In this the lust, in that the avarice
Were means, not ends; ambition was the vice.
That very Caesar, born in Scipio's days,
Had aimed, like him, by chastity at praise.
Lucullus, when frugality could charm,
Had roasted turnips in the Sabine farm.
220   In vain th' observer eyes the builder's toil,
But quite mistakes the scaffold for the pile.

    In this one passion man can strength enjoy,
As fits give vigour just when they destroy.
Time, that on all things lays his lenient hand,
Yet tames not this; it sticks to our last sand.
Consistent in our follies and our sins,
Here honest Nature ends as she begins.

    Old politicians chew on wisdom past,
And totter on in bus'ness to the last;
230   As weak, as earnest; and as gravely out,
As sober Lanesb'rough dancing in the gout.

    Behold a rev'rend sire, whom want of grace
Has made the father of a nameless race,
Shoved from the wall perhaps, or rudely pressed
By his own son, that passes by unblessed:
Still to his wench he crawls on knocking knees,
And envies ev'ry sparrow that he sees.

    A salmon's belly, Helluo, was thy fate;
The doctor called, declares all help too late:
240   'Mercy!' cries Helluo, 'mercy on my soul!
Is there no hope? – Alas! – then bring the jowl.'

    The frugal crone, whom praying priests attend,
Still tries to save the hallowed taper's end,

Collects her breath, as ebbing life retires,
For one puff more, and in that puff expires.
    'Odious! in woollen! 'twould a saint provoke
(Were the last words that poor Narcissa spoke);
No, let a charming chintz, and Brussels lace
Wrap my cold limbs, and shade my lifeless face:
One would not, sure, be frightful when one's dead –   250
And – Betty – give this cheek a little red.'
    The courtier smooth, who forty years had shined
An humble servant to all human kind,
Just brought out this, when scarce his tongue could
            stir,
'If – where I'm going – I could serve you, sir?'
    'I give and I devise (old Euclio said,
And sighed) my lands and tenements to Ned.'
Your money, sir; 'My money, sir, what, all?
Why – if I must – (then wept) I give it Paul.'
The manor, sir? – 'The manor! hold, he cried;   260
Not that – I cannot part with that' – and died.
    And you! brave COBHAM, to the latest breath
Shall feel your ruling passion strong in death:
Such in those moments as in all the past,
'Oh, save my Country, Heav'n!' shall be your last.

Epistle II

TO
A Lady

ARGUMENT
Of the Characters *of* WOMEN

Of the characters of women (considered only as contradistin-
guished from the other sex). That these are yet more inconsistent
and incomprehensible than those of men, of which instances
are given even from such characters as are plainest and most
strongly marked; as the Affected, v. 7, etc., *the* Soft-natured, *v.*

29; *the* Cunning, v. 45; *the* Whimsical, v. 53; *the* Wits and
Refiners, v. 87, *the* Stupid and Silly, v. 101. *How contrarieties
run through them all.*

*But though the particular characters of this sex are more
various than those of men, the general characteristic, as to the
ruling passion, is more uniform and confined. In what that lies,
and whence it proceeds, etc. Men are best known in public life,
women in private, v. 199. What are the aims and the fate of the
sex, both as to* Power *and* Pleasure? *v. 219, 231, etc. Advice for
their true interest, v. 249. The picture of an estimable woman,
made up of the best kind of contrarieties, v. 269, etc.*

    Nothing so true as what you once let fall,
'Most women have no characters at all.'
Matter too soft a lasting mark to bear,
And best distinguished by black, brown, or fair.
    How many pictures of one nymph we view,
All how unlike each other, all how true!
Arcadia's countess, here in ermined pride,
Is there, Pastora by a fountain side.
Here Fannia, leering on her own good man,
And there, a naked Leda with a swan.
Let then the fair one beautifully cry,
In Magdalen's loose hair and lifted eye,
Or dressed in smiles of sweet Cecilia shine,
With simp'ring angels, palms, and harps divine;
Whether the charmer sinner it, or saint it,
If Folly grow romantic, I must paint it.
    Come then, the colours and the ground prepare!
Dip in the rainbow, trick her off in air;
Chuse a firm cloud before it fall, and in it
Catch, e'er she change, the Cynthia of this minute.
    Rufa, whose eye quick-glancing o'er the park
Attracts each light gay meteor of a spark,
Agrees as ill with Rufa studying Locke
As Sappho's diamonds with her dirty smock,
Or Sappho at her toilet's greasy task,
With Sappho fragrant at an ev'ning mask:

So morning insects that in muck begun,
Shine, buzz, and fly-blow in the setting sun.
   How soft is Silia! fearful to offend,
The frail one's advocate, the weak one's friend: 30
To her, Calista proved her conduct nice,
And good Simplicius asks of her advice.
Sudden, she storms! she raves! You tip the wink,
But spare your censure; Silia does not drink.
All eyes may see from what the change arose,
All eyes may see – a pimple on her nose.
   Papillia, wedded to her am'rous spark,
Sighs for the shades – 'How charming is a park!'
A park is purchased; but the fair he sees
All bathed in tears – 'Oh odious, odious trees!'   40
   Ladies like variegated tulips show:
'Tis to their changes half their charms we owe;
Their happy spots the nice admirer take,
Fine by defect, and delicately weak.
'Twas thus Calypso once each heart alarmed,
Awed without virtue, without beauty charmed;
Her tongue bewitched as odly as her eyes,
Less wit than mimic, more a wit than wise;
Strange graces still, and stranger flights she had,
Was just not ugly, and was just not mad;   50
Yet ne'er so sure our passion to create
As when she touched the brink of all we hate.
   Narcissa's nature, tolerably mild,
To make a wash, would hardly stew a child;
Has ev'n been proved to grant a lover's pray'r,
And paid a tradesman once to make him stare;
Gave alms at Easter, in a Christian trim,
And made a widow happy, for a whim.
Why then declare good nature is her scorn,
When 'tis by that alone she can be borne?   60
Why pique all mortals, yet affect a name?
A fool to pleasure, yet a slave to fame:
Now deep in Taylor and the *Book of Martyrs*,
Now drinking citron with his Grace and Chartres.

Now conscience chills her, and now passion burns,
And atheism and religion take their turns;
A very heathen in the carnal part,
Yet still a sad, good Christian at her heart.
    See Sin in state, majestically drunk;
70 Proud as a peeress, prouder as a punk;
Chaste to her husband, frank to all beside,
A teeming mistress, but a barren bride.
What then? let blood and body bear the fault,
Her head's untouched, that noble seat of thought:
Such this day's doctrine – in another fit
She sins with poets through pure love of wit.
What has not fired her bosom or her brain?
Caesar and Tall-boy, Charles and Charlemagne.
As Helluo, late dictator of the feast,
80 The nose of hautgout, and the tip of taste,
Critiqued your wine, and analysed your meat,
Yet on plain pudding deigned at home to eat;
So Philomedé, lect'ring all mankind
On the soft passion, and the taste refined,
Th'address, the delicacy – stoops at once,
And makes her hearty meal upon a dunce.
    Flavia's a wit, has too much sense to pray;
To toast our wants and wishes is her way;
Nor asks of God, but of her stars, to give
90 The mighty blessing, 'while we live, to live'.
Then all for death, that opiate of the soul!
Lucretia's dagger, Rosamonda's bowl.
Say, what can cause such impotence of mind?
A spark too fickle, or a spouse too kind.
Wise wretch! with pleasures too refined to please,
With too much spirit to be e'er at ease,
With too much quickness ever to be taught,
With too much thinking to have common thought:
You purchase pain with all that joy can give,
100 And die of nothing but a rage to live.
    Turn then from wits; and look on Simo's mate,
No ass so meek, no ass so obstinate;

Or her, that owns her faults, but never mends,
Because she's honest, and the best of friends;
Or her, whose life the church and scandal share,
For ever in a passion, or a pray'r;
Or her, who laughs at Hell, but (like her Grace)
Cries, 'Ah! how charming if there's no such place!'
Or who in sweet vicissitude appears
Of mirth and opium, ratafie and tears,   110
The daily anodyne, and nightly draught,
To kill those foes to fair ones, Time and Thought.
Woman and Fool are two hard things to hit;
For true no-meaning puzzles more than wit.
    But what are these to great Atossa's mind?
Scarce once herself, by turns all womankind!
Who, with herself, or others, from her birth
Finds all her life one warfare upon earth:
Shines in exposing knaves, and painting fools,
Yet is, whate'er she hates and ridicules.   120
No thought advances, but her eddy brain
Whisks it about, and down it goes again.
Full sixty years the world has been her trade,
The wisest fool much time has ever made.
From loveless youth to unrespected age,
No passion gratified except her rage.
So much the fury still outran the wit,
The pleasure missed her, and the scandal hit.
Who breaks with her, provokes revenge from Hell,
But he's a bolder man who dares be well.   130
Her ev'ry turn with violence pursued,
Nor more a storm her hate than gratitude:
To that each passion turns, or soon or late;
Love, if it makes her yield, must make her hate.
Superiors? death! and equals? what a curse!
But an inferior not dependent? worse.
Offend her, and she knows not to forgive;
Oblige her, and she'll hate you while you live;
But die, and she'll adore you – then the bust
And temple rise – then fall again to dust.   140

Last night, her lord was all that's good and great;
A knave this morning, and his will a cheat.
Strange! by the means defeated of the ends,
By spirit robbed of pow'r, by warmth of friends,
By wealth of follow'rs! without one distress
Sick of herself through very selfishness!
Atossa, cursed with ev'ry granted pray'r,
Childless with all her children, wants an heir.
To heirs unknown descends th'unguarded store
150   Or wanders, Heav'n-directed, to the poor.
    Pictures like these, dear madam, to design
Asks no firm hand, and no unerring line;
Some wand'ring touches, some reflected light,
Some flying stroke alone can hit 'em right:
For how should equal colours do the knack?
Chameleons who can paint in white and black?
    'Yet Cloe sure was formed without a spot' –
Nature in her then erred not, but forgot.
'With ev'ry pleasing, ev'ry prudent part,
160   Say, what can Cloe want?' – she wants a heart.
She speaks, behaves, and acts just as she ought,
But never, never, reached one gen'rous thought.
Virtue she finds too painful an endeavour,
Content to dwell in decencies for ever.
So very reasonable, so unmoved,
As never yet to love, or to be loved.
She, while her lover pants upon her breast,
Can mark the figures on an Indian chest;
And when she sees her friend in deep despair,
170   Observes how much a chintz exceeds mohair.
Forbid it Heav'n, a favour or a debt
She e'er should cancel – but she may forget.
Safe is your secret still in Cloe's ear;
But none of Cloe's shall you ever hear.
Of all her dears she never slandered one,
But cares not if a thousand are undone.
Would Cloe know if you're alive or dead?
She bids her footman put it in her head.

Cloe is prudent – would you too be wise?
Then never break your heart when Cloe dies.   180
     One certain portrait may (I grant) be seen,
Which Heav'n has varnished out, and made a queen:
THE SAME FOR EVER! and described by all
With truth and goodness, as with crown and ball.
Poets heap virtues, painters gems at will,
And show their zeal, and hide their want of skill;
'Tis well—but, artists! who can paint or write,
To draw the naked is your true delight.
That robe of quality so struts and swells,
None see what parts or nature it conceals: 190
Th'exactest traits of body or of mind,
We owe to models of an humble kind.
If Queensberry to strip there's no compelling,
'Tis from a handmaid we must take a Helen.
From peer or bishop 'tis no easy thing
To draw the man who loves his God, or King;
Alas! I copy (or my draught would fail)
From honest Mah'met, or plain Parson Hale.
     But grant, in public men sometimes are shown,
A woman's seen in private life alone: 200
Our bolder talents in full light displayed;
Your virtues open fairest in the shade.
Bred to disguise, in public 'tis you hide;
There, none distinguish 'twixt your shame or pride,
Weakness or delicacy; all so nice
That each may seem a virtue, or a vice.
     In men, we various ruling passions find;
In women, two almost divide the kind:
Those, only fixed, they first or last obey,
The love of pleasure, and the love of sway.   210
     That, Nature gives; and where the lesson taught
Is but to please, can pleasure seem a fault?
Experience, this; by man's oppression cursed,
They seek the second not to lose the first.
     Men, some to bus'ness, some to pleasure take;
But ev'ry Woman is at heart a rake:

Men, some to quiet, some to public strife;
But ev'ry lady would be queen for life.
    Yet mark the fate of a whole sex of queens!
220 Pow'r all their end, but beauty all the means:
In youth they conquer with so wild a rage,
As leaves them scarce a subject in their age.
For foreign glory, foreign joy, they roam;
No thought of peace or happiness at home.
But Wisdom's triumph is well-timed retreat,
As hard a science to the fair as Great!
Beauties, like tyrants, old and friendless grown,
Yet hate repose, and dread to be alone,
Worn out in public, weary ev'ry eye,
230 Nor leave one sigh behind them when they die.
    Pleasures the sex, as children birds, pursue,
Still out of reach, yet never out of view;
Sure, if they catch, to spoil the toy at most,
To covet flying, and regret when lost;
At last, to follies youth could scarce defend,
It grows their age's prudence to pretend;
Ashamed to own they gave delight before,
Reduced to feign it, when they give no more:
As hags hold sabbaths, less for joy than spite,
240 So these their merry, miserable Night;
Still round and round the ghosts of beauty glide,
And haunt the places where their honour died.
    See how the world its veterans rewards!
A youth of frolics, an old age of cards;
Fair to no purpose, artful to no end,
Young without lovers, old without a friend;
A fop their passion, but their prize a sot,
Alive, ridiculous, and dead, forgot!
    Ah! friend! to dazzle let the vain design;
250 To raise the thought, and touch the heart be thine!
That charm shall grow, while what fatigues the Ring
Flaunts and goes down, an unregarded thing:
So when the sun's broad beam has tired the sight,
All mild ascends the moon's more sober light,

Serene in virgin modesty she shines,
And unobserved the glaring orb declines.
  Oh! blest with temper, whose unclouded ray
Can make tomorrow cheerful as today;
She, who can love a sister's charms, or hear
Sighs for a daughter with unwounded ear;   260
She, who ne'er answers till a husband cools,
Or, if she rules him, never shows she rules;
Charms by accepting, by submitting sways,
Yet has her humour most, when she obeys;
Let fops or Fortune fly which way they will;
Disdains all loss of tickets, or codille;
Spleen, vapours, or smallpox, above them all,
And mistress of herself, though china fall.
  And yet, believe me, good as well as ill,
Woman's at best a contradiction still.   270
Heav'n, when it strives to polish all it can
Its last best work, but forms a softer man;
Picks from each sex, to make the fav'rite blessed,
Your love of pleasure, our desire of rest:
Blends, in exception to all gen'ral rules,
Your taste of follies, with our scorn of fools,
Reserve with frankness, art with truth allied,
Courage with softness, modesty with pride,
Fixed principles, with fancy ever new;
Shakes all together, and produces – You.   280
  Be this a woman's fame; with this unblessed,
Toasts live a scorn, and queens may die a jest.
This Phoebus promised (I forget the year)
When those blue eyes first opened on the sphere;
Ascendant Phoebus watched that hour with care,
Averted half your parents' simple pray'r,
And gave you beauty, but denied the pelf
That buys your sex a tyrant o'er itself.
The gen'rous god, who wit and gold refines,
And ripens spirits as he ripens mines,   290
Kept dross for duchesses, the world shall know it,
To you gave sense, good humour, and a poet.

Epistle III

TO

Allen Lord Bathurst

ARGUMENT
Of the Use *of* RICHES

That it is known to few, most falling into one of the extremes,
Avarice *or* Profusion, v. 1, etc. *The point discussed, whether the*
invention of Money *has been more commodious or pernicious*
to mankind, v. 21 to 77. *That Riches, either to the* avaricious
or the prodigal, *cannot afford happiness, scarcely necessaries,*
v. 85 to 106. *That Avarice is an absolute frenzy, without an*
end or purpose, v. 107 etc. *Conjectures about the motives of*
avaricious men, v. 113 to 153. *That the conduct of men, with*
respect to Riches, can only be accounted for by the ORDER OF
PROVIDENCE, *which works the general good out of extremes,*
and brings all to its great end by perpetual revolutions, v. 161
to 178. *How a miser acts upon principles which appear to him*
reasonable, v. 179. *How a* Prodigal *does the same,* v. 199. *The*
due Medium, and true use of Riches, v. 219. *The* Man of Ross,
v. 250. *The fate of the* Profuse *and the* Covetous, *in two ex-*
amples; both miserable in Life and in Death, v. 300, etc. *The*
Story of Sir Balaam, v. 339 *to the end.*

Who shall decide, when doctors disagree,
And soundest casuists doubt, like you and me?
You hold the word, from Jove to Momus giv'n,
That Man was made the standing jest of Heav'n;
And gold but sent to keep the fools in play,
For some to heap, and some to throw away.
But I, who think more highly of our kind
(And surely, Heav'n and I are of a mind),
Opine, that Nature, as in duty bound,
10   Deep hid the shining mischief under ground;

But when by Man's audacious labour won,
Flamed forth this rival to its sire the sun,
Then careful Heav'n supplied two sorts of men,
To squander these, and those to hide again.
    Like doctors thus, when much dispute has passed,
We find our tenets just the same at last.
Both fairly owning, riches in effect
No grace of Heav'n or token of th'Elect;
Giv'n to the fool, the mad, the vain, the evil,
To Ward, to Waters, Chartres, and the Devil.   20
    What Nature wants, commodious gold bestows,
'Tis thus we eat the bread another sows:
But how unequal it bestows, observe,
'Tis thus we riot, while who sow it, starve.
What Nature wants (a phrase I much distrust)
Extends to luxury, extends to lust:
Useful, I grant, it serves what life requires,
But dreadful too, the dark assassin hires;
Trade it may help, society extend,
But lures the pirate, and corrupts the friend;   30
It raises armies in a nation's aid,
But bribes a senate, and the land's betrayed.
In vain may heroes fight, and patriots rave,
If secret gold saps on from knave to knave.
Once, we confess, beneath the patriot's cloak,
From the cracked bag the dropping guinea spoke,
And jingling down the back stairs, told the crew,
'Old Cato is as great a rogue as you.'
Blest paper-credit! last and best supply!
That lends Corruption lighter wings to fly!   40
Gold imped by thee can compass hardest things,
Can pocket states, can fetch or carry kings;
A single leaf shall waft an army o'er,
Or ship off senates to a distant shore;
A leaf, like Sibyl's, scatter to and fro
Our fates and fortunes, as the winds shall blow:
Pregnant with thousands flits the scrap unseen,
And silent sells a king, or buys a queen.

Oh! that such bulky bribes as all might see,
50   Still, as of old, incumbered villainy!
Could France or Rome divert our brave designs,
With all their brandies or with all their wines?
What could they more than knights and squires
              confound,
Or water all the Quorum ten miles round?
A statesman's slumbers how this speech would spoil!
'Sir, Spain has sent a thousand jars of oil;
Huge bales of British cloth blockade the door;
A hundred oxen at your levee roar.'
      Poor Avarice one torment more would find;
60   Nor could Profusion squander all, in kind.
Astride his cheese Sir Morgan might we meet,
And Worldly crying coals from street to street,
Whom with a wig so wild, and mien so mazed,
Pity mistakes for some poor tradesman crazed.
Had Colepepper's whole wealth been hops and hogs,
Could he himself have sent it to the dogs?
His Grace will game: to White's a bull be led,
With spurning heels and with a butting head.
To White's be carried, as to ancient games,
70   Fair coursers, vases, and alluring dames.
Shall then Uxorio, if the stakes he sweep,
Bear home six whores, and make his lady weep?
Or soft Adonis, so perfumed and fine,
Drive to St James's a whole herd of swine?
Oh filthy check on all industrious skill,
To spoil the nation's last great trade, quadrille!
Since then, my Lord, on such a world we fall,
What say you? 'Say? Why take it, gold and all.'
      What riches give us let us then enquire:
Meat, fire, and clothes. What more? meat, clothes,
80   and fire.
Is this too little? would you more than live?
Alas! 'tis more than Turner finds they give.
Alas! 'tis more than (all his visions past)
Unhappy Wharton, waking, found at last!

What can they give? to dying Hopkins, heirs;
To Chartres, vigour; Japhet, nose and ears?
Can they, in gems bid pallid Hippia glow,
In Fulvia's buckle ease the throbs below,
Or heal, old Narses, thy obscener ail,
With all th'embroid'ry plastered at thy tail?   90
They might (were Harpax not too wise to spend)
Give Harpax self the blessing of a friend;
Or find some doctor that would save the life
Of wretched Shylock, spite of Shylock's wife;
But thousands die, without or this, or that,
Die, and endow a college, or a cat;
To some, indeed, Heav'n grants the happier fate
T'enrich a bastard, or a son they hate.

   Perhaps you think the poor might have their part?
Bond damns the poor, and hates them from his heart.   100
The grave Sir Gilbert holds it for a rule
That 'ev'ry man in want is knave or fool'.
'God cannot love (says Blunt, with tearless eyes)
The wretch he starves' – and piously denies;
But the good bishop, with a meeker air,
Admits, and leaves them, Providence's care.

   Yet, to be just to these poor men of pelf,
Each does but hate his neighbour as himself;
Damned to the mines, an equal fate betides
The slave that digs it, and the slave that hides.   110
Who suffer thus, mere charity should own,
Must act on motives pow'rful, though unknown:
Some war, some plague, or famine they foresee,
Some revelation hid from you and me.
Why Shylock wants a meal, the cause is found:
He thinks a loaf will rise to fifty pound.
What made directors cheat in South Sea year?
To live on ven'son when it sold so dear.
Ask you why Phryne the whole auction buys?
Phryne foresees a general excise.   120
Why she and Sappho raise that monstrous sum?
Alas! they fear a man will cost a plum.

Wise Peter sees the world's respect for gold,
And therefore hopes this nation may be sold:
Glorious ambition! Peter, swell thy store,
And be what Rome's great Didius was before.

The crown of Poland, venal twice an age,
To just three millions stinted modest Gage.
But nobler scenes Maria's dreams unfold,
130   Hereditary realms, and worlds of gold.
Congenial souls! whose life one av'rice joins,
And one fate buries in th'Asturian mines.

Much injur'd Blunt! why bears he Britain's hate?
A wizard told him in these words our fate:
'At length corruption, like a gen'ral flood,
(So long by watchful ministers withstood)
Shall deluge all; and av'rice creeping on,
Spread like a low-born mist, and blot the sun;
Statesman and Patriot ply alike the stocks,
140   Peeress and butler share alike the box,
And judges job, and bishops bite the town,
And mighty dukes pack cards for half a crown.
See Britain sunk in lucre's sordid charms,
And France revenged of ANNE'S and EDWARD'S
            arms!'

'Twas no court-badge, great scriv'ner! fired thy brain,
Nor lordly luxury, nor City gain:
No, 'twas thy righteous end (ashamed to see
Senates degen'rate, Patriots disagree,
And nobly wishing party-rage to cease)
150   To buy both sides, and give thy country peace.

'All this is madness,' cries a sober sage;
But who, my friend, has reason in his rage?
The ruling passion, be it what it will,
The ruling passion conquers Reason still.
Less mad the wildest whimsy we can frame
Than ev'n that passion, if it has no aim;
For though such motives folly you may call,
The folly's greater to have none at all.

Hear then the truth: "Tis Heav'n each passion sends,
And diff'rent men directs to diff'rent ends.   160
Extremes in Nature equal good produce,
Extremes in Man concur to gen'ral use.'
Ask we what makes one keep, and one bestow?
That Pow'r who bids the ocean ebb and flow;
Bids seed-time, harvest, equal course maintain
Through reconciled extremes of drought and rain;
Builds life on death, on change duration founds,
And gives th'eternal wheels to know their rounds.

Riches, like insects, when concealed they lie,
Wait but for wings, and in their season fly.   170
Who sees pale Mammon pine amidst his store,
Sees but a backward steward for the poor;
This year a reservoir, to keep and spare;
The next, a fountain, spouting through his heir,
In lavish streams to quench a country's thirst,
And men and dogs shall drink him till they burst.

Old Cotta shamed his fortune and his birth,
Yet was not Cotta void of wit or worth:
What though (the use of barb'rous spits forgot)
His kitchen vied in coolness with his grot?   180
His court with nettles, moats with cresses stored,
With soups unbought and salads blessed his board?
If Cotta lived on pulse, it was no more
Than Brahmins, saints, and sages did before;
To cram the rich was prodigal expense,
And who would take the poor from Providence?
Like some lone Chartreux stands the good old Hall,
Silence without, and fasts within the wall;
No raftered roofs with dance and tabor sound,
No noontide bell invites the country round: 190
Tenants with sighs the smokeless towers survey,
And turn th'unwilling steeds another way;
Benighted wanderers, the forest o'er,
Curse the saved candle, and unop'ning door,
While the gaunt mastiff growling at the gate
Affrights the beggar whom he longs to eat.

Not so his son, he marked this oversight,
And then mistook reverse of wrong for right
(For what to shun will no great knowledge need,
But what to follow, is a task indeed).
Yet sure, of qualities deserving praise,
More go to ruin fortunes, than to raise.
Whole slaughtered hecatombs, and floods of wine
Fill the capacious squire, and deep divine!
Yet no mean motive this profusion draws,
His oxen perish in his country's cause;
'Tis GEORGE and LIBERTY that crowns the cup,
And zeal for that great House which eats him up.
The woods recede around the naked seat,
The sylvans groan – no matter – for the fleet:
Next goes his wool – to clothe our valiant bands,
Last, for his country's love, he sells his lands.
To town he comes, completes the nation's hope,
And heads the bold train-bands, and burns a pope.
And shall not Britain now reward his toils,
Britain, that pays her patriots with her spoils?
In vain at court the bankrupt pleads his cause,
His thankless country leaves him to her laws.

The sense to value riches, with the art
T'enjoy them, and the virtue to impart,
Not meanly, nor ambitiously pursued,
Not sunk by sloth, not raised by servitude:
To balance fortune by a just expense,
Join with economy, magnificence;
With splendour, charity; with plenty, health;
Oh teach us, BATHURST! yet unspoiled by wealth!
That secret rare, between th' extremes to move
Of mad good-nature, and of mean self-love.

To worth or want well-weighed, be bounty giv'n,
And ease, or emulate, the care of Heav'n
(Whose measure full o'erflows on human race),
Mend Fortune's fault, and justify her grace.
Wealth in the gross is death, but life diffused;
As poison heals, in just proportion used,

In heaps, like ambergris, a stink it lies,
But well-dispersed, is incense to the skies.
    Who starves by nobles, or with nobles eats?
The wretch that trusts them, and the rogue that cheats.
Is there a Lord, who knows a cheerful noon
Without a fiddler, flatt'rer, or buffoon?   240
Whose table, wit, or modest merit share,
Un-elbowed by a gamester, pimp, or play'r?
Who copies yours, or OXFORD's better part,
To ease th'oppressed, and raise the sinking heart?
Wheree'er he shines, oh Fortune, gild the scene,
And angels guard him in the golden Mean!
There, English Bounty yet awhile may stand,
And Honour linger e'er it leaves the land.
    But all our praises why should Lords engross?
Rise, honest Muse! and sing the MAN of ROSS: 250
Pleased Vaga echoes through her winding bounds,
And rapid Severn hoarse applause resounds.
Who hung with woods yon mountain's sultry brow?
From the dry rock who bade the waters flow?
Not to the skies in useless columns tossed,
Or in proud falls magnificently lost,
But clear and artless, pouring through the plain
Health to the sick, and solace to the swain.
Whose causeway parts the vale with shady rows?
Whose seats the weary traveller repose?   260
Who taught that heav'n-directed spire to rise?
'The MAN of ROSS,' each lisping babe replies.
Behold the marketplace with poor o'erspread!
The MAN of ROSS divides the weekly bread:
He feeds yon alms-house, neat, but void of state,
Where Age and Want sit smiling at the gate;
Him portioned maids, apprenticed orphans blest,
The young who labour, and the old who rest.
Is any sick? the MAN of ROSS relieves,
Prescribes, attends, the med'cine makes, and gives.   270
Is there a variance? enter but his door,
Balked are the courts, and contest is no more.

Despairing quacks with curses fled the place,
And vile attorneys, now an useless race.
　　'Thrice happy man! enabled to pursue
What all so wish, but want the pow'r to do!
Oh say, what sums that gen'rous hand supply?
What mines, to swell that boundless charity?'
　　Of debts, and taxes, wife and children clear,
280　This man possessed – five hundred pounds a year.
Blush, Grandeur, blush! proud courts, withdraw
　　　　your blaze!
Ye little stars! hide your diminished rays.
　　'And what? no monument, inscription, stone?
His race, his form, his name almost unknown?'
　　Who builds a church to God, and not to fame,
Will never mark the marble with his name:
Go search it there, where to be born and die,
Of rich and poor makes all the history;
Enough, that Virtue filled the space between;
290　Proved, by the ends of being, to have been.
When Hopkins dies, a thousand lights attend
The wretch, who living saved a candle's end.
Should'ring God's altar a vile image stands,
Belies his features, nay extends his hands;
That live-long wig which Gorgon's self might own
Eternal buckle takes in Parian stone.
Behold what blessings wealth to life can lend!
And see, what comfort it affords our end.
　　In the worst inn's worst room, with mat half-hung,
300　The floors of plaster, and the walls of dung,
On once a flock-bed, but repaired with straw,
With tape-tied curtains, never meant to draw,
The George and Garter dangling from that bed
Where tawdry yellow strove with dirty red,
Great Villers lies – alas! how changed from him,
That life of pleasure, and that soul of whim!
Gallant and gay, in Cliveden's proud alcove,
The bow'r of wanton Shrewsbury and love;

Or just as gay, at Council, in a ring
Of mimicked statesmen, and their merry king.   310
No wit to flatter, left of all his store!
No fool to laugh at, which he valued more.
There, victor of his health, of fortune, friends,
And fame, this lord of useless thousands ends.
    His Grace's fate sage Cutler could foresee,
And well (he thought) advised him, 'Live like me.'
As well his Grace replied, 'Like you, Sir John?
That I can do, when all I have is gone.'
Resolve me, Reason, which of these is worse,
Want with a full, or with an empty purse?   320
Thy life more wretched, Cutler, was confessed,
Arise, and tell me, was thy death more blest?
Cutler saw tenants break, and houses fall,
For very want; he could not build a wall.
His only daughter in a stranger's pow'r,
For very want; he could not pay a dow'r.
A few grey hairs his rev'rend temples crowned,
'Twas very want that sold them for two pound.
What ev'n denied a cordial at his end,
Banished the doctor, and expelled the friend?   330
What but a want, which you perhaps think mad,
Yet numbers feel the want of what he had!
Cutler and Brutus, dying both exclaim,
'Virtue! and Wealth! what are ye but a name!'
    Say, for such worth are other worlds prepared?
Or are they both, in this, their own reward?
A knotty point! to which we now proceed.
But you are tired – I'll tell a tale—'Agreed.'
    Where London's column, pointing at the skies,
Like a tall bully, lifts the head, and lies;   340
There dwelt a Citizen of sober fame,
A plain good man, and Balaam was his name,
Religious, punctual, frugal, and so forth;
His word would pass for more than he was worth.
One solid dish his week-day meal affords,
An added pudding solemnized the Lord's:

Constant at church, and Change; his gains were sure,
His givings rare, save farthings to the poor.

The Dev'l was piqued such saintship to behold,
350   And longed to tempt him like good Job of old,
But Satan now is wiser than of yore,
And tempts by making rich, not making poor.

Roused by the Prince of Air, the whirlwinds sweep
The surge, and plunge his father in the deep;
Then full against his Cornish lands they roar,
And two rich shipwrecks bless the lucky shore.

Sir Balaam now, he lives like other folks,
He takes his chirping pint, and cracks his jokes;
'Live like yourself,' was soon my Lady's word;
360   And lo! two puddings smoked upon the board.

Asleep and naked as an Indian lay,
An honest factor stole a gem away:
He pledged it to the knight; the knight had wit,
So kept the diamond, and the rogue was bit.
Some scruple rose, but thus he eased his thought,
'I'll now give sixpence where I gave a groat;
Where once I went to church, I'll now go twice –
And am so clear too of all other vice.'

The Tempter saw his time; the work he plied;
370   Stocks and subscriptions pour on ev'ry side,
Till all the Demon makes his full descent
In one abundant show'r of cent per cent,
Sinks deep within him, and possesses whole,
Then dubs Director, and secures his soul.

Behold Sir Balaam, now a man of spirit,
Ascribes his gettings to his parts and merit;
What late he called a blessing, now was wit,
And God's good Providence, a lucky hit.
Things change their titles, as our manners turn:
380   His compting-house employed the Sunday-morn;
Seldom at church ('twas such a busy life)
But duly sent his family and wife.

There (so the Dev'l ordained) one Christmastide
My good old Lady catched a cold, and died.
  A nymph of quality admires our knight;
He marries, bows at Court, and grows polite:
Leaves the dull cits, and joins (to please the fair)
The well-bred cuckolds in St James's air:
First, for his son a gay commission buys,
Who drinks, whores, fights, and in a duel dies;   390
His daughter flaunts a viscount's tawdry wife;
She bears a coronet and pox for life.
In Britain's senate he a seat obtains,
And one more pensioner St Stephen gains.
My Lady falls to play; so bad her chance,
He must repair it; takes a bribe from France;
The House impeach him; Coningsby harangues;
The Court forsake him, and Sir Balaam hangs.
Wife, son, and daughter, Satan! are thy own,
His wealth, yet dearer, forfeit to the Crown: 400
The Devil and the King divide the prize,
And sad Sir Balaam curses God and dies.

Epistle IV

TO
Richard Boyle, Earl of Burlington

ARGUMENT
Of the Use of RICHES

*The vanity of Expense in people of wealth and quality. The
abuse of the word* Taste, v. 13. *That the first principle and
foundation, in this as in everything else, is* Good Sense, v. 40.
The chief proof of it is to follow Nature, *even in works of mere
luxury and elegance. Instanced in* Architecture *and* Gardening,
where all must be adapted to the genius *and* use *of the* place,
and the beauties not forced into it, but resulting from it, v. 50.

How men are disappointed in their most expensive undertak-
ings, for want of this true foundation, without which nothing
can please long, *if at all; and the best* examples *and* rules *will*
but be perverted into something burdensome *or ridiculous,*
v. 65, etc. to 92. *A description of the* false taste *of* Magnifi-
cence; *the first grand error of which is to imagine that* Greatness
consists in the size *and* dimension, *instead of the* Proportion
and Harmony *of the* whole, v. 97, *and the second, either in*
joining together parts incoherent, *or too* minutely resembling,
or in the repetition *of the* same *too frequently,* v. 105, etc. *A*
word or two of false Taste in Books, *in* Music, *in* Painting, *even*
in Preaching *and* Prayer, *and lastly in* Entertainments, v. 133,
etc. *Yet* PROVIDENCE *is justified in giving wealth to be squan-*
dered in this manner, since it is dispersed to the poor and
laborious part of mankind, v. 169. *What are the* proper objects
of Magnificence, and proper field for the expense of great men,
v. 177, etc. *and finally, the great and public works which*
become a Prince, v. 191, *to the end.*

> 'Tis strange, the miser should his cares employ
> To gain those riches he can ne'er enjoy.
> Is it less strange, the prodigal should waste
> His wealth, to purchase what he ne'er can taste?
> Not for himself he sees, or hears, or eats;
> Artists must choose his pictures, music, meats:
> He buys for Topham drawings and designs,
> For Pembroke statues, dirty gods, and coins;
> Rare monkish manuscripts for Hearne alone,
> And books for Mead, and butterflies for Sloane.
> Think we all these are for himself? no more
> Than his fine wife, alas! or finer whore.
>   For what has Virro painted, built, and planted?
> Only to show, how many tastes he wanted.
> What brought Sir Visto's ill got wealth to waste?
> Some demon whispered, 'Visto! have a taste.'
> Heav'n visits with a taste the wealthy fool,
> And needs no rod but Ripley with a rule.

10

See! sportive fate, to punish awkward pride
Bids Bubo build, and sends him such a guide: 20
A standing sermon, at each year's expense,
That never coxcomb reached magnificence!
    You show us Rome was glorious, not profuse,
And pompous buildings once were things of use.
Yet shall (my Lord) your just, your noble rules
Fill half the land with imitating fools,
Who random drawings from your sheets shall take,
And of one beauty many blunders make;
Load some vain church with old theatric state,
Turn arcs of triumph to a garden gate;   30
Reverse your ornaments, and hang them all
On some patched dog-hole eked with ends of wall;
Then clap four slices of pilaster on't,
That laced with bits of rustic, makes a front;
Or call the winds through long arcades to roar,
Proud to catch cold at a Venetian door:
Conscious they act a true Palladian part,
And if they starve, they starve by rules of art.
    Oft have you hinted to your brother Peer
A certain truth, which many buy too dear: 40
Something there is, more needful than expense,
And something previous ev'n to taste – 'tis sense:
Good sense, which only is the gift of Heav'n,
And though no science, fairly worth the sev'n:
A light, which in yourself you must perceive;
Jones and Le Nôtre have it not to give.
    To build, to plant, whatever you intend,
To rear the column, or the arch to bend,
To swell the terrace, or to sink the grot,
In all, let Nature never be forgot;   50
But treat the goddess like a modest fair,
Nor over-dress, nor leave her wholly bare;
Let not each beauty ev'rywhere be spied,
Where half the skill is decently to hide.
He gains all points who pleasingly confounds,
Surprises, varies, and conceals the bounds.

Consult the genius of the place in all,
That tells the waters or to rise, or fall,
Or helps th'ambitious hill the heav'ns to scale,
60 Or scoops in circling theatres the vale;
Calls in the country, catches op'ning glades,
Joins willing woods, and varies shades from shades;
Now breaks, or now directs, th' intending lines,
Paints as you plant, and as you work, designs.

Still follow sense, of ev'ry art the soul;
Parts answ'ring parts shall slide into a whole,
Spontaneous beauties all around advance,
Start ev'n from difficulty, strike from chance.
Nature shall join you; time shall make it grow
70 A work to wonder at – perhaps a STOWE.

Without it, proud Versailles! thy glory falls,
And Nero's terraces desert their walls.
The vast parterres a thousand hands shall make,
Lo! COBHAM comes, and floats them with a lake;
Or cut wide views through mountains to the plain,
You'll wish your hill or sheltered seat again.
Ev'n in an ornament its place remark,
Nor in an hermitage set Dr Clarke.

Behold Villario's ten-years' toil complete;
80 His arbours darken, his espaliers meet;
The wood supports the plain, the parts unite,
And strength of shade contends with strength of light;
A waving glow the bloomy beds display,
Blushing in bright diversities of day,
With silver-quiv'ring rills meander'd o'er –
Enjoy them, you! Villario can no more.
Tired of the scene parterres and fountains yield,
He finds at last he better likes a field.

Through his young woods how pleased Sabinus strayed,
90 Or sat delighted in the thick'ning shade,
With annual joy the red'ning shoots to greet,
Or see the stretching branches long to meet.
His son's fine taste an op'ner vista loves,
Foe to the dryads of his father's groves;

One boundless green, or flourished carpet views,
With all the mournful family of yews;
The thriving plants ignoble broomsticks made,
Now sweep those alleys they were born to shade.
    At Timon's villa let us pass a day,
Where all cry out, 'What sums are thrown away!'   100
So proud, so grand, of that stupendous air,
Soft and agreeable come never there.
Greatness, with Timon, dwells in such a draught
As brings all Brobdingnag before your thought.
To compass this, his building is a town,
His pond an ocean, his parterre a down:
Who but must laugh, the master when he sees?
A puny insect, shiv'ring at a breeze.
Lo! what huge heaps of littleness around!
The whole, a laboured quarry above ground.   110
Two cupids squirt before; a lake behind
Improves the keenness of the northern wind.
His gardens next your admiration call,
On ev'ry side you look, behold the wall!
No pleasing intricacies intervene,
No artful wildness to perplex the scene;
Grove nods at grove, each alley has a brother,
And half the platform just reflects the other.
The suff'ring eye inverted Nature sees,
Trees cut to statues, statues thick as trees,   120
With here a fountain, never to be played,
And there a summer-house, that knows no shade.
Here Amphitrite sails through myrtle bow'rs;
There gladiators fight, or die, in flow'rs;
Un-watered see the drooping sea horse mourn,
And swallows roost in Nilus' dusty urn.
    My Lord advances with majestic mien,
Smit with the mighty pleasure, to be seen:
But soft – by regular approach – not yet –
First through the length of yon hot terrace sweat,   130
And when up ten steep slopes you've dragged your thighs,
Just at his study door he'll bless your eyes.

His study! with what authors is it stored?
In books, not authors, curious is my Lord;
To all their dated backs he turns you round:
These Aldus printed, those Du Sueil has bound.
Lo some are vellum, and the rest as good
For all his Lordship knows, but they are wood.
For Locke or Milton 'tis in vain to look,
140 These shelves admit not any modern book.
    And now the chapel's silver bell you hear,
That summons you to all the pride of pray'r:
Light quirks of music, broken and unev'n,
Make the soul dance upon a jig to Heav'n.
On painted ceilings you devoutly stare,
Where sprawl the saints of Verrio or Laguerre,
On gilded clouds in fair expansion lie,
And bring all Paradise before your eye.
To rest, the cushion and soft dean invite,
150 Who never mentions Hell to ears polite.
    But hark! the chiming clocks to dinner call;
A hundred footsteps scrape the marble hall;
The rich buffet well-coloured Serpents grace,
And gaping tritons spew to wash your face.
Is this a dinner? this a genial room?
No, 'tis a temple, and a hecatomb,
A solemn sacrifice, performed in state,
You drink by measure, and to minutes eat.
So quick retires each flying course, you'd swear
160 Sancho's dread doctor and his wand were there.
Between each act the trembling salvers ring,
From soup to sweet-wine, and 'God bless the King.'
In plenty starving, tantalized in state,
And complaisantly helped to all I hate,
Treated, caressed, and tired, I take my leave,
Sick of his civil pride from morn to eve;
I curse such lavish cost, and little skill,
And swear no day was ever passed so ill.
    Yet hence the poor are clothed, the hungry fed;
170 Health to himself, and to his infants bread

The lab'rer bears: what his hard heart denies,
His charitable vanity supplies.
　　Another age shall see the golden ear
Imbrown the slope, and nod on the parterre,
Deep harvests bury all his pride has planned,
And laughing Ceres reassume the land.
　　Who then shall grace, or who improve the soil?
Who plants like BATHURST, or who builds like BOYLE.
'Tis use alone that sanctifies expense,
And splendour borrows all her rays from sense.   180
　　His father's acres who enjoys in peace,
Or makes his neighbours glad, if he increase;
Whose cheerful tenants bless their yearly toil,
Yet to their Lord owe more than to the soil;
Whose ample lawns are not ashamed to feed
The milky heifer and deserving steed;
Whose rising forests, not for pride or show,
But future buildings, future navies grow:
Let his plantations stretch from down to down,
First shade a country, and then raise a town.   190
　　You too proceed! make falling arts your care,
Erect new wonders, and the old repair;
Jones and Palladio to themselves restore,
And be whate'er Vitruvius was before:
Till kings call forth th' ideas of your mind
(Proud to accomplish what such hands designed):
Bid harbours open, public ways extend,
Bid temples, worthier of the god, ascend,
Bid the broad arch the dang'rous flood contain,
The mole projected break the roaring main;   200
Back to his bounds their subject sea command,
And roll obedient rivers through the land.
These honours, peace to happy Britain brings;
These are imperial works, and worthy kings.

The Fourth Satire of Dr John Donne Versified

> Quid vetat, ut nosmet Lucili scripta legentes
> Quaerere, num illius, num rerum dura negarit
> Versiculos natura magis factos, et euntes
> Mollius?

Well, if it be my time to quit the stage,
Adieu to all the follies of the age!
I die in charity with fool and knave,
Secure of peace at least beyond the grave.
I've had my purgatory here betimes,
And paid for all my satires, all my rhymes.
The poet's hell, its tortures, fiends, and flames,
To this were trifles, toys, and empty names.

    With foolish pride my heart was never fired,
10 Nor the vain itch t' admire, or be admired:
I hoped for no commission from his Grace;
I bought no benefice, I begged no place;
Had no new verses, nor new suit to show,
Yet went to court! – the Dev'l would have it so.
But as the fool, that in reforming days
Would go to mass in jest (as story says),
Could not but think, to pay his fine was odd,
Since 'twas no formed design of serving God:
So was I punished, as if full as proud
20 As prone to ill, as negligent of good,
As deep in debt, without a thought to pay, ⎫
As vain, as idle, and as false, as they   ⎬
Who live at court, for going once that way! ⎭

    Scarce was I entered, when behold! there came
A thing which Adam had been posed to name;
Noah had refused it lodging in his ark,
Where all the race of reptiles might embark:
A verier monster than on Afric's shore
The sun e'er got, or slimy Nilus bore,

Or Sloane, or Woodward's wondrous shelves contain;   30
Nay, all that lying travellers can feign.
The watch would hardly let him pass at noon,
At night, would swear him dropped out of the moon:
One whom the mob, when next we find or make
A popish plot, shall for a Jesuit take;
And the wise Justice, starting from his chair,
Cry, by your priesthood, tell me what you are?
     Such was the wight: th' apparel on his back
Though coarse, was rev'rend, and though bare, was black.
The suit, if by the fashion one might guess,   40
Was velvet in the youth of good Queen Bess,
But mere tuff-taffety what now remained:
So Time, that changes all things, had ordained!
Our sons shall see it leisurely decay,
First turn plain rash, then vanish quite away.
     This thing has travelled, speaks each language too,
And knows what's fit for ev'ry state to do;
Of whose best phrase and courtly accent joined
He forms one tongue exotic and refined.
Talkers, I've learned to bear; Motteux I knew,   50
Henley himself I've heard, nay Budgell too;
The doctor's wormwood style, the hash of tongues
A pedant makes, the storm of Gonson's lungs,
The whole artill'ry of the terms of war,
And (all those plagues in one) the bawling bar:
These I could bear; but not a rogue so civil
Whose tongue will compliment you to the Devil.
A tongue that can cheat widows, cancel scores,
Make Scots speak treason, cozen subtlest whores,
With royal favourites in flatt'ry vie,   60
And Oldmixon and Burnet both out-lie.
     He spies me out. I whisper, 'Gracious God!
What sin of mine could merit such a rod?
That all the shot of dullness now must be
From this thy blunderbuss discharged on me!'

'Permit,' he cries, 'no stranger to your fame,
To crave your sentiment, if —— 's your name.
What speech esteem you most?' 'The King's,' said I.
'But the best words?' – 'O, sir, the dictionary.'
70   'You miss my aim; I mean the most acute
And perfect speaker?' – 'Onslow, past dispute.'
'But sir, of writers?' – 'Swift for closer style,
And Hoadley for a period of a mile.'
'Why, yes, 'tis granted, these indeed may pass
Good common linguists, and so Panurge was;
Nay, troth, th' Apostles (though perhaps too rough)
Had once a pretty gift of tongues enough.
Yet these were all poor gentlemen! I dare
Affirm, 'twas travel made them what they were.'
80   Thus others' talents having nicely shown,
He came by sure transition to his own;
Till I cried out, 'You prove yourself so able,
Pity! you was not druggerman at Babel:
For had they found a linguist half so good,
I make no question but the tow'r had stood.'

'Obliging sir! for courts you sure were made;
Why then for ever buried in the shade?
Spirits like you, believe me, should be seen;
The King would smile on you – at least the Queen?'
90   'Ah, gentle sir! you courtiers so cajole us –
But Tully has it, *Nunquam minus solus*:
But as for courts, forgive me if I say
No lessons now are taught the Spartan way.
Though in his pictures lust be full displayed,
Few are the converts Aretine has made;
And though the court show vice exceeding clear,
None should, by my advice, learn virtue there.'
At this entranced, he lifts his hands and eyes,
Squeaks like a high-stretched lutestring, and replies:
100   'Oh 'tis the sweetest of all earthly things
To gaze on princes, and to talk of kings!'
'Then happy man who shows the tombs!' said I,
'He dwells amidst the royal family;

He, ev'ry day, from king to king can walk,
Of all our Harries, all our Edwards talk,
And get, by speaking truth of monarchs dead,
What few can of the living, ease and bread.'
'Lord! sir, a mere mechanic! strangely low,
And coarse of phrase – your English all are so.
How elegant your Frenchman?' – 'Mine, d'ye mean?   110
I have but one, I hope the fellow's clean.'
'Oh! sir, politely so! nay, let me die,
Your only wearing is your paduasoy.'
'Not sir, my only – I have better still,
And this, you see, is but my dishabille' –
Wild to get loose, his patience I provoke,
Mistake, confound, object, at all he spoke;
But as coarse iron, sharpened, mangles more,
And itch most hurts, when angered to a sore,
So when you plague a fool, 'tis still the curse,   120
You only make the matter worse and worse.

He passed it o'er; affects an easy smile
At all my peevishness, and turns his style.
He asks, 'What news?' I tell him of new plays,
New eunuchs, harlequins, and operas.
He hears; and as a still, with simples in it,
Between each drop it gives, stays half a minute,
Loath to enrich me with too quick replies,
By little, and by little, drops his lies.
Mere household trash! of birthnights, balls, and shows,   130
More than ten Holinsheds, or Halls, or Stows.
When the Queen frowned, or smiled, he knows; and what
A subtle minister may make of that.
Who sins with whom? who got his pension rug,
Or quickened a reversion by a drug?
Whose place is quartered out, three parts in four,
And whether to a bishop, or a whore?
Who, having lost his credit, pawned his rent,
Is therefore fit to have a government?

140 Who, in the secret, deals in stocks secure,
And cheats th' unknowing widow, and the poor:
Who makes a trust, or charity, a job,
And gets an act of Parliament to rob?
Why turnpikes rise, and now no cit nor clown
Can gratis see the country, or the town?
Shortly no lad shall chuck, or lady vole,
But some excising courtier will have toll.
He tells what strumpet places sells for life,
What squire his lands, what citizen his wife.
150 And last (which proves him wiser still than all)
What lady's face is not a whited wall?

As one of Woodward's patients, sick, and sore,
I puke, I nauseate – yet he thrusts in more;
Trims Europe's balance, tops the statesman's part,
And talks *Gazettes* and *Post Boys* o'er by heart.
Like a big wife at sight of loathsome meat
Ready to cast, I yawn, I sigh, and sweat.
Then as a licensed spy, whom nothing can
Silence, or hurt, he libels the Great Man;
160 Swears every place entailed for years to come,
In sure succession to the Day of Doom:
He names the price for ev'ry office paid,
And says our wars thrive ill, because delayed:
Nay, hints 'tis by connivance of the court
That Spain robs on, and Dunkirk's still a port.
Not more amazement seized on Circe's guests,
To see themselves fall endlong into beasts,
Than mine, to find a subject staid and wise
Already half turned traitor by surprise.
170 I feared th' infection slide from him to me,
As in the pox, some give it, to get free;
And quick to swallow me, methought I saw
One of our giant statues ope its jaw!
In that nice moment, as another lie
Stood just a-tilt, the Minister came by.
Away he flies. He bows, and bows again,
And close as Umbra, joins the dirty train.

Not Fannius' self more impudently near,
When half his nose is in his patron's ear.
I quaked at heart; and still afraid to see   180
All the court filled with stranger things than he,
Ran out as fast as one that pays his bail,
And dreads more actions, hurries from a jail.
　　Bear me, some god! oh quickly bear me hence
To wholesome solitude, the nurse of sense,
Where contemplation prunes her ruffled wings,
And the free soul looks down to pity kings!
There sober thought pursued th' amusing theme,
Till fancy coloured it, and formed a dream.
A vision hermits can to Hell transport,   190
And forc'd ev'n me to see the damned at court.
Not Dante, dreaming all th' infernal state,
Beheld such scenes of envy, sin, and hate.
Base fear becomes the guilty, not the free;
Suits tyrants, plunderers, but suits not me.
Shall I, the terror of this sinful town,
Care if a liveried lord or smile or frown?
Who cannot flatter, and detest who can,
Tremble before a noble serving-man?
O my fair mistress, Truth! shall I quit thee   200
For huffing, braggart, puffed nobility?
Thou who, since yesterday, hast rolled o'er all
The busy, idle blockheads of the ball,
Hast thou, oh sun! beheld an emptier sort
Than such as swell this bladder of a court?
Now pox on those who show a court in wax!
It ought to bring all courtiers on their backs.
Such painted puppets, such a varnished race
Of hollow gewgaws, only dress and face,
Such waxen noses, stately, staring things,   210
No wonder some folks bow, and think them kings.
　　See! where the British youth, engaged no more
At Fig's, at White's, with felons, or a whore,
Pay their last duty to the court, and come
All fresh and fragrant to the drawing room:

In hues as gay, and odours as divine
As the fair fields they sold to look so fine.
'That's velvet for a king!' the flatt'rer swears;
'Tis true, for ten days hence 'twill be King Lear's.
220   Our court may justly to our stage give rules,
That helps it both to fools' coats and to fools.
And why not players strut in courtiers' clothes?
For these are actors too, as well as those:
Wants reach all states; they beg but better dressed,
And all is splendid poverty at best.

    Painted for sight, and essenced for the smell,
Like frigates fraught with spice and cochine'l,
Sail in the ladies: how each pirate eyes
So weak a vessel, and so rich a prize!
230   Top-gallant he, and she in all her trim,
He boarding her, she striking sail to him.
'Dear countess! you have charms all hearts to hit!'
And 'Sweet Sir Fopling! you have so much wit!'
Such wits and beauties are not praised for nought,
For both the beauty and the wit are bought.
'Twould burst ev'n Heraclitus with the spleen
To see those antics, Fopling and Courtin:
The Presence seems, with things so richly odd,
The mosque of Mahound, or some queer pagod.
240   See them survey their limbs by Durer's rules,
Of all beau-kind the best proportioned fools!
Adjust their clothes, and to confession draw
Those venial sins, an atom, or a straw:
But oh! what terrors must distract the soul
Convicted of that mortal crime, a hole!
Or should one pound of powder less bespread
Those monkey tails that wag behind their head!
Thus finished, and corrected to a hair,
They march, to prate their hour before the fair.
250   So first to preach a white-gloved chaplain goes,
With band of lily, and with cheek of rose,
Sweeter than Sharon, in immaculate trim,
Neatness itself impertinent in him.

Let but the ladies smile, and they are blest;
Prodigious! how the things protest, protest.
Peace, fools! or Gonson will for papists seize you,
If once he catch you at your 'Jesu! Jesu!'
   Nature made ev'ry fop to plague his brother,
Just as one beauty mortifies another.
But here's the captain, that will plague them both;   260
Whose air cries 'Arm!' whose very look's an oath,
Though his soul's bullet, and his body buff!
Damn him, he's honest, sir – and that's enough.
He spits fore-right; his haughty chest before,
Like batt'ring rams, beats open ev'ry door;
And with a face as red, and as awry,
As Herod's hang-dogs in old tapestry,
Scarecrow to boys, the breeding woman's curse,
Has yet a strange ambition to look worse;
Confounds the civil, keeps the rude in awe,   270
Jests like a licensed fool, commands like law.
   Frighted, I quit the room, but leave it so
As men from jails to execution go,
For hung with deadly sins I see the wall,
And lined with giants, deadlier than them all:
Each man an Ascapart, of strength to toss,
For quoits, both Temple Bar and Charing Cross.
Scared at the grisly forms, I sweat, I fly,
And shake all o'er, like a discovered spy.
   Courts are too much for wits so weak as mine;   280
Charge them with Heaven's artill'ry, bold divine!
From such alone the great rebukes endure,
Whose satire's sacred, and whose rage secure.
'Tis mine to wash a few light stains; but theirs
To deluge sin, and drown a court in tears.
Howe'er, what's now apocrypha, my wit,
In time to come, may pass for holy writ.

An Epistle to Dr Arbuthnot

Neque sermonibus vulgi dederis te, nec in praemiis humanis spem posueris rerum tuarum; suis te oportet illecebris ipsa virtus trahat ad verum decus. Quid de te alii loquantur, ipsi videant, sed loquentur tamen.

ADVERTISEMENT

This paper is a sort of bill of complaint, begun many years since, and drawn up by snatches as the several occasions offered. I had no thoughts of publishing it, till it pleased some persons of rank and fortune (the authors of *Verses to the imitator of Horace*, and of an *Epistle to a doctor of divinity from a nobleman at Hampton Court*) to attack, in a very extraordinary manner, not only my writings (of which, being public, the public is judge), but my person, morals, and family; whereof, to those who know me not, a truer information may be requisite. Being divided between the necessity to say something of myself, and my own laziness to undertake so awkward a task, I thought it the shortest way to put the last hand to this epistle. If it have anything pleasing, it will be that by which I am most desirous to please, the truth and the sentiment; and if anything offensive, it will be only to those I am least sorry to offend, the vicious or the ungenerous.

Many will know their own pictures in it, there being not a circumstance but what is true; but I have, for the most part, spared their names, and they may escape being laughed at if they please.

I would have some of them know it was owing to the request of the learned and candid friend to whom it is inscribed that I make not as free use of theirs as they have done of mine. However, I shall have this advantage and honour on my side, that whereas, by their proceeding, any abuse may be directed at any man, no injury can possibly be done by mine, since a nameless character can never be found out but by its truth and likeness.

'Shut, shut the door, good John!' fatigued, I said;
'Tie up the knocker, say I'm sick, I'm dead.'
The dog-star rages! nay, 'tis past a doubt
All Bedlam, or Parnassus, is let out:
Fire in each eye, and papers in each hand,
They rave, recite, and madden round the land.

    What walls can guard me, or what shades can hide?
They pierce my thickets, through my grot they glide,
By land, by water, they renew the charge,
They stop the chariot, and they board the barge.   10
No place is sacred, not the church is free,
E'vn Sunday shines no sabbath day to me:
Then from the Mint walks forth the man of rhyme,
Happy to catch me, just at dinner time.

    Is there a parson much bemused in beer,
A maudlin poetess, a rhyming peer,
A clerk foredoomed his father's soul to cross,
Who pens a stanza when he should engross?
Is there, who locked from ink and paper, scrawls
With desp'rate charcoal round his darken'd walls?   20
All fly to Twit'nam, and in humble strain
Apply to me to keep them mad or vain.
Arthur, whose giddy son neglects the laws,
Imputes to me and my damned works the cause;
Poor Cornus sees his frantic wife elope,
And curses wit, and poetry, and Pope.

    Friend to my life (which did not you prolong,
The world had wanted many an idle song),
What drop or nostrum can this plague remove?
Or which must end me, a fool's wrath or love?   30
A dire dilemma! either way I'm sped;
If foes, they write, if friends, they read me dead.
Seized and tied down to judge, how wretched I!
Who can't be silent, and who will not lie.
To laugh were want of goodness and of grace,
And to be grave exceeds all power of face.
I sit with sad civility, I read
With honest anguish and an aching head,

And drop at last, but in unwilling ears,
40 This saving counsel, 'Keep your piece nine years.'
     'Nine years!' cries he, who high in Drury Lane,
Lulled by soft zephyrs through the broken pane,
Rhymes ere he wakes, and prints before term ends,
Obliged by hunger and request of friends.
'The piece, you think, is incorrect? why, take it,
I'm all submission: what you'd have it, make it.'
     Three things another's modest wishes bound,
My friendship, and a prologue, and ten pound.
     Pitholeon sends to me: 'You know his Grace,
50 I want a patron; ask him for a place.'
Pitholeon libelled me – 'but here's a letter
Informs you, sir, 'twas when he knew no better.
Dare you refuse him? Curll invites to dine,
He'll write a journal, or he'll turn divine.'
Bless me! a packet – 'Tis a stranger sues,
A virgin tragedy, an orphan Muse.'
If I dislike it, 'Furies, death, and rage!'
If I approve, 'Commend it to the stage.'
There (thank my stars) my whole commission ends,
60 The play'rs and I are, luckily, no friends.
Fired that the house rejects him, "Sdeath, I'll print it,
And shame the fools – your interest, sir, with Lintot.'
Lintot, dull rogue! will think your price too much:
'Not, sir, if you revise it, and retouch.'
All my demurs but double his attacks;
At last he whispers, 'Do, and we go snacks.'
Glad of a quarrel, straight I clap the door;
'Sir, let me see your works and you no more.'
     'Tis sung, when Midas' ears began to spring
70 (Midas, a sacred person and a king),
His very minister who spied them first
(Some say his queen) was forced to speak or burst.
And is not mine, my friend, a sorer case,
When ev'ry coxcomb perks them in my face?

'Good friend, forbear! you deal in dang'rous things;
I'd never name queens, ministers, or kings;
Keep close to ears, and those let asses prick,
'Tis nothing' – Nothing! if they bite and kick?
Out with it, *Dunciad*! let the secret pass,
That secret to each fool, that he's an ass.   80
The truth once told (and wherefore should we lie?),
The queen of Midas slept, and so may I.
    You think this cruel? take it for a rule,
No creature smarts so little as a fool.
Let peals of laughter, Codrus, round thee break,
Thou unconcerned canst hear the mighty crack:
Pit, box, and gallery in convulsions hurled,
Thou stand'st unshook amidst a bursting world.
Who shames a scribbler? break one cobweb through,
He spins the slight self-pleasing thread anew: 90
Destroy his fib or sophistry in vain;
The creature's at his dirty work again,
Throned in the centre of his thin designs,
Proud of a vast extent of flimsy lines!
Whom have I hurt? has poet yet, or peer,
Lost the arched eyebrow or Parnassian sneer?
And has not Colley still his lord and whore?
His butchers Henley? his freemasons Moore?
Does not one table Bavius still admit?
Still to one bishop Philips seem a wit?   100
Still Sappho – 'Hold! for God's sake – you'll offend.
No names – be calm – learn prudence of a friend:
I too could write, and I am twice as tall;
But foes like these' – One flatt'rer's worse than all.
Of all mad creatures, if the learn'd are right,
It is the slaver kills, and not the bite.
A fool quite angry is quite innocent;
Alas! 'tis ten times worse when they repent.
    One dedicates in high heroic prose,
And ridicules beyond a hundred foes;   110
One from all Grub Street will my fame defend,
And, more abusive, calls himself my friend.

This prints my letters, that expects a bribe,
And others roar aloud, 'Subscribe, subscribe!'
   There are who to my person pay their court:
I cough like Horace; and, though lean, am short;
Ammon's great son one shoulder had too high,
Such Ovid's nose, and 'Sir! you have an eye –.'
Go on, obliging creatures! make me see
120   All that disgraced my betters met in me.
Say, for my comfort, languishing in bed,
'Just so immortal Maro held his head';
And when I die, be sure you let me know
Great Homer died three thousand years ago.
   Why did I write? what sin to me unknown
Dipped me in ink, my parents', or my own?
As yet a child, nor yet a fool to fame,
I lisped in numbers, for the numbers came;
I left no calling for this idle trade,
130   No duty broke, no father disobeyed:
The Muse but served to ease some friend, not wife,
To help me through this long disease, my life,
To second, Arbuthnot! thy art and care,
And teach the being you preserved to bear.
   'But why then publish?' Granville the polite,
And knowing Walsh, would tell me I could write;
Well natured Garth inflamed with early praise,
And Congreve loved, and Swift endured my lays;
The courtly Talbot, Somers, Sheffield read,
140   Ev'n mitred Rochester would nod the head,
And St John's self (great Dryden's friends before)
With open arms received one poet more.
Happy my studies, when by these approved!
Happier their author, when by these beloved!
From these the world will judge of men and books,
Not from the Burnets, Oldmixons, and Cooks.
   Soft were my numbers; who could take offence
While pure description held the place of sense?
Like gentle Fanny's was my flow'ry theme,
150   A painted mistress, or a purling stream.

Yet then did Gildon draw his venal quill;
I wished the man a dinner, and sat still;
Yet then did Dennis rave in furious fret;
I never answered; I was not in debt.
If want provoked, or madness made them print,
I waged no war with Bedlam or the Mint.
    Did some more sober critic come abroad,
If wrong, I smiled, if right, I kissed the rod.
Pains, reading, study, are their just pretence,
And all they want is spirit, taste, and sense.   160
Commas and points they set exactly right,
And 'twere a sin to rob them of their mite.
Yet ne'er one sprig of laurel graced these ribalds,
From slashing Bentley down to piddling Tibbalds:
Each wight who reads not, and but scans and spells,
Each word-catcher that lives on syllables,
E'vn such small critics some regard may claim,
Preserved in Milton's or in Shakespeare's name.
Pretty! in amber to observe the forms
Of hairs, or straws, or dirt, or grubs, or worms!   170
The things, we know, are neither rich nor rare,
But wonder how the devil they got there.
    Were others angry, I excused them too;
Well might they rage, I gave them but their due.
A man's true merit 'tis not hard to find;
But each man's secret standard in his mind,
That casting-weight pride adds to emptiness,
This, who can gratify? for who can guess?
The bard whom pilfered pastorals renown,
Who turns a Persian tale for half a crown,   180
Just writes to make his barrenness appear,
And strains from hard-bound brains eight lines a year;
He who still wanting, though he lives on theft,
Steals much, spends little, yet has nothing left;
And he who now to sense, now nonsense leaning,
Means not, but blunders round about a meaning;
And he whose fustian's so sublimely bad,
It is not poetry, but prose run mad:

All these, my modest satire bade translate,
And owned that nine such poets made a Tate.
How did they fume, and stamp, and roar, and chafe!
And swear not Addison himself was safe.
   Peace to all such! but were there one whose fires
True genius kindles, and fair fame inspires,
Blessed with each talent and each art to please,
And born to write, converse, and live with ease;
Should such a man, too fond to rule alone,
Bear, like the Turk, no brother near the throne;
View him with scornful, yet with jealous eyes,
And hate for arts that caused himself to rise;
Damn with faint praise, assent with civil leer,
And without sneering, teach the rest to sneer;
Willing to wound, and yet afraid to strike,
Just hint a fault, and hesitate dislike;
Alike reserved to blame or to commend,
A tim'rous foe, and a suspicious friend;
Dreading ev'n fools, by flatterers besieged,
And so obliging that he ne'er obliged;
Like Cato, give his little senate laws,
And sit attentive to his own applause;
While wits and templars ev'ry sentence raise,
And wonder with a foolish face of praise –
Who but must laugh if such a man there be?
Who would not weep, if Atticus were he?
   What though my name stood rubric on the walls,
Or plastered posts, with claps, in capitals?
Or smoking forth, a hundred hawkers' load,
On wings of winds came flying all abroad?
I sought no homage from the race that write;
I kept, like Asian monarchs, from their sight:
Poems I heeded (now berhymed so long)
No more than thou, great George! a birthday song.
I ne'er with wits or witlings passed my days
To spread about the itch of verse and praise;

190

200

210

220

Nor like a puppy daggled through the town
To fetch and carry sing-song up and down;
Nor at rehearsals sweat, and mouthed, and cried,
With handkerchief and orange at my side;
But sick of fops, and poetry, and prate,
To Bufo left the whole Castalian state.   230
    Proud as Apollo on his forkèd hill
Sat full blown Bufo, puffed by ev'ry quill:
Fed with soft dedication all day long,
Horace and he went hand in hand in song.
His library (where busts of poets dead,
And a true Pindar stood without a head)
Received of wits an undistinguished race,
Who first his judgement asked, and then a place:
Much they extolled his pictures, much his seat,
And flattered ev'ry day, and some days eat: 240
Till grown more frugal in his riper days,
He paid some bards with port, and some with praise;
To some a dry rehearsal was assigned,
And others (harder still) he paid in kind.
Dryden alone (what wonder?) came not nigh;
Dryden alone escaped this judging eye:
But still the great have kindness in reserve;
He helped to bury whom he helped to starve.
    May some choice patron bless each grey goose quill!
May ev'ry Bavius have his Bufo still!   250
So when a statesman wants a day's defence,
Or envy holds a whole week's war with sense,
Or simple pride for flattery makes demands,
May dunce by dunce be whistled off my hands!
Blest be the great! for those they take away,
And those they left me – for they left me Gay;
Left me to see neglected genius bloom,
Neglected die, and tell it on his tomb;
Of all thy blameless life the sole return
My verse, and Queensberry weeping o'er thy urn!   260
    Oh let me live my own, and die so too!
('To live and die is all I have to do');

Maintain a poet's dignity and ease,
And see what friends, and read what books I please;
Above a patron, though I condescend
Sometimes to call a minister my friend.
I was not born for courts or great affairs;
I pay my debts, believe, and say my prayers;
Can sleep without a poem in my head,
Nor know if Dennis be alive or dead.

    Why am I asked what next shall see the light?
Heav'ns! was I born for nothing but to write?
Has life no joys for me? or (to be grave)
Have I no friend to serve, no soul to save?
'I found him close with Swift' – 'Indeed? no doubt
(Cries prating Balbus) something will come out.'
'Tis all in vain, deny it as I will:
'No, such a genius never can lie still';
And then for mine obligingly mistakes
The first lampoon Sir Will or Bubo makes.
Poor guiltless I! and can I choose but smile,
When every coxcomb knows me by my style?

    Cursed be the verse, how well soe'er it flow,
That tends to make one worthy man my foe,
Give virtue scandal, innocence a fear,
Or from the soft-eyed virgin steal a tear!
But he who hurts a harmless neighbour's peace,
Insults fall'n worth, or beauty in distress,
Who loves a lie, lame slander helps about,
Who writes a libel, or who copies out;
That fop whose pride affects a patron's name,
Yet absent, wounds an author's honest fame;
Who can your merit selfishly approve,
And show the sense of it without the love;
Who has the vanity to call you friend,
Yet wants the honour, injured, to defend;
Who tells whate'er you think, whate'er you say,
And, if he lie not, must at least betray;
Who to the dean and silver bell can swear,
And sees at Cannons what was never there;

270
280
290
300

Who reads but with a lust to misapply,
Make satire a lampoon, and fiction lie:
A lash like mine no honest man shall dread,
But all such babbling blockheads in his stead.

   Let Sporus tremble – 'What? that thing of silk,
Sporus, that mere white curd of asses' milk?'
Satire or sense, alas! can Sporus feel?
Who breaks a butterfly upon a wheel?
   Yet let me flap this bug with gilded wings,
This painted child of dirt, that stinks and stings;   310
Whose buzz the witty and the fair annoys,
Yet wit ne'er tastes, and beauty ne'er enjoys:
So well-bred spaniels civilly delight
In mumbling of the game they dare not bite.
Eternal smiles his emptiness betray,
As shallow streams run dimpling all the way.
Whether in florid impotence he speaks,
And, as the prompter breathes, the puppet squeaks,
Or at the ear of Eve, familiar toad,
Half froth, half venom, spits himself abroad   320
In puns, or politics, or tales, or lies,
Or spite, or smut, or rhymes, or blasphemies;
His wit all see-saw between that and this,
Now high, now low, now master up, now miss,
And he himself one vile antithesis.
Amphibious thing! that acting either part,
The trifling head, or the corrupted heart,
Fop at the toilet, flatt'rer at the board,
Now trips a lady, and now struts a lord.
Eve's tempter thus the rabbins have expressed: 330
A cherub's face, a reptile all the rest;
Beauty that shocks you, parts that none will trust,
Wit that can creep, and pride that licks the dust.
   Not Fortune's worshipper, nor fashion's fool,
Not lucre's madman, nor ambition's tool,
Not proud nor servile; be one poet's praise,
That if he pleased, he pleased by manly ways;

That flatt'ry, ev'n to kings, he held a shame,
And thought a lie in verse or prose the same;
340   That not in fancy's maze he wandered long,
But stooped to truth, and moralized his song;
That not for fame, but virtue's better end,
He stood the furious foe, the timid friend,
The damning critic, half-approving wit,
The coxcomb hit, or fearing to be hit;
Laughed at the loss of friends he never had,
The dull, the proud, the wicked, and the mad;
The distant threats of vengeance on his head,
The blow unfelt, the tear he never shed;
350   The tale revived, the lie so oft o'erthrown,
Th' imputed trash and dullness not his own;
The morals blackened when the writings 'scape,
The libelled person, and the pictured shape;
Abuse on all he loved, or loved him, spread,
A friend in exile, or a father dead;
The whisper, that to greatness still too near,
Perhaps yet vibrates on his sovereign's ear –
Welcome for thee, fair Virtue! all the past:
For thee, fair Virtue! welcome ev'n the last!
360   'But why insult the poor? affront the great?'
A knave's a knave to me in ev'ry state;
Alike my scorn, if he succeed or fail,
Sporus at court, or Japhet in a jail;
A hireling scribbler, or a hireling peer,
Knight of the post corrupt, or of the shire;
If on a pillory, or near a throne,
He gain his prince's ear, or lose his own.
Yet soft by nature, more a dupe than wit,
Sappho can tell you how this man was bit:
370   This dreaded sat'rist Dennis will confess
Foe to his pride, but friend to his distress:
So humble, he has knocked at Tibbald's door,
Has drunk with Cibber, nay, has rhymed for Moore.
Full ten years slandered, did he once reply?
Three thousand suns went down on Welsted's lie.

To please a mistress one aspersed his life;
He lashed him not, but let her be his wife:
Let Budgell charge low Grub Street on his quill,
And write whate'er he pleased, except his will;
Let the two Curlls of town and court abuse   380
His father, mother, body, soul, and muse:
Yet why? that father held it for a rule
It was a sin to call our neighbour fool;
That harmless mother thought no wife a whore;
Hear this, and spare his family, James Moore!
Unspotted names, and memorable long!
If there be force in virtue, or in song.
    Of gentle blood (part shed in Honour's cause,
While yet in Britain Honour had applause)
Each parent sprung – 'What fortune, pray?' – Their own;   390
And better got than Bestia's from the throne.
Born to no pride, inheriting no strife,
Nor marrying discord in a noble wife,
Stranger to civil and religious rage,
The good man walked innoxious through his age:
No courts he saw, no suits would ever try,
Nor dared an oath, nor hazarded a lie.
Unlearn'd, he knew no schoolman's subtle art,
No language but the language of the heart.
By nature honest, by experience wise,   400
Healthy by temp'rance and by exercise;
His life, though long, to sickness passed unknown,
His death was instant and without a groan.
O grant me thus to live, and thus to die!
Who sprung from kings shall know less joy than I.
    O friend! may each domestic bliss be thine!
Be no unpleasing melancholy mine:
Me, let the tender office long engage
To rock the cradle of reposing age,
With lenient arts extend a mother's breath,   410
Make languor smile, and smooth the bed of death;
Explore the thought, explain the asking eye,

And keep a while one parent from the sky!
On cares like these if length of days attend,
May Heav'n, to bless those days, preserve my friend!
Preserve him social, cheerful, and serene,
And just as rich as when he served a queen.
  Whether that blessing be denied or giv'n,
Thus far was right; the rest belongs to Heav'n.

[IMITATIONS OF HORACE]

Satire, II, i

To Mr Fortescue

P. There are (I scarce can think it, but am told),
There are to whom my satire seems too bold,
Scarce to wise Peter complaisant enough,
And something said of Chartres much too rough.
The lines are weak, another's pleased to say;
Lord Fanny spins a thousand such a day.
Tim'rous by nature, of the rich in awe,
I come to counsel learnèd in the law:
You'll give me, like a friend both sage and free,
Advice; and (as you use) without a fee.
  Fr. I'd write no more.
                          P. Not write? but then I think,
And for my soul I cannot sleep a wink.
I nod in company, I wake at night;
Fools rush into my head, and so I write.
  Fr. You could not do a worse thing for your life.
Why, if the night seem tedious – take a wife;
Or rather, truly, if your point be rest,
Lettuce and cowslip wine; *probatum est*.

But talk with Celsus, Celsus will advise
Hartshorn, or something that shall close your eyes.   20
Or if you needs must write, write Caesar's praise;
You'll gain at least a knighthood, or the bays.

   P. What? like Sir Richard, rumbling, rough, and fierce,
With arms, and George, and Brunswick, crowd the verse;
Rend with tremendous sound your ears asunder,
With gun, drum, trumpet, blunderbuss, and thunder?
Or nobly wild, with Budgell's fire and force,
Paint angels trembling round his falling horse?

   Fr. Then all your Muse's softer art display,
Let Carolina smooth the tuneful lay;   30
Lull with Amelia's liquid name the Nine,
And sweetly flow through all the royal line.

   P. Alas! few verses touch their nicer ear;
They scarce can bear their laureate twice a year;
And justly Caesar scorns the poet's lays;
It is to history he trusts for praise.

   Fr. Better be Cibber, I'll maintain it still,
Than ridicule all taste, blaspheme quadrille,
Abuse the city's best good men in metre,
And laugh at peers that put their trust in Peter.   40
Ev'n those you touch not, hate you.

                  P. What should ail 'em?

   Fr. A hundred smart in Timon and in Balaam:
The fewer still you name, you wound the more;
Bond is but one, but Harpax is a score.

   P. Each mortal has his pleasure: none deny
Scarsdale his bottle, Darty his ham-pie;
Ridotta sips and dances till she see
The doubling lustres dance as fast as she:
Fox loves the senate, Hockley Hole his brother,
Like in all else, as one egg to another.   50
I love to pour out all myself, as plain
As downright Shippen, or as old Montaigne:
In them, as certain to be loved as seen,
The soul stood forth, nor kept a thought within;

In me what spots (for spots I have) appear
Will prove at least the medium must be clear.
In this impartial glass, my Muse intends
Fair to expose myself, my foes, my friends;
Publish the present age, but where my text
60   Is vice too high, reserve it for the next;
My foes shall wish my life a longer date,
And ev'ry friend the less lament my fate.
My head and heart thus flowing through my quill,
Verse-man or prose-man, term me which you will,
Papist or Protestant, or both between,
Like good Erasmus, in an honest mean,
In moderation placing all my glory,
While Tories call me Whig, and Whigs a Tory.

        Satire's my weapon, but I'm too discreet
70   To run amuck, and tilt at all I meet;
I only wear it in a land of Hectors,
Thieves, supercargoes, sharpers, and directors.
Save but our army! and let Jove encrust
Swords, pikes, and guns, with everlasting rust!
Peace is my dear delight – not Fleury's more:
But touch me, and no minister so sore.
Whoe'er offends, at some unlucky time
Slides into verse, and hitches in a rhyme,
Sacred to ridicule his whole life long,
80   And the sad burden of some merry song.

        Slander or poison dread from Delia's rage;
Hard words or hanging, if your judge be Page;
From furious Sappho scarce a milder fate,
Poxed by her love, or libelled by her hate.
Its proper pow'r to hurt each creature feels;
Bulls aim their horns, and asses lift their heels;
'Tis a bear's talent not to kick, but hug;
And no man wonders he's not stung by pug.
So drink with Walters, or with Chartres eat,
90   They'll never poison you, they'll only cheat.

        Then, learned sir! (to cut the matter short)
Whate'er my fate, or well or ill at court,

Whether old age, with faint but cheerful ray,
Attends to gild the evening of my day,
Or death's black wing already be displayed
To wrap me in the universal shade;
Whether the darkened room to Muse invite,
Or whitened wall provoke the skewer to write:
In durance, exile, Bedlam, or the Mint,
Like Lee or Budgell, I will rhyme and print.   100

    Fr. Alas, young man, your days can ne'er be long:
In flow'r of age you perish for a song!
Plums and directors, Shylock and his wife,
Will club their testers now to take your life.

    P. What? armed for virtue when I point the pen,
Brand the bold front of shameless, guilty men,
Dash the proud gamester in his gilded car,
Bare the mean heart that lurks beneath a star;
Can there be wanting, to defend her cause,
Lights of the church, or guardians of the laws?   110
Could pensioned Boileau lash in honest strain
Flatt'rers and bigots ev'n in Louis' reign?
Could laureate Dryden pimp and friar engage,
Yet neither Charles nor James be in a rage?
And I not strip the gilding off a knave,
Unplaced, unpensioned, no man's heir, or slave?
I will, or perish in the gen'rous cause:
Hear this, and tremble! you, who 'scape the laws.
Yes, while I live, no rich or noble knave
Shall walk the world, in credit, to his grave: 120
To VIRTUE ONLY and HER FRIENDS, A FRIEND,
The world beside may murmur, or commend.
Know, all the distant din that world can keep
Rolls o'er my grotto, and but soothes my sleep.

    There my retreat the best companions grace,
Chiefs out of war, and statesmen out of place:
There St John mingles with my friendly bowl
The feast of reason and the flow of soul;
And he, whose lightning pierced th' Iberian lines,
Now forms my quincunx, and now ranks my vines,   130

Or tames the genius of the stubborn plain,
Almost as quickly as he conquered Spain.
  Envy must own, I live among the great
No pimp of pleasure, and no spy of state,
With eyes that pry not, tongue that ne'er repeats,
Fond to spread friendships, but to cover heats;
To help who want, to forward who excel;
This all who know me, know; who love me, tell;
And who unknown defame me, let them be
140 Scribblers or peers, alike are mob to me.
This is my plea, on this I rest my cause –
What saith my counsel learned in the laws?
  Fr. Your plea is good; but still I say, beware!
Laws are explained by men – so have a care.
It stands on record that in Richard's times
A man was hanged for very honest rhymes.
Consult the statute: *quart.* I think it is,
Edwardi sext. or *prim. et quint. Eliz.*
See *Libels, Satires* – here you have it – read.
150   *P.* Libels and satires! lawless things indeed!
But grave epistles, bringing vice to light,
Such as a king might read, a bishop write,
Such as Sir Robert would approve – *Fr.* Indeed!
The case is altered – you may then proceed.
In such a cause the plaintiff will be hissed,
My lords the judges laugh, and you're dismissed.

Satire, II, ii

To Mr Bethel

What, and how great, the virtue and the art
To live on little with a cheerful heart
(A doctrine sage, but truly none of mine),
Let's talk, my friends, but talk before we dine;

Not when a gilt buffet's reflected pride
Turns you from sound philosophy aside;
Not when from plate to plate your eyeballs roll,
And the brain dances to the mantling bowl.

Hear Bethel's sermon, one not versed in schools,
But strong in sense, and wise without the rules.   10
'Go work, hunt, exercise! (he thus began)
Then scorn a homely dinner if you can.
Your wine locked up, your butler strolled abroad,
Or fish denied (the river yet unthawed);
If then plain bread and milk will do the feat,
The pleasure lies in you, and not the meat.'

Preach as I please, I doubt our curious men
Will choose a pheasant still before a hen;
Yet hens of Guinea full as good I hold,
Except you eat the feathers, green and gold.   20
Of carps and mullets why prefer the great
(Though cut in pieces ere my lord can eat),
Yet for small turbots such esteem profess?
Because God made these large, the other less.

Oldfield, with more than harpy throat endued,
Cries, 'Send me, gods! a whole hog barbecued!'
O blast it, south winds! till a stench exhale,
Rank as the ripeness of a rabbit's tail.
By what criterion do you eat, d'ye think,
If this is prized for sweetness, that for stink?   30
When the tired glutton labours through a treat,
He finds no relish in the sweetest meat;
He calls for something bitter, something sour,
And the rich feast concludes extremely poor.
Cheap eggs, and herbs, and olives still we see;
Thus much is left of old simplicity!

The robin-redbreast till of late had rest,
And children sacred held a martin's nest,
Till beccaficos sold so dev'lish dear
To one that was, or would have been, a peer.   40
Let me extol a cat on oysters fed,
I'll have a party at the Bedford Head;

Or ev'n to crack live crawfish recommend;
I'd never doubt at court to make a friend!
 'Tis yet in vain, I own, to keep a pother
About one vice, and fall into the other:
Between excess and famine lies a mean;
Plain, but not sordid, though not splendid, clean.
 Avidien or his wife (no matter which,
50 For him you'll call a dog, and her a bitch)
Sell their presented partridges and fruits,
And humbly live on rabbits and on roots;
One half-pint bottle serves them both to dine,
And is at once their vinegar and wine.
But on some lucky day (as when they found
A lost bank-bill, or heard their son was drowned)
At such a feast, old vinegar to spare
Is what two souls so generous cannot bear:
Oil, though it stink, they drop by drop impart,
60 But souse the cabbage with a bounteous heart.
 He knows to live, who keeps the middle state,
And neither leans on this side, nor on that;
Nor stops, for one bad cork, his butler's pay,
Swears, like Albutius, a good cook away;
Nor lets, like Naevius, ev'ry error pass,
The musty wine, foul cloth, or greasy glass.
 Now hear what blessings temperance can bring
(Thus said our friend, and what he said I sing):
First health: the stomach (crammed from ev'ry dish,
70 A tomb of boiled and roast, and flesh and fish,
Where bile, and wind, and phlegm, and acid jar,
And all the man is one intestine war)
Remembers oft the schoolboy's simple fare,
The temp'rate sleeps, and spirits light as air.
 How pale, each worshipful and rev'rend guest
Rise from a clergy, or a City feast!
What life in all that ample body, say?
What heav'nly particle inspires the clay?
The soul subsides, and wickedly inclines
80 To seem but mortal, ev'n in sound divines.

On morning wings, how active springs the mind
That leaves the load of yesterday behind!
How easy ev'ry labour it pursues!
How coming to the poet ev'ry Muse!
Not but we may exceed, some holy time,
Or tired in search of truth, or search of rhyme;
Ill health some just indulgence may engage,
And more, the sickness of long life, old age:
For fainting age what cordial drop remains,
If our intemp'rate youth the vessel drains?   90

   Our fathers praised rank venison. You suppose,
Perhaps, young men! our fathers had no nose?
Not so: a buck was then a week's repast,
And 'twas their point, I ween, to make it last,
More pleased to keep it till their friends could come,
Than eat the sweetest by themselves at home.
Why had not I in those good times my birth,
Ere coxcomb-pies or coxcombs were on earth?

   Unworthy he, the voice of fame to hear,
That sweetest music to an honest ear   100
(For 'faith, Lord Fanny! you are in the wrong,
The world's good word is better than a song),
Who has not learned fresh sturgeon and ham-pie
Are no rewards for want, and infamy!
When luxury has licked up all thy pelf,
Cursed by thy neighbours, thy trustees, thyself,
To friends, to fortune, to mankind a shame,
Think how posterity will treat thy name;
And buy a rope, that future times may tell
Thou hast at least bestowed one penny well.   110

   'Right,' cries his Lordship, 'for a rogue in need
To have a taste, is insolence indeed:
In me 'tis noble, suits my birth and state,
My wealth unwieldy, and my heap too great.'
Then, like the sun, let bounty spread her ray,
And shine that superfluity away.
Oh impudence of wealth! with all thy store,
How dar'st thou let one worthy man be poor?

Shall half the new-built churches round thee fall?
120 Make quays, build bridges, or repair Whitehall;
Or to thy country let that heap be lent,
As Marlborough's was, but not at five per cent.
    Who thinks that Fortune cannot change her mind
Prepares a dreadful jest for all mankind.
And who stands safest? tell me, is it he
That spreads and swells in puffed prosperity,
Or blessed with little, whose preventing care
In peace provides fit arms against a war?
    Thus Bethel spoke, who always speaks his thought,
130 And always thinks the very thing he ought.
His equal mind I copy what I can,
And as I love, would imitate the man.
In South Sea days, not happier, when surmised
The lord of thousands, than if now excised;
In forest planted by a father's hand,
Than in five acres now of rented land.
Content with little, I can piddle here
On broccoli and mutton, round the year;
But ancient friends (though poor, or out of play)
140 That touch my bell, I cannot turn away.
'Tis true, no turbots dignify my boards,
But gudgeons, flounders, what my Thames affords;
To Hounslow Heath I point, and Bansted Down,
Thence comes your mutton, and these chicks my own;
From yon old walnut tree a show'r shall fall,
And grapes, long ling'ring on my only wall,
And figs from standard and espalier join;
The devil is in you if you cannot dine.
Then cheerful healths (your mistress shall have place),
150 And, what's more rare, a poet shall say grace.
    Fortune not much of humbling me can boast
Though double taxed, how little have I lost!
My life's amusements have been just the same,
Before, and after standing armies came.

My lands are sold, my father's house is gone;
I'll hire another's; is not that my own,
And yours, my friends? through whose free opening gate
None comes too early, none departs too late
(For I, who hold sage Homer's rule the best,
Welcome the coming, speed the going guest.)   160
   'Pray heav'n it last!' cries Swift, 'as you go on;
I wish to God this house had been your own.
Pity! to build, without a son or wife:
Why, you'll enjoy it only all your life.'
Well, if the use be mine, can it concern one
Whether the name belong to Pope or Vernon?
What's property? dear Swift! you see it alter
From you to me, from me to Peter Walter;
Or in a mortgage prove a lawyer's share,
Or in a jointure vanish from the heir;   170
Or in pure equity (the case not clear)
The Chanc'ry takes your rents for twenty year:
At best, it falls to some ungracious son,
Who cries, 'My father's damned, and all's my own.'
Shades, that to Bacon could retreat afford,
Become the portion of a booby lord;
And Helmsley, once proud Buckingham's delight,
Slides to a scriv'ner or a City knight.
Let lands and houses have what lords they will,
Let us be fixed, and our own masters still.   180

Epistle, I, i

To Lord Bolingbroke

St John, whose love indulged my labours past,
Matures my present, and shall bound my last!
Why will you break the sabbath of my days?
Now sick alike of envy and of praise.

Public too long, ah let me hide my age!
See modest Cibber now has left the stage:
Our gen'rals now, retired to their estates,
Hang their old trophies o'er the garden gates,
In life's cool evening satiate of applause,
Nor fond of bleeding ev'n in Brunswick's cause.

    A voice there is, that whispers in my ear
('Tis reason's voice, which sometimes one can hear),
'Friend Pope! be prudent, let your Muse take breath,
And never gallop Pegasus to death;
Lest stiff and stately, void of fire or force,
You limp, like Blackmore, on a Lord Mayor's horse.'

    Farewell then verse, and love, and ev'ry toy,
The rhymes and rattles of the man or boy;
What right, what true, what fit, we justly call,
Let this be all my care – for this is all;
To lay this harvest up, and hoard with haste
What ev'ry day will want, and most, the last.

    But ask not, to what doctors I apply;
Sworn to no master, of no sect am I:
As drives the storm, at any door I knock,
And house with Montaigne now, or now with Locke.
Sometimes a Patriot, active in debate,
Mix with the world, and battle for the state;
Free as young Lyttelton, her cause pursue,
Still true to virtue, and as warm as true;
Sometimes with Aristippus, or St Paul,
Indulge my candour, and grow all to all:
Back to my native moderation slide,
And win my way by yielding to the tide.

    Long, as to him who works for debt, the day;
Long as the night to her whose love's away;
Long as the year's dull circle seems to run
When the brisk minor pants for twenty-one;
So slow th' unprofitable moments roll
That lock up all the functions of my soul,
That keep me from myself, and still delay
Life's instant business to a future day:

That task which, as we follow, or despise,
The eldest is a fool, the youngest wise;
Which done, the poorest can no wants endure,
And which not done, the richest must be poor.
  Late as it is, I put myself to school,
And feel some comfort not to be a fool.
Weak though I am of limb, and short of sight,
Far from a lynx, and not a giant quite,   50
I'll do what Mead and Cheselden advise
To keep these limbs, and to preserve these eyes.
Not to go back, is somewhat to advance,
And men must walk at least before they dance.
  Say, does thy blood rebel, thy bosom move
With wretched av'rice, or as wretched love?
Know, there are words, and spells, which can control,
Between the fits, this fever of the soul;
Know, there are rhymes, which fresh and fresh applied,
Will cure the arrant'st puppy of his pride.   60
Be furious, envious, slothful, mad, or drunk,
Slave to a wife, or vassal to a punk,
A Switz, a High Dutch, or a Low Dutch bear;
All that we ask is but a patient ear.
  'Tis the first virtue, vices to abhor,
And the first wisdom, to be fool no more,
But to the world no bugbear is so great
As want of figure, and a small estate.
To either India see the merchant fly,
Scared at the spectre of pale poverty!   70
See him, with pains of body, pangs of soul,
Burn through the tropic, freeze beneath the pole!
Wilt thou do nothing for a nobler end,
Nothing to make philosophy thy friend?
To stop thy foolish views, thy long desires,
And ease thy heart of all that it admires?
  Here, Wisdom calls: 'Seek virtue first, be bold!
As gold to silver, virtue is to gold.'
There, London's voice: 'Get money, money still!
And then let virtue follow, if she will.'   80

This, this the saving doctrine preached to all,
From low St James's up to high St Paul;
From him whose quills stand quivered at his ear,
To him who notches sticks at Westminster.

Barnard in spirit, sense, and truth abounds;
'Pray then, what wants he?' Fourscore thousand pounds,
A pension, or such harness for a slave
As Bug now has, and Dorimant would have.
Barnard, thou art a cit, with all thy worth;
90   But wretched Bug, his Honour, and so forth.

Yet every child another song will sing,
'Virtue, brave boys! 'tis virtue makes a king.'
True, conscious honour is to feel no sin;
He's armed without that's innocent within:
Be this thy screen, and this thy wall of brass;
Compared to this, a minister's an ass.

And say, to which shall our applause belong,
This new court jargon, or the good old song?
The modern language of corrupted peers,
100   Or what was spoke at Cressy and Poitiers?
Who counsels best? who whispers, 'Be but great,
With praise or infamy, leave that to fate;
Get place and wealth, if possible, with grace;
If not, by any means get wealth and place.'
For what? to have a box where eunuchs sing,
And foremost in the circle eye a king.
Or he, who bids thee face with steady view
Proud fortune, and look shallow greatness through, }
And, while he bids thee, sets th' example too?
110   If such a doctrine, in St James's air,
Should chance to make the well-dressed rabble stare;
If honest Schutz take scandal at a spark
That less admires the palace than the park;
Faith, I shall give the answer Reynard gave:
'I cannot like, dread sir! your royal cave;
Because I see, by all the tracks about,
Full many a beast goes in, but none comes out.'

Adieu to Virtue if you're once a slave:
Send her to Court, you send her to her grave.
    Well, if a king's a lion, at the least   120
The people are a many-headed beast;
Can they direct what measures to pursue
Who know themselves so little what to do?
Alike in nothing but one lust of gold,
Just half the land would buy, and half be sold:
Their country's wealth our mightier misers drain,
Or cross, to plunder provinces, the main;
The rest, some farm the poor-box, some the pews;
Some keep assemblies, and would keep the stews;
Some with fat bucks on childless dotards fawn;   130
Some win rich widows by their chine and brawn;
While with the silent growth of ten per cent
In dirt and darkness hundreds stink content.
    Of all these ways, if each pursues his own,
Satire, be kind, and let the wretch alone;
But show me one who has it in his pow'r
To act consistent with himself an hour.
Sir Job sailed forth, the evening bright and still,
'No place on earth (he cried) like Greenwich Hill!'
Up starts a palace: lo! th' obedient base   140
Slopes at its foot, the woods its sides embrace,
The silver Thames reflects its marble face.
Now let some whimsy, or that devil within
Which guides all those who know not what they mean,
But give the knight (or give his lady) spleen;
'Away, away! take all your scaffolds down,
For snug's the word, my dear! we'll live in town.'
    At am'rous Flavio is the stocking thrown?
That very night he longs to lie alone.
The fool whose wife elopes some thrice a quarter,   150
For matrimonial solace dies a martyr.
Did ever Proteus, Merlin, any witch,
Transform themselves so strangely as the rich?
'Well, but the poor' – the poor have the same itch:

They change their weekly barber, weekly news,
Prefer a new japanner to their shoes,
Discharge their garrets, move their beds, and run
(They know not whither) in a chaise and one;
They hire their sculler, and when once aboard,
160   Grow sick, and damn the climate – like a lord.
     You laugh, half-beau, half-sloven if I stand,
My wig all powder, and all snuff my band;
You laugh, if coat and breeches strangely vary,
White gloves, and linen worthy Lady Mary!
But when no prelate's lawn, with hair-shirt lined,
Is half so incoherent as my mind,
When (each opinion with the next at strife,
One ebb and flow of follies all my life),
I plant, root up; I build, and then confound;
170   Turn round to square, and square again to round;
You never change one muscle of your face,
You think this madness but a common case;
Nor once to Chanc'ry, nor to Hales apply,
Yet hang your lip to see a seam awry!
Careless how ill I with myself agree,
Kind to my dress, my figure, not to me.
Is this my guide, philosopher, and friend?
This, he who loves me, and who ought to mend?
Who ought to make me (what he can, or none),
180   That man divine whom wisdom calls her own;
Great without title, without fortune blessed;
Rich ev'n when plundered, honoured while oppressed;
Loved without youth, and followed without power,
At home though exiled; free, though in the Tower:
In short, that reas'ning, high, immortal thing,
Just less than Jove, and much above a king;
Nay, half in Heav'n – except (what's mighty odd)
A fit of vapours clouds this demigod.

Epistle, II, i

ADVERTISEMENT

The reflections of Horace, and the judgements passed in his epistle to Augustus, seemed so seasonable to the present times that I could not help applying them to the use of my own country. The author thought them considerable enough to address them to his prince, whom he paints with all the great and good qualities of a monarch upon whom the Romans depended for the increase of an absolute empire. But to make the poem entirely English, I was willing to add one or two of those virtues which contribute to the happiness of a free people, and are more consistent with the welfare of our neighbours.

This epistle will show the learned world to have fallen into two mistakes: one, that Augustus was a patron of poets in general; whereas he not only prohibited all but the best writers to name him, but recommended that care even to the civil magistrate, *Admonebat praetores, ne paterentur nomen suum obsolefieri,* etc., the other, that this piece was only a general discourse of poetry; whereas it was an apology for the poets, in order to render Augustus more their patron. Horace here pleads the cause of his contemporaries: first, against the taste of the town, whose humour it was to magnify the authors of the preceding age; secondly, against the court and nobility, who encouraged only the writers for the theatre; and lastly, against the emperor himself, who had conceived them of little use to the government. He shows (by a view of the progress of learning, and the change of taste among the Romans) that the introduction of the polite arts of Greece had given the writers of his time great advantages over their predecessors; that their morals were much improved, and the licence of those ancient poets restrained; that satire and comedy were become more just and useful; that whatever extravagancies were left on the stage were owing to the ill taste of the nobility; that poets, under due regulations, were in many respects useful to the state; and concludes, that it was upon them the emperor himself must depend for his fame with posterity.

We may farther learn from this Epistle, that Horace made his court to this great prince by writing with a decent freedom toward him, with a just contempt of his low flatterers, and with a manly regard to his own character.

To Augustus

Ne rubeam, pingui donatus munere!

While you, great patron of mankind! sustain
The balanced world, and open all the main;
Your country, chief, in arms abroad defend,
At home with morals, arts, and laws amend;
How shall the Muse, from such a monarch, steal
An hour, and not defraud the public weal?
  Edward and Henry, now the boast of fame,
And virtuous Alfred, a more sacred name,
After a life of gen'rous toils endured,
The Gaul subdued, or property secured,
Ambition humbled, mighty cities stormed,
Or laws established, and the world reformed;
Closed their long glories with a sigh, to find
Th' unwilling gratitude of base mankind!
All human virtue, to its latest breath,
Finds envy never conquered but by death;
The great Alcides, ev'ry labour past,
Had still this monster to subdue at last.
Sure fate of all, beneath whose rising ray
Each star of meaner merit fades away!
Oppressed we feel the beam directly beat;
Those suns of glory please not till they set.
  To thee the world its present homage pays,
The harvest early, but mature the praise:
Great friend of Liberty! in kings a name
Above all Greek, above all Roman fame:
Whose word is truth, as sacred and revered
As Heaven's own oracles from altars heard.

Wonder of kings! like whom, to mortal eyes,
None e'er has risen, and none e'er shall rise.   30

   Just in one instance, be it yet confessed
Your people, sir, are partial in the rest;
Foes to all living worth except your own,
And advocates for folly dead and gone.
Authors, like coins, grow dear as they grow old;
It is the rust we value, not the gold.
Chaucer's worst ribaldry is learned by rote,
And beastly Skelton heads of houses quote.
One likes no language but the *Faery Queen*;
A Scot will fight for *Christ's Kirk o' the Green*;   40
And each true Briton is to Ben so civil,
He swears the Muses met him at the Devil.

   Though justly Greece her eldest sons admires,
Why should not we be wiser than our sires?
In ev'ry public virtue we excel,
We build, we paint, we sing, we dance as well;
And learnèd Athens to our art must stoop,
Could she behold us tumbling through a hoop.

   If time improve our wit as well as wine,
Say at what age a poet grows divine?   50
Shall we, or shall we not, account him so,
Who died, perhaps, a hundred years ago?
End all dispute, and fix the year precise
When British bards begin t' immortalize?

   'Who lasts a century can have no flaw;
I hold that wit a classic, good in law.'

   Suppose he wants a year, will you compound?
And shall we deem him ancient, right and sound,
Or damn to all eternity at once,
At ninety-nine, a modern and a dunce?   60

   'We shall not quarrel for a year or two;
By Courtesy of England, he may do.'

   Then, by the rule that made the horsetail bare,
I pluck out year by year, as hair by hair,
And melt down ancients like a heap of snow,
While you, to measure merits, look in Stow,

And estimating authors by the year
Bestow a garland only on a bier.

70 Shakespeare (whom you and every playhouse bill
Style the divine, the matchless, what you will)
For gain, not glory, winged his roving flight,
And grew immortal in his own despite.
Ben, old and poor, as little seemed to heed
The life to come, in ev'ry poet's creed.
Who now reads Cowley? if he pleases yet
His moral pleases, not his pointed wit;
Forgot his epic, nay Pindaric art,
But still I love the language of his heart.

80 'Yet surely, surely these were famous men!
What boy but hears the sayings of old Ben?
In all debates where critics bear a part,
Not one but nods, and talks of Jonson's art,
Of Shakespeare's nature, and of Cowley's wit;
How Beaumont's judgement checked what Fletcher writ;
How Shadwell hasty, Wycherley was slow;
But for the passions, Southerne sure, and Rowe.
These, only these, support the crowded stage
From eldest Heywood down to Cibber's age.'

90 All this may be; the people's voice is odd,
It is, and it is not, the voice of God.
To *Gammer Gurton* if it give the bays,
And yet deny the *Careless Husband* praise,
Or say our fathers never broke a rule;
Why then, I say, the public is a fool.
But let them own that greater faults than we
They had, and greater virtues, I'll agree.
Spenser himself affects the obsolete,
And Sidney's verse halts ill on Roman feet;
Milton's strong pinion now not Heav'n can bound,

100 Now serpent-like, in prose he sweeps the ground;
In quibbles, angel and archangel join,
And God the Father turns a school-divine.
Not that I'd lop the beauties from his book,
Like slashing Bentley with his desp'rate hook;

Or damn all Shakespeare, like th' affected fool
At court, who hates whate'er he read at school.
   But for the wits of either Charles's days,
The mob of gentlemen who wrote with ease,
Sprat, Carew, Sedley, and a hundred more
(Like twinkling stars the miscellanies o'er),   110
One simile that solitary shines
In the dry desert of a thousand lines,
Or lengthened thought that gleams through many a page,
Has sanctified whole poems for an age.
I lose my patience, and I own it too,
When works are censured, not as bad, but new;
While if our elders break all reason's laws,
These fools demand not pardon, but applause.
   On Avon's bank, where flow'rs eternal blow,
If I but ask, if any weed can grow,   120
One tragic sentence if I dare deride
Which Betterton's grave action dignified,
Or well-mouthed Booth with emphasis proclaims
(Though but perhaps a muster-roll of names),
How will our fathers rise up in a rage
And swear all shame is lost in George's age!
You'd think no fools disgraced the former reign,
Did not some grave examples yet remain,
Who scorn a lad should teach his father skill,
And, having once been wrong, will be so still.   130
He, who to seem more deep than you or I
Extols old bards, or Merlin's prophecy,
Mistake him not; he envies, not admires,
And to debase the sons, exalts the sires.
Had ancient times conspired to disallow
What then was new, what had been ancient now?
Or what remained, so worthy to be read
By learnèd critics, of the mighty dead?
   In days of ease, when now the weary sword
Was sheathed, and luxury with Charles restored;   140
In ev'ry taste of foreign courts improved,
'All by the king's example lived and loved.'

Then peers grew proud in horsemanship t' excel,
Newmarket's glory rose, as Britain's fell;
The soldier breathed the gallantries of France,
And ev'ry flow'ry courtier writ romance.
Then marble, soften'd into life, grew warm,
And yielding metal flowed to human form:
Lely on animated canvas stole
150   The sleepy eye, that spoke the melting soul.
No wonder then, when all was love and sport,
The willing Muses were debauched at court;
On each enervate string they taught the note
To pant, or tremble through a eunuch's throat.
       But Britain, changeful as a child at play,
Now calls in princes, and now turns away.
Now Whig, now Tory, what we loved we hate;
Now all for pleasure, now for church and state;
Now for prerogative, and now for laws;
160   Effects unhappy! from a noble cause.
       Time was, a sober Englishman would knock
His servants up, and rise by five o'clock,
Instruct his family in ev'ry rule,
And send his wife to church, his son to school.
To worship like his fathers was his care;
To teach their frugal virtues to his heir;
To prove that luxury could never hold,
And place on good security his gold.
Now times are changed, and one poetic itch
170   Has seized the court and City, poor and rich.
Sons, sires, and grandsires, all will wear the bays;
Our wives read Milton, and our daughters plays;
To theatres and to rehearsals throng,
And all our grace at table is a song.
I, who so oft renounce the Muses, lie,
Not —'s self e'er tells more fibs than I;
When sick of Muse, our follies we deplore,
And promise our best friends to rhyme no more;
We wake next morning in a raging fit
180   And call for pen and ink to show our wit.

He served a 'prenticeship who sets up shop;
Ward tried on puppies, and the poor, his drop;
Ev'n Radcliffe's doctors travel first to France,
Nor dare to practise till they've learned to dance;
Who builds a bridge that never drove a pile?
(Should Ripley venture, all the world would smile).
But those who cannot write, and those who can,
All rhyme, and scrawl, and scribble, to a man.

Yet, sir, reflect; the mischief is not great;
These madmen never hurt the church or state: 190
Sometimes the folly benefits mankind,
And rarely av'rice taints the tuneful mind.
Allow him but his plaything of a pen,
He ne'er rebels, or plots, like other men:
Flight of cashiers, or mobs, he'll never mind,
And knows no losses while the Muse is kind.
To cheat a friend, or ward, he leaves to Peter,
The good man heaps up nothing but mere metre,
Enjoys his garden and his book in quiet;
And then – a perfect hermit in his diet.   200

Of little use the man, you may suppose,
Who says in verse what others say in prose;
Yet let me show a poet's of some weight,
And (though no soldier) useful to the state.
What will a child learn sooner than a song?
What better teach a foreigner the tongue?
What's long or short, each accent where to place,
And speak in public with some sort of grace?
I scarce can think him such a worthless thing,
Unless he praise some monster of a king;   210
Or virtue or religion turn to sport,
To please a lewd or unbelieving court.
Unhappy Dryden! – In all Charles's days
Roscommon only boasts unspotted bays;
And in our own (excuse some courtly stains)
No whiter page than Addison remains.
He from the taste obscene reclaims our youth,
And sets the passions on the side of truth,

Forms the soft bosom with the gentlest art,
And pours each human virtue in the heart.
Let Ireland tell how wit upheld her cause,
Her trade supported, and supplied her laws;
And leave on Swift this grateful verse engraved,
'The rights a court attacked, a poet saved.'
Behold the hand that wrought a nation's cure
Stretched to relieve the idiot and the poor,
Proud vice to brand, or injured worth adorn,
And stretch the ray to ages yet unborn.
Not but there are, who merit other palms;
Hopkins and Sternhold glad the heart with psalms;
The boys and girls whom charity maintains
Implore your help in these pathetic strains;
How could devotion touch the country pews
Unless the gods bestowed a proper muse?
Verse cheers their leisure, verse assists their work,
Verse prays for peace, or sings down pope and Turk.
The silenced preacher yields to potent strain,
And feels that grace his pray'r besought in vain;
The blessing thrills through all the lab'ring throng,
And Heav'n is won by violence of song.
      Our rural ancestors, with little blest,
Patient of labour when the end was rest,
Indulged the day that housed their annual grain
With feasts, and off'rings, and a thankful strain.
The joy their wives, their sons, and servants share,
Ease of their toil, and partners of their care;
The laugh, the jest, attendants on the bowl,
Smoothed ev'ry brow, and opened ev'ry soul;
With growing years the pleasing licence grew,
And taunts alternate innocently flew.
But times corrupt, and Nature, ill inclined,
Produced the point that left a sting behind,
Till friend with friend, and families at strife,
Triumphant malice raged through private life.
Who felt the wrong, or feared it, took th' alarm,
Appealed to law, and Justice lent her arm.

At length, by wholesome dread of statutes bound,
The poets learned to please, and not to wound.
Most warped to flatt'ry's side; but some, more nice,
Preserved the freedom, and forbore the vice.   260
Hence Satire rose, that just the medium hit,
And heals with morals what it hurts with wit.
We conquered France, but felt our captive's charms;
Her arts victorious triumphed o'er our arms;
Britain to soft refinements less a foe,
Wit grew polite, and numbers learned to flow.
Waller was smooth; but Dryden taught to join ⎫
The varying verse, the full resounding line,   ⎬
The long majestic march, and energy divine;   ⎭
Though still some traces of our rustic vein   270
And splay-foot verse remained, and will remain.
Late, very late, correctness grew our care,
When the tired nation breathed from civil war;
Exact Racine, and Corneille's noble fire,
Showed us that France had something to admire.
Not but the tragic spirit was our own,
And full in Shakespeare, fair in Otway shone;
But Otway failed to polish or refine,
And fluent Shakespeare scarce effaced a line.
Ev'n copious Dryden wanted, or forgot,   280
The last and greatest art, the art to blot.
   Some doubt if equal pains or equal fire
The humbler muse of comedy require?
But in known images of life I guess
The labour greater, as th' indulgence less.
Observe how seldom ev'n the best succeed:
Tell me if Congreve's fools are fools indeed?
What pert low dialogue has Farquhar writ!
How Van wants grace, who never wanted wit!
The stage how loosely does Astraea tread,   290
Who fairly puts all characters to bed!
And idle Cibber, how he breaks the laws,
To make poor Pinky eat with vast applause!

But fill their purse, our poet's work is done,
Alike to them, by pathos or by pun.
    O you! whom Vanity's light bark conveys
On Fame's mad voyage by the wind of praise,
With what a shifting gale your course you ply,
Forever sunk too low, or borne too high!
300   Who pants for glory finds but short repose;
A breath revives him, or a breath o'erthrows.
Farewell the stage! if just as thrives the play
The silly bard grows fat, or falls away.
    There still remains, to mortify a wit,
The many-headed monster of the pit:
A senseless, worthless, and unhonoured crowd,
Who, to disturb their betters, mighty proud,
Clatt'ring their sticks before ten lines are spoke,
Call for the farce, the bear, or the Black Joke.
310   What dear delight to Britons farce affords!
Ever the taste of mobs, but now of lords
(Taste, that eternal wanderer, which flies
From heads to ears, and now from ears to eyes).
The play stands still; damn action and discourse,
Back fly the scenes, and enter foot and horse;
Pageants on pageants, in long order drawn,
Peers, heralds, bishops, ermine, gold, and lawn;
The Champion too! and, to complete the jest,
Old Edward's armour beams on Cibber's breast!
320   With laughter sure Democritus had died,
Had he beheld an audience gape so wide.
Let bear or elephant be e'er so white,
The people, sure, the people are the sight!
Ah luckless poet! stretch thy lungs and roar,
That bear or elephant shall heed thee more;
While all its throats the gallery extends,
And all the thunder of the pit ascends!
Loud as the wolves, on Orcas' stormy steep,
Howl to the roarings of the northern deep:
330   Such is the shout, the long applauding note,
At Quin's high plume, or Oldfield's petticoat;

Or when from court a birthday suit bestowed
Sinks the lost actor in the tawdry load.
Booth enters – hark! the universal peal!
'But has he spoken?' Not a syllable.
'What shook the stage, and made the people stare?'
Cato's long wig, flower'd gown, and lacquered chair.

   Yet lest you think I rally more than teach,
Or praise malignly arts I cannot reach,
Let me for once presume t' instruct the times,   340
To know the poet from the man of rhymes:
'Tis he who gives my breast a thousand pains,
Can make me feel each passion that he feigns;
Enrage, compose, with more than magic art,
With pity, and with terror, tear my heart,
And snatch me o'er the earth, or through the air,
To Thebes, to Athens, when he will, and where.

   But not this part of the poetic state
Alone deserves the favour of the great.
Think of those authors, sir, who would rely   350
More on a reader's sense, than gazer's eye.
Or who shall wander where the Muses sing?
Who climb their mountain, or who taste their spring?
How shall we fill a library with wit,
When Merlin's cave is half unfurnished yet?

   My liege! why writers little claim your thought,
I guess, and, with their leave, will tell the fault:
We poets are (upon a poet's word)
Of all mankind, the creatures most absurd:
The season when to come, and when to go,   360
To sing, or cease to sing, we never know;
And if we will recite nine hours in ten,
You lose your patience, just like other men.
Then too we hurt ourselves when, to defend
A single verse, we quarrel with a friend;
Repeat unasked; lament, the wit's too fine
For vulgar eyes, and point out ev'ry line:
But most, when straining with too weak a wing,
We needs will write epistles to the king;

370   And from the moment we oblige the town,
Expect a place or pension from the crown;
Or dubbed historians by express command,
T' enrol your triumphs o'er the seas and land,
Be called to court to plan some work divine,
As once for Louis, Boileau and Racine.
     Yet think, great sir! (so many virtues shown)
Ah think! what poet best may make them known?
Or choose at least some minister of grace
Fit to bestow the laureate's weighty place.
380   Charles, to late times to be transmitted fair,
Assigned his figure to Bernini's care;
And great Nassau to Kneller's hand decreed
To fix him graceful on the bounding steed;
So well in paint and stone they judged of merit:
But kings in wit may want discerning spirit.
The hero William, and the martyr Charles,
One knighted Blackmore, and one pensioned Quarles,
Which made old Ben and surly Dennis swear
'No Lord's anointed, but a Russian bear.'
390   Not with such majesty, such bold relief,
The forms august of king, or conquering chief,
E'er swelled on marble, as in verse have shined
(In polished verse) the manners and the mind.
Oh! could I mount on the Maeonian wing,
Your arms, your actions, your repose to sing!
What seas you traversed, and what fields you fought!
Your country's peace, how oft, how dearly bought!
How barb'rous rage subsided at your word,
And nations wondered while they dropped the sword!
400   How, when you nodded, o'er the land and deep
Peace stole her wing, and wrapped the world in sleep,
Till earth's extremes your mediation own,
And Asia's tyrants tremble at your throne –
But verse, alas! your Majesty disdains,
And I'm not used to panegyric strains.
The zeal of fools offends at any time,
But most of all, the zeal of fools in rhyme.

Besides, a fate attends on all I write,
That when I aim at praise they say I bite.
A vile encomium doubly ridicules;   410
There's nothing blackens like the ink of fools.
If true, a woeful likeness; and if lies,
'Praise undeserved is scandal in disguise.'
Well may he blush, who gives it, or receives;
And when I flatter, let my dirty leaves
(Like journals, odes, and such forgotten things,
As Eusden, Philips, Settle, writ of kings)
Clothe spice, line trunks, or fluttering in a row,
Befringe the rails of Bedlam and Soho.

Epistle, II, ii

Ludentis speciem dabit et torquebitur.

Dear Colonel, Cobham's and your country's friend!
You love a verse; take such as I can send.
   A Frenchman comes, presents you with his boy,
Bows and begins – 'This lad, sir, is of Blois:
Observe his shape how clean! his locks how curled!
My only son, I'd have him see the world.
His French is pure; his voice too – you shall hear –
Sir, he's your slave, for twenty pound a year.
Mere wax as yet, you fashion him with ease,
Your barber, cook, upholst'rer; what you please: 10
A perfect genius at an opera song –
To say too much might do my honour wrong.
Take him with all his virtues on my word;
His whole ambition was to serve a lord;
But, sir, to you with what would I not part?
Though faith, I fear 'twill break his mother's heart.
Once (and but once) I caught him in a lie,
And then, unwhipped, he had the grace to cry:

The fault he has I fairly shall reveal,
20 (Could you o'erlook but that) – it is to steal.'
    If, after this, you took the graceless lad,
Could you complain, my friend, he proved so bad?
Faith, in such case, if you should prosecute,
I think Sir Godfrey should decide the suit;
Who sent the thief that stole the cash away,
And punished him that put it in his way.
    Consider then, and judge me in this light;
I told you when I went, I could not write;
You said the same; and are you discontent
30 With laws to which you gave your own assent?
Nay, worse, to ask for verse at such a time!
D'ye think me good for nothing but to rhyme?
    In Anna's wars a soldier, poor and old,
Had dearly earned a little purse of gold:
Tired in a tedious march, one luckless night
He slept, poor dog! and lost it to a doit.
This put the man in such a desp'rate mind, ⎫
Between revenge, and grief, and hunger joined, ⎬
Against the foe, himself, and all mankind, ⎭
40 He leapt the trenches, scaled a castle wall,
Tore down a standard, took the fort and all.
'Prodigious well!' his great commander cried,
Gave him much praise, and some reward beside.
Next pleased his Excellence a town to batter
(Its name I know not, and 'tis no great matter);
'Go on, my friend (he cried), see yonder walls!
Advance and conquer! go where glory calls!
More honours, more rewards, attend the brave.'
Don't you remember what reply he gave?
50 'D'ye think me, noble gen'ral, such a sot?
Let him take castles who has ne'er a groat.'
    Bred up at home, full early I begun
To read in Greek the wrath of Peleus' son.
Besides, my father taught me from a lad
The better art, to know the good from bad
(And little sure imported to remove,
To hunt for truth in Maudlin's learned grove).

But knottier points we knew not half so well
Deprived us soon of our paternal cell;
And certain laws, by suff'rers thought unjust,   60
Denied all posts of profit or of trust:
Hopes after hopes of pious papists failed,
While mighty William's thund'ring arm prevailed.
For right hereditary taxed and fined,
He stuck to poverty with peace of mind;
And me, the Muses helped to undergo it;
Convict a papist he, and I a poet.
But (thanks to Homer) since I live and thrive,
Indebted to no prince or peer alive,
Sure I should want the care of ten Munros,   70
If I would scribble rather than repose.

Years foll'wing years steal something ev'ry day;
At last they steal us from ourselves away.
In one our frolics, one amusements end,
In one a mistress drops, in one a friend.
This subtle thief of life, this paltry time,
What will it leave me, if it snatch my rhyme?
If ev'ry wheel of that unwearied mill
That turned ten thousand verses, now stands still.

But after all, what would ye have me do,   80
When out of twenty I can please not two?
When this, heroics only deigns to praise,
Sharp satire that, and that Pindaric lays?
One likes the pheasant's wing, and one the leg;
The vulgar boil, the learnèd roast an egg;
Hard task to hit the palate of such guests,
When Oldfield loves what Dartineuf detests!

But grant I may relapse, for want of grace,
Again to rhyme, can London be the place?
Who there his Muse, or self, or soul attends,   90
In crowds, and courts, law, business, feasts, and friends?
My counsel sends to execute a deed;
A poet begs me I will hear him read:
'In Palace Yard at nine you'll find me there –
At ten for certain, sir, in Bloomsb'ry Square –

Before the lords at twelve my cause comes on –
There's a rehearsal, sir, exact at one.' –
'Oh, but a wit can study in the streets,
And raise his mind above the mob he meets.'
100 Not quite so well however as one ought;
A hackney coach may chance to spoil a thought;
And then a nodding beam, or pig of lead,
God knows, may hurt the very ablest head.
Have you not seen, at Guildhall's narrow pass,
Two aldermen dispute it with an ass?
And peers give way, exalted as they are,
Ev'n to their own s-r-v–nce in a car?

   Go, lofty poet! and in such a crowd
Sing thy sonorous verse – but not aloud.
110 Alas! to grottos and to groves we run
To ease and silence, ev'ry Muse's son:
Blackmore himself, for any grand effort,
Would drink and doze at Tooting or Earl's Court.
How shall I rhyme in this eternal roar?
How match the bards whom none e'er matched before?
The man who, stretched in Isis' calm retreat,
To books and study gives sev'n years complete,
See! strewed with learnèd dust, his nightcap on,
He walks, an object new beneath the sun!
120 The boys flock round him, and the people stare: ⎤
So stiff, so mute some statue you would swear, ⎬
Stepped from its pedestal to take the air. ⎦
And here, while town, and court, and City roars,
With mobs, and duns, and soldiers, at their doors,
Shall I in London act this idle part,
Composing songs for fools to get by heart?

   The Temple late two brother sergeants saw,
Who deemed each other oracles of law;
With equal talents, these congenial souls,
130 One lulled th' Exchequer, and one stunned the Rolls;
Each had a gravity would make you split,
And shook his head at Murray, as a wit.

'Twas, 'Sir, your law' – and 'Sir, your eloquence',
'Yours, Cowper's manner' – and 'Yours, Talbot's sense.'
    Thus we dispose of all poetic merit,
Yours Milton's genius, and mine Homer's spirit.
Call Tibbald Shakespeare, and he'll swear the Nine,
Dear Cibber! never matched one ode of thine.
Lord! how we strut through Merlin's cave, to see
No poets there, but Stephen, you, and me.   140
Walk with respect behind, while we at ease
Weave laurel crowns, and take what names we please.
'My dear Tibullus!' if that will not do,
'Let me be Horace, and be Ovid you:
Or, I'm content, allow me Dryden's strains,
And you shall rise up Otway for your pains.'
Much do I suffer, much, to keep in peace
This jealous, waspish, wronghead, rhyming race;
And much must flatter, if the whim should bite,
To court applause by printing what I write: 150
But let the fit pass o'er; I'm wise enough
To stop my ears to their confounded stuff.
    In vain bad rhymers all mankind reject,
They treat themselves with most profound respect;
'Tis to small purpose that you hold your tongue,
Each, praised within, is happy all day long.
But how severely with themselves proceed
The men who write such verse as we can read?
Their own strict judges, not a word they spare
That wants or force, or light, or weight, or care,   160
Howe'er unwillingly it quits its place,
Nay, though at court (perhaps) it may find grace:
Such they'll degrade; and sometimes, in its stead,
In downright charity revive the dead;
Mark where a bold expressive phrase appears,
Bright through the rubbish of some hundred years;
Command old words, that long have slept, to wake,
Words that wise Bacon or brave Raleigh spake;
Or bid the new be English, ages hence
(For use will father what's begot by sense),   170

Pour the full tide of eloquence along,
Serenely pure, and yet divinely strong,
Rich with the treasures of each foreign tongue;
Prune the luxuriant, the uncouth refine,
But show no mercy to an empty line;
Then polish all, with so much life and ease,
You think 'tis nature, and a knack to please;
'But ease in writing flows from art, not chance,
As those move easiest who have learned to dance.'

180   If such the plague and pains to write by rule,
Better (say I) be pleased, and play the fool;
Call, if you will, bad rhyming a disease,
It gives men happiness, or leaves them ease.
There lived *in primo Georgii* (they record)
A worthy member, no small fool, a lord;
Who, though the House was up, delighted sate,
Heard, noted, answered, as in full debate:
In all but this a man of sober life,
Fond of his friend, and civil to his wife;

190   Not quite a madman, though a pasty fell,
And much too wise to walk into a well.
Him the damned doctors and his friends immured,
They bled, they cupped, they purged; in short they cured
Whereat the gentleman began to stare –
'My friends?' he cried, 'pox take you for your care!
That from a Patriot of distinguished note
Have bled and purged me to a simple vote.'

Well, on the whole, plain prose must be my fate:
Wisdom (curse on it) will come soon or late.

200   There is a time when poets will grow dull;
I'll e'en leave verses to the boys at school.
To rules of poetry no more confined,
I learn to smooth and harmonize my mind,
Teach ev'ry thought within its bounds to roll,
And keep the equal measure of the soul.

Soon as I enter at my country door,
My mind resumes the thread it dropped before;

Thoughts which at Hyde Park Corner I forgot,
Meet and rejoin me in the pensive grot:
There all alone, and compliments apart,   210
I ask these sober questions of my heart.

  If, when the more you drink, the more you crave,
You tell the doctor; when the more you have,
The more you want, why not, with equal ease,
Confess as well your folly as disease?
The heart resolves this matter in a trice,
'Men only feel the smart, but not the vice.'

  When golden angels cease to cure the evil,
You give all royal witchcraft to the devil;
When servile chaplains cry that birth and place   220
Endue a peer with honour, truth, and grace,
Look in that breast, most dirty Duke! be fair,
Say, can you find out one such lodger there?
Yet still, not heeding what your heart can teach,
You go to church to hear these flatt'rers preach.

  Indeed, could wealth bestow or wit or merit,
A grain of courage, or a spark of spirit,
The wisest man might blush, I must agree,
If vile Van-muck loved sixpence more than he.

  If there be truth in law, and use can give   230
A property, that's yours on which you live.
Delightful Abscourt, if its fields afford
Their fruits to you, confesses you its lord:
All Worldly's hens, nay partridge, sold to town,
His ven'son too, a guinea makes your own:
He bought at thousands what, with better wit,
You purchase as you want, and bit by bit;
Now, or long since, what diff'rence will be found:
You pay a penny, and he paid a pound.

  Heathcote himself, and such large-acred men,   240
Lords of fat E'sham, or of Lincoln Fen,
Buy every stick of wood that lends them heat,
Buy every pullet they afford to eat;
Yet these are wights who fondly call their own
Half that the devil o'erlooks from Lincoln town.

The laws of God, as well as of the land,
Abhor a perpetuity should stand:
Estates have wings, and hang in fortune's pow'r,
Loose on the point of ev'ry wav'ring hour,
250   Ready, by force, or of your own accord,
By sale, at least by death, to change their lord.
Man? and *forever?* wretch! what wouldst thou have?
Heir urges heir, like wave impelling wave.
All vast possessions (just the same the case
Whether you call them villa, park, or chase),
Alas, my Bathurst! what will they avail?
Join Cotswood hills to Sapperton's fair dale,
Let rising granaries and temples here,
There mingled farms and pyramids appear,
260   Link towns to towns with avenues of oak,
Enclose whole downs in walls, 'tis all a joke!
Inexorable death shall level all,
And trees, and stones, and farms, and farmer fall.

    Gold, silver, iv'ry, vases sculptured high,
Paint, marble, gems, and robes of Persian dye,
There are who have not – and, thank Heav'n, there are
Who, if they have not, think not worth their care.

    Talk what you will of taste, my friend, you'll find
Two of a face as soon as of a mind.
270   Why, of two brothers, rich and restless one
Ploughs, burns, manures, and toils from sun to sun;
The other slights, for women, sports, and wines,
All Townshend's turnips, and all Grosvenor's mines;
Why one like Bubb with pay and scorn content,
Bows and votes on, in court and Parliament;
One, driv'n by strong benevolence of soul,
Shall fly, like Oglethorpe, from pole to pole:
Is known alone to that directing Pow'r
Who forms the genius in the natal hour;
280   That God of Nature, who, within us still,
Inclines our action, not constrains our will;
Various of temper, as of face or frame,
Each individual: his great end the same.

Yes, sir, how small soever be my heap,
A part I will enjoy, as well as keep.
My heir may sigh, and think it want of grace
A man so poor would live without a place,
But sure no statute in his favour says,
How free, or frugal, I shall pass my days;
I who at some times spend, at others spare,   290
Divided between carelessness and care.
'Tis one thing madly to disperse my store;
Another, not to heed to treasure more;
Glad, like a boy, to snatch the first good day,
And pleased if sordid want be far away.

What is't to me (a passenger, God wot)
Whether my vessel be first-rate or not?
The ship itself may make a better figure,
But I that sail am neither less nor bigger.
I neither strut with ev'ry favouring breath,   300
Nor strive with all the tempest in my teeth;
In pow'r, wit, figure, virtue, fortune, placed
Behind the foremost, and before the last.

'But why all this of avarice? I have none.'
I wish you joy, sir, of a tyrant gone;
But does no other lord it at this hour
As wild and mad? the avarice of power?
Does neither rage inflame, nor fear appal?
Not the black fear of death, that saddens all?
With terrors round, can reason hold her throne,   310
Despise the known, nor tremble at th' unknown?
Survey both worlds, intrepid and entire,
In spite of witches, devils, dreams, and fire?
Pleased to look forward, pleased to look behind,
And count each birthday with a grateful mind?
Has life no sourness, drawn so near its end?
Canst thou endure a foe, forgive a friend?
Has age but melted the rough parts away,
As winter fruits grow mild ere they decay?
Or will you think, my friend, your business done,   320
When of a hundred thorns, you pull out one?

Learn to live well, or fairly make your will;
You've played, and loved, and ate, and drank your fill.
Walk sober off, before a sprightlier age
Comes titt'ring on, and shoves you from the stage:
Leave such to trifle with more grace and ease,
Whom folly pleases, and whose follies please.

Ode, IV, i

To Venus

Again? new tumults in my breast?
Ah spare me, Venus! let me, let me rest!
    I am not now, alas! the man
As in the gentle reign of my Queen Anne.
    Ah sound no more thy soft alarms,
Nor circle sober fifty with thy charms.
    Mother too fierce of dear desires!
Turn, turn to willing hearts your wanton fires:
    To number five direct your doves,
There spread round Murray all your blooming loves;
    Noble and young, who strikes the heart
With ev'ry sprightly, ev'ry decent part;
    Equal, the injured to defend,
To charm the mistress, or to fix the friend.
    He, with a hundred arts refined,
Shall stretch thy conquests over half the kind;
    To him each rival shall submit,
Make but his riches equal to his wit.
    Then shall thy form the marble grace,
(Thy Grecian form) and Chloe lend the face.
    His house, embosomed in the grove,
Sacred to social life and social love,
    Shall glitter o'er the pendant green,
Where Thames reflects the visionary scene:

Thither the silver sounding lyres
Shall call the smiling loves, and young desires;
    There every Grace and Muse shall throng,
Exalt the dance, or animate the song;
    There youths and nymphs, in consort gay,
Shall hail the rising, close the parting day.   30
    With me, alas! those joys are o'er;
For me the vernal garlands bloom no more.
    Adieu! fond hope of mutual fire,
The still believing, still renewed desire;
    Adieu! the heart-expanding bowl,
And all the kind deceivers of the soul!
    But why? ah tell me, ah too dear!
Steals down my cheek th' involuntary tear?
    Why words so flowing, thoughts so free,
Stop, or turn nonsense, at one glance of thee?   40
    Thee, dressed in fancy's airy beam,
Absent I follow through th' extended dream;
    Now, now I seize, I clasp thy charms,
And now you burst (ah, cruel!) from my arms,
    And swiftly shoot along the mall,
    Or softly glide by the canal,
    Now shown by Cynthia's silver ray,
And now on rolling waters snatched away.

Ode, IV, ix

Lest you should think that verse shall die
    Which sounds the silver Thames along,
Taught on the wings of truth to fly
    Above the reach of vulgar song;

Though daring Milton sits sublime,
    In Spenser native muses play;
Nor yet shall Waller yield to time,
    Nor pensive Cowley's moral lay.

Sages and chiefs long since had birth
10   Ere Caesar was, or Newton named;
These raised new empires o'er the earth,
          And those new heav'ns and systems framed.

Vain was the chief's and sage's pride!
They had no poet, and they died!
In vain they schemed, in vain they bled!
They had no poet, and are dead!

EPILOGUE TO THE SATIRES

Dialogue I

Fr. Not twice a twelvemonth you appear in print,
And when it comes, the court see nothing in't;
You grow correct that once with rapture writ,
And are, besides, too moral for a wit.
Decay of parts, alas! we all must feel –
Why now, this moment, don't I see you steal?
'Tis all from Horace; Horace long before ye
Said 'Tories called him Whig, and Whigs a Tory',
And taught his Romans, in much better metre,
10   'To laugh at fools who put their trust in Peter.'
      But Horace, sir, was delicate, was nice;
Bubo observes, he lashed no sort of vice:
Horace would say, Sir Billy served the crown,
Blunt could do business, Higgins knew the town;
In Sappho touch the failings of the sex,
In rev'rend bishops note some small neglects,
And own the Spaniard did a waggish thing
Who cropped our ears, and sent them to the king.
His sly, polite, insinuating style
20   Could please at court, and make Augustus smile;

An artful manager, that crept between
His friend and shame, and was a kind of screen.
But 'faith, your very friends will soon be sore;
Patriots there are, who wish you'd jest no more –
And where's the glory? 'twill be only thought
The Great Man never offered you a groat.
Go see Sir Robert –

               P. See Sir Robert! – hum –
And never laugh – for all my life to come?
Seen him I have, but in his happier hour
Of social pleasure, ill exchanged for pow'r;   30
Seen him, uncumbered with a venal tribe,
Smile without art, and win without a bribe.
Would he oblige me? let me only find
He does not think me what he thinks mankind.
Come, come, at all I laugh he laughs, no doubt;
The only diff'rence is – I dare laugh out.

   Fr. Why, yes: with Scripture still you may be free;
A horse laugh, if you please, at honesty;
A joke on Jekyl, or some odd Old Whig,
Who never changed his principle, or wig;   40
A Patriot is a fool in ev'ry age,
Whom all lord chamberlains allow the stage:
These nothing hurts; they keep their fashion still,
And wear their strange old virtue as they will.

   If any ask you, 'Who's the man, so near
His Prince, that writes in verse, and has his ear?'
Why, answer 'Lyttelton!' and I'll engage
The worthy youth shall ne'er be in a rage;
But were his verses vile, his whisper base,
You'd quickly find him in Lord Fanny's case.   50
Sejanus, Wolsey, hurt not honest Fleury,
But well may put some statesmen in a fury.

   Laugh then at any, but at fools or foes;
These you but anger, and you mend not those.
Laugh at your friends, and if your friends are sore,
So much the better, you may laugh the more.

To vice and folly to confine the jest
Sets half the world, God knows, against the rest,
Did not the sneer of more impartial men
60 At sense and virtue balance all again.
Judicious wits spread wide the ridicule,
And charitably comfort knave and fool.
    P. Dear sir, forgive the prejudice of youth:
Adieu distinction, satire, warmth, and truth!
Come, harmless characters that no one hit;
Come, Henley's oratory, Osborne's wit!
The honey dropping from Favonio's tongue,
The flow'rs of Bubo, and the flow of Young!
The gracious dew of pulpit eloquence,
70 And all the well-whipped cream of courtly sense;
The first was Hervey's, Fox's next, and then
The Senate's, and then Hervey's once again.
O come! that easy Ciceronian style,
So Latin, yet so English all the while,
As, though the pride of Middleton and Bland,
All boys may read, and girls may understand!
Then might I sing without the least offence,
And all I sung should be the nation's sense;
Or teach the melancholy muse to mourn,
80 Hang the sad verse on Carolina's urn,
And hail her passage to the realms of rest,
All parts performed, and all her children blest!
So – satire is no more – I feel it die –
No gazetteer more innocent than I –
And let, a God's name, ev'ry fool and knave
Be graced through life, and flattered in his grave.
    Fr. Why so? if satire knows its time and place,
You still may lash the greatest – in disgrace:
For merit will by turns forsake them all.
90 Would you know when? exactly when they fall.
But let all satire in all changes spare
Immortal Selkirk, and grave De la Ware!
Silent and soft, as saints remove to Heav'n,
All ties dissolved and ev'ry sin forgiv'n,

These may some gentle, ministerial wing
Receive, and place for ever near a king!
There, where no passion, pride, or shame transport,
Lulled with the sweet nepenthe of a court:
There where no father's, brother's, friend's disgrace
Once break their rest, or stir them from their place;   100
But past the sense of human miseries,
All tears are wiped for ever from all eyes;
No cheek is known to blush, no heart to throb,
Save when they lose a question, or a job.
    P. Good heav'n forbid, that I should blast their glory,
Who know how like Whig ministers to Tory,
And when three sov'reigns died could scarce be vexed,
Consid'ring what a gracious prince was next.
Have I, in silent wonder, seen such things
As pride in slaves, and avarice in kings?   110
And at a peer or peeress shall I fret,
Who starves a sister, or forswears a debt?
Virtue, I grant you, is an empty boast;
But shall the dignity of vice be lost?
Ye gods! shall Cibber's son, without rebuke,
Swear like a lord, or Rich out-whore a duke?
A fav'rite's porter with his master vie,
Be bribed as often, and as often lie?
Shall Ward draw contracts with a statesman's skill?
Or Japhet pocket, like his Grace, a will?   120
Is it for Bond or Peter (paltry things)
To pay their debts, or keep their faith, like kings?
If Blount dispatched himself, he played the man,
And so mayst thou, illustrious Passeran!
But shall a printer, weary of his life,
Learn from their books to hang himself and wife?
This, this, my friend, I cannot, must not bear;
Vice thus abused, demands a nation's care;
This calls the Church to deprecate our sin,
And hurls the thunder of the laws on gin.   130

Let modest Foster, if he will, excel
Ten metropolitans in preaching well;
A simple Quaker, or a Quaker's wife,
Outdo Landaff in doctrine – yea, in life:
Let humble Allen, with an awkward shame,
Do good by stealth, and blush to find it fame.
Virtue may choose the high or low degree,
'Tis just alike to Virtue, and to me;
Dwell in a monk, or light upon a king,
She's still the same belov'd, contented thing.
Vice is undone, if she forgets her birth,
And stoops from angels to the dregs of earth:
But 'tis the fall degrades her to a whore;
Let greatness own her, and she's mean no more.
Her birth, her beauty, crowds and courts confess,
Chaste matrons praise her, and grave bishops bless;
In golden chains the willing world she draws,
And hers the gospel is, and hers the laws;
Mounts the tribunal, lifts her scarlet head,
And sees pale virtue carted in her stead.
Lo! at the wheels of her triumphal car,
Old England's genius, rough with many a scar,
Dragged in the dust! his arms hang idly round,
His flag inverted trails along the ground!
Our youth, all liv'ried o'er with foreign gold,
Before her dance; behind her crawl the old!
See thronging millions to the pagod run,
And offer country, parent, wife, or son!
Hear her black trumpet through the land proclaim
That 'not to be corrupted is the shame'.
In soldier, churchman, patriot, man in pow'r,
'Tis av'rice all, ambition is no more!
See all our nobles begging to be slaves!
See all our fools aspiring to be knaves!
The wit of cheats, the courage of a whore,
Are what ten thousand envy and adore:

All, all look up, with reverential awe,
At crimes that 'scape, or triumph o'er the law.
While truth, worth, wisdom, daily they decry –
'Nothing is sacred now but villainy.'   170
    Yet may this verse (if such a verse remain)
Show there was one who held it in disdain.

Dialogue II

Fr. 'Tis all a libel – Paxton, sir, will say.
    P. Not yet, my friend! tomorrow 'faith it may;
And for that very cause I print today.
How should I fret to mangle every line
In rev'rence to the sins of Thirty-nine!
Vice with such giant strides comes on amain,
Invention strives to be before in vain;
Feign what I will, and paint it e'er so strong,
Some rising genius sins up to my song.
    Fr. Yet none but you by name the guilty lash;   10
Ev'n Guthrie saves half Newgate by a dash.
Spare then the person, and expose the vice.
    P. How, sir! not damn the sharper, but the dice?
Come on then, satire! gen'ral, unconfined,
Spread thy broad wing, and souse on all the kind.
Ye statesmen, priests, of one religion all!
Ye tradesmen, vile, in army, court, or hall!
Ye rev'rend atheists! *Fr.* Scandal! name them, who?
    P. Why that's the thing you bid me not to do.
Who starved a sister, who forswore a debt,   20
I never named; the town's inquiring yet.
The pois'ning dame – *Fr.* You mean – *P.* I don't.
        Fr. You do.
    P. See, now I keep the secret, and not you!
The bribing statesman – *Fr.* Hold! too high you go.
    P. The bribed elector – *Fr.* There you stoop too low.

     P. I fain would please you, if I knew with what;
Tell me, which knave is lawful game, which not?
Must great offenders, once escaped the crown,
Like royal harts, be never more run down?
30   Admit your law to spare the knight requires,
As beasts of nature may we hunt the squires?
Suppose I censure – you know what I mean –
To save a bishop, may I name a dean?
     Fr. A dean, sir? no: his fortune is not made;
You hurt a man that's rising in the trade.
     P. If not the tradesman who set up today,
Much less the 'prentice who tomorrow may.
Down, down, proud satire! though a realm be spoiled,
Arraign no mightier thief than wretched Wild;
40   Or, if a court or country's made a job,
Go drench a pickpocket, and join the mob.
     But sir, I beg you (for the love of vice!)
The matter's weighty, pray consider twice:
Have you less pity for the needy cheat,
The poor and friendless villain, than the great?
Alas! the small discredit of a bribe
Scarce hurts the lawyer, but undoes the scribe.
Then better sure it charity becomes
To tax directors, who (thank God) have plums;
50   Still better, ministers; or if the thing
May pinch ev'n there – why, lay it on a king.
     Fr. Stop! stop!
                 P. Must satire, then, nor rise nor fall?
Speak out, and bid me blame no rogues at all.
     Fr. Yes, strike that Wild, I'll justify the blow.
     P. Strike? why the man was hanged ten years ago:
Who now that obsolete example fears?
Ev'n Peter trembles only for his ears.
     Fr. What, always Peter? Peter thinks you mad;
You make men desp'rate, if they once are bad
60   Else might he take to virtue some years hence –
     P. As Selkirk, if he lives, will love the prince.

Fr. Strange spleen to Selkirk!
                        P. Do I wrong the man?
God knows, I praise a courtier where I can.
When I confess, there is who feels for fame,
And melts to goodness, need I Scarb'rough name?
Pleased let me own, in Esher's peaceful grove
(Where Kent and Nature vie for Pelham's love)
The scene, the master, op'ning to my view,
I sit and dream I see my Craggs anew!
    Ev'n in a bishop I can spy desert;   70
Secker is decent, Rundle has a heart;
Manners with candour are to Benson giv'n,
To Berkeley, every virtue under Heav'n.
    But does the court a worthy man remove?
That instant, I declare, he has my love:
I shun his zenith, court his mild decline;
Thus Somers once and Halifax were mine.
Oft in the clear, still mirror of retreat
I studied Shrewsbury, the wise and great;
Carleton's calm sense and Stanhope's noble flame   80
Compared, and knew their gen'rous end the same.
How pleasing Atterbury's softer hour!
How shined the soul, unconquered in the Tow'r!
How can I Pult'ney, Chesterfield forget,
While Roman spirit charms, and Attic wit?
Argyle, the state's whole thunder born to wield,
And shake alike the senate and the field,
Or Wyndham, just to freedom and the throne,
The master of our passions, and his own.
Names which I long have loved, nor loved in vain,   90
Ranked with their friends, not numbered with their train;
And if yet higher the proud list should end,
Still let me say, 'No follower, but a friend.'
    Yet think not friendship only prompts my lays;
I follow Virtue; where she shines, I praise:
Point she to priest or elder, Whig or Tory,
Or round a Quaker's beaver cast a glory.
I never (to my sorrow I declare)
Dined with the Man of Ross, or my Lord May'r.

100   Some, in their choice of friends (nay, look not grave)
      Have still a secret bias to a knave;
      To find an honest man, I beat about,
      And love him, court him, praise him, in or out.
          Fr. Then why so few commended?
                                        P. Not so fierce;
      Find you the virtue, and I'll find the verse.
      But random praise – the task can ne'er be done;
      Each mother asks it for her booby son,
      Each widow asks it for the best of men,
      For him she weeps, for him she weds again.
110   Praise cannot stoop, like satire, to the ground;
      The number may be hanged, but not be crowned.
      Enough for half the greatest of these days
      To 'scape my censure, not expect my praise.
      Are they not rich? what more can they pretend?
      Dare they to hope a poet for their friend?
      What Richelieu wanted, Louis scarce could gain,
      And what young Ammon wished, but wished in vain.
      No pow'r the Muse's friendship can command;
      No pow'r, when virtue claims it, can withstand.
120   To Cato, Virgil paid one honest line;
      O let my country's friends illumine mine!
      – What are you thinking? *Fr.* Faith, the thought's no sin;
      I think your friends are out, and would be in.
          P. If merely to come in, sir, they go out,
      The way they take is strangely round about.
          Fr. They too may be corrupted, you'll allow?
          P. I only call those knaves who are so now.
      Is that too little? come, then, I'll comply –
      Spirit of Arnall! aid me while I lie:
130   Cobham's a coward, Polwarth is a slave,
      And Lyttelton a dark designing knave,
      St John has ever been a wealthy fool –
      But let me add, Sir Robert's mighty dull,
      Has never made a friend in private life,
      And was, besides, a tyrant to his wife.
          But pray, when others praise him, do I blame?
      Call Verres, Wolsey, any odious name?

Why rail they then, if but a wreath of mine,
Oh, all-accomplished St John! deck thy shrine?
    What! shall each spur-galled hackney of the day,   140
When Paxton gives him double pots and pay,
Or each new-pensioned sycophant, pretend
To break my windows if I treat a friend;
Then wisely plead to me they meant no hurt,
But 'twas my guest at whom they threw the dirt?
Sure, if I spare the minister, no rules
Of honour bind me not to maul his tools;
Sure, if they cannot cut, it may be said
His saws are toothless, and his hatchet's lead.
    It angered Turenne, once upon a day,   150
To see a footman kicked that took his pay:
But when he heard th' affront the fellow gave,
Knew one a man of honour, one a knave,
The prudent gen'ral turned it to a jest,
And begged he'd take the pains to kick the rest;
Which not at present having time to do –
    Fr. Hold sir! for God's sake, where's th' affront to you?
Against your worship when had Selkirk writ?
Or Page poured forth the torrent of his wit?
Or grant the bard whose distich all commend   160
('In pow'r a servant, out of pow'r a friend')
To Walpole guilty of some venial sin,
What's that to you, who ne'er was out nor in?
    The priest whose flattery bedropped the crown,
How hurt he you? he only stained the gown.
And how did, pray, the florid youth offend,
Whose speech you took, and gave it to a friend?
    P. Faith, it imports not much from whom it came; }
Whoever borrowed could not be to blame, }
Since the whole House did afterwards the same. }   170
Let courtly wits to wits afford supply,
As hog to hog in huts of Westphaly;
If one, through nature's bounty or his lord's,
Has what the frugal dirty soil affords,
From him the next receives it, thick or thin,

As pure a mess almost as it came in;
The blessèd benefit, not there confined,
Drops to the third, who nuzzles close behind;
From tail to mouth, they feed and they carouse;
180   The last full fairly gives it to the House.
        Fr. This filthy simile, this beastly line,
Quite turns my stomach – *P.* So does flatt'ry mine;
And all your courtly civet-cats can vent,
Perfume to you, to me is excrement.
But hear me further – Japhet, 'tis agreed,
Writ not, and Chartres scarce could write or read,
In all the courts of Pindus guiltless quite;
But pens can forge, my friend, that cannot write;
And must no egg in Japhet's face be thrown,
190   Because the deed he forged was not my own?
Must never patriot then declaim at gin
Unless, good man! he has been fairly in;
No zealous pastor blame a failing spouse
Without a staring reason on his brows?
And each blasphemer quite escape the rod,
Because the insult's not on man, but God?
        Ask you what provocation I have had?
The strong antipathy of good to bad.
When truth or virtue an affront endures,
200   Th' affront is mine, my friend, and should be yours.
Mine, as a foe professed to false pretence,
Who think a coxcomb's honour like his sense;
Mine, as a friend to ev'ry worthy mind;
And mine as man, who feel for all mankind.
        Fr. You're strangely proud.
                                        P. So proud, I am no slave; ⎫
So impudent, I own myself no knave;   ⎬
So odd, my country's ruin makes me grave.   ⎭
Yes, I am proud; I must be proud to see
Men not afraid of God, afraid of me;
210   Safe from the bar, the pulpit, and the throne,
Yet touched and shamed by ridicule alone.

O sacred weapon! left for truth's defence,
Sole dread of folly, vice, and insolence!
To all but Heav'n-directed hands denied,
The Muse may give thee, but the gods must guide.
Rev'rent I touch thee! but with honest zeal,
To rouse the watchmen of the public weal,
To Virtue's work provoke the tardy Hall,
And goad the prelate, slumb'ring in his stall.
Ye tinsel insects! whom a court maintains,   220
That counts your beauties only by your stains,
Spin all your cobwebs o'er the eye of day!
The Muse's wing shall brush you all away.
All his Grace preaches, all his Lordship sings,
All that makes saints of queens, and gods of kings;
All, all but truth, drops dead-born from the press,
Like the last *Gazette*, or the last Address.
  When black ambition stains a public cause,
A monarch's sword when mad vainglory draws,
Not Waller's wreath can hide the nation's scar,   230
Nor Boileau turn the feather to a star.
  Not so when diademed with rays divine,
Touched with the flame that breaks from Virtue's shrine,
Her priestess Muse forbids the good to die,
And opes the temple of Eternity.
There other trophies deck the truly brave
Than such as Anstis casts into the grave;
Far other stars than * * * and * * * wear,
And may descend to Mordington from Stair;
(Such as on Hough's unsullied mitre shine,   240
Or beam, good Digby! from a heart like thine).
Let envy howl, while Heav'n's whole chorus sings,
And bark at honour not conferred by kings;
Let flatt'ry sickening see the incense rise,
Sweet to the world, and grateful to the skies:
Truth guards the poet, sanctifies the line,
And makes immortal, verse as mean as mine.
  Yes, the last pen for freedom let me draw,
When truth stands trembling on the edge of law.

250   Here, last of Britons! let your names be read;
        Are none, none living? let me praise the dead,
        And for that Cause which made your fathers shine,
        Fall by the votes of their degen'rate line.
            Fr. Alas! alas! pray end what you began,
        And write next winter more *Essays on Man.*

The Dunciad

To Dr Jonathan Swift

Tandem Phoebus adest, morsusque inferre parantem
Congelat, et patulos, ut erant, indurat hiatus.

Book the First

ARGUMENT

*The Proposition, the Invocation, and the Inscription. Then the
original of the great empire of Dullness, and cause of the con-
tinuance thereof. The College of the Goddess in the City, with
her private Academy for Poets in particular; the governors of
it, and the four Cardinal Virtues. Then the poem hastes into the
midst of things, presenting her, on the evening of a Lord May-
or's day, revolving the long succession of her sons, and the
glories past and to come. She fixes her eye on Bays to be the
instrument of that great event which is the subject of the poem.
He is described pensive among his books, giving up the cause,
and apprehending the period of her Empire: after debating
whether to betake himself to the Church, or to gaming, or to
party-writing, he raises an altar of proper books, and (making
first his solemn prayer and declaration) purposes thereon to
sacrifice all his unsuccessful writings. As the pile is kindled, the
Goddess beholding the flame from her seat, flies and puts it out
by casting upon it the poem of Thulè. She forthwith reveals
herself to him, transports him to her Temple, unfolds her Arts,
and initiates him into her Mysteries; then announcing the death*

of Eusden *the poet laureate, anoints him, carries him to court,
and proclaims him successor.*

The Mighty Mother, and her son who brings
The Smithfield Muses to the ear of kings,
I sing. Say you, her instruments the Great!
Called to this work by Dullness, Jove, and Fate;
You by whose care, in vain decried and cursed,
Still Dunce the second reigns like Dunce the first;
Say how the Goddess bade Britannia sleep,
And poured her spirit o'er the land and deep.

In eldest time, e'er mortals writ or read,
E'er Pallas issued from the Thund'rer's head,   10
Dullness o'er all possessed her ancient right,
Daughter of Chaos and eternal night:
Fate in their dotage this fair idiot gave,
Gross as her sire, and as her mother grave,
Laborious, heavy, busy, bold, and blind,
She ruled, in native anarchy, the mind.

Still her old empire to restore she tries,
For, born a goddess, Dullness never dies.

O thou! whatever title please thine ear,
Dean, Drapier, Bickerstaff, or Gulliver!   20
Whether thou choose Cervantes' serious air,
Or laugh and shake in Rab'lais' easy chair,
Or praise the court, or magnify mankind,
Or thy grieved country's copper chains unbind;
From thy Boeotia though her Pow'r retires,
Mourn not, my SWIFT, at aught our realm acquires,
Here pleased behold her mighty wings outspread
To hatch a new Saturnian age of lead.

Close to those walls where Folly holds her
     throne,
And laughs to think Monroe would take her down,   30
Where o'er the gates, by his famed father's hand
Great Cibber's brazen, brainless brothers stand;
One cell there is, concealed from vulgar eye,
The cave of Poverty and Poetry.

Keen, hollow winds howl through the bleak recess,
Emblem of Music caused by Emptiness.
Hence bards, like Proteus long in vain tied down,
Escape in monsters, and amaze the town.
Hence Miscellanies spring, the weekly boast
40   Of Curll's chaste press, and Lintot's rubric post:
Hence hymning Tyburn's elegiac lines,
Hence Journals, Medleys, Merc'ries, Magazines:
Sepulchral lies, our holy walls to grace,
And New Year Odes, and all the Grub Street race.

In clouded majesty here Dullness shone;
Four guardian Virtues, round, support her throne:
Fierce champion Fortitude, that knows no fears
Of hisses, blows, or want, or loss of ears:
Calm Temperance, whose blessings those partake
50   Who hunger, and who thirst for scribbling sake:
Prudence, whose glass presents th' approaching jail;
Poetic Justice, with her lifted scale,
Where, in nice balance, truth with gold she weighs,
And solid pudding against empty praise.

Here she beholds the Chaos dark and deep
Where nameless Somethings in their causes sleep,
Till genial Jacob, or a warm third day,
Call forth each mass, a poem, or a play;
How hints, like spawn, scarce quick in embryo lie,
60   How new-born nonsense first is taught to cry,
Maggots half-formed in rhyme exactly meet,
And learn to crawl upon poetic feet.
Here one poor word an hundred clenches makes,
And ductile dullness new meanders takes;
There motley images her fancy strike,
Figures ill paired, and similies unlike.
She sees a mob of metaphors advance,
Pleased with the madness of the mazy dance:
How Tragedy and Comedy embrace;
70   How Farce and Epic get a jumbled race;
How Time himself stands still at her command,
Realms shift their place, and ocean turns to land.

Here gay description Egypt glads with showers,
Or gives to Zembla fruits, to Barca flowers;
Glitt'ring with ice here hoary hills are seen,
There, painted valleys of eternal green,
In cold December fragrant chaplets blow,
And heavy harvests nod beneath the snow.
   All these, and more, the cloud-compelling Queen
Beholds through fogs, that magnify the scene.   80
She, tinselled o'er in robes of varying hues,
With self-applause her wild creation views;
Sees momentary monsters rise and fall,
And with her own fools-colours gilds them all.
   'Twas on the day, when * * rich and grave,
Like Cimon, triumphed both on land and wave
(Pomps without guilt, of bloodless swords and maces,
Glad chains, warm furs, broad banners, and broad faces).
Now night descending, the proud scene was o'er,
But lived, in Settle's numbers, one day more.   90
Now May'rs and Shrieves all hushed and satiate lay,
Yet eat, in dreams, the custard of the day;
While pensive poets painful vigils keep,
Sleepless themselves, to give their readers sleep.
Much to the mindful Queen the feast recalls
What City swans once sung within the walls;
Much she revolves their arts, their ancient praise,
And sure succession down from Heywood's days.
She saw, with joy, the line immortal run,
Each sire imprest and glaring in his son: 100
So watchful Bruin forms, with plastic care,
Each growing lump, and brings it to a bear.
She saw old Prynne in restless Daniel shine,
And Eusden eke out Blackmore's endless line;
She saw slow Philips creep like Tate's poor page,
And all the mighty mad in Dennis rage.
   In each she marks her image full expressed,
But chief in BAYS's monster-breeding breast;
Bays, formed by nature stage and Town to bless,
And act, and be, a coxcomb with success.   110

Dullness with transport eyes the lively Dunce,
Rememb'ring she herself was pertness once.
Now (shame to Fortune!) an ill run at play
Blanked his bold visage, and a thin third day:
Swearing and supperless the hero sate,
Blasphemed his gods, the dice, and damned his fate;
Then gnawed his pen, then dashed it on the ground,
Sinking from thought to thought, a vast profound!
Plunged for his sense, but found no bottom there,
120   Yet wrote and floundered on, in mere despair.
Round him much embryo, much abortion lay,
Much future Ode, and abdicated Play;
Nonsense precipitate, like running lead,
That slipped through cracks and zig-zags of the head;
All that on Folly Frenzy could beget,
Fruits of dull heat, and sooterkins of Wit.
Next, o'er his books his eyes began to roll,
In pleasing memory of all he stole,
How here he sipped, how there he plundered snug
130   And sucked all o'er, like an industrious bug.
Here lay poor Fletcher's half-eat scenes, and here
The frippery of crucified Molière;
There hapless Shakespeare, yet of Tibbald sore,
Wished he had blotted for himself before.
The rest on outside merit but presume,
Or serve (like other fools) to fill a room;
Such with their shelves as due proportion hold,
Or their fond parents dressed in red and gold;
Or where the pictures for the page atone,
140   And Quarles is saved by beauties not his own.
Here swells the shelf with Ogilby the great;
There, stamped with arms, Newcastle shines complete;
Here all his suff'ring brotherhood retire,
And 'scape the martyrdom of jakes and fire:
A Gothic library! of Greece and Rome
Well purged, and worthy Settle, Banks, and Broome.
     But, high above, more solid Learning shone,
The classics of an age that heard of none;

There Caxton slept, with Wynkyn at his side,
One clasped in wood, and one in strong cow-hide;   150
There, saved by spice, like mummies, many a year,
Dry bodies of Divinity appear:
De Lyra there a dreadful front extends,
And here the groaning shelves Philemon bends.

  Of these twelve volumes, twelve of amplest size,
Redeemed from tapers and defrauded pies,
Inspired he seizes; these an altar raise.
An hecatomb of pure, unsullied lays
That altar crowns; a folio Commonplace
Founds the whole pile, of all his works the base.   160
Quartos, octavos, shape the less'ning pyre;
A twisted birthday ode completes the spire.

  Then he: 'Great Tamer of all human art!
First in my care, and ever at my heart;
Dullness! whose good old cause I yet defend,
With whom my Muse began, with whom shall end;
E'er since Sir Fopling's periwig was praise,
To the last honours of the butt and bays:
O thou! of bus'ness the directing soul!
To this our head like bias to the bowl,   170
Which, as more pond'rous, made its aim more true,
Obliquely waddling to the mark in view:
O! ever gracious to perplexed mankind,
Still spread a healing mist before the mind,
And lest we err by Wit's wild dancing light,
Secure us kindly in our native night.
Or, if to Wit a coxcomb make pretence,
Guard the sure barrier between that and Sense;
Or quite unravel all the reas'ning thread,
And hang some curious cobweb in its stead!   180
As, forced from wind-guns, lead itself can fly,
And pond'rous slugs cut swiftly through the sky;
As clocks to weight their nimble motion owe,
The wheels above urged by the load below:

Me Emptiness, and Dullness could inspire,
And were my elasticity, and fire.
Some Daemon stole my pen (forgive th'offence)
And once betrayed me into common sense:
Else all my prose and verse were much the same;
190   This, prose on stilts, that, poetry fall'n lame.
Did on the stage my fops appear confined?
My life gave ampler lessons to mankind.
Did the dead letter unsuccessful prove?
The brisk example never failed to move.
Yet sure had Heav'n decreed to save the State,
Heav'n had decreed these works a longer date.
Could Troy be saved by any single hand,
This grey-goose weapon must have made her stand.
What can I now? my Fletcher cast aside,
200   Take up the Bible, once my better guide?
Or tread the path by vent'rous heroes trod,
This box my thunder, this right hand my god?
Or chaired at White's amidst the doctors sit,
Teach oaths to gamesters, and to nobles wit?
Or bidst thou rather Party to embrace?
(A friend to Party thou, and all her race;
'Tis the same rope at different ends they twist;
To Dullness Ridpath is as dear as Mist.)
Shall I, like Curtius, desp'rate in my zeal,
210   O'er head and ears plunge for the Commonweal?
Or rob Rome's ancient geese of all their glories,
And cackling save the monarchy of Tories?
Hold – to the Minister I more incline;
To serve his cause, O Queen! is serving thine.
And see! thy very Gazetteers give o'er,
Ev'n Ralph repents, and Henley writes no more.
What then remains? Ourself. Still, still remain
Cibberian forehead, and Cibberian brain.
This brazen brightness, to the squire so dear;
220   This polished hardness, that reflects the peer;

This arch absurd, that wit and fool delights;
This mess, tossed up of Hockley Hole and White's;
Where dukes and butchers join to wreathe my crown,
At once the bear and fiddle of the town.
    'O born in sin, and forth in folly brought!
Works damned, or to be damned! (your father's fault),
Go, purified by flames ascend the sky,
My better and more Christian progeny!
Unstained, untouched, and yet in maiden sheets;
While all your smutty sisters walk the streets.   230
Ye shall not beg, like gratis-given Bland,
Sent with a pass, and vagrant through the land;
Not sail, with Ward, to ape-and-monkey climes,
Where vile mundungus trucks for viler rhymes;
Not sulphur-tipped, emblaze an alehouse fire;
Not wrap up oranges, to pelt your sire!
O! pass more innocent, in infant state,
To the mild Limbo of our father Tate,
Or peaceably forgot, at once be blest
In Shadwell's bosom with eternal rest!   240
Soon to that mass of Nonsense to return,
Where things destroyed are swept to things unborn.'
    With that, a tear (portentous sign of grace!)
Stole from the master of the sev'nfold face,
And thrice he lifted high the Birthday brand,
And thrice he dropped it from his quiv'ring hand;
Then lights the structure, with averted eyes:
The rolling smokes involve the sacrifice.
The op'ning clouds disclose each work by turns,
Now flames the Cid, and now Perolla burns;   250
Great Caesar roars, and hisses in the fires;
King John in silence modestly expires;
No merit now the dear Nonjuror claims,
Molière's old stubble in a moment flames.
Tears gushed again, as from pale Priam's eyes
When the last blaze sent Ilion to the skies.
Roused by the light, old Dullness heaved the head;
Then snatched a sheet of Thulè from her bed,

Sudden she flies, and whelms it o'er the pyre;
260   Down sink the flames, and with a hiss expire.
      Her ample presence fills up all the place;
A veil of fogs dilates her awful face:
Great in her charms! as when on shrieves and may'rs
She looks, and breathes herself into their airs.
She bids him wait her to her sacred Dome:
Well pleased he entered, and confessed his home.
So spirits ending their terrestrial race
Ascend, and recognize their native place.
This the Great Mother dearer held than all
270   The clubs of quidnuncs, or her own Guildhall:
Here stood her opium, here she nursed her Owls,
And here she planned th' imperial seat of Fools.
      Here to her chosen all her works she shows:
Prose swelled to verse, verse loit'ring into prose;
How random thoughts now meaning chance to find,
Now leave all memory of sense behind;
How Prologues into Prefaces decay,
And these to Notes are frittered quite away;
How Index-learning turns no student pale,
280   Yet holds the eel of science by the tail;
How, with less reading than makes felons scape,
Less human genius than God gives an ape,
Small thanks to France, and none to Rome or Greece,
A past, vamped, future, old, revived, new piece,
'Twixt Plautus, Fletcher, Shakespeare, and Corneille,
Can make a Cibber, Tibbald, or Ozell.
      The Goddess then, o'er his anointed head,
With mystic words, the sacred opium shed.
And lo! her bird (a monster of a fowl,
290   Something betwixt a Heideggre and owl)
Perched on his crown, 'All hail! and hail again,
My son! the promised land expects thy reign.
Know, Eusden thirsts no more for sack or praise;
He sleeps among the dull of ancient days;

Safe, where no critics damn, no duns molest,
Where wretched Withers, Ward, and Gildon rest,
And high-born Howard, more majestic sire,
With Fool of Quality compleats the choir.
Thou Cibber! thou, his laurel shalt support,
Folly, my son, has still a friend at court. 300
Lift up your gates, ye princes, see him come!
Sound, sound ye viols, be the cat-call dumb!
Bring, bring the madding bay, the drunken vine;
The creeping, dirty, courtly ivy join.
And thou! his aide de camp, lead on my sons,
Light-armed with points, antitheses, and puns.
Let bawdry, billingsgate, my daughters dear,
Support his front, and oaths bring up the rear;
And under his, and under Archer's wing,
Gaming and Grub Street skulk behind the King. 310
    'O! when shall rise a monarch all our own,
And I, a nursing-mother, rock the throne,
'Twixt Prince and people close the curtain draw,
Shade him from light, and cover him from law;
Fatten the courtier, starve the learnèd band,
And suckle armies, and dry-nurse the land:
'Till senates nod to lullabies divine,
And all be sleep, as at an Ode of thine.'

    She ceased. Then swells the Chapel Royal throat:
'God save King Cibber!' mounts in ev'ry note. 320
Familiar White's, 'God save King Colley!' cries;
'God save King Colley!' Drury Lane replies;
To Needham's quick the voice triumphal rode,
But pious Needham dropped the name of God;
Back to the Devil the last echoes roll,
And 'Coll!' each butcher roars at Hockley Hole.
    So when Jove's block descended from on high
(As sings thy great forefather Ogilby),
Loud thunder to its bottom shook the bog,
And the hoarse nation croaked, 'God save King Log!' 330

Book the Second

*The King being proclaimed, the solemnity is graced with public
games and sports of various kinds; not instituted by the Hero,
as by Aeneas in Virgil, but for greater honour by the Goddess
in person (in like manner as the games Pythia, Isthmia, etc.
were anciently said to be ordained by the Gods, and as Thetis
herself appearing, according to Homer, Odyss. 24. proposed
the prizes in honour of her son Achilles). Hither flock the poets
and critics, attended, as is but just, with their patrons and
booksellers. The Goddess is first pleased, for her disport, to
propose games to the Booksellers, and setteth up the Phantom
of a poet, which they contend to overtake. The Races described,
with their divers accidents. Next, the game for a Poetess. Then
follow the Exercises for the Poets, of tickling, vociferating, div-
ing: the first holds forth the arts and practices of Dedicators,
the second of Disputants and fustian Poets, the third of pro-
found, dark, and dirty Party-writers. Lastly, for the Critics, the
Goddess proposes (with great propriety) an exercise, not of
their parts, but their patience, in hearing the works of two
voluminous authors, one in verse, and the other in prose, delib-
erately read, without sleeping: the various effects of which,
with the several degrees and manners of their operation, are
here set forth; till the whole number, not of Critics only, but of
spectators, actors, and all present, fall fast asleep; which natur-
ally and necessarily ends the games.*

> High on a gorgeous seat, that far outshone
> Henley's gilt tub, or Fleckno's Irish throne,
> Or that where on her curls the public pours,
> All-bounteous, fragrant grains and golden show'rs,
> Great Cibber sate. The proud Parnassian sneer,
> The conscious simper, and the jealous leer,
> Mix on his look; all eyes direct their rays
> On him, and crowds turn coxcombs as they gaze.

His peers shine round him with reflected grace,
New-edge their dullness, and new-bronze their face.   10
So from the sun's broad beam, in shallow urns
Heav'n's twinkling sparks draw light, and point
    their horns.

  Not with more glee, by hands pontific crowned,
With scarlet hats wide-waving circled round,
Rome in her Capitol saw Querno sit,
Throned on sev'n hills, the Antichrist of wit.

  And now the Queen, to glad her sons, proclaims
By herald hawkers, high heroic games.
They summon all her race: an endless band
Pours forth, and leaves unpeopled half the land.   20
A motley mixture! in long wigs, in bags,
In silks, in crapes, in garters, and in rags,
From drawing rooms, from colleges, from garrets,
On horse, on foot, in hacks, and gilded chariots:
All who true Dunces in her cause appeared,
And all who knew those Dunces to reward.

  Amid that area wide they took their stand,
Where the tall maypole once o'er-looked the Strand;
But now (so ANNE and piety ordain)
A church collects the saints of Drury Lane.   30

  With Authors, Stationers obeyed the call
(The field of glory is a field for all);
Glory, and gain, th'industrious tribe provoke,
And gentle Dullness ever loves a joke.
A Poet's form she placed before their eyes,
And bade the nimblest racer seize the prize;
No meagre, muse-rid mope, adust and thin,
In a dun nightgown of his own loose skin,
But such a bulk as no twelve bards could raise,
Twelve starveling bards of these degen'rate days.   40
All as a partridge plump, full-fed, and fair,
She formed this image of well-bodied air;
With pert flat eyes she windowed well its head,
A brain of feathers, and a heart of lead;

And empty words she gave, and sounding strain,
But senseless, lifeless! idol void and vain!
Never was dashed out, at one lucky hit,
A fool, so just a copy of a wit;
So like, that critics said, and courtiers swore,
50   A wit it was, and called the phantom More.
       All gaze with ardour: some a poet's name,
Others a sword-knot and laced suit inflame.
But lofty Lintot in the circle rose:
'This prize is mine; who tempt it are my foes;
With me began this genius, and shall end.'
He spoke: and who with Lintot shall contend?
       Fear held them mute. Alone, untaught to fear,
Stood dauntless Curll; 'Behold that rival here!
The race by vigour, not by vaunts is won;
60   So take the hindmost, Hell.' – He said, and run.
Swift as a bard the bailiff leaves behind,
He left huge Lintot, and outstripped the wind.
As when a dabchick waddles through the copse
On feet and wings, and flies, and wades, and hops;
So lab'ring on, with shoulders, hands, and head,
Wide as a windmill all his figure spread,
With arms expanded Bernard rows his state,
And left-legg'd Jacob seems to emulate.
Full in the middle way there stood a lake,
70   Which Curll's Corinna chanced that morn to make
(Such was her wont, at early dawn to drop
Her evening cates before his neighbour's shop);
Here fortuned Curll to slide; loud shout the band,
And 'Bernard! Bernard!' rings through all the Strand.
Obscene with filth the miscreant lies bewrayed,
Fall'n in the plash his wickedness had laid:
Then first (if poets aught of truth declare)
The caitiff vaticide conceived a pray'r.
       'Hear Jove! whose name my bards and I adore
80   As much at least as any god's, or more;
And him and his, if more devotion warms,
Down with the Bible, up with the Pope's Arms.'

A place there is, betwixt earth, air, and seas,
Where, from ambrosia, Jove retires for ease.
There in his seat two spacious vents appear,
On this he sits, to that he leans his ear,
And hears the various vows of fond mankind;
Some beg an eastern, some a western wind:
All vain petitions, mounting to the sky,
With reams abundant this abode supply;   90
Amused he reads, and then returns the bills
Signed with that ichor which from gods distils.
    In office here fair Cloacina stands,
And ministers to Jove with purest hands.
Forth from the heap she picked her vot'ry's pray'r,
And placed it next him, a distinction rare!
Oft had the Goddess heard her servant's call
From her black grottos near the Temple-wall,
List'ning delighted to the jest unclean
Of link-boys vile, and watermen obscene;   100
Where as he fished her nether realms for wit,
She oft had favoured him, and favours yet.
Renewed by ordure's sympathetic force,
As oiled with magic juices for the course,
Vig'rous he rises; from th' effluvia strong
Imbibes new life, and scours and stinks along;
Repasses Lintot, vindicates the race,
Nor heeds the brown dishonours of his face.
    And now the victor stretched his eager hand
Where the tall Nothing stood, or seemed to stand;   110
A shapeless shade, it melted from his sight
Like forms in clouds, or visions of the night.
To seize his papers, Curll, was next thy care;
His papers light, fly diverse, tossed in air;
Songs, sonnets, epigrams the winds uplift,
And whisk 'em back to Evans, Young, and Swift.
Th'embroidered suit at least he deemed his prey;
That suit an unpaid tailor snatched away.
No rag, no scrap, of all the beau, or wit,
That once so fluttered, and that once so writ.   120

Heav'n rings with laughter; of the laughter vain,
Dullness, good Queen, repeats the jest again.
Three wicked imps, of her own Grub Street choir,
She decked like Congreve, Addison, and Prior;
Mears, Warner, Wilkins run: delusive thought!
Breval, Bond, Besaleel, the varlets caught.
Curll stretches after Gay, but Gay is gone,
He grasps an empty Joseph for a John:
So Proteus, hunted in a nobler shape,
130 Became, when seized, a puppy, or an ape.
To him the Goddess: 'Son! thy grief lay down,
And turn this whole illusion on the town.
As the sage dame, experienced in her trade,
By names of toasts retails each battered jade
(Whence hapless Monsieur much complains at Paris
Of wrongs from Duchesses and Lady Mary's);
Be thine, my stationer! this magic gift;
Cook shall be Prior, and Concanen, Swift:
So shall each hostile name become our own,
140 And we too boast our Garth and Addison.'
With that she gave him (piteous of his case,
Yet smiling at his rueful length of face)
A shaggy tap'stry, worthy to be spread
On Codrus' old, or Dunton's modern bed;
Instructive work! whose wry-mouthed portraiture
Displayed the fates her confessors endure.
Earless on high stood unabashed De Foe,
And Tutchin flagrant from the scourge below.
There Ridpath, Roper, cudgelled might ye view,
150 The very worsted still looked black and blue.
Himself among the storied chiefs he spies
As from the blanket high in air he flies,
And 'Oh! (he cried) what street, what lane but knows
Our purgings, pumpings, blankettings, and blows?
In ev'ry loom our labours shall be seen,
And the fresh vomit run for ever green!'
See in the circle next, Eliza placed,
Two babes of love close clinging to her waist;

Fair as before her works she stands confessed,
In flow'rs and pearls by bounteous Kirkall dressed.   160
The Goddess then: 'Who best can send on high
The salient spout, far-streaming to the sky;
His be yon Juno of majestic size,
With cow-like udders, and with ox-like eyes.
This china jordan let the chief o'ercome
Replenish, not ingloriously, at home.'
Osborne and Curll accept the glorious strife
(Though this his son dissuades, and that his wife).
One on his manly confidence relies,
One on his vigour and superior size.   170
First Osborne leaned against his lettered post;
It rose, and laboured to a curve at most.
So Jove's bright bow displays its wat'ry round
(Sure sign, that no spectator shall be drowned).
A second effort brought but new disgrace,
The wild meander washed the Artist's face:
Thus the small jet, which hasty hands unlock,
Spurts in the gard'ner's eyes who turns the cock.
Not so from shameless Curll; impetuous spread
The stream, and smoking flourished o'er his head.   180
So (famed like thee for turbulence and horns)
Eridanus his humble fountain scorns;
Through half the heav'ns he pours the'exalted urn;
His rapid waters in their passage burn.

　　Swift as it mounts, all follow with their eyes:
Still happy Impudence obtains the prize.
Thou triumph'st, victor of the high-wrought day,
And the pleased dame, soft-smiling, lead'st away.
Osborne, through perfect modesty o'ercome,
Crowned with the jordan, walks contented home.   190

　　But now for Authors nobler palms remain;
Room for my Lord! three jockeys in his train;
Six huntsmen with a shout precede his chair;
He grins, and looks broad nonsense with a stare.
His Honour's meaning Dullness thus expressed:
'He wins this patron, who can tickle best.'

He chinks his purse, and takes his seat of state:
With ready quills the Dedicators wait;
Now at his head the dextrous task commence,
And, instant, Fancy feels th' imputed sense;
Now gentle touches wanton o'er his face,
He struts Adonis, and affects grimace:
Rolli the feather to his ear conveys,
Then his nice taste directs our Operas:
Bentley his mouth with classic flatt'ry opes,
And the puffed orator bursts out in tropes.
But Welsted most the poet's healing balm
Strives to extract from his soft, giving palm;
Unlucky Welsted! thy unfeeling master,
The more thou ticklest, gripes his fist the faster.
    While thus each hand promotes the pleasing pain,
And quick sensations skip from vein to vein;
A youth unknown to Phoebus, in despair,
Puts his last refuge all in Heav'n and pray'r.
What force have pious vows! The Queen of Love
His sister sends, her vot'ress, from above.
As taught by Venus, Paris learnt the art
To touch Achilles' only tender part;
Secure, through her, the noble prize to carry,
He marches off, his Grace's Secretary.
    'Now turn to diff'rent sports (the Goddess cries)
And learn, my sons, the wond'rous pow'r of Noise.
To move, to raise, to ravish ev'ry heart,
With Shakespeare's nature, or with Jonson's art,
Let others aim: 'tis yours to shake the soul
With thunder rumbling from the mustard bowl,
With horns and trumpets now to madness swell,
Now sink in sorrows with a tolling bell;
Such happy arts attention can command
When fancy flags, and sense is at a stand.
Improve we these. Three cat-calls be the bribe
Of him, whose chatt'ring shames the monkey tribe,
And his this drum, whose hoarse heroic bass
Drowns the loud clarion of the braying Ass.'

200

210

220

230

Now thousand tongues are heard in one loud din:
The monkey-mimics rush discordant in;
'Twas chatt'ring, grinning, mouthing, jabb'ring all,
And Noise and Norton, Brangling and Breval,
Dennis and Dissonance, and captious Art,
And Snip-snap short, and Interruption smart,   240
And Demonstration thin, and Theses thick,
And Major, Minor, and Conclusion quick.
'Hold (cried the Queen), a cat-call each shall win;
Equal your merits! equal is your din!
But that this well-disputed game may end,
Sound forth my Brayers, and the welkin rend.'
    As when the long-eared milky mothers wait
At some sick miser's triple-bolted gate,
For their defrauded, absent foals they make
A moan so loud, that all the guild awake;   250
Sore sighs Sir Gilbert, starting at the bray,
From dreams of millions, and three groats to pay.
So swells each windpipe; Ass intones to Ass,
Harmonic twang! of leather, horn, and brass;
Such as from lab'ring lungs th' Enthusiast blows,
High sound, attemp'red to the vocal nose,
Or such as bellow from the deep Divine;
There Webster! pealed thy voice, and Whitfield! thine.
But far o'er all, sonorous Blackmore's strain;
Walls, steeples, skies, bray back to him again.   260
In Tot'nam Fields the brethren, with amaze,
Prick all their ears up, and forget to graze;
Long Chanc'ry Lane retentive rolls the sound,
And courts to courts return it round and round;
Thames wafts it thence to Rufus' roaring hall,
And Hungerford re-echoes bawl for bawl.
All hail him victor in both gifts of song,
Who sings so loudly, and who sings so long.
    This labour past, by Bridewell all descend
(As morning pray'r, and flagellation end),   270
To where Fleet Ditch with disemboguing streams
Rolls the large tribute of dead dogs to Thames:

The king of dikes! than whom no sluice of mud
With deeper sable blots the silver flood.
'Here strip, my children! here at once leap in,
Here prove who best can dash through thick and thin,
And who the most in love of dirt excel,
Or dark dexterity of groping well.
Who flings most filth, and wide pollutes around
280   The stream, be his the Weekly Journals bound,
A pig of lead to him who dives the best;
A peck of coals apiece shall glad the rest.'
    In naked majesty Oldmixon stands,
And Milo-like surveys his arms and hands;
Then sighing, thus, 'And am I now three score?
Ah why, ye gods! should two and two make four?'
He said, and climbed a stranded lighter's height,
Shot to the black abyss, and plunged downright.
The senior's judgement all the crowd admire,
290   Who but to sink the deeper, rose the higher.
    Next Smedley dived; slow circles dimpled o'er
The quaking mud, that closed, and oped no more.
All look, all sigh, and call on Smedley lost;
'Smedley' in vain resounds through all the coast.
    Then * essayed; scarce vanished out of sight,
He buoys up instant, and returns to light:
He bears no token of the sabler streams,
And mounts far off among the swans of Thames.
    True to the bottom, see Concanen creep,
300   A cold, long-winded native of the deep:
If perserverance gain the diver's prize,
Not everlasting Blackmore this denies:
No noise, no stir, no motion can'st thou make,
Th' unconscious stream sleeps o'er thee like a lake.
    Next plunged a feeble, but a desp'rate pack,
With each a sickly brother at his back:
Sons of a day! just buoyant on the flood,
Then numbered with the puppies in the mud.
Ask ye their names? I could as soon disclose
310   The names of these blind puppies as of those.

Fast by, like Niobe (her children gone)
Sits Mother Osborne, stupefied to stone!
And monumental brass this record bears,
'These are, – ah no! these were, the Gazetteers!'
    Not so bold Arnall; with a weight of skull
Furious he dives, precipitately dull.
Whirlpools and storms his circling arm invest,
With all the might of gravitation blest.
No crab more active in the dirty dance,
Downward to climb, and backward to advance,   320
He brings up half the bottom on his head,
And loudly claims the Journals and the lead.
    The plunging Prelate, and his pond'rous Grace,
With holy envy gave one layman place.
When lo! a burst of thunder shook the flood.
Slow rose a form, in majesty of mud,
Shaking the horrors of his sable brows,
And each ferocious feature grim with ooze.
Greater he looks, and more than mortal stares;
Then thus the wonders of the deep declares.   330
    First he relates, how sinking to the chin,
Smit with his mien, the mud-nymphs suck'd him in:
How young Lutetia, softer than the down,
Nigrina black, and Merdamante brown,
Vied for his love in jetty bow'rs below,
As Hylas fair was ravished long ago.
Then sung, how shown him by the nut-brown maids
A branch of Styx here rises from the shades,
That tinctured as it runs with Lethe's streams,
And wafting vapours from the Land of Dreams   340
(As under seas Alphaeus' secret sluice
Bears Pisa's off'rings to his Arethuse)
Pours into Thames: and hence the mingled wave
Intoxicates the pert, and lulls the grave;
Here brisker vapours o'er the Temple creep,
There, all from Paul's to Aldgate drink and sleep.
    Thence to the banks where rev'rend Bards repose,
They led him soft; each rev'rend Bard arose;

And Milbourne chief, deputed by the rest,
350 Gave him the cassock, surcingle, and vest.
'Receive (he said) these robes which once were mine;
Dullness is sacred in a sound divine.'

He ceased, and spread the robe; the crowd confess
The rev'rend Flamen in his lengthened dress.
Around him wide a sable army stand,
A low-born, cell-bred, selfish, servile band,
Prompt or to guard or stab, to saint or damn;
Heav'n's Swiss, who fight for any god, or man.

Through Lud's famed gates, along the well-known Fleet
360 Rolls the black troop, and overshades the street,
Till show'rs of Sermons, Characters, Essays,
In circling fleeces whiten all the ways:
So clouds replenished from some bog below
Mount in dark volumes, and descend in snow.
Here stopped the Goddess; and in pomp proclaims
A gentler exercise to close the games.

'Ye Critics! in whose heads, as equal scales,
I weigh what author's heaviness prevails;
Which most conduce to soothe the soul in slumbers,
370 My Henley's periods, or my Blackmore's numbers;
Attend the trial we propose to make:
If there be man who o'er such works can wake,
Sleep's all-subduing charms who dares defy,
And boasts Ulysses' ear with Argus' eye:
To him we grant our amplest pow'rs to sit
Judge of all present, past, and future wit;
To cavil, censure, dictate, right or wrong,
Full and eternal privilege of tongue.'

Three College Sophs, and three pert Templars came,
380 The same their talents, and their tastes the same;
Each prompt to query, answer, and debate,
And smit with love of Poesy and Prate.
The pond'rous books two gentle readers bring;
The heroes sit, the vulgar form a ring.
The clam'rous crowd is hushed with mugs of mum,
Till all tuned equal, send a gen'ral hum.

Then mount the Clerks, and in one lazy tone
Through the long, heavy, painful page drawl on;
Soft creeping, words on words, the sense compose;
At ev'ry line they stretch, they yawn, they doze.   390
As to soft gales top-heavy pines bow low
Their heads, and lift them as they cease to blow:
Thus oft they rear, and oft the head decline,
As breathe, or pause, by fits, the airs divine.
And now to this side, now to that they nod,
As verse, or prose, infuse the drowsy god.
Thrice Budgele aimèd to speak, but thrice suppressed
By potent Arthur, knocked his chin and breast.
Toland and Tindal, prompt at priests to jeer,
Yet silent bowed to Christ's No Kingdom here.   400
Who sate the nearest, by the words o'ercome,
Slept first; the distant nodded to the hum.
Then down are rolled the books; stretched o'er 'em lies
Each gentle Clerk, and mutt'ring seals his eyes.
As what a Dutchman plumps into the lakes,
One circle first, and then a second makes;
What Dullness dropped among her sons imprest
Like motion from one circle to the rest;
So from the midmost the nutation spreads
Round and more round, o'er all the sea of heads.   410
At last Centlivre felt her voice to fail,
Motteux himself unfinished left his tale,
Boyer the state, and Law the stage gave o'er,
Morgan and Mandeville could prate no more;
Norton, from Daniel and Ostroea sprung,
Blessed with his father's front, and mother's tongue,
Hung silent down his never-blushing head;
And all was hushed, as Folly's self lay dead.
    Thus the soft gifts of Sleep conclude the day,
And stretched on bulks, as usual, Poets lay.   420
Why should I sing what bards the nightly Muse
Did slumb'ring visit, and convey to stews;
Who prouder marched with magistrates in state
To some famed roundhouse, ever open gate!

How Henley lay inspired beside a sink,
And to mere mortals seemed a priest in drink,
While others, timely, to the neighb'ring Fleet
(Haunt of the Muses) made their safe retreat.

Book the Third

ARGUMENT

After the other persons are disposed in their proper places of rest, the Goddess transports the King to her Temple, and there lays him to slumber with his head on her lap; a position of marvellous virtue, which causes all the visions of wild enthusiasts, projectors, politicians, inamoratos, castle-builders, chemists, and poets. He is immediately carried on the wings of Fancy, and led by a mad poetical Sibyl, to the Elysian *shade; where, on the banks of* Lethe, *the souls of the dull are dipped by* Bavius *before their entrance into this world. There he is met by the ghost of* Settle, *and by him made acquainted with the wonders of the place, and with those which he himself is destined to perform. He takes him to a* Mount of Vision, *from whence he shows him the past triumphs of the Empire of Dullness, then the present, and lastly the future: how small a part of the world was ever conquered by Science, how soon those conquests were stopped, and those very nations again reduced to her dominion. Then distinguishing the island of* Great Britain, *shows by what aids, by what persons, and by what degrees it shall be brought to her Empire. Some of the persons he causes to pass in review before his eyes, describing each by his proper figure, character, and qualifications. On a sudden the scene shifts, and a vast number of miracles and prodigies appear, utterly surprising and unknown to the King himself, till they are explained to be the wonders of his own reign now commencing. On this subject* Settle *breaks into a congratulation, yet not unmixed with concern, that his own times were but the types of these. He prophesies how first the nation shall be*

overrun with Farces, Operas, *and* Shows; *how the throne of*
Dullness shall be advanced over the Theatres, *and set up even*
at Court; *then how her sons shall preside in the seats of* Arts
and Sciences: *giving a glimpse, or Pisgah-sight of the future*
fullness of her Glory, the accomplishment whereof is the sub-
ject of the fourth and last book.

But in her Temple's last recess enclosed,
On Dullness' lap th' anointed head reposed.
Him close she curtains round with vapours blue,
And soft besprinkles with Cimmerian dew.
Then raptures high the seat of sense o'erflow,
Which only heads refined from reason know.
Hence, from the straw where Bedlam's prophet nods,
He hears loud oracles, and talks with gods;
Hence the fool's paradise, the statesman's scheme,
The air-built castle, and the golden dream,   10
The maid's romantic wish, the chemist's flame,
And poet's vision of eternal fame.
    And now, on Fancy's easy wing conveyed,
The King descending, views th' Elysian shade.
A slipshod Sibyl led his steps along,
In lofty madness meditating song;
Her tresses staring from poetic dreams,
And never washed, but in Castalia's streams.
Taylor, their better Charon, lends an oar,
(Once swan of Thames, though now he sings no more).   20
Benlowes, propitious still to blockheads, bows,
And Shadwell nods the poppy on his brows.
Here, in a dusky vale where Lethe rolls,
Old Bavius sits, to dip poetic souls,
And blunt the sense, and fit it for a skull
Of solid proof, impenetrably dull.
Instant, when dipped, away they wing their flight,
Where Brown and Mears unbar the gates of light,
Demand new bodies, and in calf's array,
Rush to the world, impatient for the day.   30

Millions and millions on these banks he views,
Thick as the stars of night, or morning dews,
As thick as bees o'er vernal blossoms fly,
As thick as eggs at Ward in pillory.
        Wond'ring he gazed: when lo! a Sage appears,
By his broad shoulders known, and length of ears,
Known by the band and suit which Settle wore
(His only suit) for twice three years before:
All as the vest, appeared the wearer's frame,
40   Old in new state, another yet the same.
Bland and familiar as in life, begun
Thus the great Father to the greater Son:
        'Oh born to see what none can see awake!
Behold the wonders of th' oblivious Lake.
Thou, yet unborn, hast touched this sacred shore;
The hand of Bavius drenched thee o'er and o'er.
But blind to former as to future fate,
What mortal knows his pre-existent state?
Who knows how long thy transmigrating soul
50   Might from Boeotian to Boeotian roll?
How many Dutchmen she vouchsafed to thrid?
How many stages through old monks she rid?
And all who since, in mild benighted days,
Mixed the Owl's ivy with the poet's bays.
As man's meanders to the vital spring
Roll all their tides, then back their circles bring;
Or whirligigs, twirled round by skilful swain,
Suck the thread in, then yield it out again:
All nonsense thus, of old or modern date,
60   Shall in thee centre, from thee circulate.
For this our Queen unfolds to vision true
Thy mental eye, for thou hast much to view:
Old scenes of glory, times long cast behind
Shall, first recalled, rush forward to thy mind;
Then stretch thy sight o'er all her rising reign,
And let the past and future fire thy brain.
        'Ascend this hill, whose cloudy point commands
Her boundless empire over seas and lands.

See, round the poles where keener spangles shine,
Where spices smoke beneath the burning Line,   70
(Earth's wide extremes) her sable flag displayed,
And all the nations covered in her shade!

  'Far eastward cast thine eye, from whence the sun
And orient Science their bright course begun:
One godlike monarch all that pride confounds,
He, whose long wall the wand'ring Tartar bounds;
Heav'ns! what a pile! whole ages perish there,
And one bright blaze turns Learning into air.

  'Thence to the south extend thy gladdened eyes;
There rival flames with equal glory rise;   80
From shelves to shelves see greedy Vulcan roll,
And lick up all their physic of the soul.

  'How little, mark! that portion of the ball
Where, faint at best, the beams of Science fall:
Soon as they dawn, from hyperborean skies
Embodied dark, what clouds of Vandals rise!
Lo! where Maeotis sleeps, and hardly flows
The freezing Tanais through a waste of snows,
The North by myriads pours her mighty sons,
Great nurse of Goths, of Alans and of Huns!   90
See Alaric's stern port! the martial frame
Of Genseric! and Attila's dread name!
See the bold Ostrogoths on Latium fall;
See the fierce Visigoths on Spain and Gaul!
See where the morning gilds the palmy shore
(The soil that arts and infant letters bore):
His conqu'ring tribes th' Arabian prophet draws,
And saving Ignorance enthrones by laws.
See Christians, Jews, one heavy sabbath keep,
And all the western world believe and sleep.   100

  'Lo! Rome herself, proud mistress now no more
Of arts, but thund'ring against heathen lore;
Her grey-haired synods damning books unread,
And Bacon trembling for his brazen head.
Padua, with sighs, beholds her Livy burn,
And ev'n th' Antipodes Vigilius mourn.

See, the Cirque falls, th' unpillared temple nods,
Streets paved with heroes, Tiber choked with gods;
Till Peter's keys some christened Jove adorn,
And Pan to Moses lends his pagan horn;
See graceless Venus to a Virgin turned,
Or Phidias broken, and Apelles burned.

   'Behold yon Isle, by palmers, pilgrims trod,
Men bearded, bald, cowled, uncowled, shod, unshod,
Peeled, patched and piebald, linsey-wolsey brothers,
Grave mummers! sleeveless some, and shirtless others.
That once was Britain – happy! had she seen
No fiercer sons, had Easter never been.
In peace, great Goddess, ever be adored;
How keen the war, if Dullness draw the sword!
Thus visit not thy own! on this blest age
Oh spread thy influence, but restrain thy rage.

   'And see, my son! the hour is on its way,
That lifts our Goddess to imperial sway;
This fav'rite isle, long severed from her reign,
Dove-like, she gathers to her wings again.
Now look through Fate! behold the scene she draws!
What aids, what armies to assert her cause!
See all her progeny, illustrious sight!
Behold, and count them, as they rise to light.
As Berecynthia, while her offspring vie
In homage to the Mother of the sky,
Surveys around her, in the blest abode,
An hundred sons, and ev'ry son a god:
Not with less glory mighty Dullness crowned
Shall take through Grub Street her triumphant round;
And her Parnassus glancing o'er at once,
Behold an hundred sons, and each a Dunce.

   'Mark first that youth who takes the foremost place,
And thrusts his person full into your face.
With all thy father's virtues blest, be born!
And a new Cibber shall the stage adorn.

   'A second see, by meeker manners known,
And modest as the maid that sips alone;

110

120

130

140

From the strong fate of drams if thou get free,
Another Durfey, Ward! shall sing in thee.
Thee shall each ale house, thee each gill house mourn,
And answ'ring gin shops sourer sighs return.

  'Jacob, the scourge of Grammar, mark with awe,   150
Nor less revere him, blunderbuss of Law.
Lo Popple's brow, tremendous to the town,
Horneck's fierce eye, and Roome's funereal frown.
Lo sneering Goode, half malice and half whim,
A fiend in glee, ridiculously grim.
Each cygnet sweet of Bath and Tunbridge race,
Whose tuneful whistling makes the waters pass:
Each songster, riddler, ev'ry nameless name,
All crowd, who foremost shall be damned to Fame.
Some strain in rhyme; the Muses, on their racks,
Scream like the winding of ten thousand jacks;   160
Some free from rhyme or reason, rule or check,
Break Priscian's head, and Pegasus's neck;
Down, down they larum, with impetuous whirl,
The Pindars, and the Miltons of a Curll.

  'Silence, ye wolves! while Ralph to Cynthia howls
And makes Night hideous—answer him, ye owls!

  'Sense, speech, and measure, living tongues and dead,
Let all give way – and Morris may be read.

  'Flow Welsted, flow! like thine inspirer, beer,
Though stale, not ripe; though thin, yet never clear;   170
So sweetly mawkish, and so smoothly dull;
Heady, not strong; o'erflowing, though not full.

  'Ah Dennis! Gildon ah! what ill-starred rage
Divides a friendship long confirmed by age?
Blockheads with reason wicked wits abhor,
But fool with fool is barb'rous civil war.
Embrace, embrace my sons! be foes no more!
Nor glad vile poets with true critics' gore.

  'Behold yon pair, in strict embraces join'd;
How like in manners, and how like in mind!   180
Equal in wit, and equally polite,
Shall this a Pasquin, that a Grumbler write;

Like are their merits, like rewards they share,
That shines a consul, this commissioner.'
    'But who is he, in closet close y-pent,
Of sober face, with learnèd dust besprent?'
'Right well mine eyes arede the myster wight,
On parchment scraps y-fed, and Wormius hight.
To future ages may thy dullness last,
As thou preserv'st the dullness of the past!
    'There, dim in clouds, the poring scholiasts mark,
Wits, who like owls, see only in the dark,
A lumberhouse of books in ev'ry head,
For ever reading, never to be read!
    'But, where each Science lifts its modern type,
Hist'ry her pot, Divinity her pipe,
While proud Philosophy repines to show,
Dishonest sight! his breeches rent below;
Imbrowned with native bronze, lo! Henley stands,
Tuning his voice, and balancing his hands.
How fluent nonsense trickles from his tongue!
How sweet the periods, neither said, nor sung!
Still break the benches, Henley! with thy strain,
While Sherlock, Hare, and Gibson preach in vain.
Oh great restorer of the good old stage,
Preacher at once, and zany of thy age!
Oh worthy thou of Egypt's wise abodes,
A decent priest, where monkeys were the gods!
But fate with butchers placed thy priestly stall,
Meek modern faith to murder, hack, and maul,
And bade thee live, to crown Britannia's praise,
In Toland's, Tindal's, and in Woolston's days.
    'Yet oh, my sons! a father's words attend
(So may the fates preserve the ears you lend):
'Tis yours, a Bacon or a Locke to blame,
A Newton's genius, or a Milton's flame.
But oh! with One, immortal One dispense,
The source of Newton's light, of Bacon's sense!
Content, each emanation of his fires
That beams on earth, each virtue he inspires,

190

200

210

220

Each art he prompts, each charm he can create,
Whate'er he gives, are giv'n for you to hate.
Persist, by all divine in Man unawed,
But, Learn, ye DUNCES! not to scorn your GOD.'
    Thus he, for then a ray of reason stole
Half through the solid darkness of his soul;
But soon the cloud returned – and thus the Sire:
'See now, what Dullness and her sons admire!
See what the charms, that smite the simple heart
Not touched by Nature, and not reached by Art.'   230
    His never-blushing head he turned aside
(Not half so pleased when Goodman prophesied),
And looked, and saw a sable sorc'rer rise,
Swift to whose hand a wingèd volume flies.
All sudden, gorgons hiss, and dragons glare,
And ten-horned friends and giants rush to war.
Hell rises, Heav'n descends, and dance on earth:
Gods, imps, and monsters, music, rage, and mirth,
A fire, a jig, a battle, and a ball,
Till one wide conflagration swallows all.   240
    Thence a new world to Nature's laws unknown
Breaks out refulgent, with a heav'n its own:
Another Cynthia her new journey runs,
And other planets circle other suns.
The forests dance, the rivers upward rise,
Whales sport in woods, and dolphins in the skies;
And last, to give the whole creation grace,
Lo! one vast egg produces human race.
    Joy fills his soul, joy innocent of thought;
'What pow'r,' he cries, 'what pow'r these wonders
            wrought?'   250
'Son, what thou seek'st is in thee! Look, and find
Each monster meets his likeness in thy mind.
Yet would'st thou more? In yonder cloud behold,
Whose sarsenet skirts are edged with flamy gold,
A matchless youth! his nod these worlds controls,
Wings the red lightning, and the thunder rolls.

Angel of Dullness, sent to scatter round
Her magic charms o'er all unclassic ground:
Yon stars, yon suns, he rears at pleasure higher,
260   Illumes their light, and sets their flames on fire.
Immortal Rich! how calm he sits at ease
'Mid snows of paper, and fierce hail of peas;
And proud his Mistress' orders to perform,
Rides in the whirlwind, and directs the storm.

      'But lo! to dark encounter in mid air
New wizards rise; I see my Cibber there!
Booth in his cloudy tabernacle shrined,
On grinning dragons thou shalt mount the wind.
Dire is the conflict, dismal is the din,
270   Here shouts all Drury, there all Lincoln's Inn;
Contending Theatres our empire raise,
Alike their labours, and alike their praise.

      'And are these wonders, son, to thee unknown?
Unknown to thee? These wonders are thy own.
These, Fate reserved to grace thy reign divine,
Foreseen by me, but ah! withheld from mine.
In Lud's old walls though long I ruled, renowned
Far as loud Bow's stupendous bells resound;
Though my own Aldermen conferred the bays,
280   To me committing their eternal praise,
Their full-fed heroes, their pacific may'rs,
Their annual trophies, and their monthly wars;
Though long my party built on me their hopes,
For writing pamphlets, and for roasting Popes;
Yet lo! in me what authors have to brag on!
Reduced at last to hiss in my own dragon.
Avert it Heav'n! that thou, my Cibber, e'er
Should'st wag a serpent-tail in Smithfield Fair!
Like the vile straw that's blown about the streets,
290   The needy poet sticks to all he meets,
Coached, carted, trod upon, now loose, now fast,
And carried off in some dog's tail at last.
Happier thy fortunes! like a rolling stone
Thy giddy dullness still shall lumber on;

Safe in its heaviness, shall never stray,
But lick up ev'ry blockhead in the way.
Thee shall the Patriot, thee the courtier taste,
And ev'ry year be duller than the last.
Till raised from booths to theatre, to Court,
Her seat imperial Dullness shall transport.   300
Already Opera prepares the way,
The sure forerunner of her gentle sway:
Let her thy heart, next drabs and dice, engage,
The third mad passion of thy doting age.
Teach thou the warb'ling Polypheme to roar,
And scream thyself as none e'er screamed before!
To aid our cause, if Heav'n thou can'st not bend,
Hell thou shalt move, for Faustus is our friend:
Pluto with Cato thou for this shalt join,
And link the Mourning Bride to Proserpine.   310
Grub Street! thy fall should men and gods conspire.
Thy stage shall stand, ensure it but from fire.
Another Aeschylus appears! prepare
For new abortions, all ye pregnant fair!
In flames, like Semele's, be brought to bed,
While op'ning Hell spouts wildfire at your head.
    'Now Bavius take the poppy from thy brow,
And place it here! here all ye heroes bow!
This, this is he, foretold by ancient rhymes:
Th' Augustus born to bring Saturnian times.   320
Signs following signs lead on the mighty year!
See! the dull stars roll round and reappear.
See, see, our own true Phoebus wears the bays!
Our Midas sits Lord Chancellor of plays!
On poets' tombs see Benson's titles writ!
Lo! Ambrose Philips is preferred for wit!
See under Ripley rise a new Whitehall,
While Jones' and Boyle's united labours fall;
While Wren with sorrow to the grave descends,
Gay dies unpensioned with a hundred friends.   330
Hibernian Politics, O Swift! thy fate,
And Pope's, ten years to comment and translate.

'Proceed, great days! till Learning fly the shore,
Till birch shall blush with noble blood no more,
Till Thames see Eton's sons for ever play,
Till Westminster's whole year be holiday,
Till Isis' elders reel, their pupils sport,
And Alma Mater lie dissolved in port!'
   'Enough! enough!' the raptured Monarch cries;
340   And through the iv'ry gate the vision flies.

Book the Fourth

ARGUMENT

The Poet being, in this Book, to declare the completion of the prophecies mentioned at the end of the former, makes a new Invocation; as the greater Poets are wont, when some high and worthy matter is to be sung. He shows the Goddess coming in her majesty, to destroy Order and Science, and to substitute the Kingdom of the Dull upon earth. How she leads captive the Sciences, and silenceth the Muses; and what they be who succeed in their stead. All her children, by a wonderful attraction, are drawn about her; and bear along with them divers others, who promote her Empire by connivance, weak resistance, or discouragement of Arts; such as Half-wits, tasteless Admirers, vain Pretenders, the Flatterers of Dunces, or the Patrons of them. All these crowd round her; one of them offering to approach her, is driven back by a Rival, but she commends and encourages both. The first who speak in form are the Genius's of the Schools, who assure her of their care to advance her cause, by confining Youth to Words, and keeping them out of the way of real Knowledge. Their Address, and her gracious Answer; with her Charge to them and the Universities. The Universities appear by their proper Deputies, and assure her that the same method is observed in the progress of Education; the speech of Aristarchus on this subject. They are driven off by a band of young Gentlemen returned from travel with their Tutors; one of whom delivers to the Goddess, in a polite oration, an account of the whole conduct and fruits of their travels: *presenting to her at the same time a young Nobleman perfectly accomplished. She receives him graciously, and indues him with the happy quality of* Want of Shame. *She sees loitering about her a number of* Indolent Persons *abandoning all business and duty, and dying with laziness: to these approaches the Antiquary* Annius, *intreating her to make them* Virtuosos, *and assign them over to him: but* Mummius, *another Antiquary, complaining of his fraudulent proceeding, she finds a method to reconcile their difference. Then enter a Troop of people fantastically adorned, offering her strange and exotic presents: amongst them, one stands forth and demands justice on another, who had deprived him of one of the greatest Curiosities in nature: but he justifies himself so well, that the Goddess gives them both her approbation. She recommends to them to find proper employment for the* Indolents *beforementioned, in the study of* Butterflies, Shells, Birds-nests, Moss, etc., *but with particular caution not to proceed beyond* Trifles, *to any useful or extensive views of* Nature, *or of the Author of Nature. Against the last of these apprehensions, she is secured by a hearty Address from the* Minute Philosophers *and* Freethinkers, *one of whom speaks in the name of the rest. The Youth thus instructed and principled, are delivered to her in a body, by the hands of* Silenus; *and then admitted to taste the cup of the* Magus *her High Priest, which causes a total oblivion of all Obligations, divine, civil, moral, or rational. To these her Adepts she sends* Priests, Attendants, *and* Comforters, *of various kinds; confers on them* Orders *and* Degrees; *and then dismissing them with a speech, confirming to each his privileges and telling what she expects from each, concludes with a* Yawn *of extraordinary virtue: the progress and effects whereof on all orders of men, and the consummation of all, in the restoration of* Night *and* Chaos, *conclude the Poem.*

> Yet, yet a moment, one dim ray of light
> Indulge, dread Chaos, and eternal Night!
> Of darkness visible so much be lent,
> As half to show, half veil the deep intent.
> Ye Pow'rs! whose Mysteries restored I sing,
> To whom Time bears me on his rapid wing,

Suspend a while your force inertly strong,
Then take at once the Poet and the Song.
  Now flamed the Dog-star's unpropitious ray,
10 Smote ev'ry brain, and withered ev'ry bay;
Sick was the sun, the owl forsook his bow'r,
The moon-struck Prophet felt the madding hour:
Then rose the seed of Chaos, and of Night,
To blot out Order, and extinguish Light,
Of dull and venal a new world to mould,
And bring Saturnian days of Lead and Gold.
  She mounts the throne; her head a cloud concealed,
In broad effulgence all below revealed
('Tis thus aspiring Dullness ever shines);
20 Soft on her lap her Laureate son reclines.
  Beneath her footstool *Science* groans in chains,
And *Wit* dreads exile, penalties, and pains.
There foamed rebellious *Logic*, gagged and bound,
There, stripped, fair *Rhet'ric* languished on the ground;
His blunted arms by *Sophistry* are borne,
And shameless *Billingsgate* her robes adorn.
Morality, by her false guardians drawn,
Chicane in furs, and *Casuistry* in lawn,
Gasps, as they straiten at each end the cord,
30 And dies, when Dullness gives her Page the word.
Mad *Mathesis* alone was unconfined,
Too mad for mere material chains to bind,
Now to pure space lifts her ecstatic stare,
Now running round the circle, finds it square.
But held in tenfold bonds the *Muses* lie,
Watched both by Envy's and by Flatt'ry's eye:
There to her heart sad Tragedy addressed
The dagger wont to pierce the Tyrant's breast;
But sober History restrained her rage,
40 And promised vengeance on a barb'rous age.
There sunk Thalia, nerveless, cold, and dead,
Had not her sister Satyr held her head:
Nor could'st thou, Chesterfield! a tear refuse;
Thou wept'st, and with thee wept each gentle Muse.

When lo! a harlot form soft sliding by,
With mincing step, small voice, and languid eye;
Foreign her air, her robe's discordant pride
In patchwork flutt'ring, and her head aside,
By singing Peers upheld on either hand,
She tripped and laughed, too pretty much to stand;   50
Cast on the prostrate Nine a scornful look,
Then thus in quaint recitativo spoke:
    'O *cara! cara!* silence all that train;
Joy to great Chaos! let Division reign:
Chromatic tortures soon shall drive them hence,
Break all their nerves, and fritter all their sense,
One trill shall harmonize joy, grief, and rage,
Wake the dull Church, and lull the ranting Stage;
To the same notes thy sons shall hum, or snore,
And all thy yawning daughters cry, *encore*.   60
Another Phoebus, thy own Phoebus, reigns,
Joys in my jigs, and dances in my chains.
But soon, ah soon Rebellion will commence,
If Music meanly borrows aid from Sense.
Strong in new arms, lo! giant Handel stands,
Like bold Briareus, with a hundred hands;
To stir, to rouse, to shake the soul he comes,
And Jove's own thunders follow Mars's drums.
Arrest him, Empress; or you sleep no more' –
She heard, and drove him to th' Hibernian shore.   70
    And now had Fame's posterior trumpet blown,
And all the nations summoned to the throne.
The young, the old, who feel her inward sway,
One instinct seizes, and transports away.
None need a guide, by sure attraction led,
And strong impulsive gravity of head;
None want a place, for all their centre found,
Hung to the Goddess, and cohered around.
Not closer, orb in orb, conglobed are seen
The buzzing bees about their dusky queen.   80
    The gath'ring number, as it moves along,
Involves a vast involuntary throng,

Who gently drawn, and struggling less and less,
Roll in her vortex, and her pow'r confess.
Not those alone who passive own her laws,
But who, weak rebels, more advance her cause.
Whate'er of dunce in College or in Town
Sneers at another, in toupee or gown;
Whate'er of mungril no one class admits,
A wit with dunces, and a dunce with wits.
90
    Nor absent they, no members of her state,
Who pay her homage in her sons, the Great;
Who false to Phoebus, bow the knee to Baal,
Or impious, preach his Word without a call.
Patrons, who sneak from living worth to dead,
Withhold the pension, and set up the head;
Or vest dull Flatt'ry in the sacred gown;
Or give from fool to fool the laurel crown.
And (last and worst) with all the cant of wit,
Without the soul, the Muse's Hypocrite.
100
    There marched the bard and blockhead, side by side,
Who rhymed for hire, and patronized for pride.
Narcissus, praised with all a parson's pow'r,
Looked a white lily sunk beneath a show'r.
There moved Montalto with superior air;
His stretched-out arm displayed a Volume fair;
Courtiers and Patriots in two ranks divide,
Through both he passed, and bowed from side to side:
But as in graceful act, with awful eye
Composed he stood, bold Benson thrust him by.
110
On two unequal crutches propped he came,
Milton's on this, on that one Johnston's name.
The decent knight retired with sober rage,
Withdrew his hand, and closed the pompous page.
But (happy for him as the times went then)
Appeared Apollo's may'r and aldermen,
On whom three hundred gold-capped youths await
To lug the pond'rous volume off in state.
    When Dullness, smiling – 'Thus revive the Wits!
120
But murder first, and mince them all to bits;

As erst Medea (cruel, so to save!)
A new Edition of old Aeson gave;
Let standard-Authors, thus, like trophies borne,
Appear more glorious as more hacked and torn,
And you, my critics! in the chequered shade,
Admire new light through holes yourselves have made.
     'Leave not a foot of verse, a foot of stone,
A page, a grave, that they can call their own;
But spread, my sons, your glory thin or thick,
On passive paper, or on solid brick.   130
So by each Bard an Alderman shall sit,
A heavy Lord shall hang at ev'ry Wit,
And while on Fame's triumphal car they ride,
Some slave of mine be pinioned to their side.'
     Now crowds on crowds around the Goddess press,
Each eager to present the first Address.
Dunce scorning Dunce beholds the next advance,
But Fop shews Fop superior complaisance.
When lo! a Spectre rose, whose index-hand
Held forth the virtue of the dreadful wand;   140
His beavered brow a birchen garland wears,
Dropping with infant's blood, and mother's tears.
O'er ev'ry vein a shudd'ring horror runs;
Eton and Winton shake through all their sons.
All flesh is humbled, Westminster's bold race
Shrink, and confess the Genius of the place;
The pale boy-senator yet tingling stands,
And holds his breeches close with both his hands.
     Then thus: 'Since Man from beast by Words is known,
Words are Man's province, Words we teach alone.   150
When Reason doubtful, like the Samian letter,
Points him two ways, the narrower is the better.
Placed at the door of Learning, youth to guide,
We never suffer it to stand too wide.
To ask, to guess, to know, as they commence,
As Fancy opens the quick springs of Sense,
We ply the Memory, we load the brain,
Bind rebel Wit, and double chain on chain;

Confine the thought, to exercise the breath,
160 And keep them in the pale of Words till death.
Whate'er the talents, or howe'er designed,
We hang one jingling padlock on the mind:
A poet the first day, he dips his quill;
And what the last? a very poet still.
Pity! the charm works only in our wall,
Lost, lost too soon in yonder House or Hall.
There truant WYNDHAM ev'ry Muse gave o'er,
There TALBOT sunk, and was a Wit no more!
How sweet an Ovid, MURRAY was our boast!
170 How many Martials were in PULT'NEY lost!
Else sure some Bard, to our eternal praise,
In twice ten thousand rhyming nights and days,
Had reached the Work, the All that mortal can;
And South beheld that Masterpiece of Man.
       'Oh (cried the Goddess) for some pedant reign!
Some gentle JAMES, to bless the land again;
To stick the Doctor's chair into the throne,
Give law to Words, or war with Words alone,
Senates and Courts with Greek and Latin rule,
180 And turn the Council to a grammar school!
For sure, if Dullness sees a grateful day,
'Tis in the shade of Arbitrary Sway.
O! if my sons may learn one earthly thing,
Teach but that one, sufficient for a king;
That which my Priests, and mine alone, maintain,
Which as it dies, or lives, we fall, or reign:
May you, may Cam, and Isis preach it long!
"The RIGHT DIVINE of Kings to govern wrong."
       Prompt at the call, around the Goddess roll
190 Broad hats, and hoods, and caps, a sable shoal:
Thick and more thick the black blockade extends,
A hundred head of Aristotle's friends.
Nor wert thou, Isis! wanting to the day,
[Though Christ Church long kept prudishly away].
Each staunch Polemic, stubborn as a rock,
Each fierce Logician, still expelling Locke,

Came whip and spur, and dashed through thin and thick
On German Crouzaz, and Dutch Burgersdyck.
As many quit the streams that murm'ring fall
To lull the sons of Marg'ret and Clare Hall,   200
Where Bentley late tempestuous wont to sport
In troubled waters, but now sleeps in port.
Before them marched that awful Aristarch;
Ploughed was his front with many a deep Remark;
His hat, which never vailed to human pride,
Walker with rev'rence took, and laid aside.
Low bowed the rest: he, kingly, did but nod;
So upright Quakers please both Man and God.
'Mistress! dismiss that rabble from your throne:
Avaunt—is Aristarchus yet unknown?   210
Thy mighty Scholiast, whose unwearied pains
Made Horace dull, and humbled Milton's strains.
Turn what they will to verse, their toil is vain,
Critics like me shall make it prose again.
Roman and Greek Grammarians! know your better:
Author of something yet more great than Letter;
While tow'ring o'er your alphabet, like Saul,
Stands our Digamma, and o'er-tops them all.
'Tis true, on Words is still our whole debate,
Disputes of *Me* or *Te*, of *aut* or *at*,   220
To sound or sink in *cano*, O or A,
Or give up Cicero to C or K.
Let Freind affect to speak as Terence spoke,
And Alsop never but like Horace joke:
For me, what Virgil, Pliny may deny,
Manilius or Solinus shall supply;
For Attic phrase in Plato let them seek,
I poach in Suidas for unlicensed Greek.
In ancient sense if any needs will deal,
Be sure I give them fragments, not a meal;   230
What Gellius or Stobaeus hashed before,
Or chewed by blind old Scholiasts o'er and o'er.
The critic eye, that microscope of Wit,
Sees hairs and pores, examines bit by bit.

How parts relate to parts, or they to whole,
The body's harmony, the beaming soul,
Are things which Kuster, Burman, Wasse shall see,
When Man's whole frame is obvious to a *flea*.
    'Ah, think not, Mistress! more true Dullness lies
240 In Folly's cap, than Wisdom's grave disguise.
Like buoys, that never sink into the flood,
On Learning's surface we but lie and nod.
Thine is the genuine head of many a House,
And much Divinity without a Νοῦς.
Nor could a BARROW work on ev'ry block,
Nor has one ATTERBURY spoiled the flock.
See! still thy own, the heavy Canon roll,
And Metaphysic smokes involve the pole.
For thee we dim the eyes, and stuff the head
250 With all such reading as was never read;
For thee explain a thing till all men doubt it,
And write about it, Goddess, and about it:
So spins the silkworm small its slender store,
And labours till it clouds itself all o'er.
    'What though we let some better sort of fool
Thrid ev'ry science, run through ev'ry school?
Never by tumbler through the hoops was shown
Such skill in passing all, and touching none.
He may indeed (if sober all this time)
260 Plague with Dispute, or persecute with Rhyme.
We only furnish what he cannot use,
Or wed to what he must divorce, a Muse;
Full in the midst of Euclid dip at once,
And petrify a Genius to a Dunce;
Or set on Metaphysic ground to prance,
Show all his paces, not a step advance.
With the same cement, ever sure to bind,
We bring to one dead level ev'ry mind.
Then take him to develop, if you can,
270 And hew the block off, and get out the Man.
But wherefore waste I words? I see advance
Whore, pupil, and laced governor from France.

Walker! our hat'— nor more he deigned to say,
But, stern as Ajax' spectre, strode away.
    In flowed at once a gay embroidered race,
And titt'ring pushed the Pedants off the place:
Some would have spoken, but the voice was drowned
By the French horn, or by the op'ning hound.
The first came forwards, with as easy mien
As if he saw St James's and the Queen.   280
When thus th'attendant Orator begun:
    'Receive, great Empress! thy accomplished Son:
Thine from the birth, and sacred from the rod,
A dauntless infant! never scared with God.
The sire saw, one by one, his virtues wake:
The mother begged the blessing of a rake.
Thou gav'st that ripeness, which so soon began,
And ceased so soon, he ne'er was boy, nor man.
Through school and college, thy kind cloud o'ercast,
Safe and unseen the young Aeneas passed;   290
Thence bursting glorious, all at once let down,
Stunned with his giddy larum half the town.
Intrepid then, o'er seas and lands he flew:
Europe he saw, and Europe saw him too.
There all thy gifts and graces we display,
Thou, only thou, directing all our way!
To where the Seine, obsequious as she runs,
Pours at great Bourbon's feet her silken sons;
Or Tiber, now no longer Roman, rolls,
Vain of Italian arts, Italian souls: 300
To happy convents, bosomed deep in vines,
Where slumber abbots, purple as their wines;
To isles of fragrance, lily-silvered vales,
Diffusing languor in the panting gales;
To lands of singing, or of dancing slaves,
Love-whisp'ring woods, and lute-resounding waves.
But chief her shrine where naked Venus keeps,
And Cupids ride the Lion of the Deeps;
Where, eased of fleets, the Adriatic main
Wafts the smooth eunuch and enamoured swain.   310

Led by my hand, he sauntered Europe round,
And gathered ev'ry vice on Christian ground;
Saw ev'ry Court, heard ev'ry King declare
His royal sense, of op'ras or the fair;
The stews and palace equally explored,
Intrigued with glory, and with spirit whored;
Tried all *hors-d'oeuvres*, all *liqueurs* defined,
Judicious drank, and greatly-daring dined,
Dropped the dull lumber of the Latin store,
320   Spoiled his own language, and acquired no more;
All classic learning lost on classic ground;
And last turned *Air*, the echo of a sound!
See now, half-cured, and perfectly well-bred,
With nothing but a solo in his head;
As much Estate, and Principle, and Wit,
As Jansen, Fleetwood, Cibber shall think fit;
Stol'n from a duel, followed by a nun,
And, if a borough choose him, not undone;
See, to my country happy I restore
330   This glorious Youth, and add one Venus more.
Her too receive (for her my soul adores);
So may the sons of sons of sons of whores
Prop thine, O Empress! like each neighbour throne,
And make a long posterity thy own.'
        Pleased, she accepts the Hero and the Dame,
Wraps in her veil, and frees from sense of shame.
        Then looked, and saw a lazy, lolling sort,
Unseen at church, at senate, or at court,
Of ever-listless loit'rers, that attend
340   No cause, no trust, no duty, and no friend.
Thee too, my Paridel! she marked thee there,
Stretched on the rack of a too easy chair,
And heard thy everlasting yawn confess
The pains and penalties of Idleness.
She pitied! but her pity only shed
Benigner influence on thy nodding head.
        But Annius, crafty Seer, with ebon wand,
And well dissembled em'rald on his hand,

False as his gems, and cankered as his coins,
Came, crammed with capon, from where Pollio dines.   350
Soft, as the wily fox is seen to creep,
Where bask on sunny banks the simple sheep,
Walk round and round, now prying here, now there,
So he; but pious, whispered first his pray'r:
    'Grant, gracious Goddess! grant me still to cheat,
O may thy cloud still cover the deceit!
Thy choicer mists on this assembly shed,
But pour them thickest on the noble head.
So shall each youth, assisted by our eyes,
See other Caesars, other Homers rise;   360
Through twilight ages hunt th' Athenian fowl
Which Chalcis gods, and mortals call an owl;
Now see an Attys, now a Cecrops clear,
Nay, Mahomet! the pigeon at thine ear;
Be rich in ancient brass, though not in gold,
And keep his Lares, though his house be sold;
To headless Phoebe his fair bride postpone,
Honour a Syrian prince above his own;
Lord of an Otho, if I vouch it true;
Blest in one Niger, till he knows of two.'   370
    Mummius o'erheard him; Mummius, Fool-renowned,
Who like his Cheops stinks above the ground,
Fierce as a startled Adder, swelled and said,
Rattling an ancient sistrum at his head:
    'Speak'st thou of Syrian princes? Traitor base!
Mine, Goddess! mine is all the hornèd race.
True, he had wit, to make their value rise;
From foolish Greeks to steal them, was as wise;
More glorious yet, from barb'rous hands to keep,
When Sallee rovers chased him on the deep.   380
Then taught by Hermes, and divinely bold,
Down his own throat he risked the Grecian gold;
Received each demigod with pious care,
Deep in his entrails – I revered them there;
I bought them, shrouded in that living shrine,
And at their second birth, they issue mine.'

'Witness great Ammon! by whose horns I swore,
(Replied soft Annius) this our paunch before
Still bears them, faithful; and that thus I eat,
390   Is to refund the medals with the meat.
To prove me, Goddess! clear of all design,
Bid me with Pollio sup, as well as dine:
There all the learn'd shall at the labour stand,
And Douglas lend his soft, obstetric hand.'
    The Goddess smiling seemed to give consent;
So back to Pollio, hand in hand, they went.
    Then thick as locusts black'ning all the ground,
A tribe, with weeds and shells fantastic crowned,
Each with some wond'rous gift approached the Pow'r,
400   A nest, a toad, a fungus, or a flow'r.
But far the foremost, two, with earnest zeal,
And aspect ardent to the Throne appeal.
    The first thus opened: 'Hear thy suppliant's call,
Great Queen, and common Mother of us all!
Fair from its humble bed I reared this Flow'r,
Suckled and cheered with air, and sun, and show'r,
Soft on the paper ruff its leaves I spread,
Bright with the gilded button tipped its head,
Then throned in glass, and named it CAROLINE:
410   Each maid cried, charming! and each youth, divine!
Did Nature's pencil ever blend such rays,
Such varied light in one promiscuous blaze?
Now prostrate! dead! behold that Caroline:
No maid cries, charming! and no youth, divine!
And lo the wretch! whose vile, whose insect lust
Laid this gay daughter of the spring in dust.
Oh punish him, or to th' Elysian shades
Dismiss my soul, where no carnation fades.'
    He ceased, and wept. With innocence of mien
420   Th' accused stood forth, and thus addressed the Queen:
    'Of all th' enamelled race, whose silv'ry wing
Waves to the tepid zephyrs of the spring,
Or swims along the fluid atmosphere,
Once brightest shined this child of heat and air.

I saw, and started from its vernal bow'r
The rising game, and chased from flow'r to flow'r.
It fled, I followed; now in hope, now pain;
It stopped, I stopped; it moved, I moved again.
At last it fixed, 'twas on what plant it pleased,
And where it fixed, the beauteous bird I seized: 430
Rose or carnation was below my care;
I meddle, Goddess! only in my sphere.
I tell the naked fact without disguise,
And, to excuse it, need but show the prize
Whose spoils this paper offers to your eye,
Fair ev'n in death! this peerless *Butterfly*.'
    'My sons! (she answered) both have done your parts:
Live happy both, and long promote our arts.
But hear a mother, when she recommends
To your fraternal care, our sleeping friends.   440
The common soul, of Heav'n's more frugal make,
Serves but to keep fools pert, and knaves awake:
A drowsy watchman, that just gives a knock,
And breaks our rest, to tell us what's o'clock.
Yet by some object ev'ry brain is stirred;
The dull may waken to a hummingbird;
The most recluse, discreetly opened, find
Congenial matter in the cockle-kind;
The mind, in metaphysics at a loss,
May wander in a wilderness of moss;   450
The head that turns at superlunar things,
Poised with a tail, may steer on Wilkins' wings.
    'O! would the sons of men once think their eyes
And Reason giv'n them but to study *Flies*!
See Nature in some partial narrow shape,
And let the Author of the Whole escape:
Learn but to trifle; or, who most observe,
To wonder at their Maker, not to serve.'
    'Be that my task (replies a gloomy Clerk,
Sworn foe to Myst'ry, yet divinely dark;   460
Whose pious hope aspires to see the day
When Moral Evidence shall quite decay,

And damns implicit faith, and holy lies,
Prompt to impose, and fond to dogmatize).
Let others creep by timid steps, and slow,
On plain Experience lay foundations low,
By common sense to common knowledge bred,
And last, to Nature's Cause through Nature led.
All-seeing in thy mists, we want no guide,
470   Mother of Arrogance, and Source of Pride!
We nobly take the high priori Road,
And reason downward, till we doubt of God:
Make Nature still encroach upon his plan,
And shove him off as far as e'er we can;
Thrust some mechanic cause into his place,
Or bind in matter, or diffuse in space.
Or, at one bound o'er-leaping all his laws,
Make God Man's image, Man the final Cause,
Find Virtue local, all Relation scorn,
480   See all in *Self*, and but for self be born:
Of naught so certain as our *Reason* still,
Of naught so doubtful as of *Soul* and *Will*.
Oh hide the God still more! and make us see
Such as Lucretius drew, a god like thee:
Wrapt up in Self, a god without a thought,
Regardless of our merit or default.
Or that bright Image to our fancy draw,
Which Theocles in raptured vision saw,
While through Poetic scenes the Genius roves,
490   Or wanders wild in academic groves;
That NATURE our Society adores,
Where Tindal dictates, and Silenus snores.'
    Roused at his name, up rose the boozy sire,
And shook from out his pipe the seeds of fire;
Then snapped his box, and stroked his belly down:
Rosy and rev'rend, though without a gown.
Bland and familiar to the throne he came,
Led up the Youth, and called the Goddess *Dame*.
Then thus: 'From priestcraft happily set free,
500   Lo! ev'ry finished son returns to thee.

First slave to words, then vassal to a name,
Then dupe to party; child and man the same:
Bounded by Nature, narrowed still by Art,
A trifling head, and a contracted heart.
Thus bred, thus taught, how many have I seen,
Smiling on all, and smiled on by a Queen.
Marked out for honours, honoured for their birth,
To thee the most rebellious things on earth:
Now to thy gentle shadow all are shrunk,
All melted down, in pension, or in punk!   510
So Kent, so Berkeley sneaked into the grave,
A monarch's half, and half a harlot's slave.
Poor Warwick nipped in Folly's broadest bloom,
Who praises now? his chaplain on his tomb.
Then take them all, oh take them to thy breast!
Thy *Magus*, Goddess! shall perform the rest.'
   With that, a WIZARD OLD his *Cup* extends,
Which whoso tastes, forgets his former friends,
Sire, ancestors, himself. Once casts his eyes
Up to a *Star*, and like Endymion dies;   520
A *Feather* shooting from another's head
Extracts his brain, and Principle is fled,
Lost is his God, his country, ev'ry thing;
And nothing left but homage to a King!
The vulgar herd turn off to roll with hogs,
To run with horses, or to hunt with dogs;
But, sad example! never to escape
Their infamy, still keep the human shape.
   But she, good Goddess, sent to ev'ry child
Firm Impudence, or Stupefaction mild;   530
And strait succeeded, leaving shame no room,
Cibberian forehead, or Cimmerian gloom.
   Kind Self-conceit to some her glass applies,
Which no one looks in with another's eyes:
But as the flatt'rer or dependant paint,
Beholds himself a Patriot, chief, or saint.
   On others Int'rest her gay liv'ry flings,
Int'rest, that waves on parti-coloured wings:

Turned to the sun, she casts a thousand dyes,
540   And, as she turns, the colours fall or rise.
    Others the syren sisters warble round,
And empty heads console with empty sound.
No more, alas! the voice of Fame they hear,
The balm of Dullness trickling in their ear.
Great Cowper, Harcourt, Parker, Raymond, King,
Why all your toils? your sons have learned to sing.
How quick Ambition hastes to ridicule!
The sire is made a peer, the son a fool.
    On some, a priest succinct in amice white
550   Attends; all flesh is nothing in his sight!
Beeves, at his touch, at once to jelly turn,
And the huge boar is shrunk into an urn:
The board with specious miracles he loads,
Turns hares to larks, and pigeons into toads.
Another (for in all what one can shine?)
Explains the *sève* and *verdeur* of the vine.
What cannot copious sacrifice atone?
Thy truffles, Perigord! thy hams, Bayonne!
With French libation, and Italian strain,
560   Wash Bladen white, and expiate Hays's stain.
Knight lifts the head, for what are crowds undone
To three essential partridges in one?
Gone ev'ry blush, and silent all reproach,
Contending princes mount them in their coach.
    Next bidding all draw near on bended knees,
The Queen confers her *Titles* and *Degrees*.
Her children first of more distinguished sort,
Who study Shakespeare at the Inns of Court,
Impale a Glow-worm, or *Vertù* profess,
570   Shine in the dignity of F. R. S.
Some, deep Freemasons, join the silent race
Worthy to fill Pythagoras's place;
Some Botanists, or Florists at the least,
Or issue members of an annual feast.
Nor past the meanest unregarded, one
Rose a Gregorian, one a Gormogon.

The last, not least in honour or applause,
Isis and Cam made Doctors of her Laws.
    Then blessing all, 'Go Children of my care!
To Practice now from Theory repair.   580
All my commands are easy, short, and full:
My Sons! be proud, be selfish, and be dull.
Guard my prerogative, assert my throne:
This nod confirms each privilege your own.
The cap and switch be sacred to his Grace;
With staff and pumps the Marquis lead the race;
From stage to stage the licensed Earl may run,
Paired with his fellow-charioteer the Sun;
The learned Baron butterflies design,
Or draw to silk Arachne's subtle line;   590
The judge to dance his brother sergeant call;
The Senator at cricket urge the ball;
The Bishop stow (pontific luxury!)
An hundred souls of turkeys in a pie;
The sturdy Squire to Gallic masters stoop,
And drown his lands and manors in a soup.
Others import yet nobler arts from France,
Teach kings to fiddle, and make senates dance.
Perhaps more high some daring son may soar,
Proud to my list to add one monarch more;   600
And nobly conscious, princes are but things
Born for First Ministers, as slaves for kings,
Tyrant supreme! shall three Estates command,
And MAKE ONE MIGHTY DUNCIAD OF THE LAND!'
    More she had spoke, but yawned – all Nature nods:
What mortal can resist the yawn of gods?
Churches and chapels instantly it reached
(St James's first, for leaden Gilbert preached);
Then catched the Schools; the Hall scarce kept awake;
The Convocation gaped, but could not speak.   610
Lost was the Nation's Sense, nor could be found,
While the long solemn unison went round.
Wide, and more wide, it spread o'er all the realm;
Ev'n Palinurus nodded at the helm;

The vapour mild o'er each Committee crept;
Unfinish'd treaties in each office slept,
And chiefless armies dozed out the campaign,
And navies yawned for orders on the main.
    O Muse! relate (for you can tell alone,
620 Wits have short memories, and Dunces none)
Relate, who first, who last resigned to rest;
Whose heads she partly, whose completely blessed;
What charms could Faction; what Ambition lull,
The Venal quiet, and entrance the Dull;
Till drowned was Sense, and Shame, and Right,
        and Wrong –
O sing, and hush the nations with thy song!

    *   *   *   *   *   *

    In vain, in vain, – the all-composing Hour
Resistless falls: The Muse obeys the Pow'r.
She comes! she comes! the sable Throne behold
630 Of *Night* primaeval, and of *Chaos* old!
Before her, *Fancy's* gilded clouds decay,
And all its varying rainbows die away.
Wit shoots in vain its momentary fires,
The meteor drops, and in a flash expires,
As one by one, at dread Medea's strain,
The sick'ning stars fade off th'ethereal plain;
As Argus' eyes by Hermes' wand opprest
Closed one by one to everlasting rest;
Thus at her felt approach, and secret might,
640 *Art* after *Art* goes out, and all is night.
See skulking *Truth* to her old cavern fled,
Mountains of Casuistry heaped o'er her head!
Philosophy, that leaned on Heav'n before,
Shrinks to her second cause, and is no more.
Physic of *Metaphysic* begs defence,
And *Metaphysic* calls for aid on *Sense!*
See Mystery to Mathematics fly!
In vain! they gaze, turn giddy, rave, and die.

Religion blushing veils her sacred fires,
And unawares *Morality* expires.   650
Nor *public* flame, nor *private*, dares to shine;
Nor *human* spark is left, nor glimpse *divine*!
Lo! thy dread Empire, CHAOS! is restored;
Light dies before thy uncreating word:
Thy hand, great Anarch! lets the curtain fall,
And universal darkness buries all.

FINIS

PROSE WRITINGS

FROM THE PREFACE
TO THE *ILIAD*

Homer is universally allowed to have had the greatest invention[1] of any writer whatever. The praise of judgement Virgil has justly contested with him, and others may have their pretensions as to particular excellencies; but his invention remains yet unrivalled. Nor is it a wonder if he has ever been acknowledged the greatest of poets, who most excelled in that which is the very foundation of poetry. It is the invention that in different degrees distinguishes all great geniuses; the utmost stretch of human study, learning, and industry, which masters everything besides, can never attain to this. It furnishes Art with all her materials, and without it judgement itself can at best but *steal wisely*. For Art is only like a prudent steward that lives on managing the riches of Nature. Whatever praises may be given to works of judgement, there is not even a single beauty in them but is owing to the invention; as in the most regular gardens, however Art may carry the greatest appearance, there is not a plant or flower but is the gift of Nature. The first can only reduce the beauties of the latter into a more obvious figure, which the common eye may better take in and is therefore more entertained with. And perhaps the reason why most critics are inclined to prefer a judicious and methodical genius to a great and fruitful one is because they find it easier for themselves to pursue their observations through an uniform and bounded walk of Art than to comprehend the vast and various extent of Nature.

Our author's work is a wild paradise where, if we cannot see all the beauties so distinctly as in an ordered garden, it is only because the number of them is infinitely greater. 'Tis like a copious nursery which contains the seeds and first productions of every kind, out of which those who followed him have but selected some particular plants, each according to his fancy, to cultivate and beautify. If some things are too luxuriant, it is owing to the richness of the soil; and if others are not arrived to perfection or maturity, it is only because they are overrun and oppressed by those of a stronger nature.

It is to the strength of this amazing invention we are to attribute that unequalled fire and rapture which is so forcible in Homer, that no man of a true poetical spirit is master of himself while he reads him. What he writes is of the most animated nature imaginable: everything moves, everything lives and is put in action. If a council be called or a battle fought, you are not coldly informed of what was said or done as from a third person; the reader is hurried out of himself by the force of the poet's imagination, and turns in one place to a hearer, in another to a spectator. The course of his verses resembles that of the army he describes: 'They pour along like a fire that sweeps the whole earth before it.'[2] 'Tis however remarkable that his fancy, which is everywhere vigorous, is not discovered immediately at the beginning of his poem in its fullest splendour; it grows in the progress both upon himself and others, and becomes on fire like a chariot wheel, by its own rapidity. Exact disposition, just thought, correct elocution, polished numbers[3] may have been found in a thousand; but this poetical *fire*, this *vivida vis animi*,[4] in a very few. Even in works where all those are imperfect or neglected, this can overpower criticism and make us admire even while we disapprove. Nay, where this appears, though attended with absurdities, it brightens all the rubbish about it, till we see nothing but its own splendour. This *fire* is discerned in Virgil, but discerned as through a glass, reflected, and more shining than warm, but everywhere equal and constant. In Lucan and Statius[5] it bursts out in sudden, short, and interrupted flashes; in Milton it glows like a furnace kept up to an uncommon fierceness by the force of art; in Shakespeare it strikes before we are aware, like an accidental fire from Heaven; but in Homer, and in him only, it burns everywhere clearly, and everywhere irresistibly.

I shall here endeavour to show how this vast invention exerts itself in a manner superior to that of any poet, through all the main constituent parts of his work, as it is the great and peculiar characteristic which distinguishes him from all other authors.

This strong and ruling faculty was like a powerful planet, which in the violence of its own course drew all things within its vortex. It seemed not enough to have taken in the whole circle of arts and the whole compass of Nature; all the inward passions and affections of mankind to supply his characters, and all the outward forms and images of things for his descriptions; but wanting yet an ampler sphere to expatiate in, he opened a new and boundless walk for his imagination and created a world for himself in the invention of *fable*.[6] That which Aristotle calls the 'soul of poetry'[7] was first breathed into it by Homer ...

The *speeches* are to be considered as they flow from the characters, being perfect or defective as they agree or disagree with the manners of those who utter them. As there is more variety of characters in the *Iliad*, so there is of speeches, than in any other poem. 'Everything in it has manners' (as Aristotle expresses it);[8] that is, everything is acted or spoken. It is hardly credible in a work of such length how small a number of lines are employed in narration. In Virgil the dramatic part is less in proportion to the narrative; and the speeches often consist of general reflections or thoughts which might be equally just in any person's mouth upon the same occasion. As many of his persons have no apparent characters, so many of his speeches escape being applied and judged by the rule of propriety. We oftener think of the author himself when we read Virgil than when we are engaged in Homer. All which are the effects of a colder invention, that interests us less in the action described: Homer makes us hearers, and Virgil leaves us readers.

If in the next place we take a view of the *sentiments*,[9] the same presiding faculty is eminent in the sublimity and spirit of his thoughts. Longinus[10] has given his opinion that it was in this part Homer principally excelled. What were alone sufficient to prove the grandeur and excellence of his sentiments in general is that they have so remarkable a parity with those of the Scripture; Duport, in his *Gnomologia Homerica*,[11] has collected innumerable instances of this sort. And it is with justice an excellent modern writer[12] allows that if Virgil has not so many thoughts that are low and vulgar, he has not so many that are sublime and noble, and that the Roman author seldom rises into very astonishing sentiments where he is not fired by the *Iliad*.

If we observe his *descriptions*, *images*, and *similes*, we shall find the invention still predominant. To what else can we ascribe that vast comprehension of images of every sort, where we see each circumstance and individual of Nature summoned together by the extent and fecundity of his imagination, to which all things, in their various views, presented themselves in an instant, and had their impressions taken off to perfection at a heat? Nay, he not only gives us the full prospects of things, but several unexpected peculiarities and side views, unobserved by any painter but Homer. Nothing is so surprising as the descriptions of his battles, which take up no less than half the *Iliad*, and are supplied with so vast a variety of incidents that no one bears a likeness to another; such different kinds of deaths that no two heroes are wounded in the same manner; and such a profusion of noble ideas that every battle rises above the last in greatness, horror, and confusion. It is certain there is not near that number of images and descriptions in any epic poet, though everyone has assisted himself with a great quantity out of him; and it is evident of Virgil, especially, that he has scarce any comparisons which are not drawn from his master.

If we descend from hence to the *expression*, we see the bright imagination of Homer shining out in the most enlivened forms of it. We acknowledge him the father of poetical diction, the first who taught that language of the gods to men. His expression is like the colouring of some great masters, which discovers itself to be laid on boldly and executed with rapidity. It is indeed the strongest and most glowing imaginable, and touched with the greatest spirit. Aristotle had reason to say he was the only poet who had found out living words;[13] there are in him more daring figures and metaphors than in any good author whatever. An arrow is 'impatient' to be on the wing, a weapon 'thirsts' to drink the blood of an enemy, and the like. Yet his expression is never too big for the sense, but justly great in proportion to it; 'tis the sentiment that swells and fills out the diction, which rises with it and forms itself about it. For in the same degree that a thought is warmer, an expression will be brighter; and as that is more strong, this will become more perspicuous, like glass in the furnace, which grows to a greater magnitude and refines to a greater clearness only as the breath within is more powerful and the heat more intense . . .

Thus, on whatever side we contemplate Homer, what principally strikes us is his *invention*. It is that which forms the character of each part of his work; and accordingly we find it to have made his fable more extensive and copious than any other, his manners more lively and strongly marked, his speeches more affecting and transported, his sentiments more warm and sublime, his images and descriptions more full and animated, his expression more raised and daring, and his numbers more rapid and various. I hope in what has been said of Virgil with regard to any of these heads, I have no way derogated from his character. Nothing is more absurd or endless than the common method of comparing eminent writers by an opposition of particular passages in them and forming a judgement from thence of their merit upon the whole. We ought to have a certain knowledge of the principal character and distinguishing excellence of each; it is in *that* we are to consider him, and in proportion to his degree in *that* we are to admire him. No author or man ever excelled all the world in more than one faculty, and as Homer has done this in invention, Virgil has in judgement. Not that we are to think Homer wanted judgement because Virgil had it in a more eminent degree, or that Virgil wanted invention because Homer possessed a larger share of it: each of these great authors had more of both than perhaps any man besides, and are only said to have less in comparison with one another. Homer was the greater genius, Virgil the better artist. In one we most admire the man, in the other the work. Homer hurries and transports us with a commanding impetuosity, Virgil leads us with an attractive majesty. Homer scatters with a generous profusion, Virgil bestows with a careful magnificence. Homer, like the Nile, pours out his riches with a sudden overflow; Virgil, like a river in its banks, with a gentle and constant stream. When we behold their battles, me thinks the two poets resemble the heroes they celebrate: Homer, boundless and irresistible as Achilles, bears all before him, and shines more and more as the tumult increases; Virgil, calmly daring like Aeneas, appears undisturbed in the midst of the action, disposes all about him, and conquers with tranquillity. And when we look upon their machines,[14] Homer seems like his own Jupiter in his terrors, shaking Olympus, scattering the lightnings, and firing the Heavens; Virgil, like the same power in his benevolence, counselling with the gods, laying plans for empires, and regularly ordering his whole creation . . .

Having now spoken of the beauties and defects of the original, it remains to treat of the translation, with the same view to the chief characteristic. As far as that is seen in the main parts of the poëm, such as the fable, manners, and sentiments, no translator can prejudice it but by wilful omissions or contractions. As it also breaks out in every particular image, description, and simile, whoever lessens or too much softens those takes off from this chief character. It is the first grand duty of an interpreter to give his author entire and unmaimed; and for the rest, the diction and versification only are his proper province, since these must be his own, but the others he is to take as he finds them.

It should then be considered what methods may afford some equivalent in our language for the graces of these in the Greek. It is certain no literal translation can be just to an excellent original in a superior language, but it is a great mistake to imagine (as many have done) that a rash paraphrase can make amends for this general defect, which is no less in danger to lose the spirit of an Ancient[15] by deviating into the modern manners of expression. If there be sometimes a darkness, there is often a light in antiquity, which nothing better preserves than a version almost literal. I know no liberties one ought to take but those which are necessary for transfusing the spirit of the original

and supporting the poetical style of the translation; and I will
venture to say there have not been more men misled in former
times by a servile dull adherence to the letter, than have been
deluded in ours by a chimerical insolent hope of raising and
improving their author. It is not to be doubted that the *fire* of
the poem is what a translator should principally regard, as it is
most likely to expire in his managing. However, it is his safest
way to be content with preserving this to his utmost in the
whole, without endeavouring to be more than he finds his
author is in any particular place. 'Tis a great secret in writing
to know when to be plain, and when poetical and figurative;
and it is what Homer will teach us if we will but follow mod-
estly in his footsteps. Where his diction is bold and lofty, let us
raise ours as high as we can; but where his is plain and humble,
we ought not to be deterred from imitating him by the fear of
incurring the censure of a mere English critic. Nothing that
belongs to Homer seems to have been more commonly mis-
taken than the just pitch of his style, some of his translators
having swelled into fustian[16] in a proud confidence of the sub-
lime, others sunk into flatness in a cold and timorous notion of
simplicity. Methinks I see these different followers of Homer,
some sweating and straining after him by violent leaps and
bounds (the certain signs of false mettle); others slowly and
servilely creeping in his train; while the poet himself is all the
time proceeding with an unaffected and equal majesty before
them. However, of the two extremes one could sooner pardon
frenzy than frigidity; no author is to be envied for such com-
mendations as he may gain by that character of style which his
friends must agree together to call simplicity, and the rest of the
world will call dullness. There is a graceful and dignified sim-
plicity, as well as a bald and sordid one, which differ as much
from each other as the air of a plain man from that of a sloven.
'Tis one thing to be tricked up,[17] and another not to be dressed
at all. Simplicity is the mean between ostentation and rusticity.

This pure and noble simplicity is nowhere in such perfection
as in the Scripture and our author. One may affirm with all
respect to the inspired writings that the Divine Spirit made use
of no other words but what were intelligible and common to

men at that time and in that part of the world; and as Homer
is the author nearest to those, his style must of course bear
a greater resemblance to the Sacred Books than that of any
other writer. This consideration (together with what has been
observed of the parity of some of his thoughts) may, methinks,
induce a translator, on the one hand, to give in to several of
those general phrases and manners of expression which have
attained a veneration even in our language, from their use in
the Old Testament; as, on the other, to avoid those which have
been appropriated to the Divinity, and in a manner consigned
to mystery and religion.

For a further preservation of this air of simplicity, a particu-
lar care should be taken to express with all plainness those
moral sentences and proverbial speeches which are so numer-
ous in this poet. They have something venerable and, as I may
say, oracular, in that unadorned gravity and shortness with
which they are delivered, a grace which would be utterly lost
by endeavouring to give them what we call a more ingenious
(that is, a more modern) turn in the paraphrase.

Perhaps the mixture of some Graecisms and old words after
the manner of Milton, if done without too much affectation,
might not have an ill effect in a version of this particular work,
which most of any other seems to require a venerable antique
cast. But certainly the use of modern terms of war and govern-
ment, such as 'platoon', 'campaign', 'junto',[18] or the like (which
some of his translators have fallen into) cannot be allowable,
those only excepted without which it is impossible to treat the
subjects in any living language.

There are two peculiarities in Homer's diction that are a sort
of marks or moles, by which every common eye distinguishes
him at first sight. Those who are not his greatest admirers look
upon them as defects, and those who are, seem pleased with
them as beauties. I speak of his compound epithets, and of his
repetitions. Many of the former cannot be done literally into
English without destroying the purity of our language. I believe
such should be retained as slide easily of themselves into an
English compound without violence to the ear or to the received
rules of composition, as well as those which have received a

sanction from the authority of our best poets, and are become familiar through their use of them, such as the cloud-compelling Jove, etc. As for the rest, whenever any can be as fully and significantly expressed in a single word as in a compounded one, the course to be taken is obvious. Some that cannot be so turned as to preserve their full image by one or two words may have justice done them by circumlocution, as the epithet εἰνοσίφυλλος to a mountain would appear little or ridiculous translated literally 'leaf-shaking', but affords a majestic idea in the periphrasis: 'the lofty mountain shakes his waving woods'. Others that admit of differing significations may receive an advantage by a judicious variation according to the occasions on which they are introduced. For example, the epithet of Apollo, ἑκηβόλος, or 'far-shooting', is capable of two explications, one literal in respect of the darts and bow, the ensigns of that god, the other allegorical with regard to the rays of the sun; therefore in such places where Apollo is represented as a god in person, I would use the former interpretation, and where the effects of the sun are described, I would make choice of the latter. Upon the whole, it will be necessary to avoid that perpetual repetition of the same epithets which we find in Homer and which, though it might be accommodated (as has been already shown) to the ear of those times, is by no means so to ours. But one may wait for opportunities of placing them where they derive an additional beauty from the occasions on which they are employed, and in doing this properly a translator may at once show his fancy and his judgement.

As for Homer's repetitions, we may divide them into three sorts: of whole narrations and speeches, of single sentences, and of one verse or hemistich.[19] I hope it is not impossible to have such a regard to these as neither to lose so known a mark of the author on the one hand, nor to offend the reader too much on the other. The repetition is not ungraceful in those speeches where the dignity of the speaker renders it a sort of insolence to alter his words, as in the messages from gods to men, or from higher powers to inferiors in concerns of state, or where the ceremonial of religion seems to require it in the solemn forms of prayers, oaths, or the like. In other cases, I believe the best rule is to be guided by the nearness or distance at which the repetitions are placed in the original. When they follow too close one may vary the expression, but it is a question whether a professed translator be authorized to omit any. If they be tedious, the author is to answer for it.

It only remains to speak of the versification. Homer (as has been said) is perpetually applying the sound to the sense, and varying it on every new subject. This is indeed one of the most exquisite beauties of poetry, and attainable by very few;[20] I know only of Homer eminent for it in the Greek, and Virgil in Latin. I am sensible it is what may sometimes happen by chance, when a writer is warm and fully possessed of his image; however, it may be reasonably believed they designed this, in whose verse it so manifestly appears in a superior degree to all others. Few readers have the ear to be judges of it, but those who have will see I have endeavoured at this beauty.

Upon the whole, I must confess myself utterly incapable of doing justice to Homer. I attempt him in no other hope but that which one may entertain without much vanity, of giving a more tolerable copy of him than any entire translation in verse has yet done. We have only those of Chapman, Hobbes, and Ogilby.[21] Chapman has taken the advantage of an immeasurable length of verse, notwithstanding which there is scarce any paraphrase more loose and rambling than his. He has frequent interpolations of four or six lines, and I remember one in the thirteenth Book of the *Odyssey*, V, 312, where he has spun twenty verses out of two. He is often mistaken in so bold a manner that one might think he deviated on purpose, if he did not in other places of his notes insist so much upon verbal trifles. He appears to have had a strong affectation of extracting new meanings out of his author, insomuch as to promise in his rhyming preface a poem of the mysteries he had revealed in Homer; and perhaps he endeavoured to strain the obvious sense to this end. His expression is involved in fustian, a fault for which he was remarkable in his original writings, as in the tragedy of *Bussy D'Ambois*, etc.[22] In a word, the nature of the man may account for his whole performance; for he appears from his preface and remarks to have been of an arrogant turn, and an enthusiast in poetry. His own boast of having finished half the *Iliad* in less than fifteen weeks shows with what negligence his version was performed. But that which is to be allowed him, and which very much contributed to cover his defects, is a daring fiery spirit that animates his translation, which is something like what one might imagine Homer himself would have writ before he arrived to years of discretion. Hobbes has given us a correct explanation of the sense in general, but for particulars and circumstances he continually lops them and often omits the most beautiful. As for its being esteemed a close translation, I doubt not many have been led into that error by the shortness of it, which proceeds not from his following the original line by line but from the contractions above-mentioned. He sometimes omits whole similes and sentences, and is now and then guilty of mistakes which no writer of his learning could have fallen into but through carelessness. His poetry, as well as Ogilby's, is too mean for criticism.

It is a great loss to the poetical world that Mr Dryden did not live to translate the *Iliad*. He has left us only the first book and a small part of the sixth, in which if he has in some places not truly interpreted the sense or preserved the antiquities, it ought to be excused on account of the haste he was obliged to write in. He seems to have had too much regard to Chapman, whose words he sometimes copies, and has unhappily followed him in passages where he wanders from the original. However, had he translated the whole work, I would no more have attempted Homer after him than Virgil, his version of whom (notwithstanding some human errors) is the most noble and spirited translation I know in any language. But the fate of great geniuses is like that of great ministers; though they are confessedly the first in the commonwealth of letters, they must be envied and calumniated only for being at the head of it.

That which in my opinion ought to be the endeavour of anyone who translates Homer is, above all things, to keep alive that spirit and fire which makes his chief character. In particular places, where the sense can bear any doubt, to follow the strongest and most poetical, as most agreeing with that character. To copy him in all the variations of his style and the

different modulations of his numbers. To preserve in the more
active or descriptive parts a warmth and elevation; in the more
sedate or narrative, a plainness and solemnity; in the speeches
a fullness and perspicuity; in the sentences a shortness and
gravity. Not to neglect even the little figures[23] and turns on the
words, nor sometimes the very cast of the periods.[24] Neither to
omit or confound any rites or customs of antiquity. Perhaps too
he ought to include the whole in a shorter compass than has
hitherto been done by any translator who has tolerably pre-
served either the sense or poetry. What I would farther
recommend to him is to study his author rather from his own
text than from any commentaries, how learned soever, or what-
ever figure they make in the estimation of the world . . .

FROM THE PREFACE
TO *THE WORKS OF*
SHAKESPEARE

It is not my design to enter into a criticism upon this author, though to do it effectually and not superficially would be the best occasion that any just writer could take to form the judgement and taste of our nation. For of all English poets Shakespeare must be confessed to be the fairest and fullest subject for criticism, and to afford the most numerous as well as most conspicuous instances both of beauties and faults[1] of all sorts. But this far exceeds the bounds of a preface, the business of which is only to give an account of the fate of his works and the disadvantages under which they have been transmitted to us. We shall hereby extenuate many faults which are his, and clear him from the imputation of many which are not: a design which, though it can be no guide to future critics to do him justice in one way, will at least be sufficient to prevent their doing him an injustice in the other.

I cannot however but mention some of his principal and characteristic excellencies, for which (notwithstanding his defects) he is justly and universally elevated above all other dramatic writers. Not that this is the proper place of praising him, but because I would not omit any occasion of doing it.

If ever any author deserved the name of an *original*, it was Shakespeare. Homer himself drew not his art so immediately from the fountains of Nature; it proceeded through Egyptian strainers and channels and came to him not without some tincture of the learning, or some cast of the models of those before him. The poetry of Shakespeare was inspiration indeed; he is not so much an imitator as an instrument of Nature; and 'tis not so just to say that he speaks from her, as that she speaks through him.

His *characters* are so much Nature herself that 'tis a sort of injury to call them by so distant a name as copies of her. Those of other poets have a constant resemblance, which shows that they received them from one another and were but multipliers of the same image: each picture, like a mock-rainbow, is but the reflection of a reflection. But every single character in Shakespeare is as much an individual as those in life itself; it is as impossible to find any two alike, and such as from their relation or affinity in any respect appear most to be twins will upon comparison be found remarkably distinct. To this life and variety of character, we must add the wonderful preservation of it, which is such throughout his plays that, had all the speeches been printed without the very names of the persons, I believe one might have applied them with certainty to every speaker.

The power over our *passions*[2] was never possessed in a more eminent degree, or displayed in so different instances. Yet all along, there is seen no labour, no pains to raise them, no preparation to guide our guess to the effect or be perceived to lead toward it. But the heart swells, and the tears burst out, just at the proper places. We are surprised the moment we weep; and yet upon reflection find the passion so just that we should be surprised if we had not wept, and wept at that very moment.

How astonishing is it again that the passions directly opposite to these, laughter and spleen,[3] are no less at his command! that he is not more a master of the great than of the ridiculous in human nature; of our noblest tendernesses, than of our vainest foibles; of our strongest emotions, than of our idlest sensations!

Nor does he only excel in the passions: in the coolness of reflection and reasoning he is full as admirable. His *sentiments*[4] are not only in general the most pertinent and judicious upon every subject, but by a talent very peculiar, something between penetration and felicity, he hits upon that particular point on which the bent of each argument turns or the force of each motive depends. This is perfectly amazing from a man of no education or experience in those great and public scenes of life which are usually the subject of his thoughts; so that he seems to have known the world by intuition, to have looked through human nature at one glance, and to be the only author that gives ground for a very new opinion, that the philosopher and even the man of the world may be *born*, as well as the poet.

It must be owned that with all these great excellencies, he has almost as great defects, and that as he has certainly written better, so he has perhaps written worse, than any other. But I think I can in some measure account for these defects from several causes and accidents[5] without which it is hard to imagine that so large and so enlightened a mind could ever have been susceptible of them. That all these contingencies should unite to his disadvantage seems to me almost as singularly unlucky, as that so many various (nay contrary) talents should meet in one man was happy and extraordinary.

It must be allowed that stage poetry, of all other, is more particularly levelled to please the populace, and its success more immediately depending upon the common suffrage. One cannot therefore wonder if Shakespeare, having at his first appearance no other aim in his writings than to procure a subsistence,[6] directed his endeavours solely to hit the taste and humour that then prevailed. The audience was generally composed of the meaner sort of people, and therefore the images of life were to be drawn from those of their own rank; accordingly we find that not our author's only, but almost all the old comedies, have their scene among tradesmen and mechanics;[7] and even their historical plays strictly follow the common old stories or vulgar[8] traditions of that kind of people. In tragedy, nothing was so sure to surprise and cause admiration as the most strange, unexpected, and consequently most unnatural events and incidents; the most exaggerated thoughts; the most verbose and bombast expression; the most pompous rhymes and thundering versification. In comedy, nothing was so sure to please as mean buffoonery, vile ribaldry, and unmannerly jests of fools and clowns. Yet even in these, our author's wit buoys up and is borne above his subject; his genius in those low parts is like some prince of a romance in the disguise of a shepherd or peasant; a certain greatness and spirit now and then break out, which manifest his higher extraction[9] and qualities.

It may be added that not only the common audience had no notion of the rules of writing, but few even of the better sort piqued themselves upon any great degree of knowledge or nicety that way, till Ben Jonson, getting possession of the stage, brought critical learning into vogue. And that this was not done without difficulty may appear from those frequent lessons (and indeed almost declamations) which he was forced to prefix to his first plays and put into the mouth of his actors, the *Grex*,[10] *Chorus*, etc., to remove the prejudices and inform the judgement of his hearers. Till then, our authors had no thoughts of writing on the model of the Ancients; their tragedies were only histories in dialogue, and their comedies followed the thread of any novel as they found it, no less implicitly than if it had been true history.

To judge therefore of Shakespeare by Aristotle's rules is like trying a man by the laws of one country who acted under those of another. He writ to the *people*, and writ at first without patronage from the better sort, and therefore without aims of pleasing them; without assistance or advice from the learned, as without the advantage of education or acquaintance among them; without that knowledge of the best models, the Ancients, to inspire him with an emulation of them; in a word, without any views of reputation and of what poets are pleased to call immortality: some or all of which have encouraged the vanity or animated the ambition of other writers.

Yet it must be observed that when his performances had merited the protection of his prince,[11] and when the encouragement of the court had succeeded to that of the town, the works of his riper years are manifestly raised above those of his former. The dates of his plays sufficiently evidence that his productions improved in proportion to the respect he had for his auditors. And I make no doubt this observation would be found true in every instance, were but editions extant from which we might learn the exact time when every piece was composed, and whether writ for the town or the court.

Another cause (and no less strong than the former) may be deduced from our author's being a *player*[12] and forming himself first upon the judgements of that body of men whereof he was a member. They have ever had a standard to themselves, upon other principles than those of Aristotle. As they live by the majority, they know no rule but that of pleasing the present humour and complying with the wit in fashion, a consideration which brings all their judgement to a short point. Players are just such judges of what is right as tailors are of what is graceful. And in this view it will be but fair to allow that most of our author's faults are less to be ascribed to his wrong judgement as a poet than to his right judgement as a player.

By these men it was thought a praise to Shakespeare that he scarce ever blotted[13] a line. This they industriously propagated, as appears from what we are told by Ben Jonson in his *Discoveries* and from the preface of Heminges and Condell to the first folio[14] edition . . .

I am inclined to think this opinion proceeded originally from the zeal of the partisans of our author and Ben Jonson, as they endeavoured to exalt the one at the expense of the other. It is ever the nature of parties to be in extremes; and nothing is so probable as that because Ben Jonson had much the most learning, it was said on the one hand that Shakespeare had none at all; and because Shakespeare had much the most wit and fancy,[15] it was retorted on the other that Jonson wanted both. Because Shakespeare borrowed nothing, it was said that Ben Jonson borrowed everything. Because Jonson did not write extempore, he was reproached with being a year about every piece; and because Shakespeare wrote with ease and rapidity, they cried he never once made a blot. Nay, the spirit of opposition ran so high that whatever those of the one side objected to the other was taken at the rebound and turned into praises, as injudiciously as their antagonists before had made them objections . . .

It is not certain that any one of his plays was published by himself. During the time of his employment in the theatre, several of his pieces were printed separately in quarto. What makes me think that most of these were not published by him is the excessive carelessness of the press; every page is so scandalously false spelled, and almost all the learned or unusual words so intolerably mangled, that it's plain there either was no corrector to the press at all or one totally illiterate . . .

If we give in to this opinion, how many low and vicious parts and passages might no longer reflect upon this great genius, but appear unworthily charged upon him? And even in those which are really his, how many faults may have been unjustly laid to his account from arbitrary additions, expunctions, transpositions of scenes and lines, confusion of characters and persons, wrong application of speeches, corruptions of innumerable passages by the ignorance, and wrong corrections of them again by the impertinence, of his first editors? From one or other of these considerations, I am verily persuaded that the greatest and grossest part of what are thought his errors would vanish, and leave his character in a light very different from that disadvantageous one in which it now appears to us.

This is the state in which Shakespeare's writings lie at present; for, since the above-mentioned folio edition, all the rest have implicitly followed it, without having recourse to any of the former, or ever making the comparison between them. It is impossible to repair the injuries already done him; too much time has elapsed, and the materials are too few. In what I have done I have rather given a proof of my willingness and desire, than of my ability, to do him justice. I have discharged the dull duty of an editor to my best judgement, with more labour than I expect thanks, with a religious abhorrence of all innovation, and without any indulgence to my private sense or conjecture. The method taken in this edition will show itself. The various readings are fairly put in the margin so that every one may compare them; and those I have preferred into the text are constantly *ex fide codicum*, upon authority. The alterations or additions which Shakespeare himself made are taken notice of as they occur. Some suspected passages which are excessively bad (and which seem interpolations by being so inserted that one can entirely omit them without any chasm, or deficience in the context) are degraded to the bottom of the page, with an asterisk referring to the places of their insertion. The scenes are marked so distinctly that every removal of place is specified, which is more necessary in this author than any other, since he shifts them more frequently; and sometimes without attending to this particular, the reader would have met with obscurities.

The more obsolete or unusual words are explained. Some of the most shining passages are distinguished by commas in the margin; and where the beauty lay not in particulars but in the whole, a star is prefixed to the scene. This seems to me a shorter and less ostentatious method of performing the better half of criticism (namely the pointing out an author's excellencies) than to fill a whole paper with citations of fine passages, with general applauses or empty exclamations at the tail of them. There is also subjoined a catalogue of those first editions by which the greater part of the various readings and of the corrected passages are authorized (most of which are such as carry their own evidence along with them). These editions now hold the place of originals, and are the only materials left to repair the deficiencies or restore the corrupted sense of the author. I can only wish that a greater number of them (if a greater were ever published) may yet be found, by a search more successful than mine, for the better accomplishment of this end.

I will conclude by saying of Shakespeare, that with all his faults and with all the irregularity of his drama, one may look upon his works, in comparison of those that are more finished and regular, as upon an ancient majestic piece of Gothic architecture, compared with a neat modern building. The latter is more elegant and glaring,[16] but the former is more strong and more solemn. It must be allowed that in one of these there are materials enough to make many of the other. It has much the greater variety and much the nobler apartments, though we are often conducted to them by dark, odd, and uncouth passages. Nor does the whole fail to strike us with greater reverence, though many of the parts are childish, ill-placed, and unequal to its grandeur.

FROM *PERI BATHOUS,*
OR: OF THE ART OF
SINKING IN POETRY

CHAPTER III

The Necessity of the Bathos, Physically Considered

Furthermore, it were great cruelty and injustice if all such authors as cannot write in the other way were prohibited from writing at all. Against this, I draw an argument from what seems to me an undoubted physical maxim, that poetry is a *natural or morbid secretion*[1] *from the brain.* As I would not suddenly stop a cold in the head or dry up my neighbour's issue,[2] I would as little hinder him from necessary writing. It may be affirmed with great truth that there is hardly any human creature past childhood but at one time or other has had some poetical evacuation,[3] and no question was much the better for it in his health; so true is the saying, *nascimur poetae.*[4] Therefore is the desire of writing properly termed *pruritus,*[5] the *titillation of the generative faculty of the brain*; and the person is said to *conceive.*[6] Now, such as conceive must *bring forth.* I have known a man thoughtful, melancholy, and raving for divers days, but forthwith grow wonderfully easy, lightsome, and cheerful upon a discharge of the peccant humour[7] in exceeding purulent metre.[8] Nor can I question but abundance of untimely deaths are occasioned by want of this laudable vent of unruly passions, yea, perhaps, in poor wretches (which is very lamentable) for mere want of pen, ink, and paper! From hence it follows that a suppression of the very worst poetry is of dangerous consequence to the State. We find by experience that the same humours which vent themselves in summer in ballads and sonnets are condensed by the winter's cold into pamphlets and speeches for and against the Ministry.[9] Nay, I know not but many times a piece of poetry may be the most innocent composition of a minister himself.

It is therefore manifest that Mediocrity ought to be allowed, yea indulged, to the good subjects of England. Nor can I conceive how the world has swallowed the contrary as a maxim upon the single authority of that Horace.[10] Why should the Golden Mean and quintessence of all virtues be deemed so offensive only in this art? Or coolness or Mediocrity be so amiable a quality in a man and so detestable in a poet?

However, far be it from me to compare these writers with those great spirits who are born with a *vivacité de pesanteur*,[11] or (as an English author calls it) an alacrity of sinking,[12] and who by strength of Nature alone can excel. All I mean is to evince the necessity of rules to these lesser geniuses, as well as the usefulness of them to the greater.

CHAPTER VIII

Of the Profound: Consisting in the Circumstances; and of Amplification and Periphrase in General

What in a great measure distinguishes other writers from ours is their choosing and separating such circumstances in a description as illustrate or elevate the subject.

The circumstances which are most natural are obvious, therefore not astonishing or peculiar. But those that are far-fetched, or unexpected, or hardly compatible, will surprise prodigiously. These therefore we must principally hunt out; but above all preserve a laudable prolixity, presenting the whole and every side at once of the image to view. For choice and distinction are not only a curb to the spirit and limit the descriptive faculty, but also lessen the book,[13] which is frequently of the worst consequence of all to our author.

When Job says in short, 'He washed his feet in butter',[14] (a circumstance some poets would have softened or passed over), hear how it is spread out by the Great Genius:

> With teats distended with their milky store,
> Such num'rous lowing herds, before my door,
> Their painful burden to unload did meet,
> That we with butter might have washed our feet.[15]

How cautious! and particular! He had (says our author) so many herds, which herds thrived so well, and thriving so well, gave so much milk, and that milk produced so much butter, that if he *did not,* he *might* have washed his feet in it.

The ensuing description of Hell is no less remarkable in the circumstances:

> In flaming heaps the raging ocean rolls,
> Whose livid waves involve despairing souls;
> The liquid burnings dreadful colours show,
> Some deeply red, and others faintly blue.[16]

Could the most minute Dutch painter have been more exact? How inimitably circumstantial is this also of a war-horse!

> His eye-balls burn, he wounds the smoking plain,
> And knots of scarlet ribbon deck his mane.[17]

Of certain cudgel-players:

> They brandish high in air their threat'ning staves,
> Their hands a woven guard of osier saves,
> In which they fix their hazel weapon's end.[18]

Who would not think the poet had passed his whole life at wakes in such laudable diversions? He even teaches us how to hold and to make a cudgel!

Periphrase[19] is another great aid to prolixity, being a diffused circumlocutory manner of expressing a known idea, which should be so mysteriously couched as to give the reader the pleasure of guessing what it is that the author can possibly mean, and a surprise when he finds it. The poet I last mentioned is incomparable in this figure:

> A waving sea of heads was round me spread,
> And still fresh streams the gazing deluge fed.[20]

Here is a waving sea of heads, which by a fresh stream of heads grows to be a gazing deluge of heads. You come at last to find it means a 'great crowd' ...

CHAPTER XI

The Figures Continued: of the Magnifying, and Diminishing Figures

A genuine writer of the Profound will take care never to magnify an object without *clouding* it at the same time. His thought will appear in a true *mist*, and very unlike what is in Nature. It must always be remembered that *darkness* is an essential quality of the Profound, or if there chance to be a glimmering, it must be as Milton expresses it, 'No light, but rather darkness visible'.[21] The chief figure of this sort is

The Hyperbole or Impossible

For instance, of a lion:

> He roared so loud, and looked so wondrous grim,
> His very shadow durst not follow him.[22]

Of a lady at dinner:

> The silver whiteness that adorns thy neck,
> Sullies the plate, and makes the napkin black.[23]

Of the same:

> The obscureness of her birth
> Cannot eclipse the lustre of her eyes,
> Which make her all one light.[24]

Of a bull-baiting:

> Up to the stars the sprawling mastiffs fly,
> And add new monsters to the frighted sky.[25]

Of a scene of misery:

> Behold a scene of misery and woe!
> Here Argus soon might weep himself quite blind,
> Ev'n though he had Briareus' hundred hands
> To wipe those hundred eyes.[26]

And that modest request of two absent lovers:

> Ye gods! annihilate but space and time,
> And make two lovers happy.[27]

The *periphrasis*, which the moderns call the *circumbendibus*,[28] whereof we have given examples in the ninth chapter and shall again in the twelfth.

To the same class of the Magnifying may be referred the following, which are so excellently modern that we have yet no name for them. In describing a country prospect:[29]

> I'd call them mountains, but can't call them so,
> For fear to wrong them with a name too low;
> While the fair vales beneath so humbly lie,
> That even humble seems a term too high.[30]

The third class remains, of the Diminishing figures: and first, the *anticlimax*, where the second line drops quite short of the first, than which nothing creates greater surprise.

On the extent of the British arms:

> Under the tropics is our language spoke,
> And part of Flanders hath received our yoke.[31]

On a warrior:

> And thou Dalhoussy the Great God of War,
> Lieutenant Colonel to the Earl of Mar.[32]

...

CHAPTER XII

Of Expression

...

The Finical,[33]

which consists of the most curious, affected, mincing metaphors; as this, of a brook dried by the sun:

> Won by the summer's importuning ray,
> Th' eloping stream did from her channel stray,
> And with enticing sunbeams stole away.[34]

Of an easy death:

> When watchful death shall on his harvest look
> And see thee ripe with age, invite the hook;
> He'll gently cut thy bending stalk, and thee
> Lay kindly in the grave, his granary.[35]

Of trees in a storm:

> Oaks with extended arms the winds defy,
> The tempest sees their strength, and sighs, and passes by.[36]

Of water simmering over the fire:

> The sparkling flames raise water to a smile,
> Yet the pleased liquor pines, and lessens all the while.[37]

Lastly I shall place THE CUMBROUS, which moves heavily under a load of metaphors and draws after it a long train of words. And the BUSKIN,[38] or Stately, frequently and with great felicity mixed with the former. For as the first is the proper engine[39] to depress what is high, so is the second to raise what is base and low to a ridiculous visibility. When both these can be done at once, then is the Bathos in perfection; as when a man is set with his head downward and his breech[40] upright, his degradation is complete: one end of him is as high as ever, only that end is the wrong one. Will not every true lover of the Profound be delighted to behold the most vulgar and low actions of life exalted in this manner?

Who knocks at the door?

> For whom thus rudely pleads my loud-tongued gate,
> That he may enter?[41]

See who is there.

> Advance the fringèd curtains of thy eyes,
> And tell me who comes yonder.[42]

Shut the door.

> The wooden guardian of our privacy
> Quick on its axle turn.

Bring my clothes.

> Bring me what Nature, tailor to the bear,
> To man himself denied: she gave me cold,
> But would not give me clothes.

Light the fire.

> Bring forth some remnant of Promethean theft,
> Quick to expand th' inclement air congealed
> By Boreas's rude breath.

Snuff the candle.

> Yon luminary amputation needs,
> Thus shall you save its half-extinguished life.

Open the letter.

> Wax! render up thy trust.[43]

Uncork the bottle and chip the bread.

> Apply thine engine to the spongy door,
> Set Bacchus from his glassy prison free,
> And strip white Ceres[44] of her nut-brown coat.

CHAPTER XV

A Receipt[45] to Make an Epic Poem

An epic poem, the critics agree, is the greatest work human nature is capable of. They have already laid down many mechanical rules for compositions of this sort, but at the same time they cut off almost all undertakers[46] from the possibility of ever performing them; for the first qualification they unanimously require in a poet is a *genius*. I shall here endeavour (for the benefit of my countrymen) to make it manifest that epic poems may be made *without a genius*, nay without learning or much reading. This must necessarily be of great use to all those who confess they never *read*, and of whom the world is convinced they never *learn*. What Molière observes of making a dinner,[47] that any man can do it with *money*, and if a professed cook cannot do it *without*, he has his art for nothing; the same may be said of making a poem. 'Tis easily brought about by him that *has* a genius, but the skill lies in doing it without one. In pursuance of this end, I shall present the reader with a plain and certain recipe by which any author in the Bathos may be qualified for this grand performance.

For the Fable[48]

Take out of any old poem, history-book, romance, or legend (for instance, Geoffrey of Monmouth[49] or Don Belianis of Greece)[50] those parts of story which afford most scope for *long descriptions*. Put these pieces together, and throw all the adventures you fancy into *one tale*. Then take a hero, whom you may choose for the sound of his name, and put him into the midst of these adventures. There let him *work*, for twelve books, at the end of which you may take him out, ready prepared to *conquer* or to *marry*, it being necessary that the conclusion of an epic poem be *fortunate*.

To make an Episode

Take any remaining adventure of your former collection in which you could no way involve your hero, or any unfortunate accident that was too good to be thrown away, and it will be of use applied to any other person, who may be lost and *evaporate* in the course of the work without the least damage to the composition.

For the Moral and Allegory

These you may extract out of the Fable afterwards, at your leisure. Be sure you *strain* them sufficiently.

For the Manners

For those of the hero, take all the best qualities you can find in the most celebrated heroes of antiquity; if they will not be reduced to a *consistency*, lay 'em all on a heap upon him. But be sure they are qualities which your Patron would be thought to have; and, to prevent any mistake which the world may be subject to, select from the alphabet those capital letters that compose his name and set them at the head of a dedication before your poem. However, do not absolutely observe the exact quantity of these virtues, it not being determined whether or no it be necessary for the hero of a poem to be an *honest man*.[51] For the under-characters, gather them from Homer and Virgil, and change the names as occasion serves.

For the Machines[52]

Take of *deities*, male and female, as many as you can use. Separate them into two equal parts, and keep Jupiter in the middle. Let Juno put him in a ferment, and Venus mollify him. Remember on all occasions to make use of volatile Mercury.[53] If you have need of *devils*, draw them out of Milton's *Paradise*, and extract your *spirits* from Tasso.[54] The use of these machines is evident; for since no epic poem can possibly subsist without them, the wisest way is to reserve them for your greatest necessities. When you cannot extricate your hero by any human means, or yourself by your own wit, seek relief from heaven, and the gods will do your business very readily. This is according to the direct prescription of Horace in his *Art of Poetry*:

Nec deus intersit, nisi dignus vindice nodus inciderit.[55]

That is to say, 'A poet should never call upon the gods for their assistance, but when he is in great perplexity.'

For the Descriptions

For a Tempest: take Eurus, Zephyr, Auster, and Boreas,[56] and cast them together in one verse. Add to these of rain, lightning and of thunder (the loudest you can) *quantum sufficit*.[57] Mix your clouds and billows well together till they foam, and thicken your description here and there with a quicksand. Brew your tempest well in your head before you set it a-blowing.

For a Battle: pick a large quantity of images and descriptions from Homer's *Iliad*, with a spice or two of Virgil, and if there remain any overplus, you may lay them by for a Skirmish. Season it well with similes, and it will make an excellent battle.

For a Burning Town: if such a description be necessary (because it is certain there is one in Virgil), old Troy is ready burnt to your hands. But if you fear that would be thought borrowed, a chapter or two of the Theory of the Conflagration,[58] well circumstanced and done into verse, will be a good *succedaneum*.[59]

As for *similes* and *metaphors*, they may be found all over the creation; the most ignorant may *gather* them, but the danger is in·*applying* them. For this advise with your Bookseller.[60]

SELECTED LETTERS

To Lady Mary Wortley Montagu,[1]
3 February 1717

Madam – I wish I could write any thing to divert you, but it is impossible in the unquiet state I am put into by your letter. It has grievously afflicted me, without affectation; and I think you would hardly have writ it in so strong terms, had you known to what a degree I feel the loss of those I value (it is only decency that hinders me from saying, of her I value). From this instant you are doubly dead to me, and all the vexation and concern I endured at your parting from England was nothing to what I suffer the moment I hear you have left Vienna. Till now I had some small hopes in God and in Fortune; I waited for accidents,[2] and had at least the faint comfort of a wish, when I thought of you. I am now – I can't tell what – I won't tell what, for it would grieve you – This letter is a piece of madness, that throws me after you in a distracted manner. I don't know which way to write, which way to send it, or if it will ever reach your hands. If it does, what can you infer from it, but what I am half afraid, and half willing, you should know: how very much I was yours, how unfortunately well I knew you, and with what a miserable constancy I shall ever remember you? . . .

You touch me very sensibly in saying you think so well of my *friendship*. In that, you do me too much *honour* – would to God you would (even at this distance) allow me to correct this period,[3] and change these phrases according to the real truth of my heart – I am foolish again, and methinks I am imitating in my ravings the dreams of spleenatic enthusiasts[4] and solitaires, who fall in love with saints, and fancy themselves in the favour of angels and spirits whom they can never see, or touch. I hope indeed that you, like one of those better beings, have a benevolence towards me; and I (on my part) really look up to you with zeal and fervour; not without some faint expectation of meeting hereafter, which is something betwixt piety and madness . . .

I am the most earnest of your well-wishers, and I was going to say your most faithful servant, but am angry at the weakness of all the terms I can use to express myself

Yours

To Teresa and Martha Blount,[5]

late 1717

Dear Ladies – I think myself obliged to desire you would not put off any diversion you may find, in the prospect of seeing me on Saturday, which is very uncertain. I take this occasion to tell you once for all, that I design no longer to be a constant companion when I have ceased to be an agreeable one. You have only had, as my friends, the privilege of knowing my unhappiness,[6] and are therefore the only people whom my company must necessarily make melancholy. I will not bring myself to you at all hours, like a skeleton, to come across your diversions and dash your pleasures. Nothing can be more shocking than to be perpetually meeting the ghost of an old acquaintance, which is all you can ever see of me.

You must not imagine this to proceed from any coldness, or the least decrease of friendship to you. If you had any love for me, I should be always glad to gratify you with an object that you thought agreeable. But as your regard is friendship and esteem, those are things that are as well, perhaps better, preserved absent than present. A man that you love is a joy to your eyes at all times; a man that you esteem is a solemn kind of thing, like a priest, only wanted at a certain hour to do his office; 'tis like oil in a salad, necessary, but of no manner of taste. And you may depend upon it, I will wait upon you[7] on every real occasion, at the first summons, as long as I live.

Let me open my whole heart to you. I have sometimes found myself inclined to be in love with you; and as I have reason to know from your temperament and conduct how miserably I should be used in that circumstance, it is worth my while to avoid it. It is enough to be disagreeable, without adding Fool to it, by constant slavery. I have heard indeed of women that have had a kindness for men of my make,[8] but it has been after enjoyment, never before; and I know to my cost you have had no taste of that talent in me, which most ladies would not only like better, but understand better, than any other I have.

I love you so well that I tell you the truth, and that has made me write this letter. I will see you less frequently this winter, as you'll less want company. When the gay part of the world is gone, I'll be ready to stop the gap of a vacant hour whenever you please. Till then I'll converse with those who are more indifferent to me, as you will with those who are more entertaining. I wish you every pleasure God and man can pour upon ye; and I faithfully promise you all the good I can do you, which is, the service of a friend, who will ever be,

Ladies, entirely yours

To Teresa and Martha Blount,
8 October 1718

Dear Ladies – nothing but your having bid me write to you often, could make me do it again without an apology. I don't know where you are, or whether you have received my letters, but conclude this can't be disagreeable to you unless you have altered your minds, a thing which in women I take to be impossible. 'Twill serve, if for nothing else, to give my services to Mr Caryll[9] (supposing you with him). If not, keep them yourselves; for services (you know) are of that nature, that like certain other common things, they'll fit everybody.

I am with my Lord Bathurst, at my bower,[10] in whose groves we had yesterday a dry walk of three hours. It is the place that of all others I fancy, and I am not yet out of humour with it, though I have had it some months. It does not cease to be agreeable to me so late in the season; the very dying of the leaves adds a variety of colours that is not unpleasant. I look upon it as a beauty I once loved, whom I should preserve a respect for in her decay. And as we should look upon a friend, with remembrance how he pleased us once, though now declined from his former gay and flourishing condition.

I write an hour or two every morning, and then ride out a-hunting upon the Downs,[11] eat heartily, talk tender senti-ments with Lord B.[12] or draw plans for houses and gardens, open avenues, cut glades, plant firs, contrive waterworks, all very fine and beautiful in our own imagination. At nights we play at Commerce, and play pretty high.[13] I do more, I bet too, for I am really rich, and must throw away my money if no deserving friend will use it. I like this course of life so well that I am resolved to stay here till I hear of somebody's being in town that is worth my coming after.

Since you are so silent in the country, I can't expect a word from you when you get to London. The first week must needs be wholly employed in making new gowns, the second in show-ing them, the third in seeing other people's, the fourth, fifth, and so on, in balls, plays, assemblies, operas, etc. How can a poor translator and hare-hunter hope for a minute's memory? Yet he comforts himself to reflect that he shall be remembered when people have forgot what colours you wore, and when those at whom you dress shall be dust! This is the pride of a poet; let me see if you dare own what is the pride of a woman. Perhaps one article of it may be to despise those who think themselves of some value, and to show your friends you can live without thinking of 'em at all. Do, keep your own secrets, that such fellows as I may laugh at ye in the valley of Jehos-aphat,[14] where cunning will be the foolishest thing in nature, and those white bums which I die to see will be shown to all the world. Now what will it avail, Ladies, if you really should do

something to make me wonder at, during the short course of
this transitory life? as long as I shall infallibly come to know, in
the enlightened state of the next world, what was the real rea-
son why you did not favour me with a line?

But I forget myself. I am talking as to women, things that
walk in the country, when possibly by this time you are got to
London and are goddesses; for how should you be less when
you are in your heaven? If so, most adorable deities, most celes-
tial beauties, hear the often repeated invocations of a poet
expecting immortality! So may no complaints of unhappy mor-
tals ever more disturb your eternal diversions! But oh dear
angels! do not on any account scratch your backsides; and oh
heavenly creatures! never leave the company to p–ss. Maintain
your dignity, blessed saints! and scorn to reveal yourselves to
fools (though it be but fair play, for they reveal themselves to
everybody). Goddesses must be all-sufficient, they can neither
want a friend nor a correspondent. How arrogant a wretch am
I then, who resolve to be one of these (if not both) to you, as
long as I have a day to live?

Dear Ladies, your most faithful, sincere servant, A. Pope

To Edward Blount,[15] 2 June 1725

You show yourself a just man and a friend in those guesses and
suppositions you make at the possible reasons of my silence,
every one of which is a true one. As to forgetfulness of you or
yours, I assure you, the promiscuous conversations of the town
serve only to put me in mind of better, and more quiet, to be
had in a corner of the world (undisturbed, innocent, serene,
and sensible) with such as you. Let no access of any distrust
make you think of me differently in a cloudy day from what
you do in the most sunshiny weather. Let the young ladies
be assured I make nothing new in my gardens without wishing
to see the print of their fairy steps in every part of 'em. I have
put the last hand to my works of this kind, in happily finishing
the subterraneous way and grotto. I there found a spring of

the clearest water, which falls in a perpetual rill that echoes
through the cavern day and night. From the River Thames,
you see through my arch up a walk of the wilderness[16] to a
kind of open temple, wholly composed of shells in the rustic
manner; and from that distance under the temple you look
down through a sloping arcade of trees, and see the sails on the
river passing suddenly and vanishing, as through a perspective
glass.[17] When you shut the doors of this grotto, it becomes
on the instant, from a luminous room, a *camera obscura*,[18] on
the walls of which all the objects of the river, hills, woods, and
boats, are forming a moving picture in their visible radiations.
And when you have a mind to light it up, it affords you a very
different scene: it is finished with shells interspersed with pieces
of looking-glass in angular forms, and in the ceiling is a star of
the same material, at which when a lamp (of an orbicular figure
of thin alabaster) is hung in the middle, a thousand pointed
rays glitter and are reflected over the place. There are connected
to this grotto by a narrower passage two porches, with niches
and seats: one toward the river, of smooth stones, full of light
and open; the other toward the arch of trees, rough with shells,
flints, and iron ore. The bottom is paved with simple pebble, as
the adjoining walk up the wilderness to the temple is to be
cockle-shells in the natural taste, agreeing not ill with the little
dripping murmur and the aquatic idea of the whole place. It
wants nothing to complete it but a good statue with an inscrip-
tion, like that beautiful antique one which you know I am so
fond of,

> *Hujus Nympha loci, sacri, custodia fontis,*
> *Dormio, dum blandæ sentio murmur aquæ.*
> *Parce meum, quisquis tangis cava marmora somnum*
> *Rumpere, seu bibas, sive lavere, tace.*[19]

> Nymph of the Grot, these sacred springs I keep,
> And to the murmur of these waters sleep;
> Whoe'er thou art, ah, gently tread the cave,
> Ah, bathe in silence, or in silence lave.[20]

You'll think I have been very poetical in this description, but it is pretty near the truth. I wish you were here to bear testimony how little it owes to art, either the place itself, or the image I give of it.

I am, etc.

To John Gay,[21] October 1730

It is true that I write to you very seldom, and have no pretence of writing which satisfies me, because I have nothing to say that can give you much pleasure: only merely that I am in being, which in truth is of little consequence to one from whose conversation I am cut off by such accidents or engagements as separate us. I continue, and ever shall, to wish you all good happiness; I wish that some lucky event might set you in a state of ease and independency all at once! and that I might live to see you as happy as this silly world and fortune can make anyone. Are we never to live together more, as we once did? I find my life ebbing apace, and my affections strengthening as my age increases; not that I am worse, but better, in my health than last winter, but my mind finds no amendment or improvement, nor support to lean upon, from those about me, and so I feel myself leaving the world as fast as it leaves me. Companions I have enough, friends few, and those too warm in the concerns of the world for me to bear pace with; or else so divided from me that they are but like the dead whose remembrance I hold in honour. Nature, temper, and habit from my youth made me have but one strong desire; all other ambitions, my person, education, constitution, religion, etc. conspired to remove far from me. That desire was to fix and preserve a few lasting, dependable friendships; and the accidents which have disappointed me in it have put a period to all my aims. So I am sunk into an idleness, which makes me neither care nor labour to be noticed by the rest of mankind; I propose no rewards to myself, and why should I take any sort of pains? Here I sit and sleep, and probably here I shall sleep till I sleep for ever, like the old man of Verona.[22] I hear of what passes in the busy world with so little attention that I forget it the next day, and as to the learned world, there is nothing passes in it. I have no more to add, but that I am with the same truth as ever,

Yours, etc.

To Jonathan Swift, 2 April 1733

You say truly that death is only terrible to us as it separates us from those we love, but I really think those have the worst of it who are left by us, if we are true friends. I have felt more (I fancy) in the loss of poor Mr Gay[23] than I shall suffer in the thought of going away myself into a state that can feel none of this sort of losses. I wished vehemently to have seen him in a condition of living independent, and to have lived in perfect indolence the rest of our days together, the two most idle, most innocent, undesigning poets of our age. I now as vehemently wish you and I might walk into the grave together, by as slow steps as you please, but contentedly and cheerfully. Whether that ever can be, or in what country, I know no more, than into what country we shall walk out of the grave. But it suffices me to know it will be exactly what region or state our Maker appoints, and that whatever *Is*, is *Right*.[24]

Our poor friend's papers are partly in my hands, and for as much as is so, I will take care to suppress things unworthy of him. As to the Epitaph,[25] I am sorry you gave a copy, for it will certainly by that means come into print, and I would correct it more, unless you will do it for me (and that I shall like as well). Upon the whole I earnestly wish your coming over hither,[26] for this reason among many others, that your influence may be joined with mine to suppress whatever we may judge proper of his papers. To be plunged in my neighbours and my papers will be your inevitable fate as soon as you come. That I am an author whose characters[27] are thought of some weight appears from the great noise and bustle that the court and town make about any I give; and I will not render them less important or interesting by sparing vice and folly, or by betraying the cause of truth and virtue. I will take care they shall be such as no man can be angry at but the persons I would have angry. You are sensible with what decency and justice I paid homage to the Royal Family, at the same time that I satirized false courtiers and spies, etc. about 'em. I have not the courage however to be such a satirist as you, but I would be as much, or more, a philosopher. You call your satires libels; I would rather call my satires epistles. They will consist more of morality than wit, and grow graver, which you will call duller. I shall leave it to my antagonists to be witty (if they can) and content myself to be useful, and in the right.

Tell me your opinion as to Lady M——'s or Lord H——'s performance?[28] They are certainly the top wits of the court, and you may judge by that single piece what can be done against me; for it was laboured, corrected, pre-commended, and post-disapproved, so far as to be disowned by themselves, after each had highly cried it up for the others. I have met with some complaints, and heard at a distance of some threats, occasioned by my satires. I sent fair messages to acquaint them where I was to be found in town, and to offer to call at their houses to satisfy them, and so it dropped. It is very poor in anyone to rail and threaten at a distance, and have nothing to say to you when they see you. – I am glad you persist and abide by so good a thing as that poem,[29] in which I am immortal for my morality. I never took any praise so kindly, and yet I think I deserve that praise better than I do any other. – When does your Collection come out, and what will it consist of? I have but last week finished another of my Epistles, in the order of the system;[30] and this week (*exercitandi gratia*[31]) I have translated, or rather parodied, another of Horace's,[32] in which I introduce you advising me about my expenses, housekeeping, etc. But these things shall lie by, till you come to carp at 'em, and alter rhymes, and grammar, and triplets, and cacophonies of all kinds.

Our Parliament will sit till midsummer, which I hope may be a motive to bring you rather in summer than so late as autumn; you use to love what I hate, a hurry of politics, etc. Courts I see not, courtiers I know not, kings I adore not, queens I compliment not; so I am never like to be in fashion, nor in dependance.

I heartily join with you in pitying our poor Lady[33] for her unhappiness, and should only pity her more, if she had more of what they at court call happiness. Come then, and perhaps we may go all together into France at the end of the season, and compare the liberties of both kingdoms. Adieu.

Believe me dear sir (with a thousand warm wishes, mixed with short sighs), ever yours

To Jonathan Swift, 19 December 1734

I am truly sorry for any complaint you have, and it is in regard to the weakness of your eyes that I write (as well as print) in folio.[34] You'll think (I know you will, for you have all the candour of a good understanding) that the thing which men of our age feel the most is the friendship of our equals; and that therefore whatever affects those who are stepped a few years before us[35] cannot but sensibly affect us who are to follow. It troubles me to hear you complain of your memory,[36] and if I am in any part of my constitution younger than you, it will be in my remembering everything that has pleased me in you, longer than perhaps you will. The two summers we passed together dwell always on my mind, like a vision which gave me a glimpse of a better life and better company than this world otherwise afforded. I am now an individual upon whom no other depends, and may go where I will, if the wretched carcase I am annexed to did not hinder me.[37] I rambled by very easy journeys this year to Lord Bathurst and Lord Peterborow, who upon every occasion commemorate, love, and wish for you. I now pass my days between Dawley, London, and this place,[38] not studious, nor idle, rather polishing old works than hewing out new. I redeem now and then a paper that hath been abandoned several years, and of this sort you'll soon see one, which I inscribe to our old friend Arbuthnot.[39]

Thus far I had written, and thinking to finish my letter the same evening, was prevented by company, and the next morning found myself in a fever, highly disordered, and so continued in bed for five days, and in my chamber till now; but so well

recovered as to hope to go abroad tomorrow, even by the
advice of Dr Arbuthnot. He himself, poor man, is much broke,[40]
though not worse than for these two last months he has been.
He took extremely kindly to your letter. I wish to God we could
once meet again, before that separation which yet I would be
glad to believe shall reunite us; but He who made us, not for
ours but his purposes, knows whether it be for the better or the
worse that the affections of this life should, or should not, con-
tinue into the other; and doubtless it is as it should be. Yet I am
sure that while I am here, and the thing that I am, I shall be
imperfect without the communication of such friends as you.
You are to me like a limb lost, and buried in another country;
though we seem quite divided, every accident makes me feel
you were once a part of me. I always consider you so much as
a friend that I forget you are an author, perhaps too much, but
'tis as I would desire you would do to me. However, if I could
inspirit you to bestow correction upon those three Treatises[41]
which you say are so near completed, I should think it a better
work than any I can pretend to of my own. I am almost at the
end of my morals, as I've been, long ago, of my wit. My system
is a short one, and my circle narrow. Imagination has no limits,
and that is a sphere in which you may move on to eternity; but
where one is confined to truth (or to speak more like a human
creature, to the appearances of truth), we soon find the short-
ness of our tether. Indeed, by the help of a metaphysical chain
of ideas, one may extend the circulation, go round and round
for ever, without making any progress beyond the point to
which Providence has pinned us. But this does not satisfy me,
who would rather say a little to no purpose than a great deal.
Lord B. is voluminous, but he is voluminous only to destroy
volumes. I shall not live, I fear, to see that work printed,[42] he is
so taken up still (in spite of the monitory hint given in the first
line of my *Essay*) with particular men, that he neglects man-
kind, and is still a creature of this world, not of the universe:
this world, which is a name we give to Europe, to England, to
Ireland, to London, to Dublin, to the court, to the castle, and
so diminishing, till it comes to our own affairs and our own
persons. When you write (either to him or to me, for we accept

it as all one), rebuke him for it, as a divine if you like it, or as a badineur if you think that more effectual.

What I write will show you that my head is yet weak. I had written to you by that gentleman from the Bath,[43] but I did not know him, and everybody that comes from Ireland pretends to be a friend of the Dean's. I am always glad to see any that are truly so, and therefore do not mistake anything I said so as to discourage your sending any such to me. Adieu.

To William Warburton,[44]
11 April 1739

Sir – I have just received from Mr Robinson two more of your *Letters*. It is in the greatest hurry imaginable that I write this, but I cannot help thanking you in particular for your third *Letter*, which is so extremely clear, short, and full, that I think Mr Crousaz ought never to have another answerer, and deserved not so good an one. I can only say you do him too much honour, and me *too much right*, so odd as the expression seems, for you have made my system as clear as I ought to have done and could not. It is indeed the same system as mine, but illustrated with a ray of your own, as they say our natural body is the same still when it is glorified. I am sure I like it better than I did before, and so will every man else. I know I meant just what you explain, but I did not explain my own meaning so well as you; you understand me as well as I do myself, but you express me better than I could express myself. Pray accept the sincerest acknowledgments of, Sir,

Your most obliged and real humble servant, A. Pope

I cannot but wish these Letters were put together in one book, and intend (with your leave) to procure a translation of part at least of them into French, but I shall not proceed a step without your consent and opinion.

Notes

Dictionary refers to *A Dictionary of the English Language*, edited by Samuel Johnson (first edition, 1755); when Johnson uses a line by Pope as his illustrative example, as he often does, this is indicated.

A few of Pope's poem titles are shortened, e.g. 'The Fourth Satire of Dr John Donne Versified', to a distinctive word or two, 'Donne'.

For full bibliographical references, see Further Reading.

Biblical passages are quoted from the King James Version, the one normally used by Pope and his contemporaries.

Quotations from foreign languages are in Latin unless otherwise indicated. English translations are by the editor of this volume.

EARLY POEMS

An Essay on Criticism

Pope published 'An Essay on Criticism' in 1711, at the age of twenty-three, yet he was able to achieve a lofty, authoritative tone and to incorporate an extraordinary range of reference, in the spirit of Horace's *Ars Poetica* and Nicolas Boileau's *Art of Poetry*. Years later Samuel Johnson said admiringly that the poem exhibits 'such extent of comprehension, such nicety of distinction, such acquaintance with mankind, and such knowledge both of ancient and modern learning, as are not often attained by the maturest age and longest experience' (*Life of Pope*, p. 94). With Horace as his chief model, Pope sought to draw together the many strands of aesthetic theory that had accumulated since ancient times, and to promote an appreciative response to literature in place of the fierce controversies that characterized the previous generation. Throughout the poem the key word 'wit' recurs dozens of times, with ever-changing nuances of implication. In addition to its modern meaning, it could indicate intelligence in general, or even genius, and Pope resisted the widespread assumption in his day that it was inferior to analytical judgement. Far from distorting the materials it works with, wit gives them a brighter lustre; it is 'Nature to advantage dressed', with 'Nature' a name for the fullness of the living universe. And far from being a didactic treatise, 'An Essay on Criticism' brilliantly exemplifies the art it describes, whether in aphorisms that have the permanence of proverbs – 'A little learning is a dang'rous thing'; 'To err is human, to forgive, divine' – or in verses whose sound and rhythm create the very quickness or heaviness they refer to. Above all, Pope encourages a generous conception of criticism, in an era when critics measured works of art dogmatically against arbitrary 'rules'. The only principles that matter, he argues, are the ones that give shape and meaning to representations of the world of experience:

> Those rules of old discovered, not devised,
> Are nature still, but nature methodized . . .

Pope has the artist's resentment of the critic who 'Seizes your fame, and puts his laws in force', and he argues eloquently for an imaginative response that can 'read each work of wit / With the same spirit that its author writ'.

Epigraph: 'If you know any rules more correct than these, share them candidly; if not, make use of these as I do' (Horace, *Epistles*, I, vi, 67–8).

4.   *sense*: Good sense, judgement.
17.   *wit*: Intelligence in general, as well as cleverness.
26.   *schools*: Pedantic universities.
27.   *coxcombs*: 'a fop; a superficial pretender to knowledge or accomplishments' (*Dictionary*).
32.   *still*: Always; also 69, 307, 437.
34.   *Maevius*: A bad poet, mentioned by Horace and Virgil. *Apollo*: Patron of poetry.
39.   *mules*: Product of a union between a horse and a donkey, a mule is barren.
40.   *witlings*: 'witling: a pretender to wit; a man of petty smartness' (*Dictionary*, citing this line).
43.   *equivocal*: Uncertain; it was thought that creatures in the Nile mud (41) might be products of 'spontaneous generation'. See also 'Donne', 27–9n.
44.   *tell*: Count (cf. US 'bank teller').
53.   *pretending*: 'to pretend: to profess presumptuously' (*Dictionary*).

60. *science*: Mode of knowledge (not just natural science); see also 224n.

62. *peculiar*: Particular; also 244.

76. *informing*: 'animating' (*Dictionary*).

77. *spirits*: Vital spirits, subtle fluids that were believed to carry energy throughout the body.

81. *as much more*: i.e. more intelligence.

84. *Muse's steed*: The winged horse Pegasus.

86. *gen'rous*: 'strong; vigorous' (*Dictionary*).

87. *mettle*: 'spirit; sprightliness; courage' (*Dictionary*, citing this line).

94. *Parnassus*: Mountain near Delphi in Greece, sacred to Apollo and the Muses.

108. *'pothecaries*: Apothecaries, or druggists, were competing with physicians for medical practice.

109. *bills*: Medical prescriptions.

112. *leaves*: Pages, with a pun on leaves of a plant.

115. *receipts*: Recipes.

120. *fable*: Story, plot.

129. *comment*: Commentary. *Mantuan Muse*: Virgil, who came from Mantua; see also 130n. and 708n.

130. *Maro*: Virgil, whose full name was Publius Virgilius Maro.

138. *Stagyrite*: Aristotle, who came from Stagira in Macedonia.

142. *happiness*: 'fortuitous elegance; unstudied grace' (*Dictionary*).

153. *faults*: Poetic effects that deviate from rigid 'rules'.

168. *Seizes*: 'takes forcible possession of by law' (*Dictionary*).

180. *Homer nods*: i.e. sometimes even Homer nods off and gets careless (from Horace's *Ars Poetica*, 359: *bonus dormitat Homerus*). *we that dream*: It is we who are nodding off.

181. *bays*: Laurel leaves, the reward of poetic excellence.

186. *consenting*: In concord, harmony.

206. *recruits*: Supplies.

208. *wants*: Is lacking.

216. *Pierian spring*: Hippocrene on Mount Olympus, sacred to the Muses.

224. *science*: Learning of all kinds.

239. *lays*: Songs.

241. *tenor*: 'continuity of state; constant mode' (*Dictionary*).

247. *dome*: Building (from Latin *domus*).

261. *verbal critic lays*: Pedant lays down rules.

267. *La Mancha's Knight*: Don Quixote, in Cervantes's novel of that name; see also 'IV Burlington', 160n.

270. *Dennis*: Critic John Dennis, long-time enemy of Pope; his early

criticisms provoked numerous allusions in Pope's poems; see 585n. below and see also 'Arbuthnot', 371n. and 'Dunciad', I, 106 and note.

276. *passions*: Emotions. *unities*: As enjoined by neoclassical dramatic theory, the three unities of time, place, and action (one day, one place, and one plot).

278. *lists*: Enclosures in which jousting combats were held.

286. *Curious*: 'difficult to please'. *exact*: 'accurate; not negligent'. *nice*: 'superfluously exact; fastidious' (all from *Dictionary*).

289. *conceit*: Clever (or too clever) metaphor or simile, as in the no longer fashionable metaphysical poets.

308. *content*: Trust.

319. *decent*: 'becoming; fit; suitable' (*Dictionary*).

321. *clown*: 'a rustic; a country fellow; a churl' (*Dictionary*).

323. *sev'ral*: Various.

324. *made pretence*: Laid claim.

328. *Fungoso*: A would-be man of fashion in Ben Jonson's *Every Man Out of His Humour*.

337. *numbers*: Metre, versification.

339. *conspire*: Unite.

347. *low*: Commonplace, vulgar.

356. *Alexandrine*: Iambic line with six stresses instead of five (as exemplified in 357).

361. *Denham ... Waller*: Seventeenth-century poets who perfected the heroic couplet. On John Denham, see also headnote to 'Windsor Forest'; on Edmund Waller, see Horace, Ode, IV, ix, 8–9n., and 'Epilogue to the Satires', II, 230n.

370. *Ajax*: Immensely powerful Greek warrior in the *Iliad*.

372. *Camilla*: A female warrior in the *Aeneid*. *scours*: 'scour: to pass swiftly over' (*Dictionary*, citing this line).

373. *main*: Level stretch of land.

374. *Timotheus*: Greek musician in the court of Alexander the Great.

376. *son of Lybian Jove*: Alexander the Great, visited the oracle of Ammon in Libya and proclaimed himself the son of Ammon ... Zeus (in Latin, Jupiter or Jove).

380. *like turns of nature*: Similar expressions of natural emotion.

383. *Dryden now*: In 1697 John Dryden wrote *Alexander's Feast, or, The Power of Music*, which was set to music by Jeremiah Clarke and later by Handel.

390. *turn*: 'the manner of adjusting the words of a sentence' (*Dictionary*).

400. *sublimes*: Exalts.

411. *own*: Lay claim to.

415. *quality*: People of rank.

419. *hackney sonneteer*: Hack writer of trivial verses.

428. *schismatics*: Religious sectarians (with stress on first syllable).

440. *school-divines*: University-trained theologians.

441. *sentences*: 'maxims; axioms, generally moral' (*Dictionary*).

444. *Scotists and Thomists*: Adherents of the opposing systems of the medieval theologians Duns Scotus and Thomas Aquinas.

445. *Duck Lane*: London street where old books were sold.

449. *proves the ready wit*: Gives ready wit an occasion to prove itself.

454. *Fondly*: Foolishly.

459. *parsons, critics, beaus*: The clergyman Jeremy Collier attacked the immorality of the stage, Gerald Langbaine criticized Dryden's plays, and the Duke of Buckingham satirized Dryden in *The Rehearsal* (on the last, see 'Dunciad', I, Argument note).

463. *Blackmores ... Milbournes*: Would-be rivals of Dryden, the physician Sir Richard Blackmore, who wrote tedious, bombastic epics, excerpts from which appear in Pope's *Peri Bathous* (see also Horace, Epistle, I, i, 16n.); and the translator Luke Milbourne.

464. *awful*: Awe-inspiring.

465. *Zoilus*: Fourth-century BC critic of Homer.

477. *betimes*: 'before long time has passed' (*Dictionary*).

509. *commence*: Begin to be.

521. *sacred*: Accursed (from *sacer*).

527. *spleen*: 'anger; spite; ill-humour' (*Dictionary*).

528. *provoking*: 'in such a manner as to raise anger' (*Dictionary*).

536. *an easy monarch*: The 'merry monarch' Charles II, noted for his anti-puritanical temperament, graceful manners, and busy love life. See also Horace, Epistle, II, i, 140n.

538. *Jilts*: Harlots, referring to Charles's numerous mistresses: *statesmen*: In addition to the Duke of Buckingham (see 459n.), Sir Charles Sedley and Sir George Etherege were also successful comic playwrights.

541. *mask*: A woman (quite possibly a prostitute) wearing a mask at the theatre.

544. *foreign reign*: William of Orange in the Netherlands, who became William III of England in 1688 when the Glorious Revolution brought his wife Mary to the English throne.

545. *Socinus*: Sixteenth-century Italian theologian who denied the divinity of Christ, and whose followers were known (and denounced) as Socinians.

551. *admired*: Wondered, marvelled.
552. *Titans*: Giant sons of earth who were overthrown by Zeus and the Olympians, and who tried in vain to conquer the heavens; by implication, deistic freethinkers who criticized orthodox beliefs; see also 'Essay on Man', IV, 73n.
553. *licensed blasphemies*: After the Licensing Act was allowed to lapse in 1695, freethinking works were published that would formerly have been censored.
563. *candour*: 'openness; kindness' (*Dictionary*).
570. *own*: Acknowledge.
578. *on no pretence*: With no matter what reasons.
580. *complacence*: 'civility; complaisance; softness of manners' (*Dictionary*); i.e. do not betray your trust by being too polite and deferential.
585. *Appius*: Dennis promoted the sublime and was known for using the word 'tremendous' (586); the allusion is unmistakable since he wrote a failed tragedy, *Appius and Virginia*.
588. *tax*: Censure. *honourable*: A person of rank (cf. 'your Honour').
591. *they can take degrees*: Awarded by Oxford and Cambridge to noblemen even when they lacked academic qualifications.
592. *satyrs*: Pope's spelling of 'satires'; probably pronounced 'sators'.
601. *lashed asleep*: 'a top sleeps when it moves with such velocity that its motion is imperceptible' (*Oxford English Dictionary*).
603. *jades*: 'horses of no spirit; worthless nags' (*Dictionary*).
606. *Still run on*: Continue to write.
617. *Dryden's Fables ... Durfey's Tales*: Dryden's *Fables Ancient and Modern* was his last book and contains some of his greatest poetry; Thomas Durfey's *Tales Tragical and Comical* was an often-derided popular work.
618. *With*: According to.
619. *Garth*: Pope's friend the physician Samuel Garth burlesqued the struggle between doctors and apothecaries in his mock-heroic *Dispensary* (which influenced 'Rape of the Lock'), and was wrongly suspected of not having written it himself.
623. *Paul's churchyard*: Booksellers had stalls outside St Paul's Cathedral.
636. *humanly*: Humanely.
641. *converse*: 'acquaintance; familiarity' (*Dictionary*).
648. *Maeonian*: Homeric (Maeonia in Asia Minor was traditionally the birthplace of Homer).
651. *Received his laws*: As laid down in the *Poetics*.

652. *conquered nature*: Aristotle wrote extensively on the physical sciences.

662. *phlegm*: 'the watery humour of the body, which is supposed to produce sluggishness or dullness' (*Dictionary*).

665. *Dionysius*: Of Halicarnassus, a Roman critic and historian (born in Asia Minor).

667. *Petronius*: Petronius Arbiter, author of the *Satyricon*, who served as *arbiter elegantiae* (judge in matters of taste) in the court of Nero.

669. *Quintilian*: Roman author of *Institutio Oratoria*, an immensely influential treatise on rhetoric.

671. *magazines*: Armouries.

675. *Longinus*: Greek rhetorician, supposed author of *On the Sublime. the Nine*: The Muses.

684. *eagles*: Roman standards in battle.

693. *Erasmus*: Dutch Renaissance humanist, liberal Catholic theologian, and opponent of Martin Luther, in the sixteenth century; author of the satiric *In Praise of Folly*.

694. *shame*: Because he attacked other priests, who deserved it.

696. *Vandals*: Like the Goths, Germanic barbarians who trashed Rome. See also 'Dunciad', III, 86–90n.

697. *Leo*: Leo X, Pope (1513–21) under whom the Renaissance was thought to have reached its high-water mark.

699. *genius*: 'protecting or ruling power' (*Dictionary*).

704. *Raphael . . . Vida*: Renaissance Italian painter and poet, respectively; Pope was familiar with Vida's *On the Art of Poetry*.

707. *Cremona*: Birthplace of Vida.

708. *Mantua*: Birthplace of Virgil, who wrote 'Mantua, alas! too close to unfortunate Cremona', which had been parcelled out to army veterans (*Eclogues*, IX, 28).

709. *Latium*: Italy; the implication is that the arts departed from Rome after it was sacked by troops of the Holy Roman Empire in 1527.

714. *Boileau*: Nicolas Boileau-Despréaux, seventeenth-century French poet, and author of an *Art of Poetry*, one of the models for 'Essay on Criticism'; see also Horace, Satire, II, i, 111n.

724. 'Nature's chief . . . well': Quoted from an *Essay on Poetry* (1682) by the Duke of Buckingham.

725. *Roscommon*: The Earl of Roscommon (d. 1685), minor poet and critic.

729. *Walsh*: William Walsh (d. 1708), Pope's friend and poetic mentor in his youth.

730. *knew*: Knew how, or knew whether.
731. *desert*: Pronounced to rhyme with 'heart'.
738. *low numbers*: Humble verses.
739. *their wants*: What they lack.

Windsor Forest

By 1707, when he was still in his teens, Pope had completed a poem describing the landscape around his home at Binfield, a few miles from Windsor. It was heavily influenced by Virgil's *Georgics* and by a seventeenth-century 'locodescriptive' poem by John Denham entitled *Cooper's Hill*, which used a hill in that area as a vantage point for surveying England's tribulations during the civil wars of the 1640s. Denham's poem contained the pair of couplets most quoted in the eighteenth century, exemplifying the balanced order that Pope likewise aspired to: he hoped that his verse might flow like the Thames:

> O could I flow like thee, and make thy stream
> My great example, as it is my theme!
> Though deep, yet clear; though gentle, yet not dull;
> Strong without rage, without o'erflowing full.

More largely, Pope admired *Cooper's Hill* for finding instructive analogies in nature; as he put it, 'The descriptions of places and images raised by the poet are still tending to some hint, or leading into some reflection, upon moral life or political institution' (Pope's footnote to the *Iliad*, Twickenham edition, VIII, p. 2361). Some years later, anticipating the end of the Duke of Marlborough's wars against France and Spain, Pope returned to the poem and added the second section (beginning at line 291). 'Windsor Forest' was published in 1713, shortly before the Peace of Utrecht ended the War of the Spanish Succession. Pope's theme is that England flourishes through a harmonious balance of opposing forces, known as *concordia discors*, symbolized in the balanced elements of the landscape. He also exploits the proximity of Windsor Castle, emblematic of the centuries-old monarchy, and the fact that Windsor Forest – 'forest' meant a protected hunting preserve, not necessarily wooded – was exploited for their own pleasure by cruel, belligerent Norman kings. Criticism of William the Conqueror and his successors alludes covertly to a more recent William, Queen Mary's consort William III, while their successor Queen Anne is hailed as a sponsor of peace, prosperity, and benevolent imperial rule.

Epigraph: 'I do not sing unbidden. Of you, Varus, all our groves of tamarisks shall sing, nor is any page more welcome to Phoebus than that which bears the name of Varus' (abridged from Virgil, *Eclogues*, VI, 9–12). The tamarisk was sacred to Phoebus Apollo, god of music and poetry.

2. *the monarch's and the Muse's seats*: Because of its proximity to Windsor Castle, and to the residence of several seventeenth-century poets.

3. *sylvan maids*: Naiads and dryads, pastoral nature spirits.

5. *Granville*: The poem is dedicated to George Granville, Lord Lansdowne, a minor poet and playwright.

8. *Live in description*: In Milton's *Paradise Lost*.

21. *lawns*: 'an open space between woods' (*Dictionary*); also 81.

26. *desert*: Deserted area, wilderness.

27. *tufted trees*: Trees in a clump, a phrase from Milton's *L'Allegro*.

31. *our oaks*: Britain's fleet of oaken ships.

33. *Olympus*: The highest mountain in Greece, home of the gods.

37–9. *Pan*: God of flocks and pastures. *Pomona*: Goddess of fruits. *Flora*: Goddess of flowers. *Ceres*: Goddess of grains.

38. *enamelled ground*: A technical term from painting, in which a layer of enamel forms the base ('ground') on which other colours may be applied; it was traditional to describe beautiful landscapes as 'enamelled'.

41. *Industry*: Industriousness, labour.

42. *Stuart*: Queen Anne (whose death in 1714 would end the Stuart line); see also 162 and note.

45. *savage laws*: The medieval Forest Laws, by which the Normans turned farmland into hunting preserves, and punished poaching by unauthorized persons even if they lived on the land.

50. *wiser . . . slaves*: i.e. wiser than humans, wild animals resisted enslavement.

52. *the elements . . . swayed*: The tyrant held sway over Nature itself (by robbing farmers of their crops).

55. *swain*: Rural labourer.

61. *Nimrod*: The tyrannical 'mighty hunter before the Lord' of Genesis 10:9.

63. *haughty Norman*: 'alluding to the destruction made in the New Forest, and the tyrannies exercised there by William I' (Pope's note).

66. *fanes*: Temples, probably recalling the destruction of the monasteries under Henry VIII.

77. *Saxon . . . Dane*: Rulers of Britain before the Norman Conquest.

80. *denied a grave*: The burial of William I was delayed because of objections by the owner of the site.

81. *second hope*: William's second son, Richard, was killed by a stag in the New Forest.

83. *Rufus*: William II, William's third son, also known as Rufus, likewise died hunting in the New Forest. See also 'Dunciad', II, 265n.

87. *unknown*: Not previously known to them, because forbidden.

90. *secret transport*: Inward rapture. *conscious*: Alert, aware.

94. *spirits*: Subtle 'animal spirits' in the blood that were believed to animate the body.

96. *Wind*: Blow.

101. *tainted*: Carrying an animal's scent.

106. *Albion*: England, from *albus* ('white'), referring to the White Cliffs of Dover.

108. *invest*: Besiege.

111. *brake*: Thicket.

119. *Arcturus*: Star in the Great Bear constellation that rises with the sun in September; it was thought to presage beneficial rain.

135. *genial*: Generative.

136. *mead*: Meadow.

142. *Tyrian dye*: Crimson or purple, as in the famous dye of ancient Tyre.

143. *volumes*: 'volume: something rolled, or convolved ... as a fold of a serpent' (*Dictionary*).

147. *Cancer*: The sun, Phoebus Apollo's chariot or 'car', enters the Crab constellation (the astrological sign for Cancer) at the summer solstice, 22 June.

150. *opening*: The cry of hounds following a scent.

159. *Arcadia*: Region in Greece associated with pastoral simplicity.

160. *immortal huntress*: Diana (Greek Artemis), goddess of the hunt and the moon.

162. *queen*: Queen Anne, who was fond of hunting.

164. *empress of the main*: Britannia ruled the seas, as Diana controlled the tides.

166. *Cynthus*: Mountain on the island of Delos, birthplace of Diana.

170. *buskined*: Wearing laced half-boots.

172. *Lodona*: A nymph whom Pope imagines changed, in the manner of Ovid's *Metamorphoses*, into the river Loddon near his home at Binfield.

176. *crescent*: The crescent moon, Diana's emblem; see 164n. *zone*: Belt.

178. *fillet*: Headband or ribbon.

186. *liquid*: Clear, transparent (*liquidus*).

200. *Cynthia*: Diana; see 166n.

207. *Still bears the name*: i.e. the Loddon.

209. *laves*: Bathes.

219. *great father*: The Thames. *floods*: Rivers.

221. *honours*: Adornments, i.e. foliage.

222. *future navies*: Ships built of oak.

227. *Po*: Eridanus, a mythological river identified by Virgil and Ovid with the Po; the name of a constellation.

230. *our earthly gods*: The royal family, residing at Windsor Castle.

233. *Jove*: Or Jupiter (the Latin name for Zeus), who rules on Mount Olympus.

242. *physic*: Medicine, extracted from plants. *spoils*: Despoils.

243. *chemic art*: The art of the chemist. *exalts*: In alchemy, refines, raises to higher power.

244. *draws*: Extracts, distils.

246. *figured worlds*: On a map, or perhaps a diagram of the zodiac.

251. *a mean*: The 'golden mean' is the midpoint between extremes of any kind, a favourite theme of Pope's; see also 'III Bathurst', 246.

255. *kindred*: The ancients believed that the soul and the stars were composed of the same substance.

257. *Scipio*: Roman general, called 'Africanus' for his defeat of Rome's rival Carthage in North Africa; he retired to a country estate after defeating Hannibal in the Second Punic War.

258. *Atticus*: Pomponius Atticus, Roman philosopher and friend of Cicero, called Atticus because of his mastery of attic Greek, likewise chose retirement. *Trumbull*: Sir William Trumbull, who retired from politics and went to Windsor Forest in 1698; a valued mentor to the youthful Pope.

259. *sacred Nine*: The Muses.

265. *Cooper's Hill*: See headnote.

272. *numbers*: Metre, versification. *Cowley*: 'Mr [Abraham] Cowley died at Chertsey, on the borders of the Forest, and was from thence conveyed to Westminster' (Pope's note); he was 48, so 'early lost' (273).

274. *sad pomp*: Cowley's body was solemnly transported down the Thames, for burial in Westminster Abbey.

275. *swans ... expire*: The 'swan song', which swans, mute until then, were supposed to sing when dying.

290. *silver star*: Emblematic of the Order of the Garter, whose meeting

place was at Windsor Castle; Pope implies that Granville deserved to be made a knight of the Garter (it never happened).

291. *Surrey*: Henry Howard, Earl of Surrey, wrote love poems while imprisoned in Windsor Castle in the sixteenth century. *sacred rage*: Poetic inspiration.

294. *lists*: See 'Essay on Criticism', 278n.

297. *Geraldine*: The mistress addressed in Surrey's poems.

298. *Myra*: The mistress addressed by Granville.

303. *Edward's acts*: Edward III rebuilt Windsor Castle in the fourteenth century and founded the Order of the Garter.

305. *monarchs chained*: Kings of Scotland and France, held prisoner at Windsor by Edward III. *Cressi*: Crécy in France, site of Edward's great victory in 1346.

306. *shield*: To affirm his claim to France, Edward put the French fleur-de-lis on his shield.

307. *Verrio*: Italian artist Antonio Verrio, commissioned by Charles II to paint scenes of British victories on the ceilings at Windsor.

311. *ill-fated Henry*: Henry VI (d. 1471), murdered and buried at Windsor.

314. *Edward*: Edward IV, his rival (d. 1483).

316. *Belerium*: Land's End in Cornwall, the south-western tip of England.

319. *Charles's tomb*: Charles I was buried ignominiously, after his execution in 1649, at Windsor by the Puritans, who refused permission for the burial service to be read.

321. *fact*: Deed, crime.

323. *purple death*: The Great Plague of 1665, which produced purple blotches and swellings.

324. *domes*: Impressive buildings; also 352n. *rolling fire*: The Great Fire that destroyed much of London in 1666.

325. *intestine wars*: Internal warfare, the civil wars.

326. *dishonest*: Dishonourable.

327. *Anna*: Queen Anne.

332. *shining horns*: Attributes of a river god.

334. *alternate*: Stressed on the second syllable.

336. *Augusta*: Roman name for London. *gold*: When London was rebuilt after the Great Fire (see 324n.), the gilt metal decorations were much admired. See also 377.

340–48. *Isis ... Darent*: English rivers ('Cole' is the Colne, and 'Vandalis' the Wandle). The Thames was often poetically described as the fruit of a union between the Thame and the Isis. The river Mole flows underground at one point. 'Danish blood' was shed near the Darent in an eleventh-century battle.

352. *domes*: Stately buildings (from *domus*). *pompous*: 'splendid; magnificent; grand' (*Dictionary*).

355. *Hail, sacred*: The speaker is Father Thames.

358. *Hermus*: In the Hermus valley in Asia Minor, grains of gold were mingled with the sands of the River Pactolus.

359. *Nilus*: The Nile, with seven mouths; its source was then unknown.

363. *Volga's banks*: Scene of recent battles between Peter the Great of Russia and Charles XII of Sweden.

368. *Iber*: The Ebro in Spain, where Marlborough fought his Iberian campaign in 1710. *Ister*: Roman name for the Danube, where Marlborough won his great victory at Blenheim in 1704.

372. *chase*: Hunt.

378. *temples rise*: After the Great Fire (see 324n.) fifty new churches were planned, though most were never built.

379–80.   *two fair cities . . . ample bow*: The commercial 'City', and the court and Parliament at Westminster, along a curving 'bow' of the Thames.

380. *Whitehall*: Royal palace destroyed by the Great Fire (and never rebuilt).

383. *sue*: 'to beg; to entreat; to petition' (*Dictionary*).

384. *bend before a British queen*: As in the time of Elizabeth I.

387. *her cross*: The red cross of St George, which appears on the Union Jack, superimposed on the crosses of St Andrew (Scotland) and St Patrick (Ireland).

389. *Tempt*: Attempt, dare.

393. *balm*: Sap from incised trees.

396. *ripening ore*: The heat of the sun ('Phoebus') was thought to ripen ore into gold.

398. *Unbounded Thames*: 'a wish that London may be made a free port' (Pope's note).

404. *feathered people*: Four Iroquois chiefs had visited London in 1710.

409. *freed Indians*: In South America, liberated from Spanish rule.

411. *race of kings*: The Incas.

420. *broken wheel*: The wheel of torture.

425. *gods*: i.e. royalty, frequently celebrated in Granville's poems.

434. *First in these fields*: 'Spring', the first of Pope's youthful sequence of pastoral poems, begins (echoing Virgil): 'First in these fields I try the sylvan strains, / Nor blush to sport on Windsor's blissful plains.'

Prologue to Mr Addison's Tragedy of Cato

At a time when he was still on good terms with Joseph Addison, Pope contributed this prologue, which was declaimed at the 1713 opening night of his hugely successful *Cato*. The tragedy presents (it would be too much to say it dramatizes) a high-principled Roman, Cato the Younger, who opposed the dictatorship of Julius Caesar and ultimately committed suicide rather than conform. In a time of great political tension, both Whigs and Tories sought to claim the play's celebration of 'Liberty' for their own. Contemporary politics aside, the theme of noble self-mastery was one that Pope would pursue throughout his poetic career.

9.   *vulgar springs*: i.e. cheap emotional effects.
23.   *gives his little senate laws*: Two decades later, in 'Arbuthnot' (209 and note), Pope cleverly adapted this line in a critique of Addison himself.
27.   *triumphal cars*: Victorious generals were accorded 'triumphs', in which chariots drew them through the streets of Rome.
41.   *scene*: The stage.
42.   *Italian song*: Opera, sung in Italian.
43.   *assert*: 'to maintain; to defend either by words or actions' (*Dictionary*).

The Rape of the Lock

'The Rape of the Lock', widely regarded as Pope's masterpiece, had a complicated history. In 1711 John Caryll, a country gentleman in the Pope family's circle of Catholic friends, told him about an incident in which Robert, Lord Petre had publicly embarrassed the beautiful Arabella Fermor by snipping off a lock of her hair. As Pope long afterward related to a friend, the two families were furious with each other, and Caryll had encouraged him to 'write a poem to make a jest of it, and laugh them together again' (Spence, *Anecdotes*, I, 44). Pope thereupon wrote a short, two-canto version of the poem, which was published in 1712. Realizing that much might still be done with the story, he later doubled it in size, adding the mock-epic 'machinery' of sylphs and gnomes and many of the most memorable episodes: the dressing scene, the boat trip on the Thames, the game of ombre, and the Cave of Spleen. This version was published in 1714, and in 1717 Pope made one further addition, Clarissa's speech in Canto V, which challenges the heroine to acknowledge that the proper goal of flirtation is marriage. In its revised form the poem brilliantly parodies the conventions of classical epic: the gods become sylphs and gnomes, and the arming of the hero becomes Belinda's dressing room; the heroic voyage is reduced to an excursion on the Thames; heroic combat to a game of cards (ombre is chosen because its rules allow Belinda to vanquish two men simultaneously); and the underworld journey to an emotional crisis of self-indulgent 'spleen'. From one point of view these epic allusions expose the triviality of the quarrel over the lock; from another, they afford a largeness of perspective that confers charm and beauty upon the social game of courtship. Seventy years later Samuel Johnson wrote: 'The subject of the poem is an event below the common incidents of common life; nothing real is introduced that is not seen so often as to be no longer regarded; yet the whole detail of a female day is here brought before us invested with so much art of decoration that, though nothing is disguised, everything is striking, and we feel all the appetite of curiosity for that from which we have a thousand times turned fastidiously away' (*Life of Pope*, p. 234). It appears, however, that the Fermor and Petre families were deeply offended by Pope's attempt to 'laugh them together again'. The heroine and hero both married other people, and by the time the 1714 version of the poem was published, Lord Petre had died of smallpox.

Dedication: *Mrs*: The title 'Mrs', short for 'Mistress', was used for unmarried as well as married women. *Rosicrucian*:   A follower of an esoteric philosophy, some of whose symbols Pope goes on to describe. As he indicates, he got most of it from *Le Comte de Gabalis*, a playful erotic fantasy by the Abbé de Villars.

Epigraph: 'I did not wish, Belinda, to violate your locks, but it gives me pleasure to have paid the tribute you begged for' (Martial, Epigram, XII, 84, substituting Belinda's name for the original).

Canto I

3.   *Caryll*: Pope's friend John Caryll, 'Secretary to Queen Mary, the wife of James II, and author of *Sir Solomon Single*, a comedy, and of several translations in Dryden's *Miscellanies*. He first suggested the subject of this poem to the author' (Pope's note); see also headnote.

6.   *lays*: Songs.

13.   *curtains*: Of the four-poster bed.

18.   *returned ... sound*: The 'repeater' watch sounded out the hour (in some cases the quarter-hour) when a button was pressed, a useful feature in the dark.

22. *morning-dream*: Imitating the messages from the gods received in dreams by Homeric heroes.

23. *birthnight*: Royal birthdays were occasions for celebration.

32. *circled green*: A 'fairy ring' of trampled grass, supposedly made by dancing fairies.

44. *the box*: In the theatre; see V, 14–19n. *the ring*: A fashionable drive in Hyde Park (Circus); also IV, 117.

45. *equipage*: Carriage with horses and attendant footmen (stressed on the final syllable).

46. *chair*: Sedan chair, carried by two servants.

55. *chariots*: Epic diction for 'carriages'; also IV, 155. Pope is echoing Dryden's translation of the *Aeneid*: 'The love of horses, which they had, alive, / And care of chariots, after death survive' (VI, 890–91).

56. *ombre*: Dramatized at length in Canto III, and see III, 27n.

58. *elements*: In accordance with the psychology based on the four elements and their prevalence in bodily 'humours', four character types are successively described in the poem as dominated by fire, water, earth, and air.

59. *sprites*: Spirits. *termagants*: 'termagant: a bawling turbulent woman' (*Dictionary*).

60. *salamander*: A lizard-like creature fabled to be able to live in fire.

62. *tea*: In Pope's time rhymed with 'away' (and III, 8).

70. *what sexes*: In *Paradise Lost*, spirits 'when they please / can either sex assume, or both' (I, 423–4).

72. *masquerades*: Masked balls, immensely popular during the eighteenth century.

73. *spark*: 'a lively, showy, splendid, gay man; it is commonly used with contempt' (*Dictionary*).

85. *garters, stars*: Emblems of knighthood. *coronets*: Insignia of dukes.

86. *Your Grace*: Polite form of address to a duke or duchess.

89. *bidden blush*: Through the use of rouge; also 143.

94. *impertinence*: 'trifle; thing of no value' (*Dictionary*).

96. *treat*: Feast.

100. *toyshop*: Equivalent to a modern gift shop; 'a shop where playthings and little nice manufactures are sold' (*Dictionary*, citing this line).

101. *sword-knots*: Decorative ribbons on the hilts of swords.

110. *main*: Sea.

115. *Shock*: Or shough, a fashionable breed of long-haired lapdog.

118. *billet-doux*: Love letter (French).

121. *toilet*: Dressing table.
127. *inferior priestess*: Her lady's maid.
131. *nicely*: Fastidiously.
134. *Arabia*: Perfume made from Arabian ingredients.
135. *tortoise . . . elephant*: Tortoise shell and ivory.
138. *Bibles*: In miniature format they were considered fashionable.
139. *awful*: Awesome.
143. *purer blush*: i.e. created by the use of rouge.
144. *keener lightnings*: Her pupils are enlarged with belladonna.
147. *plait*: Arrange in folds.
148. *Betty*: Generic name for a lady's maid.

Canto II

4. *Launched*: Belinda's party is travelling by boat up the Thames to Hampton Court.
7. *sparkling cross*: Arabella Fermor, who had been educated in a French convent, wore such a cross.
25. *springes*: Snares; two syllables, pronounced 'sprindges'.
32. *force . . . fraud*: Thomas Hobbes wrote in *Leviathan* (I, xiii): 'Force and fraud are in war the two cardinal virtues.'
35. *Phoebus*: The sun.
38. *gilt*: Books in elegant gilt leather bindings.
47. *secure*: 'free from danger; safe' (*Dictionary*).
51. *zephyrs*: Breezes.
53. *careful*: Full of cares.
56. *repair*: 'to go to; to betake himself' (*Dictionary*).
70. *Superior by the head*: An epic hero would be taller than his followers.
73. *sylphids*: Female sylphs.
74. *genii . . . demons*: Guardian spirits.
77. *purest aether*: The pure air above the moon.
84. *painted bow*: Rainbow.
86. *glebe*: Farmland.
97. *wash*: Liquid cosmetics.
99. *invention*: Creativity (*invenire*).
100. *furbelow*: 'a piece of stuff plaited and puckered together . . . on the petticoats or gowns of women' (*Dictionary*).
103. *slight*: Trickery (as in 'sleight of hand').
105. *Diana's law*: Chastity.
113. *drops*: Diamond earrings.
115. *Crispissa*: Curls (from *crispere*).
118. *petticoat*: A skirt, intended to be visible, beneath a gown.

120. *ribs of whale*: Petticoats were given their shape by whalebone stays.

124. *the fair*: The fair lady.

128. *bodkin*: 'an instrument to draw a thread or ribbon through a loop' (*Dictionary*, citing this line), and see also IV, 98 and note.

129. *pomatums*: Ointments.

131. *alum styptics*: Astringent ointments made from alum (a compound of aluminium and potassium), used to quench bleeding.

132. *rivelled*: 'rivel: to contract into wrinkles and corrugations' (*Dictionary*).

133. *Ixion*: Punished by Zeus, for his love of Hera, by being bound for eternity on a turning wheel.

134. *whirling mill*: Device for beating chocolate.

Canto III

4.   *Hampton*: The royal palace at Hampton Court, twelve miles up the Thames from London, favoured by Queen Anne.

7.   *three realms*: England, Scotland, and Ireland; the union of England and Scotland in 1707 created the United Kingdom.

23. *Exchange*: The Royal Exchange in London, the central venue for commerce and banking.

27. *ombre*: Card game for three players with forty cards. As 'ombre' (from Spanish *hombre*, man), Belinda has the right to call trumps.

29. *join*: Pronounced to rhyme with 'nine'.

30. *sacred Nine*: The Muses.

33. *matadore*: The three highest-ranking cards; see also 49–53n.

41. *succinct*: Short.

42. *halberts*: Or halberds, ceremonial weapons combining a spear and a battleaxe.

44. *velvet plain*: The card table; as also 'the verdant field' (52), and 'the level green' (80 and note).

46. *Let spades . . . they were*: Recalling 'God said, Let there be light, and there was light' (Genesis 1:3).

49–53. *Spadillio . . . Manillio . . . Basto*: The three matadore cards: the ace and deuce of spades, and the ace of clubs.

59. *rebel knave*: The knave of spades.

61. *Pam*: The knave of clubs, highest card in the game of lu (or loo).

74. *the globe*: In contemporary playing cards, the king of clubs held a globe. This and other pictorial details would have been familiar to Pope's first readers.

80. *the level green*: The card table is covered with green baize, with a pun on the grassy 'green' where fallen soldiers would lie.

84. *habit*: Clothing.
92. *codille*: Defeat of the 'ombre' player. Belinda and the Baron have each won four tricks, and she needs one more in order not to lose.
94. *nice trick*: Nicely judged trick, with a pun on 'trickery'.
106. *berries crackle*: Coffee beans ground in the coffee mill.
107. *shining altars of Japan*: Lacquered or 'japanned' tables.
109. *grateful*: Pleasing.
111. *At once*: At one and the same time.
117. *Coffee*: Coffee-houses were popular venues for gossip and politics.
122. *Scylla's fate*: Greek princess who betrayed her father Nisus by pulling a sacred hair from his head, and was punished by being metamorphosized into a bird.
132. *engine*: 'any instrument' (*Dictionary*, citing this line).
142. *ideas*: Images.
147. *forfex*: Scissors (Latin), playfully elevated epic diction.
152. *But airy substance . . . again*: 'See Milton, Book 6, of Satan cut asunder by the angel Michael' (Pope's note).
164. *coach and six*: Carriage drawn by six horses.
165. *Atalantis*: *The New Atalantis* (1709), by Mary Delarivière Manley, a novel that retailed scandalous stories about thinly-disguised contemporary celebrities.
171. *date*: 'end; conclusion' (*Dictionary*).
173. *labour of the gods*: The walls of Troy were said to have been built by Apollo and Poseidon.

Canto IV

1–2. *anxious cares . . . secret passions*: Recalls Dido's passion in Dryden's translation of the *Aeneid*: 'But anxious cares already seized the queen; / She fed within her veins a flame unseen' (IV, 1–2).
4. *their charms survive*: i.e. they outlive their youthful beauty.
8. *manteau*: Fashionable outer garment, incongruously associated here with Cynthia (Diana), goddess of chastity and the hunt.
16. *Spleen*: Mental illness, known as 'melancholy', which was thought to originate in disorders of the spleen; see also 60 and note.
18. *vapour*: Melancholic attacks of the spleen were known as 'the vapours'.
20. *dreaded east*: East winds, generally chilly in England, were thought to encourage melancholia.
24. *Pain at her side*: i.e. in the spleen. *Megrim*: Migraine.
25. *wait*: Wait upon.

34. *airs*: 'an affected or laboured manner or gesture' (*Dictionary*).
43. *spires*: Spirals.
45. *Elysian scenes*: Like those of the happy Elysian fields of the after-life; see also 'Dunciad', IV, 417n.
46. *machines*: The elaborate scenic machinery of the theatre.
51. *pipkin*: Small pot. *Homer's tripod*: Impressive kettle awarded as a prize at epic games.
52. *goose-pie*: 'alludes to a real fact; a lady of distinction imagined herself in this condition' (Pope's note).
56. *spleenwort*: Fern thought to have curative powers (carried by Umbriel as Aeneas carried a golden bough in the underworld).
60. *hysteric or poetic fit*: Alluding to the age-old connection between melancholy and genius.
62. *physic*: Medicine.
69. *citron-waters*: Brandy with lemon peel. *inflame*: i.e. red-faced from drinking too much.
71. *airy horns*: Imagined infidelities, which would generate a cuck-old's horns.
75. *costive*: Constipated.
77. *chagrin*: 'ill humour; vexation; fretfulness; peevishness. It is pro-nounced *shagreen*' (*Dictionary*).
82. *Ulysses . . . winds*: In *Odyssey*, X.
89. *Thalestris*: Queen of the Amazons.
98. *bodkin*: 'an instrument to dress the hair' (*Dictionary*, citing this line), and see II, 128 and note.
99. *paper-durance*: Curling papers, held in place with strips of lead.
101. *fillets*: Headbands or ribbons.
109. *toast*: 'a celebrated woman whose health is often drunk' (*Dictionary*).
114. *Exposed through crystal*: The Baron will wear the lock set into a ring.
117. *Hyde Park Circus*: The 'ring'; see I, 44 and note.
118. *the sound of Bow*: Within earshot of the bells of St Mary-le-Bone (Bow), and therefore in the commercial City of London (as contrasted with the Westminster of fashion and politics).
124. *nice conduct of a clouded cane*: Skilful flourishing of a walking stick with a head of mottled amber.
126. *case*: Subject at hand.
128. *Z—ds*: Zounds, from 'God's wounds'. *Gad*: Polite form of 'God', to avoid swearing.
135. *honours*: 'ornament; decoration' (*Dictionary*).
156. *bohea*: See 'Epistle to Mrs Teresa Blount', 15n.

162. *patch-box*: Box for beauty patches, worn on the face.
164. *Poll*: A parrot, often called 'Polly'.

Canto V

2.   *fate and Jove*: Recalling Aeneas' refusal to stay with Dido: 'His hardened heart nor prayers nor threat'ning move, / Fate, and the god, had stopped his ears' (Dryden's *Aeneid*, IV, 636–7).

7.   *Clarissa*: 'a new character introduced in the subsequent editions, to open more clearly the moral of the poem, in a parody of the speech of Sarpedon to Glaucus in Homer' (Pope's note). For Pope's translation of Sarpedon's speech, see Excerpts from the *Iliad*, Book XII.

14–19. *Why bows ... front-box grace*: At the theatre, ladies sat in the front boxes facing the stage, gentlemen in the side-boxes, and ordinary people in the pit.

20. *smallpox*: Frequently disfiguring or fatal in the eighteenth century, when inoculation was just being introduced.

21. *housewife's*: Pronounced 'hussif's'.

37. *virago*: 'a female warrior; a woman with the qualities of a man' (*Dictionary*).

39. *side in parties*: Take sides.

47. *Latona*: Mother of Apollo and Diana.

53. *sconce*: Candle holder on a wall. 'Minerva in like manner, during the battle of Ulysses with the suitors in the *Odyssey*, perches on a beam of the roof to behold it' (Pope's note).

57. *press*: 'crowd; tumult; throng' (*Dictionary*, citing this line).

62. *Dapperwit*: Character in *Love in a Wood* (1672) by William Wycherley.

63. *Sir Fopling*: Title character, a fatuous would-be wit, in *The Man of Mode, or, Sir Fopling Flutter* (1676), by George Etheredge.

64. *'Those eyes are made so killing'*: 'the words in a song in the opera of *Camilla*' (Pope's note). Buononcini's opera was extremely popular in London.

65. *Meander's*: River in Asia Minor, which gave its name to rivers with a winding course.

66. *as he sings he dies*: The 'swan song'; see 'Windsor Forest' 275 and note.

74. *the wits mount up*: i.e. they weigh even less than the ladies' hairs.

78. *die*: With the old double entendre on 'orgasm'.

83. *just*: 'exact; proper; accurate' (*Dictionary*).

113. *the lunar sphere*: Imitating Astolfo's journey to the moon in Ariosto's *Orlando Furioso*, in search of Orlando's lost wits.

126. *Proculus*: Romulus was fabled to have been taken up into the heavens in a cloud; a senator named Julius Proculus claimed to have seen him in a vision.

127. *liquid*: Clear, transparent (*liquidus*).

128. *trail of hair*: The tail of the comet Berenices (whose name derives from a Greek word for 'long-haired').

129. *Berenice*: Egyptian queen whose lock of hair was said to have been metamorphosed into the constellation Coma Berenices.

133. *beau monde*: High society (French). *the Mall*: Fashionable walk in St James's Park.

136. *Rosamonda's lake*: Pond in the park.

137. *Partridge*: 'John Partridge was a ridiculous star-gazer, who in his almanacs every year never failed to predict the downfall of the Pope and the king of France, then at war with the English' (Pope's note). Swift had skewered Partridge in the *Bickerstaff Papers*.

138. *Galileo's eyes*: Through the telescope.

140. *Louis*: Louis XIV.

142. *sphere*: Pronounced to rhyme with 'hair'.

Epistle to Mrs Teresa Blount

On Teresa Blount, see Selected Letters, note 5. The title refers to the coronation of George I in 1714. For 'Mrs', see 'Rape of the Lock', Dedication note.

1. *fond*: 'foolishly tender; injudiciously indulgent' (*Dictionary*).

3. *roll a melting eye*: i.e. flirt.

4. *spark*: See 'Rape of the Lock', I, 73n.

7. *Zephalinda*: A romance name, which Teresa Blount liked to use in letters.

11. *plain-work*: 'needlework as distinguished from embroidery' (*Dictionary*, citing this line).

13. *assembly*: Public social gathering.

15. *bohea*: 'a species of tea, of higher colour and more astringent taste than green tea' (*Dictionary*). 'Bohea' and 'tea' were pronounced 'bohay' and 'tay'.

18. *dine exact at noon*: i.e. far earlier than in fashionable London.

23. *rack*: 'to torment; to harass' (*Dictionary*).

24. *whisk*: The card game whist. *sack*: Sweet sherry.

26. *buss*: Kiss.

32. *triumphs*: i.e. romantic conquests.

36. *gartered knights*: Holders of the high distinction of the Order of the Garter.
38. *flirt*: Dismissive gesture with a fan.
41. *your slave*: i.e. Pope himself.
43. *abstracted from the crew*: Daydreaming rather than noticing the throng.
46. *Parthenia*: Another romance name, connoting virginity; Martha Blount, Teresa's sister, sometimes called herself 'Parthenissa'.
47. *Gay*: Pope's friend, the poet and playwright John Gay, author of *The Beggar's Opera*. See also 'Arbuthnot', 258n. and 260n.; 'Dunciad', III, 330n.; and Selected Letters, note 21.
48. *chairs*: Sedan chairs, carried by two servants. *coxcomb*: See 'Essay on Criticism', 27n.

Eloisa to Abelard

The twelfth-century theologian Peter Abelard fell in love with his student Héloïse, who gave birth to a son. To satisfy her outraged father, who was a canon of Notre Dame Cathedral, they entered into a secret marriage, but when Abelard lodged Héloïse in a convent her father believed he had abandoned her and hired thugs to castrate him. Abelard subsequently became a Benedictine monk and founded a monastery, the Paraclete (a name for the Holy Spirit); still later he gave it as a convent to Héloïse, who presided there over a community of nuns. In the seventeenth century their letters (written in Latin) were published, and a 1713 English translation by John Hughes was the principal source for 'Eloisa to Abelard'. More generally, Pope followed the model of Ovid's *Heroides*, verse letters imagined as written by famous women. Eloisa analyses her spiritual struggle with bitter clarity; when the poem was published in 1717, Pope hinted to both Martha Blount and Lady Mary Wortley Montagu that the final lines alluded to his own frustrated erotic yearnings.

Argument: *several*: Separate, different.

1. *awful*: Awe-inspiring; also 143.
4. *vestal*: A vestal virgin was a priestess in ancient Rome; thus, a nun.
10. *holy silence*: Monastic vow of silence.
12. *idea*: Image (not, as in modern usage, 'concept').
20. *grots*: Ornamental garden grotto, such as Pope had at Twickenham. *horrid*: 'hideous; dreadful; shocking' (*Dictionary*); bristling (*horridus*).

22. *statues . . . weep*: As condensed moisture runs down them.
56. *Excuse*: 'to disengage from an obligation' (*Dictionary*).
62. *Mind*: God.
63. *attemp'ring*: Tempering, moderating.
66. *truths divine*: 'he was her preceptor in philosophy and divinity' (Pope's note).
81. *jealous God*: Cupid (Greek Eros).
90. *fond*: Doting.
102. *poniard*: Dagger.
104. *common*: In common, shared. *pain*: 'penalty, punishment' (*Dictionary*).
126. *partial*: i.e. partial to you.
129. *thy flock*: Of monks.
133. *these hallowed walls*: The monastery of the Paraclete; see head-note.
135–6. *stores . . . floors*: i.e. no rich man's money paid for expensive decoration.
138. *bribed*: In the hope that pious bequests would earn entrance to heaven.
142. *domes*: Buildings (from *domus*).
144. *dim windows*: Coloured with stained glass.
152–3. *father*: Priest. *brother*: Monastic brother, monk. *sister*: Nun.
158. *rills*: Brooks.
162. *visionary*: Seeing visions.
169. *floods*: Streams or rivers.
177–8. *believed . . . man*: Others believe that Eloisa is a faithful spouse of God, but inwardly she confesses that she still loves Abelard.
190. *science*: Knowledge, learning.
191. *the sense*: Awareness of the sin.
195. *a passion to resign*: To give up the passion of love.
212. *Obedient slumbers . . . weep*: Pope's note says the line was borrowed from Richard Crashaw's *Description of a Religious House*.
219. *Spouse*: Christ; nuns are 'brides of Christ'.
220. *white*: Robed in white. *hymeneals*: Wedding songs.
229. *all-conscious night*: Wholly conscious, because dreams know no bounds.
258. *The torch of Venus burns not*: Because he has been castrated. In the first and second editions (1717, 1720), these lines followed: 'Cut from the root my perished joys I see, / And love's warm tide for ever stopped in thee.' Pope deleted them, after they were criticized as too suggestive.

261. *lasting flames*: Roman funerary urns were supplied with lamps intended to burn perpetually.

267. *matin*: Matins, the first office, or service, of the monastic day.

270. *ev'ry bead*: Of the rosary. *too soft*: Because tears of love, not repentance.

271. *censer*: Incense container.

282. *dispute my heart*: Dispute with heaven for my heart; Abelard was highly skilled in the art of academic disputation.

284. *idea of the skies*: Images of Heaven.

288. *fiends*: Devils.

300. *Faith ... immortality*: Through faith, the believer is in possession of eternal life even before death.

321. *office*: The funeral service.

343. *one kind grave*: 'Abelard and Eloisa were interred in the same grave, or in monuments adjoining, in the monastery of the Paraclete. He died in the year 1142, she in 1163' (Pope's note).

354. *dreadful sacrifice*: The re-enactment of Christ's sacrifice in the Eucharist.

359. *some future bard*: Pope himself.

361. *whole years in absence*: Lady Mary Wortley Montagu, with whom Pope was infatuated at this time, was living in Istanbul, where her husband was ambassador. *deplore*: 'to lament; to bewail' (*Dictionary*).

Elegy to the Memory of an Unfortunate Lady

Attempts to identify the subject of the poem and her heartless relatives have always been unsuccessful, and the lady may be a composite of various originals, or even entirely imaginary. At any rate the elegy expresses, as Pope's biographer Maynard Mack says, 'taut feelings of injustice and deprivation' that are unusual in his work (*Alexander Pope: A Life*, p. 319). The philosopher David Hume knew the poem by heart.

4. *visionary sword*: With which the lady killed herself, seen as if in a vision.

8. *a Roman's part*: Suicide, considered appropriate by the Romans in certain circumstances.

9. *reversion*: Right of succession or inheritance.

14. *glorious fault*: Rebellion by Lucifer's fallen angels against God, and by the Titans against the Olympian gods (see also 'Essay on Criticism', 552n.).

28. *race*: Relatives.

35. *ball*: The globe.
39. *passengers*: Passers-by.
41. *Furies*: Goddesses of vengeance in Greek mythology.
55. *sable weeds*: Black clothing indicating mourning.
59. *loves*: Sculpted cupids (Greek Eros).
61. *no sacred earth*: Suicides could not be buried in consecrated ground.
64. *green turf ... breast*: As in an inscription common on tomb-stones, *sit tibi terra levis*.
66. *blow*: Bloom.
68. *The ground, now sacred*: Her remains have sanctified the ground where she was buried.
77. *lays*: Songs.

From the Iliad

Pope laboured mightily on his *Iliad* translation, poring over commentaries and diligently improving his competence in Greek, and when the first instalment came out in 1715 it was acclaimed a masterpiece. His work was standard for a full century, and so long as the rhythms and music of the heroic couplet were admired, it remained, as Johnson called it, 'that poetical wonder, ... a performance which no age or nation can pretend to equal' (*Life of Pope*, p. 236). With canny business acumen, Pope bypassed the booksellers and sold an expensive edition by advance subscription; the *Iliad* and its sequel, the *Odyssey* – completed in 1726, over a decade after the project began – earned him £10,000 and assured his financial security. For the *Odyssey*, however, he employed a pair of obscure poets, William Broome and Elijah Fenton, to do half of the translation, and when this became known it encouraged critics to suggest that he was not altogether different from humbler writers whom he liked to disparage for writing for money.

[From the description of the first battle, Book IV]

In a note to this passage, Pope indicated the effects he hoped to convey: 'This is the first battle in Homer, and it is worthy observation with what grandeur it is described, and raised by one circumstance above another, till all is involved in horror and tumult. The simile of the winds, rising by degrees into a general tempest, is an image of the progress of his own spirit in this description. We see first an innumerable army moving in order, and are amused with the pomp and silence, then wakened with the noise and clamour; next they join, the adverse gods are let down among them; the imaginary persons of Terror, Flight, Discord succeed to reinforce them; then all is undistinguished fury and a confusion of horrors, only that at different openings we behold the distinct deaths of several heroes, and then are involved again in the same confusion.' (*amused*: Entertained. *join*: Join battle.)

486. *Sedate*: 'calm; quiet; still' (*Dictionary*).
488. *Those only heard*: i.e. only those are heard.
499. *These ... incites*: The Trojan army is supported by Mars (in Greek, Ares), and the Greek army by Minerva (Athena).
504. *horrid*: See 'Eloisa to Abelard', 20n.
535. *spurns*: 'spurn: to kick; to strike or drive with the foot' (*Dictionary*).
546. *Ide*: Mount Ida above Troy, where Simoïsius' parents were shepherds.
557. *honours*: Poetical term for beautiful hair, or here, by analogy, leaves.
565. *corse*: Corpse.

[The council of deities, Book VIII]

4. *Olympus*: See 'Windsor Forest', 33n.
16. *Tartarean gulf*: A place of punishment and torture, even lower than Hades, in the underworld.
22. *th' Almighty*: Pope frequently borrows the language of Christian theology for Jove, as he acknowledged in his note: 'Homer in this whole passage plainly shows his belief of one supreme, omnipotent God, whom he introduces with a majesty and superiority worthy the great Ruler of the universe.'
26. *main*: Sea.
28. *Thund'rer*: A frequent Homeric epithet for Zeus (in Latin, Jove).
36. *rev'rend*: Reverent.
38. *Wisdom*: Attribute of Athena.
40. *own*: Acknowledge.
44. *Argives*: Men of Argos, a region in southern Greece ruled by the Greek commander Agamemnon.
47. *cloud-compelling*: Another epithet for Zeus, the sky-god. *suit*: 'a petition; an address of entreaty' (*Dictionary*).
60. *fane*: Temple.
61. *car*: Chariot.

[Sarpedon's speech, Book XII]

348. *Sarpedon*: Stressed on the second syllable.
350. *son*: Zeus was Sarpedon's father.
354. *ductile*: 'easy to be drawn out into length, or expanded' (*Dictionary*).

356. *Lycian*: From Lycia, a Greek settlement in Asia Minor, of which Sarpedon was king.

359. *savage*: The savage lion.

366. *gen'rous*: 'strong; vigorous' (*Dictionary*).

368. *aspiring*: Rising.

396. *Or let*: Either let.

399. *pursue*: Follow.

[Vulcan forges the shield of Achilles, Book XVIII]

479. *lame artist*: Vulcan (in Greek, Hephaestos), blacksmith and god of fire, was a son of Zeus and his wife Juno (Hera); after a quarrel Zeus threw him from Olympus, and his landing on the island of Lemnos left him lame.

489. *science*: Knowledge.

492. *Thetis*: A nereid or sea goddess, mother of the Greek hero Achilles. *sate*: Sat.

506. *a man's embrace*: After Thetis resisted Zeus' courtship, he forced her to marry a mortal, Peleus.

508. *The mighty fine*: i.e. death.

509. *a godlike hero*: Achilles.

515. *secret woe*: Furious because Agamemnon had taken away his concubine, Achilles was sulking in his tent instead of joining his comrades in battle.

517. *the Grecian suffrage*: Approval of Agamemnon's action by the rest of the Greeks.

522. *his friend*: His best friend Patroclus fought disguised in Achilles' armour, and his death enraged Achilles and brought him back into the fight.

525. *Phoebus*: Apollo. *Hector had the name*: i.e. the Trojan hero Hector got credit for killing Patroclus, but it was really Apollo's doing.

526. *resigns*: Yields, gives up.

528. *short-lived*: Thetis knows that Achilles is fated to die in a later battle.

548. *better hand*: Right hand.

550. *doubling*: i.e. the sounds are redoubled by echoes.

556. *godlike ... rose*: i.e. images produced by the god's labours appear in relief.

561-4. *Pleiads ... Bear*: Constellations; the 'axle of the sky' is the North Star, to which the Bear (known in modern times as the Plough and the Big Dipper) points.

566. *Nor bathes ... the main*: The Bear constellation never sets into the sea, but remains always visible above the horizon.

570. *hymeneal*: Wedding.

574. *cithern*: Lute-like stringed instrument.

579. *discharged*: Paid.

587. *Alternate*: Stressed on the second syllable; also '[The reception of Hector's body . . .]', 902.

589. *talents*: The talent was a unit of weight, varying from country to country.

593. *leaguered*: Besieged.

599. *Pallas*: Athena.

602. *superior by the head*: See 'Rape of the Lock', II, 70n.

604. *flood*: River.

608. *swains*: Rustic labourers.

609. *reeds*: Pan pipes, made by shepherds from hollow reeds.

619. *confessed*: Revealed.

625. *came out*: i.e. appeared in vivid relief on the shield.

628. *hind*: Farm labourer.

629. *shares*: Ploughshares.

636. *sable looked*: i.e. appeared convincingly dark, although made of gold.

644. *gripe*: Grip.

656. *pales*: 'pale: any enclosure' (*Dictionary*).

660. *purple product*: The grape harvest.

662. *the fate of Linus*: Linus, whose name personifies a dirge or lamentation, was a foundling raised by shepherds and later torn to pieces by dogs.

666. *low*: Bellow.

670. *sour*: Heavy, coarse.

677. *the eye . . . leads*: i.e. leads the viewer's eye.

678. *meads*: Meadows.

679. *cots*: Cottages.

682–3. *Gnossus . . . Daedalean art*: Cnossus or Knossos, founded by Minos in Crete. The artificer Daedalus built the famous labyrinth to imprison the Minotaur, the half-bull monster to which Queen Pasiphaë gave birth after mating with a bull.

685. *simars*: Cymars, loose diaphanous garments.

687. *locks*: Of hair.

689. *depend*: Hang down.

702. *last hand*: Final touches.

704. *buckler*: Shield.

706. *cuirass*: Armour covering the torso.

707. *greaves*: Armour for the shin. *helm*: Helmet.

[*The reception of Hector's body in*
Troy, Book XXIV]

886. *wain*: Wagon.

887. *the slain*: The Trojan hero Hector, son of King Priam, had been
slain in battle by Achilles, avenging the death of Patroclus. After
dragging the corpse through the dust around the city of Troy,
Achilles at first refused to return it, but relented after a personal
plea by the aged Priam.

888. *wife and mother*: Hector's wife Andromache, who had begged
him not to go to his death, and his mother Hecuba.

898. *wait*: Observe, watch.

902. *Alternately*: Stressed on the second syllable.

912. *only son*: Their little boy Astyanax, who had burst into tears at
the sight of his father's armour.

916. *Ilion*: Troy.

926. *pressed the plain*: i.e. died in battle on the plain of Troy.

929. *hurl thee headlong*: Prophetic of Astyanax' fate soon afterward,
when a Greek warrior threw him to his death lest he grow up to
be king.

934–5. *Why gav'st . . . last command*: Pope notes that he borrowed
these lines from a brief Homeric translation by William Con-
greve, and he dedicated the entire work to his friend's memory.

942. *sustains her part*: i.e. Hecuba takes up the lament.

949. *Stygian coast*: The bank of the river Styx, boundary between the
world of the living and the underworld of Hades.

952. *tomb of him*: Of Patroclus.

965. *Since Paris brought me*: Helen (of Troy) ran away from her hus-
band, King Menelaus of Sparta, with the Trojan prince Paris; in
Homeric tradition the Trojan War began when the Greeks
attempted to recover her.

980. *at home*: In Sparta.

LATER POEMS

[TWO EPIGRAMS]

Epigram. Engraved on the Collar of a Dog

1.   *Kew*: Kew Palace near Richmond, ten miles outside London;
Pope gave the dog to the Prince of Wales.

Epitaph. Intended for Sir Isaac Newton

2. *Let Newton be*: Adapting Genesis 1:3 (see 'Rape of the Lock', III, 46n.); Newton studied the properties of light in his widely read *Optics*.

An Essay on Man

Well aware that he was gaining a reputation as a fierce satirist, Pope sought in 'An Essay on Man' to achieve a major philosophical work in the time-honoured genre of theodicy, whose purpose was to 'vindicate the ways of God to Man' (I, 16). But whereas Milton, in *Paradise Lost*, aspired to 'justify the ways of God to men' (I, 26) by narrating the story of original sin, Pope avoided theology, sternly rebuked humans for questioning the perfect governance of the universe, and argued that apparent evils were necessary elements in a well-balanced whole – 'All partial evil, universal good' – with the consequence that 'Whatever IS, is RIGHT' (I, 292–4). This was a version of the philosophy known as 'optimism', according to which we inhabit the best or 'optimal' of all possible worlds, even if it is often painful for us; the claim was that if anything were altered to make our own lives happier, the perfect adjustment of the 'whole' would suffer.

Much to Pope's surprise, many critics felt that his poem was irreligious, or at best a version of deistic natural religion that took little notice of Christian teachings. Certainly few theologians would have agreed with his claim, in the Argument to Epistle I, that '*Man is not to be deemed* imperfect', or with his approval of the self-love that preachers denounced as sinful pride: 'Thus God and Nature linked the gen'ral frame, / And bade self-love and social be the same' (III, 317–18). Pope was therefore deeply grateful when the clergyman William Warburton came forward to argue the poem's fundamental orthodoxy (see Selected Letters, note 44). Still, even Pope's admirers continued to hold that he was no philosopher (he did indeed owe his argument in part to his friend Bolingbroke, 'master of the poet, and the song', IV, 374) and that the poem's real merits were those of metaphor and imagery. Samuel Johnson wrote years later, 'He tells us much that every man knows, and much that he does not know himself.' But Johnson added, 'Surely a man of no very comprehensive search may venture to say that he has heard all this before, but it was never till now recommended by such a blaze of embellishment or such sweetness of melody. The vigorous contraction of some thoughts, the luxuriant amplification of others, the incidental illustrations, and sometimes the dignity, sometimes the softness of the verses, enchain philosophy, suspend criticism, and oppress judgement by overpowering pleasure' (*Life of Pope*, pp. 243–4).

The Design

'*come home . . . bosoms*': From the Dedicatory Epistle to the 1625 edition of Francis Bacon's *Essays*. *the charts which are to follow*: Apparently refers to poems Pope expected to write in the never-realized *Opus Magnum*. *deduce*: 'to draw in a regular connected series' (*Dictionary*).

Epistle I

Argument: *conceiting*: Conceiving.

1.   ST JOHN: Lord Bolingbroke's family name; the poem is dedicated to him. See also Horace, Satire, II, i, 127n.

5.   *Expatiate*: 'to range at large; to rove without any prescribed limits' (*Dictionary*).

9–10.   *beat . . . covert*: In hunting, to find game by 'beating' both open country and wooded thickets.

11.   *latent*: 'hidden; concealed; secret' (*Dictionary*).

12.   *sightless soar*: i.e. try to soar higher than human faculties permit.

15.   *candid*: 'fair; open; ingenuous' (*Dictionary*).

23–8.   *He, who . . . as we are*: i.e. only such a person, who however does not exist, could do these things.

25.   *system*: As in the 'solar system'; also 89.

27.   *varied being*: Various modes of existence.

29.   *bearings*: 'bearing: the site or place of anything with respect to something else' (*Dictionary*, citing this line).

30.   *nice*: 'formed with minute exactness' (*Dictionary*).

31.   *thy*: The reader's.

33.   *chain*: The Great Chain of Being, which supposedly connected all existing things without any gaps; alluding also to the golden chain of Zeus 'whose strong embrace holds heav'n, and earth, and main' (Pope's *Iliad*, VIII, 26); also 237.

41.   *argent fields*: Sky filled with silvery stars.

42.   *Jove's*: Jupiter's. *satellites*: Pronounced with four syllables as 'satéllities'.

45.   *full or not coherent*: i.e. there will be a gap unless the chain is complete.

55.   *single*: Single movement.

60.   *a part we see*: Echoing 1 Corinthians 13:12: 'now I know in part, but then shall I know even as I also am known'.

64. *Egypt's god*: Apis, the sacred bull of Memphis; contrasted with the 'ox', sacrificial 'victim' of religious sacrifice.

67–8. *doing . . . deity*: A characteristically compressed Popean summary: 'doing' refers to the 'actions' and 'suff'ring' to 'passions' (66); 'checked' and 'impelled' to the horse that Man either 'restrains' or 'drives' (61–2); 'slave' to the ox in its role as 'victim' and 'deity' to the ox as 'god' (64).

73. *a certain sphere*: i.e. heaven after death.

76. *As who*: As he who.

79. *From brutes . . . know*: i.e. what men know is hidden from animals, and what disembodied spirits know is hidden from men.

81. *riot*: 'wild and loose festivity' (*Dictionary*).

87. *equal*: Impartial; also 111.

88. *a sparrow fall*: 'Are not two sparrows sold for a farthing? and one of them shall not fall on the ground without your Father' (Matthew 10:29).

97. *from home*: Away from home, i.e. heaven.

99. *Indian*: In the Americas.

102. *walk*: 'a length of space, or circuit through which one walks' (*Dictionary*).

110. *seraph's fire*: The angelic seraphim were associated with fire; see also 278n.

117. *gust*: 'sense of tasting' (*Dictionary*, citing this line).

121. *the balance and the rod*: The scales of justice and the rod of punishment.

126. *angels would be gods*: The angels who followed Satan in his rebellion.

129. *who but wishes*: Whoever so much as wishes.

133. *genial*: Generative.

140. *canopy*: Placed above a throne.

142. *livid deaths*: Plagues, whose victims turned bluish or 'livid' in colour, were supposedly provoked by the sun's heat.

145. *the first Almighty Cause*: God.

147. *some change*: i.e. deterioration since the Fall of Man.

156. *Borgia*: Cesare Borgia (d. 1507), Italian duke notorious for treachery and cunning. *Catiline*: Conspirator against the Roman republic; also II, 199; IV, 240.

160. *Ammon*: See 'Essay on Criticism', 376n.

163. *those, in these*: These moral things, those natural things.

169. *elemental strife*: The classical concept of endless interaction among the four 'elements'; see also II, 111n. and III, 219–22n.

174. *less than angel*: 'thou hast made him a little lower than the angels' (Psalm 8:5).

181. *compensated*: Stressed on the second syllable. *of course*: In the normal course of events.

199. *effluvia*: Invisible particles, transmitting odours.

202. *music of the spheres*: Harmony supposedly emitted by the planets, heard by angels but inaudible to humans.

204. *zephyr*: Gentle breeze. *rill*: Brook.

212. *lynx's beam*: Beams of sight were thought to be emitted by the eye; the lynx supposedly had exceptionally acute vision.

213. *lioness between*: The senses of sight and hearing were supposedly weak in lions, which therefore hunted by ear.

214. *sagacious*: 'quick of scent' (*Dictionary*). *tainted*: Imbued with an animal's smell.

215. *the flood*: Rivers and seas.

219. *nice*: Careful, skilful, precise.

220. *healing dew*: Honey was thought to have medicinal properties.

222. *half-reas'ning elephant*: 'the largest of all quadrupeds, of whose sagacity, faithfulness, prudence, and even understanding, many surprising relations are given' (*Dictionary*).

223. *that*: i.e. instinct. *barrier*: Accented on the second syllable, rhyming with 'near'.

227. *join*: Pronounced to rhyme with 'line'.

234. *quick*: Alive.

240. *glass*: Microscope or telescope. *thee*: Man.

248. *amazing*: 'wonderful; astonishing' (*Dictionary*).

261. *repined*: Resented, complained.

262. *engines*: Instruments to carry out the intentions of the mind.

278. *burns*: In Christian theology, the seraphim ('burning ones' in Hebrew) are the highest order of angels.

280. *equals all*: Makes all equal.

281. *nor order imperfection name*: i.e. do not say that order is imperfect.

283. *kind*: Appropriate.

285. *sphere*: Pronounced 'sphare'.

288. *mortal hour*: The hour of death.

293. *in erring reason's spite*: In spite of erring reason.

Epistle II

Argument: *principle*: 'ground of action; motive' (*Dictionary*).

1.   *scan*: Examine closely (and presumptuously).

3–18.   *Placed on this isthmus . . . the world*: Adapts, in a much less tragic mode, Blaise Pascal's account of man in the *Pensées* as 'judge of all things, imbecile worm of earth, depository of truth, sewer of uncertainty and error: the glory and refuse of the universe'.

5.   *too much knowledge*: Because the ancient Sceptic philosophers denied the possibility of valid knowledge.

6.   *stoic's pride*: Because Stoics aspired to a godlike indifference to suffering.

11.   *his reason such*: Such is his reason.

20–22. *measure earth . . . regulate the sun*: References to the much-publicized work of contemporary scientists.

23.   *empyreal sphere*: Plato held that archetypal 'ideas' or forms occupied the outermost sphere of the Ptolemaic universe, the 'empyrean'.

26.   *quitting sense*: Escaping from the body in a mystical trance, as later Neoplatonists taught.

27–8.   *eastern . . . sun*: Pope had in mind a sage who whirled his head dizzily in order to imitate the movement of heavenly bodies.

35.   *rules . . . bind*: Newton showed that the orbits of comets, previously thought irregular, obeyed laws.

43.   *science*: Knowledge of all kinds.

44.   *equipage*: 'accoutrements' (*Dictionary*); the accent is on the final syllable.

46.   *learning's luxury, or idleness*: i.e. learning misused as ostentatious display, or to while away the time.

55.   *this . . . that*: i.e. reason ('this') is not intrinsically good, nor is self-love intrinsically bad.

59.   *acts*: Impels.

60.   *balance*: The balance-wheel of a watch; the 'spring' (59) is the mainspring whose energy is given regularity by the wheel.

63.   *peculiar*: Particular.

72.   *Reason's at distance*: Reason is stronger when its objects are distant.

78.   *still*: Always.

81.   *schoolmen*: 'versed in the niceties and subtleties of academical disputation' (*Dictionary*).

84.   *wit*: Intelligence in general.

89–90. *that . . . This*: Self-love and reason.

91.   *or wrong or rightly*: Either wrong or rightly.

94.   *real*: Pronounced as two syllables.

95.   *divide*: Divide with other people, share.

98.   *List*: Enlist.

99. *Those that imparted*: i.e. those passions, when reason's care has been imparted to them.

105. *in act*: Into action.

108. *card*: The dial of a sailor's compass.

111. *Passions, like elements*: The four elements of classical theory, represented in the four fluids or 'humours' of the body; so long as they were equally balanced and 'tempered', no passion (see 117–18 and note) could gain disproportionate power; see also 139 and 159 and notes.

112. *his*: God's.

117–18. *Love ... grief*: The six principal 'passions' in traditional psychology.

132. *Aaron's serpent*: When Aaron threw down his rod before Pharaoh, it became a serpent (Exodus 7).

139. *vital humour*: As in 111, but perhaps also with a suggestion of the 'animal spirits' that were thought to animate or vitalize the body.

144. *peccant*: 'corrupt; bad; offensive to the body; injurious to health; it is chiefly used in medical writers' (*Dictionary*).

149. *sway*: 'power; rule; dominion' (*Dictionary*).

150. *weak queen*: i.e. reason, weak even though her rule or 'sway' is legitimate.

159–60. *small humours ... driv'n them out*: Gout, which produces excruciating pain in the feet and legs, supposedly attracted 'morbid' humours there from the rest of the body.

166. *sev'ral*: Different.

175. *Eternal Art*: i.e. Providence. *educing*: Bringing out, extracting.

177. *mercury*: Psychic volatility, stabilized or 'fixed' by a ruling passion.

181. *ungrateful*: Unresponsive.

182. *savage stocks*: Vigorous but infertile trunks to which fruit trees are grafted.

186. *spleen*: 'melancholy; hypochondriacal humours' (*Dictionary*).

187–94. *anger ... shame*: Pope invokes six of the Seven Deadly Sins – anger, avarice, sloth, lust, envy, and pride – but substitutes 'shame' for gluttony; he suggests that each can have positive effects.

197. *bias*: In bowls (lawn bowling), 'the weight lodged on one side of a bowl, which turns it from the straight line' (*Dictionary*).

198. *Nero*: Notoriously cruel Roman emperor. *Titus*: Benevolent emperor; see also IV, 146n.

200. *Decius ... Curtius*: Romans who sacrificed their lives in battle for their country.

203. *joined*: Rhymes with 'mind'.

209. *nice*: Subtle.

222–4. *York ... Zembla*: The river Tweed lies north of the city of York; the Orkney islands ('Orcades', pronounced as three syllables) north of the Scottish mainland; and the island of Novaya Zemlya north of Russia.

228. *own*: Admit.

230. *hard*: Hardened (as, by analogy, people grow hardened to vice).

231. *vicious*: Prone to vices in general, not necessarily malice.

237. *sev'ral*: Respective, separate.

241. *happy*: Fortunate.

247. *defects*: Accented on the second syllable.

257. *its*: Life's.

261. *pelf*: Riches.

262. *change*: Exchange.

269. *chemist*: Alchemist, seeking to turn base metals into gold.

279. *Scarfs*: Badges of office. *garters*: Emblems of the high honour of the Order of the Garter.

280. *beads*: Rosaries.

288. *bubble*: In addition to the literal meaning, 'anything which wants solidity and firmness; anything that is more specious than real' (*Dictionary*).

Epistle III

1. *Universal Cause*: God as the 'first cause' of everything that exists.

4. *trim*: 'dress; ornaments' (*Dictionary*).

9. *plastic*: 'having the power to give form' (*Dictionary*).

15. *vegetables*: Pronounced as four syllables: veg-e-ta-bles.

29. *wanton*: Playful.

33. *pours his throat*: Pours out his song.

38. *vindicate*: Lay claim to (from *vindicare*).

42. *lord of all*: Man.

50. *Be Man the wit*: i.e. Man is the sole intelligent being.

53. *stooping*: Plunging down on its prey.

56. *Philomela*: The nightingale.

61. *vain*: Full of vanity.

63. *learnèd hunger*: Man has learned to cultivate domestic animals to satisfy his hunger.

64. *savage*: i.e. wild animals.

65. *he dooms his feast*: Whom he has doomed to be his meal.

68. *by touch ethereal slain*: 'Several of the ancients, and many Orientals at this day, esteemed those who were struck by lightning

as sacred persons, and the particular favourites of Heaven'
(Pope's note).

74.   *makes him hope it*: In anticipation of immortality.

79.   *with reason, or with instinct*: i.e. human or animal.

83.   *unerring guide*: Instinct in animals was thought to embody the
      direct influence of God ('In this 'tis God directs (98)), and hence
      was superior to unreliable human reason.

86.   *pressed*: Impressed into service, as in the army or navy.

90.   *wide or short*: Wide of the mark or falling short.

91.   *quick*: 'active; sprightly; ready' (*Dictionary*).

93.   *This*: Instinct.

98.   *this . . . that*: Instinct and reason.

102. *Build on the wave . . . the sand*: The halcyon is 'a bird, of which
      it is said that she breeds in the sea, and that there is always a
      calm during her incubation' (*Dictionary*); kingfishers nest in
      sandy riverbanks.

104. *De Moivre*: Abraham de Moivre, brilliant French mathematician
      who lived in England in Pope's time.

105. *stork*: 'a bird of passage famous for the regularity of its depart-
      ure' (*Dictionary*).

115. *ether*: 'an element more fine and subtle than air; the matter of the
      highest regions above' (*Dictionary*).

118. *vital flame*: 'A fine, warm, igneous substance, supposed to reside
      in the hearts of animals, as necessary to life, or rather, as that
      which constitutes life itself' (Pope's note). *genial*: Generative.

124. *their race*: i.e. their offspring.

132. *bands*: Bonds (of family).

134. *At once*: At one and the same time.

135. *With choice we fix*: i.e. in the choice of a spouse.

140. *nat'ral . . . habitual*: i.e. natural love for infants, and habitual for
      grown children ('brood', 139).

142. *helpless . . . began*: The parents enfeebled by age.

144. *That . . . age*: Memory looks back to youth, foresight anticipates
      age.

146. *preserved the kind*: i.e. preserved the human race by sexual
      desire and marital love.

148. *The state of Nature*: Before civilization began.

154. *No murder . . . fed*: Animals were not killed for clothing or food.

155. *the resounding wood*: The only temple was the forest, filled with
      natural sounds.

162. *butcher . . . tomb*: i.e. of flesh that is killed and eaten.

165. *just disease*: Disease that is deserved, as a result of intemperate living.

177. *nautilus . . . sail*: 'nautilus: a shell furnished with something analogous to oars and a sail' (*Dictionary*); the chambered nautilus, buoyant enough to float on the ocean surface, was thought to spread a membrane in order to catch the wind.

183. *small people*: Here, species of insect.

184. *ant's . . . bees*: Ants were believed to live in democratic equality, while bees served their queen in a 'realm' or monarchy (from French *royaume*).

219–22. *furrow . . . eagle*: Pope invokes successively the classical elements: earth, fire, water, and air.

225. *explored*: Detected.

230. *never sought but one*: i.e. reason deduces that there must have been a single Creator, not multiple gods.

232. *saw that all was right*: Cf. 'And God saw every thing that he had made, and, behold, it was very good' (Genesis 1:31).

233. *To virtue . . . trod*: i.e. progressed through pleasure to virtue.

234. *owned*: Acknowledged.

236. *right divine*: The divine right of kings, repudiated in England after the Glorious Revolution of 1688 deposed James II; see also 'Dunciad', IV, 188n.

240. *but*: i.e. could but be, could only be.

242. *enormous*: 'irregular; out of measure; not regulated by any stated measures' (*Dictionary*).

246. *taught the tyrant awe*: i.e. taught him how to inspire awe.

249. *She*: Superstition.

253. *earth . . . skies*: Earthquakes and storms, attributed to supernatural causes.

256. *made her devils*: i.e. imagined them.

257–8. *Gods . . . lust*: These passionate, changeable, and unjust gods are the Olympians of classical mythology.

265. *flamen*: Roman priest. *living food*: Animal sacrifice.

267. *Heav'n's own thunders*: Interpreting the natural phenomenon of thunder in the 'heavens' as a supernatural omen.

268. *engine*: Instrument of revenge against the priest's 'foe'.

286. *moral*: Morality, ethical principles.

290. *nor to*: Neither to. *strings*: As in a musical instrument.

292. *strike the other*: Touching or striking one string causes sympathetic vibrations in the others.

294. *a well-mixed state*: A government, like Britain's, that combines

monarchy with electoral representation (preferable to the unmixed extremes of absolute rule and total democracy).

296. *consent*: 'concord; agreement' (*Dictionary*).

305. *modes of faith*: i.e. competing sects. *graceless*: 'without grace; wicked; hopelessly corrupt; abandoned' (*Dictionary*).

311. *gen'rous*: Fertile.

315. *act*: Cause (the soul) to act.

Epistle IV

10. *flaming mine*: Alluding to the belief that minerals were ripened by the heat of the sun (Phoebus).

11. *Parnassian laurels*: Symbolic of poetic achievement, from Mount Parnassus, seat of the Muses.

12. *iron harvests*: Victories in battle (in 'the field').

14. *culture*: Cultivation, as in agriculture.

15. *sincere*: 'pure; unmingled' (*Dictionary*).

18. ST JOHN: See I, 1n.

30. *All states . . . conceive*: All conditions of life can attain it, and all minds conceive it.

37. *what happiness we justly call*: i.e. what we rightly call happiness.

40. *kind*: Humankind.

45. *Abstract*: Take away.

59. *In who*: i.e. in those who.

73-4. *sons of earth . . . skies*: Recalling the rebellion of the Titans, who piled up mountains in attempting to reach and overthrow Zeus.

78. *mere*: 'this or that only; such and nothing else' (*Dictionary*).

80. *competence*: 'such a fortune as, without exuberance, is equal to the necessities of life' (*Dictionary*).

81. *consists*: Is consistent.

92. *One they must want*: They must still lack one happiness.

99. *Falkland*: Lucius Cary, Viscount Falkland, killed in battle during the Civil War.

100. *Turenne*: The Vicomte de Turenne, Marshal of France, one of the greatest generals of the seventeenth century, killed in battle in 1675.

101. *Sidney*: Sir Philip Sidney, Elizabethan poet, killed (1586) like the others in a relatively insignificant battle.

104-6. *Digby . . . the sire*: Robert Digby, a friend of Pope's, who died in 1726 at the age of 40, and whose father (see 'Epilogue to the Satires', II, 241n.) was still living at 74 when the poem was published.

107. *bishop*: Bishop Belsunce, who remained in Marseilles in 1720 throughout a plague epidemic, which was thought to be transmitted by infected air ('each gale was death' (108)); Marseilles is pronounced as three syllables.

110. *a parent*: Pope's mother died in June 1733, at the age of 91.

116. *improved*: In an ironic sense.

118. *Abel ... Cain*: Cain murdered his brother Abel (Genesis 4).

120. *dire disease*: Syphilis, then incurable.

123. *Aetna ... a sage*: The philosopher Empedocles, studying an eruption of Mount Etna in Sicily, got too close and died; Pope may be recalling a tradition that he deliberately threw himself in to prove that he had become a god.

126. *Bethel*: Hugh Bethel, a Member of Parliament, a country gentleman in Yorkshire, and an old friend of Pope's, who had journeyed to Italy in the hope of relieving his asthma.

130. *Chartres*: Francis Charteris, a notorious gambler and rake whose sexual 'vigour' was sapped by debauchery; he was condemned to death in 1730 for raping a servant, and his subsequent pardon was widely thought to have been due to bribery. *reserve the hanging wall*: i.e. will a church that is about to fall down wait until its collapse can crush a villain like Charteris?

137. *Calvin*: John Calvin, Protestant reformer who broke with Roman Catholicism in 1630, and whose theology became widely influential under the name of Calvinism.

139. *rod*: Of punishment.

146. *Caesar ... Titus*: Julius Caesar is taken as an example of a ruthless conqueror, and the Emperor Titus, who lamented wasting any day in which he accomplished nothing good, as his opposite.

153. *tempts the main*: Risks going to sea in hope of profit.

160. *private*: i.e. private citizen.

166. *stand*: Stop, make a stand.

170. *coach and six*: Carriage with six horses, suggestive of great wealth.

171. *gown*: As worn by clergymen, academics, and judges.

175. *an individual*: The same person as child and as adult.

192. *wants*: Lacks.

193. *condition*: Rank or station in life.

199. *cowl*: Monastic hood.

201. *monarch*: Probably referring to Philip V of Spain, who abdicated in 1724 and retired briefly to a monastery (his son's death forced him to resume the throne).

203. *fellow*: 'a word of contempt: the foolish mortal; the mean wretch; the sorry rascal' (*Dictionary*, citing this line).

204. *leather*: The apron worn by cobblers. *prunello*: 'a kind of stuff of which the clergymen's gowns are made' (*Dictionary*, citing this line).

205. *strings*: Identified by Pope in a note as 'honours', such as the ribbons of a knightly order.

208. *Lucrece*: Virtuous Roman matron who committed suicide after being raped by Tarquin. See also 'II A Lady', 92n.

212. *the Flood*: i.e. Noah's.

214. *own*: Admit.

216. *Howards*: A great aristocratic family, which included the dukes of Norfolk.

220. *Macedonia's madman*: Alexander the Great, obsessed with conquering the world. *the Swede*: Charles XII of Sweden, a spectacular recent conqueror who was killed in battle in 1718.

225. *politic*: 'artful; cunning' (*Dictionary*, citing this line).

235. *Aurelius*: Marcus Aurelius Antoninus, Roman emperor and Stoic philosopher.

236. *Socrates*: The great philosopher was executed by the Athenians for allegedly corrupting the minds of his young followers.

240. *Tully*: Marcus Tullius Cicero, Roman writer and politician, author of celebrated orations in the trial of Catiline (I, 156), and eventually executed for his opposition to Mark Antony.

244. *Eugene*: Prince Eugene of Savoy, commander of the army of the Austrian Empire, who fought alongside the Duke of Marlborough in the War of the Spanish Succession.

246. *Rubicon*: River in northern Italy which Caesar crossed against the orders of the Roman senate, which became proverbial for taking an irrevocable step.

247. *feather*: The quill pen of a writer ('wit'). *rod*: Perhaps a general's baton.

252. *hung on high*: As the corpses of traitors and criminals were once publicly displayed.

256. *huzzas*: Hurrahs.

257. *Marcellus*: A friend of Cicero's, who ended his life in exile.

259. *parts*: 'qualities; powers; faculties; accomplishments' (*Dictionary*).

260. *you*: Bolingbroke.

270. *'mount*: Amount.

277. *ribbons*: Honorary distinctions (cf. 205).

278. *Umbra*: Shadow (Latin), often applied to flatterers and intriguers. *Sir Billy*: Dismissive name for any foolish knight.

279. *yellow dirt*: i.e. gold.

280. *Gripus*: Grasping, miserly (Latin).

281. *Bacon*: Francis Bacon, essayist and philosopher of science, who became Lord Chancellor under James I but was subsequently convicted of corruption.

282. *meanest*: 'mean: contemptible; despicable' (*Dictionary*).

284. *Cromwell*: See 'I Cobham', 88n.

288. *scale*: Ladder (as in French *échelle*).

290. *those . . . betray*: i.e. people who ruined the kings ('those') who trusted them, and betrayed the queens ('these') who loved them.

299. *wealth ill fated*: Pope seems to have had in mind Marlborough, who grew immensely rich through his military campaigns and was accused by the Tories (as in 'Windsor Forest') of protracting the war for his own profit.

307. *enormous*: Excessive; cf. III, 242n.

308. *tale*: 'Tally' as well as 'story'.

336. *But touches*: That doesn't touch.

365. *straight*: Straightway, immediately.

373. *genius*: Guardian spirit (again addressing Bolingbroke).

378. *fall with dignity*: As Bolingbroke left office when George I dismissed him in 1714; see also Horace, Satire, II, i, 127n. *temper*: 'calmness of mind; moderation' (*Dictionary*).

385. *bark*: Small seagoing vessel.

389. *pretend*: Profess, proclaim.

Epistles to Several Persons

The four poems collected by Pope under this title (renamed, after his death, *Moral Essays* by his editor William Warburton) were published from 1731 to 1735, coinciding with 'An Essay on Man', which came out in 1733–4. 'Burlington' and, a year later, 'Bathurst' were the first to be published, but were reprinted afterward by Pope in the sequence given here. The subtitles indicate the ways in which he hoped they would take their place in a never-realized *Opus Magnum*. '*Of . . . the* Characters *of* MEN' ('Cobham') advances the concept of the 'ruling passion', also treated in the 'Essay on Man'. '*Of the* Characters *of* WOMEN' ('A Lady') claims that women are prone to histrionic variability and in that sense have 'no characters at all': their personalities may be vivid, but they lack the stable and predictable 'character' of traditional psychology. The first of the two poems on '*Of the* Use *of* RICHES' contrasts wise stewardship with prodigal extravagance, yet claims that both extremes are beneficial to society as a whole; the second addresses the narrower subject of true and false taste in architecture and other arts.

Epigraph: 'The work should have brevity, so that the thought may run freely and not entangle itself in words that are burdensome to weary ears. The style should be sometimes serious and often humorous, in keeping with the role of an orator or poet, and at other times of a wit who holds back his strength and wisely diminishes it' (Horace, Satire, I, 9–14).

Epistle I

To Sir Richard Temple, Lord Cobham

Dedication: Richard Temple, Viscount Cobham, was a Whig politician who nevertheless opposed the policies of the Walpole administration. He had been dismissed from his post as an army general in retribution for supporting an investigation into government corruption, and Pope, who visited Cobham's estate at Stowe in Buckinghamshire shortly afterward, dedicated this poem to him as a tribute to his independence and integrity.

5.   *coxcomb*: See 'Essay on Criticism', 27n.
7.   *passenger*: Passer-by.
14.   *these*: i.e. these observations.
15.   *peculiar*: Specific, unique.
18.   *moss*: 'There are about 300 sorts of moss observed by naturalists' (Pope's note); today approximately 12,000 species.
37.   *stay*: Pause.
39.   *sedate*: 'calm; quiet; serene' (*Dictionary*).
42.   *spring*: Source of energy, as in the mainspring driving a clock.
43.   *determined*: 'determine: to direct to any certain point' (*Dictionary*).
46.   *sense*: i.e. the senses.
54.   CHANDOS: Wealthy duke, patron of the arts, whose estate at Cannons was mistakenly believed to be the original for Timon's villa in 'IV Burlington', 99; Pope is here attempting to make amends to the offended Chandos.
55.   *Shylock*: Any (unscrupulous) usurer, after the character in Shakespeare's *The Merchant of Venice*.
56.   *at squat*: Squatting.
57.   *gen'rous*: 'magnanimous; open of heart' (*Dictionary*). *Manly*: An attractively plain-spoken character in *The Plain Dealer* (1676) by Pope's friend Wycherley.
59.   *Umbra*: See 'Essay on Man', IV, 278n.
60.   *vulgar*: Common.
62.   *spleen*: Misanthropy, probably referring to Swift, whose indignation at human folly was the source of wit.

64. *bent*: 'turn of the temper, or disposition' (*Dictionary*).
65. *contraries*: Accented on the first syllable.
72. *place*: Public office.
73. *hazard*: Gambling with dice.
75. *borough*: Town or city parliamentary constituency, where candidates were expected to treat the electors to drink.
76. *Hackney*: London borough, where the candidate would be 'friendly' to the electors. *Whitehall*: The seat of government, where the Member of Parliament would ignore their wishes after the election was over.
77. *Catius*: An epicure from Horace's Satire, II, iv.
78. *Thinks who*: i.e. thinks that he who.
81. *Patritio*: A Patriot; see "III Bathurst', 139n.
85. *picquette*: Picquet, a card game.
86. *Newmarket*: Site in Suffolk of a celebrated racecourse, made fashionable by Charles II.
87. *Montaigne*: Michel de Montaigne, sixteenth-century writer whose *Essays* expressed scepticism about the possibility of certain knowledge; see also Horace, Satire, II, i, 52n. *Charron*: Pierre Charron, Montaigne's friend, author of a treatise *Of Wisdom* that was likewise sceptical. Both accepted the Roman Catholic religion; it is not known why Pope considered Charron 'more sage'.
88. *Otho*: Roman emperor for three months in 69 AD, who committed suicide after defeat in battle. *Cromwell*: Oliver Cromwell, who rose from obscurity to lead the victorious Puritan army and then to rule England as Lord Protector after the execution of Charles I; since he retained the simple manners of a country gentleman, he apparently seemed a 'buffoon' to Pope.
89. *leaden saint*: 'Louis XI of France wore in his hat a leaden image of the Virgin Mary, which when he swore by, he feared to break his oath' (Pope's note); 'revere' was pronounced 'revar'.
90. *godless regent ... star*: The Duke of Orleans, regent of France while Louis XV was a minor, was irreligious but believed in astrology.
91. *bigot ... genius*: 'Philip V of Spain, who, after renouncing the throne for religion, resumed it to gratify his queen; and Victor Amadeus II, king of Sardinia, who resigned the crown, and in trying to reassume it, was imprisoned till his death' (Pope's note).
93. *a woman, child, or dotard*: Then in power: Russia was ruled by the Czarina Anna, Louis XV had ascended the French throne in 1715 at the age of 5, and Pope Clement XII was 82.

94. *just*: No less then, positively.

97. *bird of passage*: Migratory bird.

104. *shave their crowns*: As monks.

107. *adust complexion*: Melancholy temperament; 'adust' indicates dry bodily humours.

108. *Charles*: In 1555 the Holy Roman Emperor Charles V abdicated and entered a Spanish monastery. *Philip*: Charles's son Philip II fought against France ('the field' is the battlefield) and sent the Spanish Armada against England.

112. *east*: The east wind tends to be damp and chilly in England, and was regarded as unhealthy.

122. *balance ... dark*: Fine distinctions can't be made among the many actions that don't stand out from the rest.

124. *policy*: 'management of affairs; stratagem' (*Dictionary*).

125. *the character to save*: i.e. to preserve the appearance of a consistent character.

131. *punk*: Whore (by implication, Cleopatra).

134. *Conduct*: 'the act of leading troops; the duty of a general' (*Dictionary*). *heroic Love*: Glorifying Caesar's liaison with Cleopatra.

136. *crape*: 'a thin stuff, loosely woven, of which the dress of the clergy is sometimes made'. *lawn*: 'fine linen, remarkable for being used in the sleeves of bishops' (*Dictionary*, citing this line for both words).

137. *chanc'lor*: The Lord Chancellor, highest judicial official in England.

138. *gownman*: Clergyman or lawyer.

141. *rate*: Rating, valuation.

142. *Heav'n's influence*: Gems were supposedly ripened by the sun's heat.

144. *here*: At court.

147. *his*: The sun's.

154. *scriv'ner*: Moneylender.

155. *churchman*: Clergyman in the Church of England, as the established church was closely allied to political power.

157. *freethinker*: 'a libertine; a contemner of religion' (*Dictionary*).

158. *Scoto*: Any Scottish merchant.

160. *by the setting sun*: i.e. by the time the sun sets.

165. *minister*: Cabinet minister.

167. *take place*: Take precedence.

171. *in what*: i.e. in what things.

172. *humours*: Temperaments.

178. *clue*: 'a guide; a direction: because men direct themselves by a clew of thread in a labyrinth' (*Dictionary*).

179. *Wharton*: Philip, Duke of Wharton, unstable and spendthrift, notable for startling changes of lifestyle; he was a convert to Catholicism and a Jacobite supporter of the exiled Stuart monarchy, and died in a Spanish monastery.

186. *parts*: 'qualities; powers; faculties; or accomplishments' (*Dictionary*).

187. *Tully*: See 'Essay on Man', IV, 240n. *Wilmot*: John Wilmot, Earl of Rochester, scandalous playboy–poet during the Restoration.

196. *still*: Always.

198. *bounty . . . made*: i.e. his free spending gained him no friends.

205. *flagitious*: 'wicked; villainous; atrocious' (*Dictionary*).

208. *prodigies*: 'prodigy: anything out of the ordinary process of nature, from which omens are drawn' (*Dictionary*).

209. *Comets are regular*: i.e. just as Newton's laws show how their 'eccentric' orbits bring them back past earth at regular intervals, so the theory of the ruling passion can explain psychological eccentricity.

211. *If second . . . take*: If they mistake secondary effects for primary causes.

212. *Catiline*: First-century Roman politician who got rich as a general ('by rapine'), was opposed by Cicero, and led a failed conspiracy against the Republic.

213. *noble dame*: Servilia, mistress of Julius Caesar and mother of his assassin Marcus Brutus.

216. *Scipio*: See 'Windsor Forest', 257n.

217. *by chastity at praise*: He would have sought to win praise for his chastity.

218. *Lucullus*: Roman epicure whose name became synonymous with lavish 'Lucullan' feasts.

219. *Sabine*: Hilly region outside Rome noted for simple living; Horace celebrated his Sabine farm.

221. *pile*: Large building.

224. *lenient*: 'assuasive; softening; mitigating' (*Dictionary*, citing this line).

225. *sand*: In an hourglass.

230. *out*: Out of order, inappropriate.

231. *Lanesb'rough*: Lanesborough was a nobleman who continued to dance, believing it good for health, even after he was crippled by gout.

233. *a nameless race*: Illegitimate children.

234. *Shoved from the wall*: The pavement close to the walls of buildings was cleaner than the street side, so bullies 'took the wall'.

237. *sparrow*: Reputed to be lecherous.

238. *salmon's belly*: A rich delicacy. *Helluo*: Glutton (Latin).

240. *soul*: Pronounced to rhyme with 'fowl'.

245. *one puff more*: The miserly old lady tries to blow out the candle for the last rites so that the stub can be used again.

246. *woollen*: In support of the British wool industry, burials had to be in wool rather than in imported silk or linen.

247. *Narcissa*: Suggestive of self-love, and referring to the actress Anne Oldfield, who often played a character named Narcissa in Colley Cibber's comedy *Love's Last Shift*.

248. *chintz*: 'cloth of cotton made in India, and printed with colours' (*Dictionary*, citing this line).

251. *Betty*: Generic name for a lady's maid; cf. 'Rape of the Lock'.

256. *devise*: Bequeath. *Euclio*: A miser in a play by Plautus.

265. *shall be your last*: Cobham did not in fact speak these words, but finding himself too weak to bring a glass of jelly to his mouth, flung it in the face of his niece and expired.

Epistle II
To A Lady

1. *you*: Martha Blount, the unnamed 'lady' to whom the epistle is addressed. See Selected Letters, note 5.

2. *no characters at all*: See headnote and Argument.

4. *black*: Dark-haired.

7-8. *ermined pride ... Pastora*: The countess has herself depicted in opulent ermine furs, and also as a simple shepherdess in a pastoral scene. 'The poet's politeness and complaisance to the sex is observable in this instance, among others, that whereas in the *Characters of Men* he has sometimes made use of real names, in the *Characters of Women* always fictitious' (Pope's note).

9. *Fannia*: Roman lady convicted of adultery.

10. *Leda*: Zeus ravished her, taking the form of a swan; the story gave painters free rein with an erotic subject.

12. *Magdalen*: Mary Magdalen (or Magdalene), mentioned only briefly in the Gospels, but according to tradition a former prostitute whom Jesus forgave; thus, another opportunity for painters to exploit an erotic subject.

13. *Cecilia*: Patron saint of music.

17. *ground*: Undercoat before applying colours.

19. *a firm cloud*: Presumably the painter makes it seem rather too substantial.

20. *Cynthia*: Goddess of the moon, hence changing minute by minute.

21. *Rufa*: Red-haired, conventionally thought to indicate sexual appetite.

22. *spark*: See 'Rape of the Lock', I, 73n.

24. *Sappho*: Greek poet; but any unchaste female poet, and usually referring to Pope's enemy Lady Mary Wortley Montagu. *dirty smock*: Lady Mary was known for slovenly dress.

26. *masked*: Masked ball.

31. *Calista*: Guilty heroine in *The Fair Penitent* by Nicholas Rowe. *nice*: 'delicate; scrupulously and minutely cautious' (*Dictionary*).

32. *Simplicius*: Any simpleton.

33. *tip the wink*: Wink knowingly.

37. *Papillia*: Butterfly (from *papilio*).

38–40. *charming ... odious*: Both were common descriptors in ladies' speech at the time. *the fair*: The fair lady.

43. *take*: 'to captivate with pleasure; to delight; to engage' (Johnson's *Dictionary*).

45. *Calypso*: Sea-nymph who bewitches Odysseus and keeps him on her island for seven years (*Odyssey*, VI).

53. *Narcissa*: i.e. a female Narcissus, in love with herself.

54. *wash*: A cosmetic preparation.

56. *paid a tradesman ... stare*: i.e. she usually buys on credit and neglects to pay, but on one occasion she did pay a tradesman, for the pleasure of seeing him stare in astonishment.

57. *trim*: 'dress; gear; ornaments' (*Dictionary*).

61. *pique*: 'to offend; to irritate' (*Dictionary*, citing this line). *affect*: 'to aim at; to endeavour after' (*Dictionary*). Despite treating people badly, Narcissa wants to have a good name.

63. *Taylor*: Jeremy Taylor, seventeenth-century author of the widely read *Holy Living* and *Holy Dying*. *Book of Martyrs*: John Foxe's sixteenth-century compilation of stories of Protestants who died for their faith.

64. *his Grace*: A duke is so addressed. *Chartres*: See 'Essay on Man', IV, 130n.

70. *punk*: Whore.

71. *frank*: 'not restrained; licentious' (*Dictionary*).

78. *Tall-boy*: An awkward lover in *The Jovial Crew* by Richard Brome; see also 'Dunciad', I, 146n. *Charles*: Stock name for a footman.

79. *Helluo*: Glutton (Latin).

80. *hautgout*: High taste (French): food so strongly flavoured (and detected as such by the nose) as to be almost spoiled.

85. *address*: Manner, deportment.

92. *Lucretia's dagger*: After being raped by the son of the Roman king Tarquin, Lucretia (in English, Lucrece) stabbed herself to death. *Rosamonda's bowl*: Rosamond Clifford, mistress of Henry II, committed suicide by poison.

101. *Simo*: An old man in Terence's comedy *Andrea*.

103. *owns*: Acknowledges.

110. *ratafie*: Or ratafia, apricot brandy.

111. *anodyne*: Painkiller.

115. *Atossa*: Ancient Persian princess, but hinting at Katherine, Duchess of Buckinghamshire, illegitimate daughter of James II.

119. *painting*: Describing accurately.

130. *be well*: Be on good terms with her.

140. *temple*: Country estates were often embellished with 'temples' in the classical style.

148. *wants an heir*: Lacks a legal heir; evidently Atossa's husband knows that he is not the father of her children.

149–50. *To heirs unknown … to the poor*: Adjusting these lines in his 1751 edition of Pope's *Works*, Warburton said that they reflect a principle that Pope 'never loses sight of … which teaches that Providence is incessantly turning the evils arising from the follies and vices of men to general good'.

155. *equal*: Flat, uniform. *knack*: Trick.

156. *Chameleons … black*: They change colour so readily that it would be impossible to depict them in black and white.

159. *part*: Quality, ability.

170. *chintz*: See 'I Cobham', 248n. *mohair*: 'thread or stuff made of camels' or other hair' (*Dictionary*, citing this line).

182. *varnished out*: Made to shine, as if with varnish.

183–4. THE SAME … *crown and ball*: Queen Elizabeth's motto was *semper eadem*, 'always the same', whereas a modern queen is 'the same' only inasmuch as painters routinely depict her with the royal attributes of a crown and orb.

191. *exactest*: Most perfect.

193. *Queensberry*: The Duchess of Queensberry, a famous beauty, yet admirably modest (thus, 'there's no compelling' her to strip).

194. *Helen*: Helen of Troy, 'the face that launched a thousand ships'. (Christopher Marlowe, *Doctor Faustus*, V, i, 92).

198. *Mah'met*: 'servant to the late king [George I], said to be the son

of a Turkish Bassa' (Pope's note). *Parson Hale*: Stephen Hales, a neighbour whom Pope admired for generous conduct of his pastoral duties as well as for his medical research.

205. *nice*: Subtle.

210. *sway*: 'power; rule; dominion' (*Dictionary*).

211. *That*: Love of pleasure.

213. *this*: Love of sway.

226. *science*: Study, discipline. *Great*: Persons in high places.

232. *Still*: Always.

239. *As hags hold sabbaths*: Witches' sabbaths were midnight rituals at which the Devil would preside.

240. *Night*: A weekly social event held at a fashionable lady's house.

247. *fop*: 'a man of small understanding and much ostentation; a pretender; a man fond of show, dress, and flutter; an impertinent'. *sot*: 'a blockhead; a dull ignorant stupid fellow; a dolt; a wretch stupefied by drinking' (both from *Dictionary*).

249. *friend*: Martha Blount.

251. *Ring*: Fashionable carriage drive in Hyde Park.

256. *declines*: Like the moon setting, a good woman will sink gently to the grave.

257. *temper*: 'calmness of mind; moderation' (*Dictionary*).

259. *a sister's charms*: Martha Blount's sister Teresa was considered more attractive.

261. *till a husband cools*: i.e. rather than quarrelling, she waits to speak until his anger has subsided.

263. *by submitting sways*: Exerts indirect power while apparently yielding.

264. *has her humour*: Succeeds in getting her way.

266. *tickets*: Lottery tickets. *codille*: The loser in the card game ombre (see 'Rape of the Lock', III, 27 and 92 and notes).

267. *spleen*: See 'Rape of the Lock', IV, 16n. *vapour*: See 'Rape of the Lock', IV, 18n. *smallpox*: See 'Rape of the Lock', V, 20n.

268. *though china fall*: Cf. 'Rape of the Lock', III, 159–60.

272. *Its last best work*: Eve was created after Adam.

274. *Your . . . our*: Women's and men's.

282. *Toasts*: See 'Rape of the Lock', IV, 109n.

283. *I forget the year*: Pope pretends not to remember how old Martha is (they were both 47 in 1735).

284. *sphere*: The world; pronounced 'sphare'.

285. *Ascendant*: Astrologically dominant at the time of a person's birth.

288. *buys . . . a tyrant*: Marriages were arranged by families; lacking

a rich dowry, Martha has been spared a disagreeable marriage
based on money.

289-90.   *The gen'rous god . . . mines*: Phoebus, god of poetry ('wit')
and of the sun, was thought to 'ripen' underground minerals
with his heat.

Epistle III
To Allen Lord Bathurst

Dedication: Lord Bathurst, one of twelve peers created in 1712 by
Queen Anne to secure a Tory majority in the House of Lords, was
a close friend and correspondent of Pope, who helped design the
landscaping of Bathurst's estate at Cirencester in Gloucestershire.

1.   *doctors*: Learned men.
2.   *casuists*: 'casuist: one that studies and settles cases of conscience'
(*Dictionary*, citing this line).
3.   *Momus*: God of ridicule.
12.   *its sire the sun*: See 'II A Lady', 289n.
17.   *owning*: Acknowledging.
18.   *th' Elect*: Persons destined to eternal salvation.
20.   *Ward*: John Ward, convicted of forgery, expelled from the House
of Commons and sentenced to the pillory. *Waters*: Peter Walter,
unscrupulous attorney and usurer; also 123 below; see also
Horace, Satire, II, i, 3. *Chartres*: See 'Essay on Man', IV, 130n.
21.   *wants*: Lacks. *commodious*: Convenient, useful.
34.   *saps*: Undermines.
36.   *guinea*: Gold coin, worth twenty-one shillings.
37.   *back stairs*: i.e. the bribe is being delivered surreptitiously.
38.   *Old Cato*: Cato the Elder, incorruptible Roman patriot.
39.   *paper-credit*: Pope was among those deeply suspicious of trans-
actions and profits that existed entirely on paper. *supply*:
Reinforcement.
41.   *imped*: Enlarged, e.g. by grafting new feathers into a bird's wing
to improve its flight.
45.   *Sibyl*: Roman prophetess who wrote her predictions on leaves,
which the wind might blow away.
53.   *confound*: Intoxicate.
54.   *water all the Quorum*: Bribe the Justices of the Peace with liquor.
58.   *levee*: Morning assembly.
60.   *in kind*: As in 'payment in kind', actual possessions (jars, oxen)
rather than money.
62.   *Worldly*: Hinting at 'Wortley', Lady Mary Wortley Montagu's

husband. *crying coals*: Like a coal-seller calling out his wares. 'Some misers of great wealth, proprietors of the coal mines, had entered at this time into an association to keep up coals to an extravagant price, whereby the poor were reduced almost to starve' (Pope's note); i.e. freeze to death.

63. *mien so mazed*: Countenance so perplexed.

65. *Colepepper*: Sir William Colepepper, who lost his fortune gambling.

66. *sent it to the dogs*: Squandered it all.

67. *His Grace*: Any duke. *game*: Gamble. *White's*: Well-known gambling club.

69. *ancient games*: Greek athletic contests, whose prizes were fine horses ('coursers'), vases, and female slaves (70).

71. *Uxorio*: A doting husband. *the stakes he sweep*: He wins the jackpot.

73. *Adonis*: Venus' lover; hence, a young man vain of his good looks.

74. *St James's*: The principal royal residence in London; see also 388n.

76. *quadrille*: Fashionable card game, which the game of financial speculation is in effect replacing.

82. *Turner*: Richard Turner, a merchant who lost a fortune through unwise investment.

84. *Wharton*: See 'I Cobham', 179n.

85. *Hopkins*: John Hopkins, 'whose rapacity obtained him the name of Vulture Hopkins; he lived worthless, but died worth three hundred thousand pounds' (Pope's note); also 291.

86. *Japhet*: Japhet Crook, a convicted forger, mutilated as punishment for an outrageous crime; he forged a will in his own favour by which he hoped to inherit several thousand pounds.

87. *Hippia*: The name suggests 'hypochondria' (familiarly called 'the hips'), a melancholy or depressive mental condition.

88. *Fulvia*: Licentious Roman lady.

89. *Narses*: Eunuch who served under the emperor Justinian I (the name incorporates 'arse').

90. *plastered*: Attached like a medicinal bandage.

91. *Harpax*: Robber (Greek).

94. *spite of Shylock's wife*: i.e. the miser's wife would prefer to be a widow, after *Merchant of Venice* (see 'I Cobham', 55n.).

96. *a cat*: 'a famous Duchess of Richmond in her last will left considerable legacies and annuities to her cats' (Pope's note).

100. *Bond*: Denis Bond expelled from the House of Commons for swindling, who profited at the expense of the poor.

101. *Sir Gilbert*: Sir Gilbert Heathcote, Lord Mayor of London and a founder of the Bank of England, regarded as the richest commoner in England.

103. *Blunt*: Sir John Blunt, director of the South Sea Company and promoter of the frenzy of speculation that led to the South Sea Bubble crash in 1720 that bankrupted its many investors; see also 145n., 150n.

107. *pelf*: Riches.

108. *hate . . . himself*: Parodying the Golden Rule: 'Thou shalt love thy neighbour as thyself' (Mark 12:31, repeated in other Gospels).

111. *own*: Admit.

118. *when it sold so dear*: 'in the extravagance and luxury of the South Sea year, the price of a haunch of venison was from three to five pounds' (Pope's note). A labourer could live for a year on not much more than £5.

120. *Phryne*: Rich Greek courtesan, and probably referring to Walpole's mistress Molly Skerrit. *excise*: Tax on commodities, a highly controversial income-producing measure of Walpole's.

121. *Sappho*: See 'II A Lady', 24n.

122. *plum*: 'in the cant of the City, the sum of one hundred thousand pounds' (*Dictionary*, citing this line); if acquired in an official post, presumably done by dishonest means.

126. *Didius*: 'a Roman lawyer, so rich as to purchase the Empire when it was set to sale' (Pope's note).

127. *crown of Poland*: The Polish throne was elective, and when it fell vacant the Polish nobility who served as electors could be bribed by would-be monarchs; see also 128–32n.

128–32.   *Gage . . . mines*: Joseph Gage offered three million pounds for the crown of Poland, but was refused, after which he married Lady Mary Herbert ('Maria') and purchased rights to the gold mines of Asturia in Spain.

131. *joins*: Pronounced to rhyme with 'mines'.

136. *ministers*: Cabinet members.

139. *Statesman*: Here, a member of the Walpole government. *Patriot*: The term preferred by members of the opposition, who regarded themselves as above ordinary politics.

140. *butler*: i.e. the peeress's butler has got rich through financial speculation. *box*: Good seat in the theatre.

141. *job*: Profit from a government appointment. *bite*: Trick, deceive.

142. *pack cards*: Stack the deck. *half a crown*: Two shillings and sixpence, a trivial sum.

144. *France revenged*: For the recent victories of British armies under Queen Anne, and in the fourteenth century under Edward III.

145. *court-badge*: Honours conferred at Court. *scriv'ner*: Money-lender (the profession in which Blunt got his start).

146. *City*: The financial and commercial centre in London, known as 'the City'.

150. *buy both sides*: Before its crash, the South Sea Company, of which Blunt was a principal director, obtained political favours from both Whig and Tory politicians.

159-62. *"Tis Heav'n . . . gen'ral use'*: Adapted from 'Essay on Man', II, 165-6, 205-6.

163. *keep . . . bestow*: Hoard, or give.

171. *Mammon*: Biblical term for riches, personified in *Paradise Lost* as 'the least erected spirit that fell / From Heav'n' (I, 679-80).

173. *spare*: 'to live frugally' (*Dictionary*).

175. *country*: Region of countryside.

180. *grot*: See 'Eloisa to Abelard', 20n.

181. *nettles . . . cresses*: Cotta dines on nettles and watercress that grow as weeds on his own property.

182. *board*: Table.

183. *pulse*: Peas and beans.

186. *take . . . Providence*: Provide charity, rather than leaving it to Providence to take care of the poor.

187. *Chartreux*: Mother house in France of the Carthusian order, noted for strict discipline.

189. *tabor*: Drum.

196. *eat*: Pronounced 'ate'.

197. *marked*: Remarked, observed.

203. *hecatombs*: Sacrifice of a hundred animals (Greek).

204. *deep divine*: Profound clergyman, implying a bottomless capacity for drink.

206. *in his country's cause*: Inasmuch as each libation is preceded by a toast to King George and liberty (207).

208. *that great House*: The House of Hanover, which came to the throne after Queen Anne's death, and was regarded by Tories as an alien (because Germanic) imposition on Britain.

209. *woods recede*: The ancient forests are cut down for sale. *seat*: Country seat, estate.

210. *sylvans*: Forest dwellers or spirits. *fleet*: The timber is sold to the Royal Navy.

211. *our valiant bands*: Soldiers.

213. *To town*: To London.

214. *train-bands*: City militia. *burns a pope*: Takes part in anti-Catholic revelry that includes burning an effigy of the pope.

216. *spoils*: i.e. of war.

224. *magnificence*: 'grandeur of appearance; splendour' (*Dictionary*).

228. *mad good-nature*: Conviviality and generosity when indulged in excess.

230. *ease, or emulate*: By charitable action, relieve Heaven of a part of its responsibility toward the needy, or at any rate imitate Heaven.

232. *Mend . . . grace*: Make up for the unequal distribution of benefits by Fortune, and thereby justify the benevolence of divine grace.

233. *but life diffused*: i.e. wealth gives life when it is shared.

234. *poison heals*: Certain substances that would be poisonous in large quantity are medicinal in controlled doses.

235. *ambergris*: Strong-smelling substance used in making perfume.

237. *Who starves by nobles*: Who is caused to starve by nobles?

242. *gamester*: Gambler with dice. *play'r*: Card player.

243. *yours*: Bathurst's. OXFORD: Edward Harley, second Earl of Oxford, who left the Harleian Library to Oxford University.

246. *the golden Mean*: See 'Windsor Forest', 251n.; all of Pope's examples are intended to recommend it.

250. *the* MAN *of* ROSS: 'The person here celebrated, who with a small estate actually performed all these good works, and whose true name was almost lost (partly by the title of the "Man of Ross" given him by way of eminence, and partly by being buried without so much as an inscription) was called Mr John Kyrle. He died in the year 1724, aged 90, and lies interred in the chancel of the church of Ross in Herefordshire' (Pope's note).

251. *Vaga*: Latin name for the River Wye, on which lies the town of Ross; the larger River Severn (252) is not far away.

258. *swain*: Rural labourer.

265. *alms-house*: 'a house devoted to the reception and support of the poor' (*Dictionary*, citing this line). *state*: Ostentation.

267. *portioned maids*: Young women whom Kyrle furnished with dowries that made it possible for them to marry.

271. *variance*: Disagreement leading to legal action.

273. *quacks*: 'quack: a vain boastful pretender to physic; one who proclaims his own medical abilities in public places' (*Dictionary*, citing this line).

274. *vile attorneys*: Lawyers of the most unscrupulous kind, who hoped to profit by a lawsuit.

280. *five hundred pounds*: A comfortable income, but far from a

fortune; Pope privately admitted that to encourage generosity, he exaggerated the extent of Kyrle's good works.

282. *little stars*: Emblems of knighthood.

287–8. *search it . . . the history*: The parish register recorded the simple facts of their births and deaths.

290. *ends of being*: True purposes of living.

292. *a candle's end*: The miser kept partly burned candles for reuse.

293. *Should'ring God's altar*: Hopkins's pompous tomb crowds against the church altar.

295. *Gorgon*: Female monster with snakes for hair, the sight of whom would turn a person to stone.

296. *buckle*: Curled hair. *Parian stone*: Superb marble from the Greek island of Paros.

300. *walls of dung*: Animal dung was mixed with straw and plaster to construct cheap masonry.

301. *flock-bed*: Bed stuffed with cloth or wool.

303. *George and Garter*: An image of St George appears in the insignia of the Order of the Garter.

305. *Villiers*: George Villiers, Duke of Buckingham, a glamorous figure in the court of Charles II; Pope follows an erroneous tradition that he died miserably. *how changed from him*: Echoing Satan's address to the fallen angel Beelzebub: 'But O how fall'n! how changed / from him . . . (*Paradise Lost*, I, 84–5).

307. *Cliveden*: 'a delightful palace on the banks of the Thames, built by the Duke of Buckingham' (Pope's note).

308. *wanton Shrewsbury*: 'the Countess of Shrewsbury, a woman abandoned to gallantries; the Earl her husband was killed by the Duke of Buckingham in a duel, and it has been said that during the combat she held the Duke's horses in the habit of a page' (Pope's note).

309. *Council*: The king's closest advisers, the privy council.

310. *their merry king*: Charles II: see 'Essay on Criticism', 536n.

312. *fool . . . valued more*: i.e. he enjoyed mockery of fools more than genuine witticisms.

314. *useless thousands*: The fortune he squandered.

315. *Cutler*: Sir John Cutler, miserly merchant.

323. *break*: Go broke.

326. *could not pay a dow'r*: Could not afford a dowry to provide his daughter with a good marriage.

328. *sold them*: Cutter was reduced to selling his hair to a wigmaker.

329. *cordial*: 'a medicine that increases the force of the heart' (*Dictionary*).

332. *Yet numbers ... he had*: Many people are so poor that they would be glad to have what still remained to him.

333. *Brutus*: The patriotic Roman who assassinated Julius Caesar.

339–40.   *London's column ... lies*: 'the Monument, built in memory of the Fire of London, with an inscription importing the city to have been burnt by the Papists' (Pope's note).

341. *Citizen*: City-dweller, a London merchant.

342. *Balaam*: Biblical name from the Book of Numbers, and castigated in 2 Peter 2:15 because he 'loved the ways of unrighteousness' (used here to suggest someone who uses religion self-servingly).

344. *more than he was worth*: Balaam was so trustworthy that he could have borrowed more than he actually owned.

346. *the Lord's*: The Lord's Day, Sunday.

347. *Change*: The Royal Exchange, where business transactions took place.

348. *farthings*: The smallest denomination of coin, worth one-quarter of a penny.

350. *Job*: God agrees to let Satan test the faith of the upright man Job.

353. *Prince of Air*: The Devil.

354. *plunge his father*: Balaam's father's drowning permits him to inherit a fortune.

356. *lucky*: The coastal inhabitants of Cornwall were thought to look forward to the plunder from shipwrecks.

358. *chirping*: Cheerful.

359. *Live like yourself*: Live in a style befitting your wealth.

362. *factor*: Mercantile agent in the colonies.

364. *the rogue was bit*: Outwitted, tricked, with a hint that 'the rogue was Pitt'. Thomas Pitt, a British administrator in India, acquired the fabulously valuable 400-carat Pitt Diamond from a Madras merchant, who in turn had got it from a sea captain who had stolen it from a slave.

366. *groat*: 'a piece valued at four pence; a proverbial name for a small sum' (*Dictionary*). Nor is the sixpence at all generous.

367–8.   *twice ... other vice*: By going twice to church, he expects to be cleared of all possible sins.

369. *Tempter*: Satan.

370. *subscriptions*: Shares in commercial ventures.

372. *cent per cent*: A profit of one hundred per cent.

374. *Director*: Member of a corporation's board of directors, for which he has in effect sold his soul.

377. *wit*: Balaam's own cleverness, rather than a blessing from Heaven.

380. *compting-house*: Counting house, commercial bookkeeping office.

382. *family*: Household servants as well as relatives.
385. *nymph of quality*: Well-born young woman.
387. *cits*: See Horace, Epistle, I, i, 89n. *the fair*: The fair sex.
388. *St James's*: The fashionable world of the court.
389. *commission*: A commission in a fashionable army regiment had to be bought.
391. *viscount*: The daughter has acquired status by marrying a nobleman.
392. *pox for life*: Venereal disease, then incurable.
393. *senate*: Grandiose classical name for the House of Commons.
394. *pensioner St Stephen*: Sir Balaam has accepted a government pension; St Stephen's Chapel, Westminster, where the House of Commons met.
395. *play . . . chance*: She has such bad luck in gambling.
397. *Coningsby*: Thomas, Earl Coningsby, a supporter of the Hanover monarchy who had moved the impeachment of Pope's friend Robert Harley, the Tory prime minister under Queen Anne.

Epistle IV
To Richard Boyle, Earl of Burlington

Dedication: Richard Boyle, third Earl of Burlington, was an architect of a number of much-admired buildings as well as patron of the arts. He published an edition of the works of the sixteenth-century Italian architect Andrea Palladio, whose attempt to recover the proportions of ancient Roman design had great influence in England, notably in Burlington's own recently completed Chiswick House in London.

6. *Artists*: Connoisseurs.
7. *He buys for Topham*: Richard Topham, a well-known connoisseur and collector of drawings; the spendthrift prodigal buys 'for' himself pictures which Topham appreciates better than their owner can.
8. *Pembroke*: Thomas Herbert, eighth Earl of Pembroke, president of the Royal Society, and noted collector.
9. *Hearne*: Thomas Hearne, medieval scholar.
10. *Mead . . . Sloane*: Richard Mead and Sir Hans Sloane, 'two eminent physicians; the one had an excellent library, the other the finest collection in Europe of natural curiosities; both men of great learning and humanity' (Pope's note). Sloane's collection became the starting point for the British Museum.
12. *wife . . . whore*: i.e. both, like the art works, are enjoyed by other men besides himself.
13. *Virro*: Contemptible patron in the fifth satire of Juvenal.

14. *wanted*: Lacked.

15. *Visto*: Alluding to artfully calculated 'vistas' through avenues of trees in contemporary gardens.

16. *demon*: Supernatural spirit.

18. *rod*: 'an instrument of correction, made of twigs tied together' (*Dictionary*), with a pun on a carpenter's measuring rod. *Ripley*: 'This man [Thomas Ripley] was a carpenter employed by a First Minister [Walpole], who raised him to an architect without any genius in the art, and after some wretched proofs of his insufficiency in public buildings made him comptroller of the Board of Works' (Pope's note).

20. *Bubo*: George Bubb Dodington, Whig politician and literary patron, a frequent target of Pope's satire. *such a guide*: As Ripley.

22. *magnificence*: 'grandeur of appearance; splendour' (*Dictionary*); in Aristotelian terms, avoiding the two extremes of shabbiness and vulgar ostentation.

23. *You*: Burlington, in his edition of Palladio.

27. *sheets*: Pages of Burlington's book.

32. *dog-hole*: 'a vile hole; a mean habitation' (*Dictionary*, citing this line).

33. *pilaster*: Rectangular column projecting from a wall.

34. *rustic*: Stone that is 'rusticated', left with a rough surface.

36. *Venetian door*: 'a door or window, so called from being much practised at Venice by Palladio and others' (Pope's note); today called a French door.

37. *Palladian part*: i.e. with the classical simplicity of Palladio's architectural style.

38. *starve*: 'to kill with cold' (*Dictionary*).

44. *science*: Knowledge of all kinds. *the sev'n*: The seven liberal arts in medieval education.

46. *Jones*: Inigo Jones, seventeenth-century architect, whose Banqueting House at Whitehall was an early example of Palladian style in England. *Le Nôtre*: André Le Nôtre, celebrated garden designer who landscaped Versailles for Louis XIV.

49. *grot*: See 'Eloisa to Abelard', 20n.

51. *fair*: Fair lady.

57. *genius . . . of the place*: Guardian spirit of a locale (*genius loci*).

58. *or to*: Either to.

60. *theatres*: Ascending tiers, like seats in a Roman theatre.

61. *Calls in the country*: Makes the surrounding countryside contribute to the aesthetic effect.

63. *intending*: Directing the eyes (*intendere oculos*).

64. *Paints*: i.e. landscape gardening is analogous to painting.

68. *Start . . . from*: Emerge from, originate in.

70. *STOWE*: The estate and gardens of Cobham in Buckinghamshire, much admired by Pope.

72. *Nero's terraces*: Elaborate gardens at the emperor's 'golden house'.

73. *parterres*: Lawns with flower beds in them. *a thousand hands*: Of labourers.

76. *You'll wish . . . sheltered seat*: i.e. after the trees are cut down, the country seat is exposed to cold winds.

78. *Dr Clarke*: Samuel Clarke, a clergyman whose bust was placed by Queen Caroline in a 'hermitage' constructed for her at Richmond Park.

79. *Villario*: i.e. the owner of a villa, a country house on the Roman model.

80. *espaliers*: Lattices on which fruit trees are trained to grow horizontally against a wall.

85. *rills*: Brooks.

89. *Sabinus*: Alluding to Horace's farm: See 'I Cobham', 219n. *strayed*: Wandered.

94. *dryads*: Wood nymphs.

95. *One . . . views*: 'The two extremes in parterres, which are equally faulty: a *boundless green*, large and naked as a field, or a *flourished carpet*, where the greatness and the nobleness of the piece is lessened by being divided into too many parts, with scrolled works and beds' (Pope's note).

96. *mournful . . . yews*: 'such little ornaments as pyramids of dark green, continually repeated, not unlike a funeral procession' (Pope's note); yew trees were common in churchyards.

99. *Timon's villa*: 'This description is intended to comprise the principles of a false taste of magnificence, and to exemplify what was said before, that nothing but good sense can obtain it' (Pope's note). To Pope's distress, Timon was wrongly thought to refer to the Duke of Chandos, who was deeply insulted: See 'I Cobham', 54 and note and 'Arbuthnot', 300.

103. *draught*: Design (as in a first draft).

104. *Brobdingnag*: Land of the giants in Swift's *Gulliver's Travels*.

106. *down*: Grassy, rolling hill; everything at Timon's estate is inappropriately grandiose.

111. *squirt*: Urinate.

112. *Improves*: An ironic allusion (since no one would want the north wind to be keener) to the claim of designers that they were 'improving' an estate.

118. *platform*: Terrace on top of a wall.

121. *played*: Made to spout water.

123. *Amphitrite*: Sea-goddess, wife of Poseidon (Roman Neptune). *myrtle*: The flower of Aphrodite (Venus).

124. *gladiators ... flow'rs*: Copies of famous Roman statues of a fighting and a dying gladiator.

126. *Nilus*: Statue of the god of the Nile, with an 'urn' from which his waters flow.

127. *mien*: 'air; look; manner' (*Dictionary*).

136. *Aldus*: Aldus Manutius, fifteenth-century Venetian printer whose Aldine editions of the classics were much prized. *Du Sueil*: Augustin Deseuil, eighteenth-century Paris bookbinder of lavish editions.

137. *vellum*: Calfskin or sheepskin, of higher quality than parchment, prepared to be used for scrolls or books.

138. *wood*: 'Many delight chiefly in the elegance of the print or of the binding; some have carried it so far as to cause the upper shelves to be filled with painted books of wood' (Pope's note).

141. *chapel*: A country house would have a private chapel.

143. *quirks*: 'quirk: loose light tune' (*Dictionary*, citing this line).

146. *sprawl the saints*: 'in painting (from which even Italy is not free) of naked figures in churches' (Pope's note). *Verrio ... Laguerre*: Painters of scenes on ceilings in British royal palaces.

150. *Who ... polite*: 'This is a fact; a reverend Dean, preaching at court, threatened the sinner with punishment in "a place which he thought it not decent to name in so polite an assembly"' (Pope's note).

153. *buffet*: 'a kind of cupboard, or set of shelves, where [silver] plate is set out to show in a place of entertainment' (*Dictionary*, citing this line).

154. *tritons*: Mermen, half-man and half-fish, named for the son of Poseidon and Amphitrite. *spew*: Vomit.

155. *genial*: Cheerful, agreeable.

156. *hecatomb*: Sacrifice of a hundred animals (Greek).

158. *to minutes eat*: In strictly timed courses; 'eat' is pronounced 'ate'.

160. *Sancho's ... wand*: In *Don Quixote*, a doctor orders each dish removed before Sancho Panza can taste it.

161. *salvers*: Trays.

162. *God bless the King*: A toast on drinking to the king's health.

163. *tantalized*: As in the myth of Tantalus in the underworld, grasping at fruit that is always just out of reach.

164. *complaisantly*: 'civilly; with desire to please; ceremoniously' (*Dictionary*, citing this line).

169. *Yet hence . . . fed*: 'The moral of the whole, where Providence is justified in giving wealth to those who squander it in this manner: a bad taste employs more hands and diffuses expense more than a good one' (Pope's note).

174. *Imbrown*: 'to make brown; to darken; to obscure' (*Dictionary*, citing this line).

176. *Ceres*: Goddess of the harvest.

178. *Who*: He who. BATHURST: Lord Bathurst, to whom Epistle III is addressed. BOYLE: See Dedication note.

186. *heifer . . . steed*: Farm animals are allowed to graze on the lawn.

188. *navies*: Warships made of oak from these woods.

189. *plantations*: Plantings of trees.

190. *country*: An area of countryside.

191. *You*: Burlington.

194. *Vitruvius*: Roman architect and author of the highly influential *De Architectura*.

197. *ways*: Roads.

200. *mole*: Stone breakwater protecting a harbour.

202. *obedient rivers*: Canals, then being constructed throughout England.

The Fourth Satire of Dr John Donne Versified

Pope's free adaptation of a satire by Donne, whose lyrics had been largely forgotten, first appeared anonymously in 1733 as 'The Impertinent, Or a Visit to the Court. A Satire. By an Eminent Hand'. As Pope's Latin epigraph indicates, by 'versifying' the original he intended to recast Donne's jolting diction and casual rhyming into his own style of couplet elegance. Donne's poem was itself an imitation, of Horace's Satire, I, ix, in which the speaker is waylaid by a literary bore; Pope encounters instead a courtier whose conversation exposes the corruption of the court milieu.

Epigraph: 'And as we read the writings of Lucilius, what forbids us to ask whether it was he himself, or the harsh nature of his subjects, that denied him more supple and better turned verses?' (Horace, Satire, I, x, 56–9).

5.   *betimes*: Early.

11.   *commission from his Grace*: Military commission bestowed by a duke (addressed as 'your Grace').

12.   *benefice*: Church living, appointment as vicar of an income-producing parish. *place*: Political appointment; also 136.

15.   *reforming days*: The early years of the Protestant Reformation.

17. *pay his fine*: The penal code prescribed a stiff fine for being present at a Catholic mass; the law was still in existence in Pope's time, though seldom enforced.

25. *Adam ... name*: After God created the animals, he 'brought them unto Adam to see what he would call them: and whatsoever Adam called every living creature, that was the name thereof' (Genesis 2:19). *posed*: Puzzled, perplexed.

27–9. *reptiles ... Nilus*: Reptiles and amphibians were thought to be spontaneously generated from the mud of the Nile. *sun e'er got*: Was ever begotten by the sun's rays.

28. *verier*: Truer.

30. *Sloane ... Woodward*: For Sloane, see 'IV Burlington', 10n. Dr John Woodward had a famous collection of miscellaneous 'curiosities'; see also 152 and n.

32. *watch*: Watchman.

34. *make*: i.e. invent.

35. *popish plot*: Recalling the scare of 1678, when it was falsely claimed that there was a Catholic conspiracy to assassinate Charles II.

37. *by your priesthood*: A judge might mistake the courtier's odd black costume for a priest's.

38. *wight*: 'a person, a being; obsolete' (*Dictionary*).

39. *bare*: Threadbare.

41. *good Queen Bess*: Elizabeth I.

42. *tuff-taffety*: Taffeta (silk) with the nap in shaggy tufts.

45. *rash*: 'satin' (*Dictionary*); i.e. the nap will be worn down until it is as smooth as satin.

50. *Motteux*: Peter Anthony (born Pierre Antoine) Motteux, a French Huguenot who lived in England, wrote plays, and translated Rabelais and Cervantes.

51. *Henley*: John Henley, preacher whose histrionic style earned him the nickname 'Orator Henley'. *Budgell*: Eustace Budgell, a minor writer, a cousin of Addison, mentioned with contempt in 'Arbuthnot', 378 and note; see also Horace, Satire, II, i, 27–8 and 100 and notes.

52. *doctor's wormwood style*: Scholar's bitter tone.

53. *Gonson*: Sir John Gonson, justice of the peace famous for delivering stern charges to juries and punitive sentences; also 256.

55. *bar*: Law courts.

58. *scores*: Debts.

59. *Make Scots speak treason*: Scots, even if disaffected from the Hanover monarchy, were proverbially cautious about exposing

themselves to risk. *cozen*: 'to cheat; to trick; to defraud' (*Dictionary*).

61. *Oldmixon*: John Oldmixon, hack writer for the Whigs and a frequent opponent of Pope; see also 'Arbuthnot', 146n. and 'Dunciad', II, 283n. *Burnet*: Either the hack writer Thomas Burnet (see 'Arbuthnot', 146n.) or Gilbert Burnet, Bishop of Salisbury, whose *History of My Own Times* (1723) Pope regarded as meretricious.

63. *rod*: See 'IV Burlington', 18n.

65. *blunderbuss*: 'a gun that is charged with many bullets, so that, without any exact aim, there is a chance of hitting the mark' (*Dictionary*).

67. —— *'s your name*: 'Pope' would fit the metre.

68. *The King's*: The King's English, but also, a sly dig at George II's German accent.

71. *Onslow*: Arthur Onslow, Speaker of the House of Commons.

72. *closer style*: i.e. tighter and more condensed, as in Swift's prose.

73. *Hoadley*: Benjamin Hoadley, Bishop of Bangor and a prolix writer. *period*: 'a complete sentence from one full stop to another' (*Dictionary*).

75. *Panurge*: Character in Rabelais' *Life of Gargantua and Pantagruel*, who speaks thirteen languages, several of them fictitious.

77. *gift of tongues*: On the day of Pentecost tongues of fire appeared above the heads of the Apostles 'and they were all filled with the Holy Ghost, and began to speak with other tongues, as the Spirit gave them utterance' (Acts 2:4).

83. *druggerman*: Properly 'dragoman', an interpreter. *Babel*: The tower at Babylon whose builders impiously sought to reach heaven, for which they were punished with a confusion of languages (Genesis 11); according to tradition the tower then collapsed.

91. *Numquam minus solus*: 'Never less alone (than when one is alone)', from *De Officiis*, III, i, by Marcus Tullius Cicero.

93. *Spartan way*: Drunkards were shown to Spartan youths as a warning against intemperance.

95. *Aretine*: Pietro Aretino, Renaissance Italian poet notorious for sonnets illustrated with obscene pictures.

102. *happy man ... tombs*: The guide who showed the royal tombs in Westminster Abbey.

108. *mechanic*: 'a low workman' (*Dictionary*).

111. *but one*: i.e. just one French servant.

112. *politely*: Elegantly.

113. *paduasoy*: Corded silk (French *soie*) in the style of Padua.

115. *dishabille*: 'loosely or negligently dressed' (*Dictionary*).

125. *eunuchs, harlequins, and operas*: Theatrical attractions regarded by traditionalists as exotic fads: eunuchs were Italian *castrati*, castrated in boyhood to preserve their soprano voices, frequently used in opera. A harlequin was a stock character, nimble and acrobatic, usually cast as a clever servant in Italian *commedia dell' arte*.

126. *simples*: Medicinal herbs.

130. *birthnights*: Royal birthdays, which were public holidays. *shows*: Probably puppet shows.

131. *Holinsheds . . . Stows*: Rafael Holinshed, Edward Hall, and John Stow were garrulous Elizabethan chroniclers.

132. *the Queen*: It was widely believed that Queen Caroline had immense influence over George II.

134. *rug*: Safe, secure (gamblers' slang).

135. *reversion*: Right of succession to an office after the death of its occupant.

138-9. *pawned . . . government*: i.e. someone who has had to pawn his income from rental properties is rescued by being given a lucrative government office.

142. *job*: Public office exploited for personal advantage; in 1732 the directors of the Charitable Corporation, intended to lend money to the poor, were convicted of embezzlement.

144. *turnpikes*: Toll roads, then held in private hands. *cit*: See Horace, Epistle, I, i, 89n. *clown*: See 'Essay on Criticism', 321n.

146. *chuck*: Play at chuck-farthing, a boys' coin-tossing game. *vole*: Win all the tricks at cards.

147. *excising courtier*: Member of the court authorized to collect a tax on some activity.

151. *whited wall*: Masked by cosmetics; cf. the Scribes and Pharisees likened by Christ to 'whitened sepulchres' (Matthew 23:27).

152. *Woodward's patients*: Woodward was fond of administering emetics to his patients.

154. *tops*: 'top: to outgo; to surpass' (*Dictionary*).

155. *Gazettes and Post Boys*: Popular newspapers.

156. *big wife*: Pregnant wife, provoked to vomit ('cast' (157)) by disgusting foods.

159. *Great Man*: A common satirists' epithet for Sir Robert Walpole, whose administration was notorious for accepting bribes.

160. *entailed*: Legally settled on an individual and his descendants.

163-5. *wars thrive ill . . . port*: Walpole's opponents charged that his reluctance to wage war abetted the growth of French power, and that he was culpably ignoring both the seizure of English merchant ships by the Spanish and the failure of the French to honour a treaty by which the fortifications of Dunkirk should have been demolished.

166. *Circe's guests*: Odysseus' mariners, transformed into pigs by her magic (*Odyssey*, X).

168. *subject*: Of the king.

171. *pox*: Venereal disease, not curable then.

173. *ope*: Open.

174. *nice*: Delicate.

175. *just a-tilt*: i.e. a barrel full of lies is tilting and about to spill over. *Minister*: Cabinet member.

177. *Umbra*: See 'Essay on Man', IV, 278n.

178. *Fannius*: Lord John Hervey: See 'Arbuthnot', Advertisement note.

183. *actions*: Legal actions.

194. *becomes*: Suits, is becoming to.

199. *serving-man*: Manservant, here used ironically for a noble but sycophantic courtier.

203. *ball*: The globe.

206. *a court in wax*: 'a famous show of the court of France in waxwork' (Pope's note).

209. *gewgaws*: Showy baubles.

213. *Fig's . . . felons*: 'Fig's, a prize-fighter's academy, where the young nobility received instruction in those days; White's was a noted gaming-house. It was also customary for the nobility and gentry to visit the condemned criminals in Newgate' (Pope's note).

217. *fair fields*: Land sold off to pay for finery.

219. *King Lear*: Cast-off aristocratic clothing was given or sold to actors, for instance, performing in Shakespeare's play.

227. *cochine'l*: Cochineal, a South American insect used to make red dye.

229. *vessel*: With a pun on woman as 'the weaker vessel' (1 Peter 3:7).

230. *Top-gallant*: The highest sails on a ship, with a pun on the courtier as a 'gallant'.

231. *striking sail*: Lowering sails in acknowledgement of defeat in battle.

233. *Sir Fopling*: See 'Rape of the Lock', V, 63n.

236. *Heraclitus*: Greek 'weeping philosopher', who would nevertheless have been provoked to laughter by Fopling and by Courtin (generic name for any court lady).

238. *Presence*: The presence chamber 'in which a great person receives company' (*Dictionary*).

239. *Mahound*: Muhammad. *pagod*: Temple of an idol in India.

240. *Durer's rules*: Albrecht Dürer wrote a *Treatise on Human Proportion*.

243–5. *venial sins . . . a hole*: i.e. they regard their actual sins as trivial (as tiny as an atom, not worth a straw), but are horrified by a hole in their clothing.

246. *one . . . less*: i.e. one less pound of powder.

249. *the fair*: Fair ladies.

251. *band*: Clergyman's collar.

252. *Sharon*: The 'rose of Sharon' in Song of Solomon 2:1.

253. *impertinent*: Inappropriate, not pertinent.

255. *protest*: Declare, with a casual invocation of God ('Jesu! Jesu!' (257)).

262. *bullet*: Unclear ('solid as a bullet'?). *buff*: Like brownish leather.

264. *fore-right*: Directly ahead.

267. *Herod's hang-dogs*: The ruffianly soldiers who crucified Christ.

268. *breeding woman's curse*: Frightening sights were thought to provoke miscarriages.

271. *licensed fool*: Medieval jester, who was permitted to speak freely.

274. *hung with deadly sins*: At Hampton Court Palace, 'the room hung with tapestry, now very ancient, representing the Seven Deadly Sins' (Pope's note). For the sins, see 'Essay on Man', II, 187–94n.

276. *Ascapart*: 'a giant famous in romances' (Pope's note).

277. *quoits*: Game similar to horseshoes in which metal rings are pitched at a stake. *Temple Bar*: Massive stone gateway that spanned Fleet Street. *Charing Cross*: Stone cross (replaced in 1675 by a statue of Charles I) marking the centre of London.

282. *great rebukes endure*: i.e. great men are willing to accept rebukes.

286. *apocrypha*: Writings not included in the Protestant Bible ('holy writ' (287)), but are in the Roman Catholic version.

An Epistle to Dr Arbuthnot

This poem, Pope's subtlest self-portrait and apologia, was composed in several stages, and Samuel Johnson rightly called it 'many fragments wrought into one design' (*Life of Pope*, p. 246). John Arbuthnot, who died a month after the poem was published in January 1735, had been a distinguished physician, an occasional writer, and Pope's collaborator in the Scriblerus Club. Pope pays tribute both to Arbuthnot's professional skill in helping him to endure 'this long disease, my life', and to his genial wit as exemplary of true satire, and as contrasted with the innuendos and lies put about by Pope's enemies. The immediate incentive was the attacks by Lady Mary Wortley Montagu and Lord John Hervey that are mentioned in the 'Advertisement'; because of their high standing in society and at court, Pope found their criticism more upsetting than the routine abuse of minor writers whom he dismissed as Grub Street 'dunces'. He also had a score to settle with the late Joseph Addison, celebrated co-author of the *Spectator,* who had encouraged him in his youth but then attempted to sabotage the translation of Homer on which Pope staked his reputation and fortune; he was covertly jealous of Pope's reputation. The portraits of Hervey as Sporus and Addison as Atticus are accordingly the highlights of 'Arbuthnot'. When he was completing it in the autumn of 1734, Pope wrote to Arbuthnot, who knew that he was suffering from a terminal illness, that it would be 'the best memorial I can leave, both of my friendship to you, and of my character'. But for all its assertiveness, 'An Epistle to Dr Arbuthnot' reveals much anxiety about the shift Pope had made from solemn 'high' verse to satire and invective, when he 'stooped to truth, and moralized [my] song'.

Epigraph: 'Pay no attention to the talk of the vulgar crowd, nor place your hopes for your exploits in human rewards; for you it is fitting that virtue itself draw you on to true glory by its own attractions. Let others say what they will about you, as in any case they will' (Cicero, *De Re Publica*, VI, xxiii).

Advertisement: *persons of rank and fortune*:   Lady Mary Wortley Montagu and Lord Hervey, whose satiric attacks had been published two years previously; the *Epistle* Pope mentions was by Hervey, and the *Verses* by Hervey and Lady Mary in collaboration: See also headnote. *sentiment*: 'a striking sentence in a composition' (*Dictionary*). *vicious*: Connoting immorality as well as malice.

1.   *John*: John Serle, Pope's gardener and servant.
3.   *dog-star*: Sirius, visible in August when poetry competitions were held in ancient Rome, and believed to cause insanity.
4.   *Bedlam*: Bethlehem Hospital for the insane. *Parnassus*: See 'Essay on Criticism', 94n.; also 96 below.
8.   *grot*: See 'Eloisa and Abelard', 20n.
10. *chariot*: Carriage. *barge*: Boat on the Thames, which flowed at the bottom of Pope's lawn.
12. *Ev'n Sunday*: Debtors could not be arrested on Sundays.

13. *the Mint*: Area south of the Thames that was a refuge for debtors.

15. *a parson*: The Reverend Laurence Eusden, Poet Laureate until
his death (1730) and a notoriously heavy drinker ('bemused in'
hints unmistakably at 'Eusden').

17. *cross*: 'to thwart; to obstruct; to hinder' (*Dictionary*).

18. *engross*: 'to copy in a large hand' (*Dictionary*, citing this line).

23. *Arthur ... son*: Arthur Moore, a politician whose son, James
Moore-Smyth, was a would-be poet; see also 98n. and 'Dun-
ciad', II, 50n.

25. *Cornus*: Cuckold (from *cornu*, horn); cuckolds conventionally
wore horns.

29. *drop or nostrum*: Patent medicines.

31. *sped*: Dispatched, killed.

40. *nine years*: As advised by Horace, *Ars Poetica*, 388–9.

41–4. *Drury Lane ... friends*: The impoverished poet lives in a cheap
garret in the seedy neighbourhood of Drury Lane; he writes for
money, but gives the conventional explanation that his friends
have implored him to publish. See also 'Dunciad', I, 322n.

43. *term*: Period during which courts were in session; books were
often published then.

48. *prologue*: To be spoken at the beginning of a play; its success
would be likelier if a famous poet introduced it.

49. *Pitholeon*: 'The name taken from a foolish poet at Rhodes, who
pretended to much Greek' (Pope's note). *his Grace*: A nobleman.

50. *place*: Official appointment.

53. *Curll*: Edmund Curll: See 'Dunciad', I, 40n.

54. *journal*: Contemporary scandal-sheet. *divine*: Clergyman.

55. *sues*: 'sue: to beg; to entreat; to petition' (*Dictionary*).

61. *house*: The theatre. *'Sdeath*: 'God's death', a mild oath.

62. *interest*: Influence. *Lintot*: Bernard Lintot, publisher of many of
Pope's works, including his Homer.

66. *snacks*: Shares.

69. *Midas*: King of Phrygia, who judged Pan to be a better singer
than Apollo, and was punished with ass's ears, a secret which
was revealed (in different versions of the story) by either a ser-
vant or his queen.

74. *perks*: Thrusts impudently.

79. *Dunciad*: The first version of Pope's satire on bad writers was
published in 1728, seven years before this poem.

85. *Codrus*: Proverbially bad poet, mentioned by Virgil and Juvenal.

87. *Pit, box, and gallery*: From front to back, the three sections of a
theatre.

94. *flimsy lines*: The spiderweb, and by analogy the 'lines' of the scribbler.

96. *Parnassian*: As if from Mount Parnassus, sacred to Apollo and the Muses.

97. *Colley*: Colley Cibber, actor and minor author, named Poet Laureate in 1730, and later the anti-hero of Pope's revised 'Dunciad'.

98. *Henley*: Delivered a sermon in praise of butchers; see 'Donne', 51n. *Moore*: Moore-Smyth, a prominent Freemason; see 23n.

99. *Bavius*: Another bad poet, in Horace and Virgil.

100. *one bishop Philips*: The minor poet Ambrose Philips was secretary to the Archbishop of Armagh; also 179 and 180 and notes.

101. *Sappho*: See 'II A Lady', 24n.

103. *twice as tall*: Arbuthnot is imagined as alluding to Pope's diminutive height.

106. *slaver*: Saliva.

111. *Grub Street*: 'originally the name of a street in Moorfields in London, much inhabited by writers of small histories, dictionaries, and temporary poems; whence any mean production is called *grubstreet*' (*Dictionary*).

113. *prints my letters*: Pope secretly connived at the supposedly unauthorized publication of his letters by Curll in 1726.

114. *Subscribe*: Expensive editions were funded by selling advance subscriptions.

116. *cough ... short*: Horace referred to his cough and his small size.

117. *Ammon's great son*: See 'Essay on Criticism', 376n.

118. *Ovid's nose*: Ovid's full name was Publius Ovidius Naso.

121. *languishing in bed*: Pope was often bedridden with his chronic illness.

122. *Maro*: Virgil, whose full name was Publius Vergilius Maro.

131. *not wife*: It was deeply disappointing to Pope that his physical condition made marriage unlikely.

133. *second*: 'to support, to assist' (*Dictionary*).

134. *teach ... to bear*: i.e. teach me to endure the existence you have preserved.

135–41. *Granville ... Walsh ... Garth*: 'persons with whom [the author] was conversant (and he adds beloved) at 16 or 17 years of age' (Pope's note). *Congreve*: The dramatist William Congreve. *Swift*: Pope's close friend Jonathan Swift. See 'Windsor Forest', 5n., and 'Essay on Criticism', 729n. and 619n., respectively. *Talbot, Somers, Sheffield*: Statesmen and patrons. *Rochester*: Francis Atterbury, Bishop of Rochester; see 355n.

and 'Dunciad', IV, 22n. *St John*: Another close friend, the politician and writer Henry St John, Viscount Bolingbroke; see also Horace, Satire, II, i, 127n.

146. *Burnets, Oldmixons . . . Cooks*: 'authors of secret and scandalous history' (Pope's note).

149. *Fanny*: One of Pope's names for Hervey, adapted from 'Fannius', a feeble Roman poet known only because Horace mentioned him with contempt (Satire, I, iv).

150. *A painted . . . stream*: As Pope remarks in a note, he has deliberately borrowed a line from Addison's poem 'A Letter from Italy' (1704), substituting 'painted mistress' for 'painted meadow'. Pope's implication is that nobody took offence at his poems when they celebrated a lady putting on make-up ('Rape of the Lock') or a pastoral stream ('Windsor Forest').

151–3. *Gildon . . . Dennis*: Charles Gildon and John Dennis, critics who had abused Pope. For Dennis, see 'Essay on Criticism', 270n.; see also 371 and note below.

157. *come abroad*: i.e. show himself.

158. *kissed the rod*: Proverbial for willingly accepting punishment.

161. *points*: Punctuation.

163. *laurel*: Traditional reward for poetic prowess.

164. *Bentley*: See Horace, Epistle, II, i, 104n. *Tibbalds*: Shakespearean editor Lewis Theobald, who criticized Pope's edition of Shakespeare and became the anti-hero of the original 'Dunciad'; see also its headnote and I, 133n.

165. *wight*: See 'Donne', 38n. *scans*: Establishes poetic metre by rote rules.

173. *Were others angry*: i.e. if others were angry.

177. *casting-weight*: That which turns the scale.

179. *pilfered pastorals*: Pope accused Ambrose Philips of plagiarizing parts of his pastoral poems.

180. *Persian tale*: Persian Tales was the title of a collection of translations by Philips. *half a crown*: A very modest payment.

183. *wanting*: Lacking, needy.

187. *fustian*: 'swelling; unnaturally pompous; ridiculously tumid; used of style' (*Dictionary*); see also 'Preface to *Iliad*', note 16.

189. *My modest satire bade translate*: Pope's satire showed other poets that they should stick to translation, since their attempts at original works were so bad.

190. *Tate*: Nahum Tate, Poet Laureate at the end of the seventeenth century, and notorious for his adaptation of *King Lear* with a happy ending.

197. *fond . . . alone*: i.e. fond of ruling all alone.
198. *the Turk*: Sultans were believed to have their close relatives murdered in order to forestall rebellion.
209. *Cato*: Roman patriot celebrated in Addison's tragedy *Cato*. See Pope's 'Prologue' to the play, 23 and note.
211. *templars*: Law students, in a London site known as the Temple after its former religious status. See also Horace, Epistle, II, ii, 127n.
214. *Atticus*: See 'Windsor Forest', 258n. (with an obvious reference here to Addison's name).
215. *rubric*: Red letters on a book's title-page.
216. *claps*: Posters 'clapped', or hung, on posts outside a bookseller's shop.
217. *hawkers's*: Street peddlers.
222. *birthday song*: The main obligation of the Poet Laureate was to write birthday and New Year odes for the monarch, who is imagined here as ignoring them.
223. *witlings*: See 'Essay on Criticism', 40n.
225. *daggled*: 'to daggle: to be in the mire; to run through wet or dirt' (*Dictionary*, citing this line).
228. *orange*: Commonly sold in theatres.
230. *Bufo*: Toad (Latin), used here to suggest a complacent patron. *Castalian*: Spring below the twin peaks of Mount Parnassus (the 'forkèd hill' (231)).
232. *puffed by ev'ry quill*: Given exaggerated praise by every quill pen.
236. *Pindar*: Greek lyric poet; the allusion 'ridicules the affectation of antiquaries who frequently exhibit the headless trunks and terms of statues for Plato, Homer, Pindar, etc.' (Pope's note).
239. *seat*: Country seat, estate.
243. *dry rehearsal*: Recitation, 'dry' because boring, and also because no port is offered.
244. *paid in kind*: He disappoints them by repaying them not with money but with poems of his own.
248. *helped to bury*: 'Mr Dryden, after having lived in exigencies, had a magnificent funeral bestowed upon him by the contribution of several persons of quality' (Pope's note).
249. *grey goose quill*: Favoured for making pens.
258. *tell it on his tomb*: Pope contributed the epitaph for John Gay's monument in Westminster Abbey, which begins: 'Of manners gentle, of affections mild; / In wit, a man; simplicity, a child; / With native humour temp'ring virtuous rage, / Formed to delight at once and lash the age.' See also 'Epistle to T. Blount', 47n.

260. *Queensberry*: During his final years Gay lived with the Duke and Duchess of Queensberry, who commissioned his monument in Westminster Abbey.

262. '*To live . . . do*': Pope quotes from *Of Prudence*, by John Denham.

276. *Balbus*: A Roman lawyer.

279. *for mine . . . mistakes*: Poems, including Pope's, often appeared anonymously at first, and he was accustomed to having others' bad verses attributed to him.

280. *Sir Will*: Sir William Yonge, Whig politician regarded as sycophantic toward Walpole. *Bubo*: See 'IV Burlington', 20n.

282. *coxcomb*: See 'Essay on Criticism', 27n.

290. *copies out*: i.e. plagiarizes.

296. *injured, to defend*: i.e. to defend you when you've been injured.

300. *Cannons*: See 'I Cobham', 54 and note and 'IV Burlington', 99 and note.

305. *Sporus*: Handsome young slave whom Nero had castrated and then married. Pope's target is Hervey; 'painted' (310) refers to his use of cosmetics.

306. *asses' milk*: Taken as a tonic by invalids, including Hervey and Pope.

308. *wheel*: 'an instrument on which criminals are tortured' (*Dictionary*).

318. *prompter*: The prime minister, Robert Walpole. *puppet*: Hervey.

319. *Eve*: Hervey's confidante Queen Caroline. *familiar toad*: 'familiar: a demon supposed to attend at call' (*Dictionary*), such as a witch's cat; in Book IV of *Paradise Lost* Satan lurks in the form of a toad at Eve's ear.

324. *master . . . miss*: Referring to Hervey's equivocal sexuality.

328. *at the board*: At table.

330. *rabbins*: Rabbis.

332. *parts*: Abilities.

343. *stood*: Withstood.

349. *The blow unfelt*: There was a false claim that Pope had been assaulted in 1728.

351. *trash*: 'profane Psalms, court poems, and many libelous things in his name, printed by Curll, etc.' (Pope's note).

353. *the pictured shape*: Caricaturists mocked Pope's deformity by picturing him as an ape.

355. *friend in exile*: Bishop Atterbury, to whom Pope remained loyal when he was accused of conspiring to restore the Stuart monarchy and then exiled to France. See also 'Dunciad', IV, 22n.

356. *still*: 'always; ever; continually' (*Dictionary*).

363. *Japhet*: Japhet Crook: See 'III Bathurst', 86n.

365. *Knight of the post*: Someone paid to give false evidence. *of the shire*: Member of Parliament elected to represent a county.

367. *lose his own*: In flagrant cases the pillory could be accompanied by cutting off the offender's ears.

369. *bit*: Tricked, cheated.

371. *friend to his distress*: When Dennis fell into poverty, Pope helped to organize a theatrical benefit performance for him.

375. *Three thousand suns*: i.e. more than ten years, with an allusion to 'Let not the sun go down upon your wrath' (Ephesians 4:26). *Welsted's lie*: Leonard Welsted, a minor poet and translator, who frequently attacked Pope; in a long footnote Pope detailed some of his lies.

378–9. *Budgell . . . will*: Another critic of Pope, suspected of having forged a will in his own favour; see also 'Donne', 51n.

380. *two Curlls*: i.e. Edmund Curll and Hervey.

383. *fool*: 'Whosoever shall say, Thou fool, shall be in danger of hell fire' (Matthew 5:22).

391. *Bestia*: Roman consul who accepted bribes, possibly alluding to the Duke of Marlborough.

396. *suits*: Lawsuits.

397. *oath*: Catholics who refused to take an oath of loyalty lost various rights; for Pope's father to have sworn the oath would have been 'a lie'.

405. *Who sprung . . . than I*: Imitated from the final line of Horace, Satire, I, iii.

410. *lenient*: 'softening, mitigating' (*Dictionary*).

412. *Explore*: Find by searching for.

415. *preserve my friend*: As Pope knew, Arbuthnot's illness was terminal; he died soon after the poem was published.

417. *served a queen*: Arbuthnot had been Queen Anne's physician.

[Imitations of Horace]

During the 1730s Pope became increasingly interested in a genre that had been popular ever since the previous century, the free adaptation of classical poems to modern British circumstances, with the original Latin text printed on facing pages (as it is in vol. IV of the Twickenham edition) for the enjoyment of readers who could appreciate the substitution of modern parallels for ancient names and events. The parallels are frequently ironic, above all in 'To Augustus', Pope's imitation of

Satire, II, i, in which the dull and philistine George II – christened, by happy coincidence, George Augustus – is implicitly contrasted with the great emperor Augustus to whom the Horatian original was addressed. In these poems Pope extended the conversational style and topical allusiveness of 'An Epistle to Dr Arbuthnot', and developed a unique blend of plain speaking, satiric innuendo, and social commentary.

In all, Pope imitated four of the eighteen Satires of Horace and five of the twenty-two Epistles. In actuality, the two categories are not really very different, since satire in the classical context derived from the word *satura*, a mixed dish or medley, and did not need to be full of ridicule and invective throughout. Modern editions usually print these poems in order of publication, interspersed with other poems from the same period, but there is no real reason to do so, since the two satires given here came out within a year of each other in 1733–4, and the three epistles likewise in 1737–8.

In addition to the conversational poems, Pope imitated two of Horace's Odes, with results that perhaps show that the lyric mode was less suited to his gifts. Ode, IV, i, first published in 1737, follows the Horatian original quite closely; IV, ix, is a fragment published after his death, and is much looser and imitates only four of the original thirteen stanzas (1–3, 7). Pope's lengthy titles (e.g. 'The First Satire of the Second Book of Horace') have been shortened (Satire, II, i).

Satire, II, i

Dedication: *Mr Fortescue*: William Fortescue held the high judiciary post of Master of the Rolls, and Pope often consulted him on legal matters; in this dialogue he is the Friend (*Fr.*), while Pope or Poet is *P*.

3.   *Peter*: Peter Walter: See 'III Bathurst', 20n.; also 40, 89 and note below. *complaisant*: 'civil; desirous to please' (*Dictionary*).

4.   *Chartres*: See 'Essay on Man', IV, 130n.

6.   *Lord Fanny*: Lord John Hervey: see 'Arbuthnot', Advertisement note and 149 and note.

15.   *for your*: i.e. to save your.

18.   *Lettuce*: Believed to inhibit sexual desire. *cowslip wine*: A soporific. *probatum est*: 'it has been proved' (i.e. tested and shown to be an effective remedy).

19.   *Celsus*: Roman medical writer, used here as a name for any physician.

20.   *Hartshorn*: Drug made from the antlers of deer (harts).

21.   *Caesar*: Ironic term for George II (but in Horace's original, a genuine compliment to the Emperor Augustus).

22. *bays*: The laurel crown of poetic excellence; hence, the title of the Poet Laureate.

23. *Sir Richard*: Blackmore: see 'Essay on Criticism', 463n.

24. *Brunswick*: George II was a descendant of the House of Brunswick in Germany.

27–8. *Budgell . . . falling horse*: Eustace Budgell, author of a poem celebrating a battle in which the king's horse was shot from under him; see also 'Donne', 51n.

30. *Carolina*: Queen Caroline, or possibly her daughter of the same name.

31. *Amelia*: Another royal daughter. *the Nine*: The Muses.

33. *nicer*: More discriminating.

34. *twice a year*: See 'Arbuthnot', 222n.

37. *Cibber*: See 'Arbuthnot', 97n.

38. *blaspheme quadrille*: Speak disparagingly of the fashionable card game.

42. *Timon . . . Balaam*: Satirized in 'IV Burlington', 99 and note, and 'III Bathurst', 342 and note. A hundred of them 'smart' because they fear that the satire is directed at them personally.

44. *Bond*: See 'III Bathurst', 100 and note: *Harpax*: Also in 'III Bathurst', 91 and note.

46. *Scarsdale*: The Earl of Scarsdale, a well-known toper. *Darty*: Charles Dartineuf, an epicure.

47. *Ridotta*: A frivolous society lady (from Italian *ridotto*, a public entertainment with music and dancing).

48. *lustres*: Glass pendants attached to chandeliers, 'doubling' because Ridotta is intoxicated and seeing double.

49. *Fox*: Stephen Fox, a Member of Parliament (called 'the senate' by analogy with Rome). *Hockley Hole*: (Also known as Hockley-in-the-Hole), site of bear-baiting, gambling, and other crude entertainments.

52. *Shippen*: William Shippen, Tory leader distinguished for his honesty and frankness. *Montaigne*: Michel de Montaigne chose provincial retirement as a refuge from the religious wars of his day; see also 'I Cobham', 87n.

60. *the next*: i.e. the next age.

66. *Erasmus*: See 'Essay on Criticism', 693n.; he was noted for taking a middle road ('moderation' (67)) in the controversies of the day.

70. *tilt*: Like a jousting knight with a lance.

71. *Hectors*: 'hector: a bully; a blustering, turbulent, pervicacious, noisy fellow' (*Dictionary*).

72. *supercargoes*: 'supercargo: an officer in the ship whose business is to manage the trade'. *sharpers*: 'sharper: a tricking fellow; a petty thief; a rascal' (*Dictionary*, citing both of these). *directors*: Heads of speculative investment companies, such as the notorious South Sea Company.

73. *Save but our army*: The advisability of maintaining a standing army was much debated; it was widely regarded as expensive and as a threat to liberty. See also 'Dunciad', I, 316n.

75. *Fleury*: André de Fleury, adviser to Louis XV of France, committed to a policy of peace.

80. *burden*: Refrain.

81. *Delia*: Possibly George II's mistress, Mary Howard.

82. *Page*: Sir Francis Page, a judge notorious for brutality and insulting language; see also 'Dunciad', IV, 30n.

83. *Sappho*: See 'II A Lady', 24n.

84. *Poxed*: Infected with venereal disease (with a sarcastic glance at Lady Mary's campaign to promote inoculation against smallpox).

88. *pug*: Pet name for a dog.

89. *Walters*: The plural brings out the pun on drinking water.

92. *or well or ill at court*: Whether or not well regarded at court.

97. *darkened room*: In a madhouse.

98. *whitened wall*: In a jail, where the prisoner lacks pen and paper but can scratch on the wall with a meat skewer.

99. *durance*: Imprisonment. *Bedlam*: Bethlehem Hospital for the insane. *the Mint*: An area south of the Thames that was a refuge for debtors. See also 'Arbuthnot', 4 and 13.

100. *Lee*: Nathaniel Lee, Restoration playwright who was committed to Bethlehem Hospital. *Budgell*: He went mad and drowned himself.

103. *Plums*: See 'III Bathurst', 122n. *Shylock*: See 'I Cobham', 55n.

104. *club their testers*: Contribute their sixpences.

106. *Brand the bold front*: Brand the forehead, as was sometimes done to criminals.

107. *gamester*: Gambler. *car*: Carriage.

108. *star*: Emblem of knighthood.

111. *Boileau*: He did not hesitate to satirize court figures even though the autocratic Louis XIV had appointed him royal historiographer; see also 'Essay on Criticism', 714 and note.

113. *pimp and friar*: In Dryden's play *The Spanish Friar*, which satirizes priests; Pope claims that it gave no offence to the crypto-Catholic Charles II and his openly Catholic brother James II (114), under

both of whom Dryden was Poet Laureate (but James did ban the play).

116. *Unplaced, unpensioned*: As a Catholic, Pope could not hold an official post or receive (as other writers often did) a government pension.

117. *gen'rous*: 'noble of mind; magnanimous; open of heart' (*Dictionary*).

121. *To* VIRTUE ... FRIEND: Directly translated from Horace's original, *Uni aequus virtuti atque ejus amicis.*

124. *grotto*: See 'Eloisa to Abelard', 20n.

127. *St John*: Henry St John (pronounced 'Sinjin'), Lord Bolingbroke, 'out of place' (126) ever since the fall of the Oxford–Bolingbroke ministry in 1714. *bowl*: 'a vessel to hold liquids, rather wide than deep; distinguished from a cup, which is rather deep than wide' (*Dictionary*).

129. *he, whose lightning*: The Earl of Peterborough, victor in battle in Spain three decades earlier.

130. *quincunx*: Four trees planted in a square around a fifth, 'when viewed by an angle of the square or parallelogram, presents equal or parallel alleys' (*Dictionary*).

133. *own*: Acknowledge.

136. *heats*: Quarrels.

137. *who want*: Those who are in want.

140. *mob*: '(contracted from *mobile*, Latin) the crowd; a tumultuous rout' (*Dictionary*).

142. *my counsel*: Fortescue, in his capacity as lawyer.

145. *Richard*: Richard III, in whose reign a poet was hanged for satirizing the king and his counselors.

147–8. *quart ... Eliz.*: Legal abbreviations for laws passed during the reigns of Edward VI and Elizabeth I.

153. *Sir Robert*: Walpole, the prime minister, who is imagined as tolerant of Pope's writings.

Satire, II, ii

Dedication: Mr Bethel: Hugh Bethel: See 'Essay on Man', IV, 126n.

8.   *mantling*: Foaming, sparkling.

9.   *schools*: Of academic philosophy.

13. *strolled*: 'stroll: to wander; to ramble; to rove' (*Dictionary*, citing this line).

16. *meat*: Food in general.

17. *doubt*: Suspect. *curious*: 'difficult to please; solicitous of perfection' (*Dictionary*).

19.   *hens of Guinea*: Small guinea fowl were considered delicacies.
20.   *Except*: Unless.
23.   *turbots*: Fish that could weigh as much as forty pounds.
25.   *Oldfield*: Identified by Pope's executor Warburton as 'an eminent glutton'. *harpy*: Rapacious mythical monster.
31.   *treat*: Feast.
37–8.   *robin-redbreast . . . martin*: Birds that were thought to bring bad luck if killed, but apparently were now ('of late') being eaten out of sheer perversity.
39.   *beccaficos*: Small birds much prized in Italy. *dear*: Expensive.
42.   *Bedford Head*: Notable eating-house.
45.   *pother*: 'bustle; tumult; flutter' (*Dictionary*, citing this line).
49.   *Avidien or his wife*: The name, implying a miser, comes from the Horatian original; Pope had in mind Edward Montagu and his wife Lady Mary.
51.   *presented*: Given them as presents.
56.   *their son*: The Montagus' ne'er-do-well son was a traveller, but didn't drown; the implication is that they would not have been sorry if he had.
61.   *knows to*: Knows how to.
64–5.   *Albutius . . . Naevius*: Names from the Horatian original.
72.   *intestine*: Civil war, with a pun on bodily intestines.
75.   *worshipful*: Honorific title for magistrates and aldermen.
76.   *City*: The eastern section of London known by this name, centre of finance and commerce.
78.   *clay*: The material body.
80.   *divines*: Clergymen.
84.   *coming*: Forthcoming.
85.   *exceed, some holy time*: Permit ourselves some excess on (religious) holidays.
88.   *And more*: i.e. and even more.
89.   *cordial*: A medicine that stimulates the heart.
94.   *ween*: Think (archaic in Pope's time).
98.   *coxcomb-pies*: Evidently pies filled with the actual rooster combs. *coxcomb*: See 'Essay on Criticism', 27n.
101.   *'faith*: Short for 'in faith'. *Lord Fanny*: Lord John Hervey: see 'Arbuthnot', Advertisement note and 149 and note.
105.   *pelf*: Riches.
106.   *trustees*: Persons in whom one puts one's trust.
109.   *buy a rope*: i.e. to hang oneself with.
119.   *new-built churches*: Fifty new churches had recently been built in London.

120. *build bridges*: London Bridge was the only one across the Thames in London, but there were plans for more. *Whitehall*: See 'Windsor Forest', 380n.

122. *Marlborough*: British commander in the wars against Louis XIV, notorious for his avarice.

123. *Who thinks*: i.e. whoever thinks.

124. *Prepares a dreadful jest*: He will inadvertently become a jest or laughingstock.

127. *preventing*: Anticipating, cautionary.

131. *equal*: 'even, uniform' (*Dictionary*).

133. *South Sea days*: When Pope and others dreamed of getting rich through investing in the South Sea Company; see also 'III Bathurst', 103n.

134. *excised*: Subjected to taxation on commodities (Walpole's excise taxes were widely resented).

136. *five acres*: The grounds of the villa Pope rented at Twickenham.

137. *piddle*: 'to trifle' (*Dictionary*).

139. *out of play*: No longer in the game, i.e. out of office.

140. *bell*: Doorbell.

141. *boards*: Dining table.

142. *gudgeons*: Small river fish.

143. *Hounslow Heath . . . Bansted Down*: Rural areas near London.

147. *standard*: A tree allowed to grow to its full height. *espalier*: See 'IV Burlington', 8on.

148. *The devil is in you*: A casual expression, meaning 'there's something wrong with you'.

149. *have place*: Take first place (in the toasts).

152. *double taxed*: Roman Catholic estates were subject to double taxation.

154. *standing armies*: See Horace, Satire, II, i, 73n.

159. *Homer's rule*: As translated by Pope: 'True friendship's laws are by this rule expressed: / Welcome the coming, speed the parting guest' (*Odyssey*, XV, 83–4).

166. *Vernon*: Thomas Vernon, from whose widow Pope leased the Twickenham property.

168. *Walter*: Peter Walter: see 'III Bathurst', 2on.

170. *jointure*: Sum of money settled upon a wife in the event that she outlived her husband (the rest of their property going legally to their heirs).

172. *Chanc'ry*: The court that heard property cases ('equity' (171)), and was notoriously slow to reach judgement.

176. *a booby lord*: Viscount Grimston, a would-be poet and owner of the estate that had once been Francis Bacon's.

177. *Helmsley*: Country estate of the Duke of Buckingham; in Pope's day the property of a banker.

178. *scriv'ner*: Moneylender. *City knight*: A man who had achieved knighthood after success in commerce.

Epistle, I, i

1. *St John*: Bolingbroke: See 'Arbuthnot', 135–41n.

2. *bound*: 'to limit; to terminate' (*Dictionary*).

3. *sabbath*: Pope seems to have been thinking of his age, 49 (7 times 7).

5. *my age*: Old age, final years.

6. *Cibber*: Colley Cibber, still Poet Laureate, but retired from acting; see also 'Arbuthnot', 97n.

10. *ev'n in Brunswick's cause*: Indicating ironically that the generals are not eager to die fighting on the Continent for George II's German relatives.

14. *Pegasus*: Winged horse of poetic inspiration.

16. *Blackmore ... horse*: Sir Richard Blackmore's epic poems move as ponderously as the docile mount of the Lord Mayor, far different from Pegasus; the line itself 'limps' with awkward metre; see also 'Essay on Criticism', 463n.

23. *doctors*: Learned men.

24. *sect*: Coterie (Pope was always a loyal Roman Catholic).

26. *Montaigne ... Locke*: For Michel de Montaigne, see 'I Cobham', 87n.; John Locke, the British popularizer of empiricist philosophy, widely read and admired in Pope's time; see also 'Dunciad', IV, 196 and note.

27. *Patriot*: See 'III Bathurst', 139n.

29. *Lyttelton*: George Lyttelton, a nobleman, opposition politician highly critical of Walpole, secretary to the Prince of Wales, and friend of Pope's. *her*: The state's.

31. *Aristippus*: Horace said that for the Greek philosopher Aristippus 'every state and circumstance of life was fitting' (Epistle, I, xvii, 23). *St Paul*: 'I am made all things to all men' (1 Corinthians 9:22).

32. *candour*: 'sweetness of temper; purity of mind; openness' (*Dictionary*).

33. *my native moderation*: St Paul wrote: 'Let your moderation be known unto all men' (Philippians 4:5).

38. *for twenty-one*: The age of attaining his majority.

42. *instant*: 'pressing; urgent; importunate' (*Dictionary*).
45. *can no wants endure*: i.e. they can want for nothing.
50. *lynx*: Reputed to have especially acute vision.
51. *Mead and Cheselden*: Richard Mead (see also 'IV Burlington', 10n.) and William Cheselden, physicians of high reputation.
57. *words, and spells*: Pope suggests that his verses might have magically curative powers.
60. *arrant'st*: 'arrant: bad in a high degree' (*Dictionary*).
62. *punk*: Whore.
63. *Switz*: Swiss. *High Dutch*: German (from *Deutsch*). *Low Dutch*: Dutch, from the Netherlands.
68. *figure*: 'distinguished appearance; eminence' (*Dictionary*).
69. *either India*: The East or West Indies.
76. *all that it admires*: i.e. covetously.
82. *low . . . high*: Probably implying a contrast between 'low church' Anglicanism, with its simplicity of worship, and the more ceremonial 'high church'; but St James's, Piccadilly is also much smaller than St Paul's Cathedral.
83. *quills*: Quill pens, the equipment of humble clerks.
84. *notches sticks*: Wooden tallies with which the Exchequer traditionally kept records of moneys owed.
85. *Barnard*: Sir John Barnard, much admired independent Member of Parliament for the City of London, who was critical of Walpole.
87. *harness*: Emblem of a knight in the Order of the Garter. *slave*: Because obsequious to the government.
88. *Bug*: Henry de Grey, Duke of Kent, apparently known (like a bedbug) for his smell. *Dorimant*: Sophisticated beau in Etherege's *The Man of Mode*.
89. *cit*: 'contracted from *citizen*: an inhabitant of a city, in an ill sense; a pert low townsman; a pragmatical trader' (*Dictionary*, citing this line).
90. *his Honour*: Any patrician who would be so addressed.
95. *screen*: Opposition term for Walpole, who 'screened' his supporters from investigation into their malfeasances. *brass*: Referring to Walpole's 'brazen' confidence.
100. *Cressy and Poitiers*: Sites of famous English victories over the French in the fourteenth century; 'Cressy' is more properly spelled 'Crécy'. Pope evidently pronounced 'Poitiers' to rhyme with 'peers'.
103. *place*: Official post.
105. *eunuchs*: See 'Donne', 125n.

106. *circle*: The most expensive seats, closest to the stage and to the royal box (George II was a fervent patron of opera).

108. *look . . . through*: See through shallow greatness.

110. *St James's*: Fashionable park.

112. *Schutz*: Augustus Schutz, a court finance official (not regarded by Pope as especially 'honest'). *spark*: See 'Rape of the Lock', I, 73n.

113. *palace*: St James's Palace.

114. *Reynard*: The fox in Aesop's fable.

115. *dread sir*: The lion, whose cave the fox wisely refuses to enter.

127. *cross . . . the main*: Cross the ocean to plunder provinces abroad.

128. *farm*: Have the right to collect the proceeds from taxation or, as here, the box in a church for contributions to the poor.

129. *assemblies*: Social gatherings. *stews*: Brothels.

130. *Some with fat bucks*: Making a present of venison, in the hope of getting an inheritance from an aged heirless man.

131. *chine and brawn*: The back and the buttock (normally used for cuts of meat).

138. *Sir Job*: Evidently implying the recipient of a political appointment or 'job'.

139. *Greenwich Hill*: Site on the Thames near London.

145. *spleen*: See 'Rape of the Lock', IV, 16n.

147. *snug's the word*: Colloquial for 'keep quiet'.

148. *Flavio*: Any attractive young man (from *flavus*, golden haired). *stocking*: On her wedding night a bride would toss her stocking among the guests, and whoever caught it was supposed to be the next to get married.

150. *elopes*: 'elope: to run away; to break loose; to escape from law or restraint' (*Dictionary*, citing this line).

152. *Proteus*: Sea-god who could take any shape. *Merlin*: Wizard in Arthur's court.

156. *japanner*: 'a shoeblacker' (*Dictionary*, citing this line).

157. *Discharge*: Vacate. *garrets*: Cheap lodgings high up under the roof.

158. *chaise and one*: Carriage drawn by a single horse.

159. *sculler*: Boatman, available for hire to carry people across the Thames.

162. *band*: Neck-band, formal collar.

164. *Lady Mary*: Lady Mary Wortley Montagu was notorious for slovenly dress.

165. *lawn*: See 'I Cobham', 136n. *hair-shirt*: Concealed undergarment 'made of hair, very rough and prickly, worn sometimes in mortification' (*Dictionary*).

169. *I plant*: In Pope's garden at Twickenham.

173. *Chanc'ry*: The Court of Chancery could take cases of insanity into consideration when deciding questions of property; see also 'Dunciad', II, 263n. *Hales*: The physician Richard Hales, who worked sympathetically with the mentally ill.

174. *hang your lip*: Look disapproving.

177. *guide, philosopher, and friend*: Bolingbroke, repeats 'Essay on Man', IV, 390.

179. *what he can, or none*: i.e. if he can't do it, nobody can.

181–2. *without title ... plundered*: Bolingbroke's noble honours had been revoked, and his estates confiscated.

184. *the Tower*: The Tower of London, where political prisoners, including Bolingbroke's former colleague Oxford, were incarcerated.

188. *fit of vapours*: See 'Rape of the Lock', IV, 18n.

Epistle, II, i

Advertisement: *prince*: i.e. king. *our neighbours*: The French, regarded as acquiescing in royal despotism. *Admonebat ... obsolefieri*: 'He [Augustus] admonished the praetors not to allow his name to be degraded' (Suetonius, *Life of Augustus*, 89).

DEDICATION: *Augustus*: With ironic reference to the disparity between Horace's Emperor Augustus and Pope's George II, christened George Augustus.

Epigraph: 'lest I should blush at being given a stupid gift' (from the Horatian original).

2. *the main*: The seas, especially the Spanish Main (the Caribbean), where the opposition claimed that Walpole's government was refusing to avenge attacks on British shipping.

3. *in arms*: George II led England into unpopular wars, with a punning reference to the 'arms' of a mistress with whom he had recently spent half a year in Germany.

4. *morals, arts, and laws*: Entirely ironic, since George had several mistresses, was indifferent to all arts except music, and had little involvement in governing his country.

7–8. *Edward ... Henry ... Alfred*: Edward III and Henry V, who won great victories over the French ('Gaul' (10)), and Alfred the Great, who defeated the Danes.

17. *Alcides*: Hercules, who had to accomplish twelve labours, the last of which was the conquest of death.

24. *mature the praise*: Implying that George II's praise has been very long delayed.

25. *friend of Liberty*: The opposition claimed that British liberties were being constantly eroded.

35. *dear*: Expensive, hence valued.

38. *Skelton*: Poet Laureate under Henry VIII, whose poems had been recently reprinted. *heads of houses*: Masters of Oxford or Cambridge colleges.

39. *Faery Queen*: The archaic style of Edmund Spenser's *Faerie Queene* was not universally admired.

40. *Christ's Kirk o' the Green*: Ballad attributed to both James I and James V of Scotland.

41. *Ben*: Ben Jonson.

42. *the Devil*: A favourite tavern of Jonson's.

48. *tumbling*: Acrobatic displays.

57. *wants*: Lacks. *compound*: Compromise.

62. *Courtesy of England*: A technical legal concession.

63. *made the horsetail bare*: The Roman general Sertorius illustrated the value of slow persistence by showing his soldiers that a horse's tail could be plucked bare by pulling one hair at a time.

65. *ancients*: Alluding to the Battle of the Books, in which Pope and Swift sided with those who argued for the enduring greatness of 'ancient' writers, while their opponents insisted that the 'moderns' had surpassed them.

66. *Stow*: John Stow, Elizabethan chronicler.

72. *in his own despite*: Despite his indifference to future fame.

74. *The life to come*: i.e. poetic immortality.

75. *Cowley*: Abraham Cowley, a poet popular in the previous century, but regarded in Pope's time as mannered and artificial.

77. *Forgot*: Forgotten. *Pindaric art*: In elaborate odes, modelled on those of the Greek Pindar.

84. *Beaumont ... Fletcher*: Francis Beaumont and John Fletcher, Elizabethan dramatists who often wrote as collaborators.

85. *Shadwell*: Thomas Shadwell, Restoration comic dramatist, Poet Laureate, and butt of Dryden's ridicule in 'Mac Flecknoe'; see also 'Dunciad', III, 22n. *Wycherley*: William Wycherley, also a dramatist, author of *The Country Wife* and *The Plain Dealer*; the implication is that it is absurd to apply the epithets 'hasty' to the tedious Shadwell and 'slow' to the witty Wycherley.

86. *passions*: Emotions. *Southerne ... Rowe*: Thomas Southerne

and Nicholas Rowe, tragic dramatists; in his youth Pope was friendly with both Wycherley and Rowe.

88. *Heywood*: John Heywood, Elizabethan dramatist (called 'eldest' to distinguish him from the later Thomas Heywood). *Cibber*: See 'Arbuthnot', 97n.; also 292 below.

91. *Gammer Gurton*: *Gammer Gurton's Needle*, an early English play, regarded in Pope's time as crude. *bays*: Laurel trophy for poetic achievement.

92. *Careless Husband*: Popular comedy by Cibber.

97. *affects the obsolete*: As in 39.

98. *Roman feet*: In *Arcadia* Sidney sometimes used the quantitative, rather than stressed, metres of Latin verse (scanned in segments known as poetic 'feet').

101. *quibbles*: Puns.

102. *school-divine*: Scholastic theologian.

104. *Bentley . . . hook*: In a recent edition of *Paradise Lost*, the classical scholar Richard Bentley presumptuously altered *Paradise Lost* in accordance with his own sense of what Milton must have written, and put rejected passages in parentheses which he called 'hooks', literalized by Pope here as a gardener's pruning hooks. See also 'Dunciad', II, 205 and note.

107. *either Charles*: Charles I and Charles II, whose reigns were separated by the Puritan interregnum.

108. *mob of gentlemen*: Deliberate oxymoron, since 'mob' normally referred to the common people.

109. *Sprat, Carew, Sedley*: Thomas Sprat, Thomas Carew, and Charles Sedley, minor writers of the seventeenth century.

110. *miscellanies*: Collections of verse by numerous writers.

115. *own*: Acknowledge.

119. *Avon*: The river in Shakespeare's native Stratford, for which he was known as 'the bard of Avon'.

122. *Betterton*: Thomas Betterton, distinguished tragic actor, a friend of Pope's youth.

123. *well-mouthed*: Notable for impressive delivery. *Booth*: Barton Booth, tragic actor and co-manager with Cibber of the Drury Lane theatre; he played the lead in Addison's *Cato* (334–7); also 334.

124. *names*: 'an absurd custom of several actors, to pronounce with emphasis the mere proper names of Greeks or Romans, which (as they call it) fill the mouth of the player' (Pope's note).

132. *Merlin's prophecy*: Prediction by the wizard Merlin that the Saxons would one day be driven out of England.

140. *with Charles restored*: After the Civil Wars and subsequent Puritan rule, Charles II, at the Restoration, brought a relaxed and permissive culture to England.

141. *foreign courts*: Charles and his courtiers had acquired French ideas and manners during their exile in France.

142. *'All ... loved'*: By George Granville, Lord Lansdowne: see 'Windsor Forest', 5n.

144. *Newmarket*: See 'I Cobham', 86n.

147. *marble ... grew warm*: As if sculptors at that time, like Pygmalion, could create statues that came to life.

149. *Lely*: Sir Peter Lely, fashionable portrait painter.

154. *eunuch's throat*: See 'Donne', 125n.

156. *Now calls in ... turns away*: Whereas Charles II was summoned from exile in 1660 to ascend the throne, his brother James II was ejected (on account of his Catholicism) in the Glorious Revolution of 1688. Pope may also imply the 'calling in' of the Elector of Hanover to be George I of England.

159. *prerogative*: Royal privilege or immunity from laws.

160. *noble cause*: i.e. liberty.

161–2. *knock ... up*: Wake up.

170. *City*: The financial and commercial district: the City of London.

176. *Not —'s self*: Deliberately unspecific: 'Cibber's' or 'Walpole's' would fit the metre.

182. *Ward*: Joshua Ward, quack doctor known for his medicinal 'drops'.

183. *Radcliffe*: John Radcliffe, distinguished physician whose bequest provided for medical students to study abroad.

184. *learned to dance*: i.e. needed to acquire the manners of gentlemen before they could set up practice as fashionable physicians.

185. *drove a pile*: i.e. had practical experience of pile-driving for bridge foundations.

186. *Ripley*: Thomas Ripley, a carpenter who, despite lack of training and talent, was given architectural commissions by Walpole.

195. *Flight of cashiers*: The chief financial officers of the South Sea Company fled England after its collapse.

197. *Peter*: Peter Walter: see 'III Bathurst', 20n.

206. *a foreigner*: George II was born in Germany, did not become an English citizen until he was twenty-two, and spoke English with a thick German accent.

212. *lewd*: Like Charles II, George was notorious for numerous mistresses. *unbelieving*: George's queen, Caroline, was thought to be a freethinker.

214. *Roscommon*: See 'Essay on Criticism', 725n.

216. *whiter*: 'white: pure; unblemished' (*Dictionary*, citing this line).

222. *supplied*: Supported or supplemented.

224. *a poet saved*: Swift became a hero in his native Ireland for exposing in the prose *Drapier's Letters* an English attempt to allow profiteers to debase the coinage.

226. *idiot . . . poor*: Swift set up a fund to assist the poor, and Pope was aware that his will provided for a hospital for the feeble-minded.

229. *palms*: Tributes.

230. *Hopkins and Sternhold*: John Hopkins and Thomas Sternhold, sixteenth-century authors of a popular metrical version of the Psalms; see also 236n.

231. *whom charity maintains*: In schools for poor and orphan children.

232. *pathetic strains*: Emotionally moving melodies.

236. *pope and Turk*: Hopkins and Sternhold included a verse translation of a hymn by Martin Luther with the line 'From Turk and Pope defend us, Lord'.

238. *grace*: Divine favour.

247. *bowl*: i.e. wine.

250. *alternate*: Stressed on the second syllable.

259. *warped*: 'warp: to turn aside from the true direction (*Dictionary*). *nice*: Fastidious.

266. *numbers*: Metre, versification.

267. *Waller . . . Dryden*: Edmund Waller and John Dryden, who developed the heroic couplet in English verse.

269. *energy*: 'strength of expression; force of signification; spirit; life' (*Dictionary*); this line, echoing Dryden's practice in emphatic triplets, has six stresses instead of five.

271. *splay-foot*: 'having the foot turned inward' (*Dictionary*, citing this line); alludes punningly to clumsy metrical 'feet'.

272. *correctness*: 'accuracy; exactness; freedom from faults' (*Dictionary*, citing this line).

274. *Racine . . . Corneille*: Jean Racine and Pierre Corneille, the greatest French dramatists of the seventeenth century. For Racine, see also 375n.

277. *Otway*: Seventeenth-century author of verse tragedies.

279. *scarce effaced a line*: See 'Preface to *Shakespeare*', note 13.

282. *doubt*: Are in doubt whether.

287. *Congreve*: William Congreve, author of *The Way of the World* and other Restoration comedies; suggests that even when he intends characters to be fools, he makes them witty.

288. *Farquhar*: George Farquhar, Restoration comic dramatist.
289. *Van*: Sir John Vanbrugh, comic dramatist and architect.
290–91. *Astraea . . . bed*: Aphra Behn, under the pen name Astraea, wrote 'loose' comedies filled with sexual innuendo.
292. *laws*: Of dramatic theory.
293. *Pinky*: William Penkethman, a comic actor who had to bolt down two chickens onstage in one of Cibber's plays.
305. *the pit*: 'the middle part of the theatre' (*Dictionary*).
308. *Clatt'ring their sticks*: Audiences were notoriously boisterous; here, banging their walking sticks in disapproval.
309. *bear*: Dancing bear. *Black Joke*: Popular tune used for indecent songs.
313. *heads . . . ears . . . eyes*: i.e. from thoughtful plays to operas, and then to pantomime and spectacle.
315. *scenes*: Theatrical scenery pulled back to reveal the inner stage.
317. *ermine*: Expensive fur lining the robes of peers. *gold*: In the costume of a herald, custodian of genealogy. *lawn*: See 'I Cobham', 136n.
318. *Champion*: The King's Champion, who rode fully armed into Westminster Hall at a royal coronation, and offered to fight anyone who would deny the new king's right to the throne.
319. *Old Edward's armour*: In a play depicting a coronation, armour from the Tower of London (apparently Edward III's) was borrowed for the actor playing the King's Champion.
320. *Democritus*: Known in ancient Athens as the laughing philosopher.
321. *gape*: With astonishment.
322. *so white*: Albino creatures were particular attractions.
328. *Orcas*: The northern tip of Scotland, facing the Orkney Islands.
331. *Quin . . . Oldfield*: Popular actors of Pope's day: James Quin often played heroes in plumed hats, and Anne Oldfield was noted for her elegant costumes and manner (see also 'I Cobham', 247n.).
332. *birthday suit*: Dress clothing worn at court on a monarch's birthday.
338. *rally*: 'to treat with slight contempt; to treat with satirical merriment' (*Dictionary*).
345. *pity . . . terror*: According to Aristotle's *Poetics*, the chief emotions aroused by tragedy.
347. *when he will, and where*: Thereby defying the neoclassical unities of time and place.
348. *this part*: i.e. drama.

350. *sir*: George II.

353. *mountain*: Mount Parnassus above Delphi, home of the Muses. *spring*: The Castalian Spring in a ravine at Delphi, sacred to Apollo and poetry.

355. *Merlin's cave*: Building in the royal gardens at Richmond that contained a collection of books.

356. *My liege*: 'My Lord', addressing the king.

372. *dubbed historians*: In former times the Poet Laureate would also have the duties of 'historiographer royal'.

375. *Boileau and Racine*: Nicolas Boileau (see also 'Essay on Criticism', 714n.) and the dramatist Racine, both appointed historiographers by Louis XIV.

378. *some minister*: Walpole appointed Cibber Poet Laureate.

380–81. *Charles ... Bernini*: The sculptor Giovanni Lorenzo Bernini made a bust of Charles I.

382. *Nassau ... Kneller*: William III was a prince of the Dutch House of Nassau before he and his wife Mary ascended the English throne. Sir Godfrey Kneller, portrait painter and friend, and sometime justice of the peace.

387–8. *William ... Quarles*: William III, described ironically as a 'hero' for his military campaigns, and Charles I, a 'martyr' because the Puritans beheaded him, respectively honoured Sir Richard Blackmore (see 'Essay on Criticism', 463n.) and the emblem-writer Francis Quarles (see also 'Dunciad', I, 140n.).

388. *Ben*: Ben Jonson. *Dennis*: John Dennis: see 'Essay on Criticism', 270n.

389. *'No ... bear'*: Unidentified.

394. *Maeonian*: See 'Essay on Criticism', 648n.

397. *dearly bought*: George's wars on the Continent were much resented.

400. *nodded*: Dozed off.

404. *your Majesty disdains*: Implying that George, unlike the Emperor Augustus, has no use for good poetry.

413. *'Praise ... disguise'*: From an anonymous poem *The Celebrated Beauties* (1709).

417. *Eusden, Philips, Settle*: Laurence Eusden, Ambrose Philips, and Elkanah Settle, minor poets who wrote flattering poems on the monarchy. For Eusden and Philips, see 'Arbuthnot', 15n. and 100n., respectively; for Settle, see 'Dunciad', I, 90 and note.

418. *Clothe spice, line trunks*: Since paper was handmade and expensive, unwanted books were torn apart to wrap spices and line trunks.

419. *Befringe* ... *Soho*: Pamphlets were hung outside used-book stalls near the Bedlam (Bethlehem) Hospital and in the district of Soho.

Epistle, II, ii

Epigraph: 'He will give the appearance of playing, and yet be in torment' (from the Horatian original).

1.   *Colonel*: probably Arthur Browne, a friend and neighbour of Pope's, whose estate was Abscourt (232). *Cobham*: See 'I Cobham', Dedication note.

4.   *Blois*: French town noted for the purity of its French.

5.   *clean*: 'elegant; neat; not unwieldy' (*Dictionary*).

10. *upholst'rer*: 'one who furnishes houses; one who fits up apartments with beds and furniture' (*Dictionary*).

24. *Sir Godfrey*: Kneller: See Epistle, II, i, 382n.

33. *Anna's wars*: The War of the Spanish Succession, during the reign of Queen Anne.

36. *doit*: Dutch coin of small value; pronounced 'dight'.

41. *standard*: Banner flown in battle.

51. *groat*: See 'III Bathurst', 366n.

53. *Peleus' son*: Achilles, whose wrath provokes the first episode of the *Iliad*.

56. *imported*: Was important, mattered.

57. *Maudlin*: Magdalen College, Oxford, pronounced 'Maudlin'.

58. *we knew not*: i.e. 'which we knew not'.

59–61. *our paternal cell ... all posts*: Anti-Catholic legislation, including laws against holding public office or purchasing land, impelled Pope's father to leave off trade and to move out of London.

63. *mighty William*: The warlike William III.

67. *Convict*: Convicted; stressed on the first syllable.

68. *thanks to Homer*: Pope's translation of Homer made him wealthy.

70. *Munros*: James Munro, distinguished London physician.

83. *Pindaric lays*: See Horace, Epistle, II, i, 77n.

87. *Oldfield*: See Horace, Satire, II, ii, 25n. *Dartineuf*: An epicure.

94–7. *Palace Yard ... rehearsal*: Widely separated areas of London, implying hurrying in four hours from the Palace of Westminster to the more northerly Bloomsbury Square, then back to the House of Lords in Westminster, and finally to a play rehearsal in Drury Lane.

96. *my cause comes on*: i.e. my case comes up in court.

102. *nodding*: Swaying, tottering. *pig*: See 'Dunciad', II, 281n.

104. *Guildhall's narrow pass*: An alley behind the Guildhall, the town hall of the City of London.

107. *s-r-v-nce*: 'sir-reverence', a euphemistic name for excrement. *car*: Normally short for 'chariot', but here, a dung cart to which the peer is obliged to give way.

110. *grottos*: See 'Eloisa to Abelard', 20n.; also 209 below.

112. *Blackmore*: See 'Essay on Criticism', 463n.

113. *Tooting or Earl's Court*: In Pope's day, villages near London (now within the city limits).

116. *Isis' calm retreat*: Oxford University, at the part of the Thames known as the Isis.

117. *sev'n years*: The period required for the BA plus the MA degree.

123. *town*: The fashionable section of London. *City*: The financial district.

124. *duns*: Bill collectors.

127. *The Temple*: The Inns of Court, legal societies that controlled admission to legal practice, at the site known as the Temple after its formerly religious status; see also 'Dunciad', IV, 568n. *brother sergeants*: Or 'serjeants', lawyers of the highest rank, who addressed each other as 'brother'.

130. *Exchequer*: The court with jurisdiction over revenue matters. *Rolls*: Repository of the records (originally rolled-up scrolls) of the Court of Chancery.

131. *make you split*: i.e. split your sides laughing.

132. *Murray*: William Murray: see Horace, Ode, IV, i, 9–10n.

134. *Cowper . . . Talbot*: William Cowper and Charles Talbot, recent Lords Chancellor, noted for eloquence.

137. *Tibbald*: See 'Arbuthnot', 164n. *the Nine*: The Muses.

138. *Cibber . . . ode*: As Laureate, Colley Cibber was required to produce official odes: See 'Arbuthnot', 97n.

139. *Merlin's cave*: See Horace, Epistle, II, i, 355n.

140. *Stephen*: Stephen Duck, librarian of Merlin's cave, a farm worker who became known as the 'thresher poet' and was taken up at court.

143. *Tibullus*: Roman elegiac poet.

153. *In vain . . . reject*: i.e. it is in vain that mankind reject bad poets.

155. *hold your tongue*: i.e. refrain from insincere praise.

160. *That wants . . . care*: That lacks either force, or light, or weight, in care.

161. *it*: The word.

163. *degrade*: Demote from its usual place.

168. *Bacon . . . Raleigh*: Francis Bacon and Walter Raleigh, early seventeenth-century writers and statesmen admired by Pope.

178–9. *'But ease . . . dance'*: Quoting (with variations) 'Essay on Criticism', 362–3.

180. *such the*: i.e. such be the.

184. *in primo Georgii*: 'in the first year of George I' (1714).

185. *member*: Of the House of Lords.

186. *the House was up*: The House of Lords was in adjournment. *sate*: Variant spelling of 'sat'.

190. *pasty*: Meat pie.

193. *cupped*: Bled (for medical purposes) with a cupping-glass. *purged*: Treated with cathartics.

196. *Patriot*: See 'III Bathurst', 139n.

206. *my country door*: At Pope's Twickenham villa.

208. *Hyde Park Corner*: In Pope's day, at the edge of London, where he would leave the city on his way home.

212. *the more you drink*: In consequence of a disease causing insatiable thirst, not alcohol.

215. *Confess . . . disease*: i.e. confess mental folly as easily as you admit physical disease.

218. *golden angels . . . evil*: The King's evil, a form of tuberculosis then called scrofula, was thought to be curable if the monarch touched the sufferer, who would be given a gold coin known as an angel (Queen Anne was the last monarch to do it).

219. *give . . . the devil*: i.e. dismiss it, 'the devil with it!'

226. *or wit*: Either wit.

229. *Van-muck*: Alluding to a rich merchant, Joshua Vanneck, who wanted to buy Bolingbroke's estate at an unacceptably low price.

230–31. *use can give/A property*: As in the saying, 'Possession is nine-tenths of the law.'

233. *you*: Anyone who gets the benefit of an estate's produce without having to own it.

234. *Worldly*: Thinly veiled reference to Edward Wortley Montagu, Lady Mary's husband.

240. *Heathcote*: Sir Gilbert Heathcote: see 'III Bathurst', 101n.

241. *E'sham*: The Vale of Evesham in Worcestershire, 'fat' because famous for fertility. *Lincoln Fen*: Marshy area in Lincolnshire that had been drained and put under cultivation.

244. *wights*: See 'Donne', 38n.

245. *the devil . . . Lincoln town*: Invoking a proverbial saying, 'He looks as the devil over Lincoln', referring to the devil carved on Lincoln Cathedral.

247. *perpetuity*: Bequeathing an estate in such a way that one's heirs are forbidden to sell it.

255. *park*: The grounds of a country estate. *chase*: Tract of hunting land.

257. *Cotswold hills*: Sheep-raising district in the west Midlands. *Sapperton*: Town near the Gloucestershire estate of Pope's friend Bathurst; Pope was interested in proposals (later successfully carried out) to link the two regions by water.

259. *pyramids*: Ornamental monuments in patricians' estates.

261. *downs*: Grassy upland.

269. *a face … a mind*: i.e. two persons' minds are no more alike than their faces.

273. *Townshend*: Charles, Viscount Townshend, who conducted agricultural experiments and became known as 'Turnip Townshend'. *Grosvenor*: Family with mines in Wales.

274. *Bubb*: See 'IV Burlington', 20n.

277. *Oglethorp*: General James Oglethorp, philanthropist who promoted the Georgia colony in America as a refuge for the poor.

278. *Is known … Pow'r*: i.e. the answer to that question is known only to God.

279. *genius*: 'nature; disposition' (*Dictionary*).

287. *place*: Government position.

290. *spare*: Save.

296. *wot*: Knows.

298. *make a better figure*: Be more graceful and attractive, with ironic reference to Pope's diminutive size and deformed body.

306. *no other*: No other tyrant passion.

312. *both worlds*: This world and the next.

Ode, IV, i

4. *Queen Anne*: She had died over twenty years previously; in the original Horace names a lover, Cynara.

6. *sober fifty*: In 1737, when the poem was first published, Pope was 49.

9–10. *number five … Murray*: The lawyer William Murray, later Earl of Mansfield and Lord Chief Justice, lived in his youth at No. 5, King's Bench Walk, and was an eloquent speaker in Parliament.

12. *part*: 'parts: qualities; powers; faculties; or accomplishments' (*Dictionary*).

14. *fix*: 'to make fast, firm, or stable' (*Dictionary*).

16. *stretch ... the kind*: Extend Venus' conquests over half of humankind.
20. *Chloe*: Any lovely nymph.
26. *loves*: Cupids.
27. *Grace*: As in the 'three Graces'.
33. *mutual fire*: Reciprocated passion.
35. *bowl*: Of wine.
47. *Cynthia*: See 'II A Lady', 20n. and 'Windsor Forest', 164n., 166n.

Ode, IV, ix

4.   *vulgar*: Commonplace.
7–8. *Waller ... Cowley's*: Edmund Waller and Abraham Cowley, contemporaries of Milton who still had some reputation in Pope's time.
11–12. *These ... those*: 'Sages' like Newton and 'chiefs' like Caesar, respectively.

Epilogue to the Satires

In this pair of linked poems, the first of which was originally entitled *One Thousand Seven Hundred and Thirty Eight: A Dialogue Something Like Horace*, Pope sought to confirm his high-minded motives as a satirist, and to identify his critics with the commercial wealth and Whig political corruption which he saw as destroying English civilization. According to Joseph Warton, who published an important edition of Pope in 1797, these poems 'were more diligently laboured and more frequently corrected than any of our author's composition', so that each time a supposedly final version came back from his copyist, Pope would revise it again until 'every line had been written twice over a second time'.

Dialogue I

1. *Fr.*: Pope's abbreviation for 'Friend'; 'P.' presumably stands for 'Pope', or possibly 'Poet'.
3. *correct*: 'revised or finished with exactness; free from faults' (*Dictionary*).
5. *parts*: Abilities, faculties.
7. *all from Horace*: Adapted from Satire, II, iii, 1–4.
8. *Tories called him Whig*: Pope is quoting himself (see Satire, II, i, 68), as well as adapting Horace.

10. *Peter*: Peter Walter: See 'III Bathurst', 20n.; also 121 below.

11. *nice*: 'scrupulously and minutely cautious' (*Dictionary*).

12. *Bubo*: Probably Bubb Dodington: see 'IV Burlington', 20n.

13. *Sir Billy*: Sir William Yonge: see 'Arbuthnot', 280n.; also 68 below.

14. *Blunt*: Sir John Blunt: see 'III Bathurst', 103n. *Huggins*: Warden of the Fleet Prison, condemned for cruelty and extortion.

15. *Sappho*: See 'II A Lady', 24n.

17. *waggish*: 'knavishly merry; merrily mischievous; frolicsome' (*Dictionary*).

18. *cropped our ears*: Referring to the incident that provoked the War of Jenkins' Ear in 1739: Jenkins, a British merchant ship captain, exhibited in Parliament an ear which Spanish coast guards had cut off.

20. *Augustus*: George II: see Horace, Epistle, II, i, Dedication note.

22. *screen*: See Horace, Epistle, I, i, 95n.

23. *'faith*: In faith.

26. *The Great Man*: Walpole. *groat*: See 'III Bathurst', 366n.

34. *what he thinks mankind*: Walpole was fond of saying that every man has his price.

36. *laugh out*: Laugh out loud.

39. *Jekyl*: Sir Joseph Jekyl, Whig politician who stood up against his party when he thought it in the wrong. *Old Whig*: i.e. not a supporter of the current Walpole government.

40. *wig*: Jekyl wore an old-fashioned voluminous wig.

41. *Patriot*: See 'III Bathurst', 139n.

42. *lord chamberlains*: In the Stage Licensing Act of 1737 (repealed 1968), this official was charged with censorship of new plays.

46. *His Prince*: Frederick Louis, the Prince of Wales, who had broken with his father; he never ascended the throne, since he died (1751) before George II did.

47. *Lyttelton*: George Lyttelton: see Horace, Epistle, I, i, 29n.

50. *Lord Fanny*: Lord John Hervey: see 'Arbuthnot', Advertisement note and 149 and note.

51. *Sejanus, Wolsey*: Powerful chief ministers of the Emperor Sejanus and of Henry VIII, respectively. *Fleury*: See Horace, Satire, II, i, 75n.

66. *Henley*: John Henley: see 'Donne', 51n.

67. *Favonio*: 'Favonius' is Latin for the mild west wind of springtime; here implies a flatterer.

71-2. *Fox's . . . Hervey's once again*: Henry Fox delivered a speech of condolence on the death of Queen Caroline that was thought to have been ghostwritten by Hervey, who later published his own Latin adaptation of it. *Senate*: Ironic classical name for the British Parliament.

75. *Middleton and Bland*: The theologian Conyers Middleton and the Eton headmaster Henry Bland, both distinguished Latinists. For Middleton, see also 'Dunciad', IV, 103–4n., and for Bland, see also 'Dunciad', I, 231n.

78. *the nation's sense*: i.e. universally approved.

80. *Hang the sad verse*: Mourning verses pinned to the coffin. *Carolina*: Queen Caroline.

82. *All parts ... blest*: Pope rejects claims that the queen had not received the sacraments on her deathbed, and that she died unreconciled with her son (and his friend), the Prince of Wales.

84. *gazetteer*: Journalist writing for a newspaper such as the *Gazette*.

85. *a God's*: In God's.

86. *graced*: 'grace: to adorn; to dignify; to embellish' (*Dictionary*).

92. *Selkirk ... De la Ware*: Noblemen whose probity Pope admired.

98. *nepenthe*: Drug causing forgetfulness, as in the *Odyssey*, IV, 220–21.

100. *place*: Government post.

102. *All tears ... eyes*: 'God shall wipe away all tears from their eyes' (Revelation 21:4).

104. *lose a question*: Have a parliamentary motion rejected. *job*: Government appointment exploited for private gain.

107–8. *three sov'reigns ... next*: During Pope's lifetime William, Mary, and Anne had died, succeeded by the despised George I.

113. *empty boast*: i.e. because they haven't got it.

115. *Cibber's son*: Theophilus Cibber, actor and minor writer, son of Colley Cibber.

116. *Rich*: John Rich, theatrical producer.

119. *Ward*: Probably John Ward: see 'III Bathurst', 20n.

120. *Japhet*: Japhet Crook: see 'III Bathurst', 86n. *his Grace*: Archbishop William Wake, who assisted George II in suppressing the politically inflammatory will of George I.

121. *Bond*: See 'III Bathurst', 100n.

122. *like kings*: The implication is that kings can break promises with impunity.

123. *If Blount dispatched himself*: Charles Blount, a deist who wrote freethinking essays and eventually killed himself, though from disappointment in love rather than philosophical principle.

124. *Passeran*: Italian deist who argued that suicide is not unethical, and had recently died in England.

125–6. *a printer . . . hang himself and wife*: 'a fact that happened in London a few years past. The unhappy man left behind him a paper justifying his action by the reasonings of some of these authors' (Pope's note).

128. *Vice thus abused*: By being flaunted by commoners, rather than by aristocrats who can expect to get away with it.

129. *deprecate*: 'to ask pardon for' (*Dictionary*).

130. *thunder . . . on gin*: Notoriously destructive of public health, the consumption of gin was controlled by an act of Parliament in 1736.

131. *Foster*: Popular Baptist preacher.

132. *metropolitans*: Archbishops.

133. *a Quaker's wife*: The Quakers were exceptional in permitting women to preach.

134. *Landaff*: Bishopric in Wales, whose occupant had ridiculed Pope.

135. *Allen*: Philanthropist Ralph Allen, Fielding's model a decade later for Squire Allworthy in *Tom Jones*.

144. *greatness*: A patron of high rank. *mean*: 'contemptible; despicable' (*Dictionary*).

149. *scarlet*: Commonly associated with sexual sin.

150. *carted*: Exposed humiliatingly in a cart, a punishment for prostitutes.

151. *car*: Chariot.

152. *genius*: 'the protecting or ruling power of men, places, or things' (*Dictionary*).

153. *arms*: Weapons.

154. *flag inverted*: Tories denounced Walpole for preferring peace to vindicating Britain's honour in war.

155. *foreign gold*: i.e. fortunes amassed by pillaging India and other colonies.

157. *pagod*: See 'Donne', 239n.

162. *ambition*: In the positive sense, aspiring to achieve something of value.

Dialogue II

1. *Paxton*: Nicholas Paxton, Treasury Solicitor, who tracked down and prosecuted slurs on the court and government; also 141.

5. *Thirty-nine*: Reference to the original title of Dialogue I, 'One Thousand Seven Hundred and Thirty Eight'.

6. *amain*: 'with vehemence; with vigour; fiercely; violently' (*Dictionary*).

7. *Invention*: Poetic imagination.

11. *Guthrie*: James Guthrie, the ordinary, or chaplain, of Newgate Prison, published convicts' confessions but tactfully replaced their names with dashes.

13. *sharper*: 'a tricking fellow; a petty thief; a rascal' (*Dictionary*).

14. *gen'ral*: i.e. not aimed at specific persons.

15. *souse*: 'to fall as a bird on its prey' (*Dictionary*). *the kind*: Humankind.

17. *hall*: i.e. hall of justice.

18. *rev'rend atheists*: Clergymen who are secretly unbelievers.

22. *The pois'ning dame*: If a specific woman is meant, she has not been identified.

25. *elector*: One of the small number of adult males eligible to vote for a Member of Parliament.

29. *royal harts*: If a hart (a stag over six years of age) was pursued by the king or queen and escaped, it could be declared a 'hart royal' that no one else was allowed to hunt.

30. *Admit . . . requires*: i.e. suppose we admit that the law requires that knights be spared.

31. *squires*: Gentry who rank below knights.

33. *dean*: The clergyman in charge of a cathedral, ranking below its bishop.

39. *Wild*: Jonathan Wild, a 'thief-taker' who controlled London crime until he was executed in 1725, notorious for delivering his henchmen to the law when he had no further use for them. Fielding and others satirized him as 'the Great Man', with an obvious analogy to Walpole.

40. *made a job*: Made an opportunity for private gain at government expense.

41. *drench*: Soak at a public pump.

42. *for the love of vice*: Ironically imitating 'for the love of God'.

49. *directors*: Profiteering managers of speculative institutions such as the South Sea Company. *plums*: See 'III Bathurst', 122n.

50. *ministers*: Cabinet ministers.

57. *Peter*: Peter Walter: see 'III Bathurst', 20n.

61. *Selkirk*: The Earl of Selkirk, as in Dialogue I, 92 and note. *the prince*: Of Wales.

64. *there is*: i.e. there does exist.

65. *Scarb'rough*: the Earl of Scarborough, admired for unwavering loyalty to the king.

67. *Kent*: William Kent, landscape gardener who laid out Pelham's estate at Esher (66) in Surrey. *Pelham*: Henry Pelham, supporter of Walpole.

70. *desert*: Merit, deservingness.
71–2. *Secker . . . Rundle . . . Benson*: Thomas Secker, Archbishop of Canterbury, and two other bishops. *decent*: Becoming, suitable.
71. *Manners*: 'ceremonious behavior; studied civility' (*Dictionary*).
73. *Berkeley*: George Berkeley, philosopher, and since 1734 Bishop of Cloyne in Ireland.
77. *Somers . . . Halifax*: Elderly noblemen who encouraged Pope as a young poet.
79–80. *Shrewsbury . . . Carleton . . . Stanhope*: Noblemen whose public service Pope admired.
82. *Atterbury*: See 'Arbuthnot', 355n.
84–8. *Pult'ney, Chesterfield . . . Argyle . . . Wyndham*: Leaders of the opposition to Walpole.
85. *Attic*: Classic Greek (also referred to as 'Attic salt').
87. *the field*: Battlefield.
91. *train*: Followers, dependants.
94. *lays*: Poems.
97. *beaver*: 'a hat of the best kind; so called from being made of the fur of beaver' (*Dictionary*). *glory*: 'lustre; brightness' (*Dictionary*).
99. *Man of Ross*: John Kyrle: see 'III Bathurst', 250n. *my Lord May'r*: Sir John Barnard: see Horace, Epistle, I, i, 85n.
103. *in or out*: i.e. in power or out of power.
107. *booby*: 'a dull, heavy, stupid fellow' (*Dictionary*).
108. *widow . . . of men*: i.e. every widow conventionally laments losing the best of men.
110. *stoop*: Swoop down, from falconry.
111. *number*: 'comparative multitude' (*Dictionary*).
114. *pretend*: Lay claim to.
116. *Richelieu*: French cardinal who was chief adviser to Louis XIII. *wanted*: Lacked. *Louis*: Louis XIV, who patronized Boileau.
117. *young Ammon*: Alexander the Great (see 'Essay on Criticism', 376n.) lamented having no Homer to celebrate his life.
120. *To Cato, Virgil paid*: Though enjoying the patronage of the Emperor Augustus, Virgil praised the fiercely republican Cato the Younger in the *Aeneid* (VIII, 670).
121. *mine*: i.e. my own poetic lines.
129. *Arnall*: William Arnall, a venal political journalist.
130. *Cobham*: See 'I Cobham', Dedication note. *Polwarth*: Henry Hume, Lord Polwarth, who as Lord Marchmont would have a long and distinguished political career.
131. *Lyttelton*: See Horace, Epistle, I, i, 29n.

132. *St John*: Bolingbroke: see Horace, Satire, II, i, 127n.

133. *Sir Robert*: Walpole.

135. *tyrant to his wife*: Walpole was well known to overlook his wife's infidelities.

137. *Verres*: Cruel and corrupt Roman governor of Sicily, with an allusion to Walpole. *Wolsey*: See Dialogue I, 51n.

140. *spur-galled hackney*: Cheap hired horse, bruised by being spurred, and, by implication, a hack writer who works for pay.

141. *pots*: Of ale.

142. *new-pensioned*: Given a permanent income with no duties attached. *pretend*: 'to put in a claim truly or falsely' (*Dictionary*).

143. *break my windows*: This recalls an incident when Bolingbroke and Bathurst were dining at Pope's villa and ruffians broke his windows.

147. *tools*: 'tool: a hireling; a wretch who acts at the command of another' (*Dictionary*), with a pun on 'mauling' a workman's tools.

149. *saws*: Pun on 'wise saws', sententious remarks.

150. *Turenne*: See 'Essay on Man', IV, 100n.

151. *took his pay*: Received wages from him.

152. *fellow*: 'a word of contempt: the foolish mortal; the mean wretch; the sorry rascal' (*Dictionary*).

159. *Page*: See Horace, Satire, II, i, 82n.; i.e. a brutal judge.

160. *the bard*: Bubb Dodington: see 'IV Burlington', 20n.; also Dialogue I, 12.

161. *'In pow'r . . . a friend'*: From a poem by Dodington, from the two-line 'distich' (160).

165. *gown*: Worn by the clergy, 'stained' by his disgraceful conduct.

166. *the florid youth*: Apparently Stephen Fox (see Horace, Satire, II, i, 49), but the point of the allusion is lost.

170. *House*: Of Commons.

172. *As hog to hog*: i.e. they consume each other's excrement. *Westphaly*: Westphalia in Germany, noted for its ham.

176. *mess*: 'a dish; a quantity of food' (*Dictionary*, citing this line).

183. *civet-cats*: Creatures from whose unpleasant secretions perfume was made.

187. *Pindus*: Mountain in Thessaly, home of the Muses.

192. *in*: In office.

194. *a staring reason on his brows*: i.e. the horns of a cuckold.

195. *rod*: Of punishment.

202. *coxcomb's*: See 'Essay on Criticism', 27n.

206. *own*: Acknowledge.

210. *the bar*: Law courts.

218. *Hall*: Westminster Hall, seat of justice but often 'tardy' to enforce it.

219. *stall*: 'the seat of a dignified clergyman in the choir' (*Dictionary*).

222. *the eye of day*: Sunlight, which easily shines through cobwebs.

227. *Gazette*: The government's official newspaper; accented on the first syllable. *Address*: Formal reply by the Lords or Commons to a speech by the king.

230. *Waller's wreath ... nation's scar*: Edmund Waller's elegy for Oliver Cromwell, whom Pope regarded as having wounded England in the civil wars of the seventeenth century.

231. *feather*: Boileau (see 'Essay on Criticism', 714n.) suggested in a poem that Louis XIV's white plume would shine like a star or comet to presage his enemies' defeat.

235. *opes*: Opens.

237. *Anstis ... grave*: The Herald at Arms, one of whose duties at a royal funeral was to cast broken staffs and ensigns of honour into the grave.

238. *stars*: Emblems of knightly orders. ***: The references are deliberately unclear, but 'George' and 'Fred'rick' – the king and his eldest son – would fit.

239. *Mordington*: Nobleman whose wife ran a gambling house. *Stair*: John Dalrymple, Earl of Stair, a general under Marlborough and later a distinguished ambassador to France.

240. *Hough*: John Hough, Bishop of Worcester, who defended the Anglican church against the Catholic James II. *mitre*: Bishop's ceremonial headdress.

241. *Digby*: William Digby, a friend of Pope's.

245. *grateful*: Pleasing.

247. *mean*: Low, not elevated.

249. *truth stands trembling*: With the threat of censorship mentioned at the beginning of the poem.

252. *Cause*: i.e. liberty.

The Dunciad

When the original three-book version of the 'Dunciad' appeared in 1728, no one quite knew what to make of it. It had roots in the parodic games of the Scriblerus Club, and there was plenty of precedent for ironic praise of bad writers, going back to Dryden's superb 'Mac Flecknoe' half a century before, in which the playwright Thomas Shadwell was pilloried as heir-apparent to the kingdom of Dullness. But 'Mac Flecknoe' was a couple of hundred lines long and focused on a single target; the 'Dunciad' was a thousand lines long (it eventually swelled to 1,750) and was filled to overflowing with the names of writers who were all, according to Pope, 'dunces'. Very loosely based on the *Aeneid*, in which Aeneas moves his kingdom from Troy to Latium, the poem traces the progress of the Goddess of Dullness from the commercial City of London to the fashionable West End, pausing along the way for a grotesque travesty of epic games. The hero, or rather anti-hero, is Lewis Theobald, a competent scholar who had made the mistake of criticizing Pope's edition of Shakespeare. In the following year a massive 'Dunciad Variorum' reprinted the poem with revisions and with massively detailed commentary, much of it attributed to the pedantic 'Martinus Scriblerus' whom the Scriblerians had delighted to impersonate.

Nor was Pope yet finished with the poem, for in 1742 an entirely new fourth book, loaded with footnotes and commentary, appeared under the title 'The New Dunciad'. Drawing on material once intended for the never-realized *Opus Magnum*, it now criticized cultural trends of all kinds, ranging from butterfly collecting to gourmet cooking. And surprisingly, there was a new king of Dullness, the actor-playwright and Poet Laureate Colley Cibber, who had made the mistake of publishing a pamphlet against Pope that included a humiliating anecdote about his early life. Johnson later commented, 'Unhappily the two heroes were of opposite characters, and Pope was unwilling to lose what he had already written; he has therefore depraved his poem by giving to Cibber the old books, the cold pedantry and sluggish pertinacity of Theobald' (*Life of Pope*, p. 186). Johnson, who began his career as an anonymous writer in what Pope despised as 'Grub Street', also objected to Pope's patrician contempt for 'dunces' whose crime was writing to earn a living (see headnote to 'From the *Iliad*').

In 1743 the fourth book was republished together with the other three, all of them revised yet again, as 'The Dunciad in Four Books'. This edition proved to be the last, and is the one given here, with the conventional title 'The Dunciad'. Since most of its targets were obscure in their own time and forgotten afterward, a reader will seldom learn much by knowing who they were (they are identified in the Notes as economically as possible). Pope's own notes to the poem are voluminous and prolix, and only a few can be included here. What makes the poem live is its inventiveness and wit, 'perhaps the best specimen that has yet appeared,' Johnson said, 'of personal satire ludicrously pompous' (*Life of Pope*, p. 241).

Epigraph: 'At last Phoebus Apollo arrived and stopped the serpent as it was about to bite, turning its open jaws to stone, and freezing the wide-open mouth' (Ovid, *Metamorphoses*, XI, 58, 60). The implication seems to be that just as Apollo prevented a serpent from devouring the severed head of the singer Orpheus, so Pope's poem can turn his enemies to stone even if they believe they have dealt him fatal blows.

Book the First

Argument: *City*: The financial district in London, known as 'the City'. *hastes into the midst*: Echoing Horace's advice that a narrative should begin *in medias res*, 'in the middle of things'. *revolving*: Reflecting on. *Bays*: Colley Cibber, recalling Buckingham's play *The Rehearsal* in which Dryden was satirized as the sententious playwright Bayes (alluding to the bay-leaf crown of the Poet Laureate); see also 108n. *period*: Conclusion. *Thulè*: Poem by Ambrose Philips: see 'Arbuthnot', 100n.; also 105 and 258 and note below. *Eusden*: The Reverend Laurence Eusden: see 'Arbuthnot', 15n.; also 104n. below.

2. *Smithfield Muses*: Implying that the vulgar amusements of the Smithfield meat market have invaded high society.
3. *you . . . the Great*: i.e. the aristocracy is complicit in the corruption of court and City.
6. *Dunce the second*: Recalling Dryden's 'Mac Flecknoe', in which 'Tom the second rules like Tom the first'; also, a covert hit at George II and George I.
10. *Pallas*: Pallas Athena, goddess of wisdom, born fully grown from the head of Zeus ('the Thunderer').
14. *Gross . . . grave*: i.e. heavy as her father Chaos, and solemn as her mother Night.
19–20. *thou . . . Gulliver*: Swift, to whom the 'Dunciad' is dedicated, was Dean of St Patrick's Cathedral in Dublin, and wrote satires under various personae: *The Drapier's Letters*, attacking a scheme to debase the coinage (the 'copper chains' (24)); 'Isaac Bickerstaff', mocking quack astrology; and Lemuel Gulliver, ostensible author of *Gulliver's Travels*.
21–2. *Cervantes . . . Rab'lais*: Pope believed that Cervantes's *Don Quixote* contained serious political satire, and that Rabelais' *Gargantua and Pantagruel* was a freewheeling fantasy.
25. *Boeotia*: Greek region renowned for stupidity; hence, Swift's native Ireland, which he despised for its supine subservience to English rule.
29–30. *those walls . . . Monroe*: The walls of the Bethlehem lunatic

asylum (known as 'Bedlam'), where Dr James Monroe attempted to cure patients of their 'folly'.

32. *Cibber's . . . brothers*: Cibber's father had carved statues of Melancholy and Madness at the gates of Bedlam; they were of stone, but 'brazen' suggests impudence.

36. *Emptiness*: i.e. empty, rumbling stomachs.

37. *Proteus*: Sea-god who constantly changes shape to resist capture; here, writers who keep changing pseudonyms to escape their creditors.

39. *Miscellanies*: Ephemeral collections of little pieces; accented on the second syllable.

40. *Curll*: Edmund Curll, publisher with whom Pope had long had a quarrel; far from being 'chaste', his products exploited scandal and obscenity; see also II, 3n., 71–2n. ff. *Lintot*: Bernard Lintot: see 'Arbuthnot', 62n. *rubric*: Red-letter pages hung up as publicity outside his shop.

41. *Tyburn*: Site of public hanging of criminals, memorialized after their deaths in cheap broadside ballads.

42. *Merc'ries*: 'Mercury' was a popular word in newspaper titles.

43. *Sepulchral lies*: Flattering epitaphs over church tombs (sepulchres).

44. *New Year Odes*: See 'Arbuthnot', 222n. *Grub Street*: See 'Arbuthnot', 111n.

45. *In clouded majesty*: Borrowed from the moon rising in *Paradise Lost*, IV, 607.

48. *want . . . of ears*: In extreme cases, offenders in the pillory might have their ears cut off.

50. *Who hunger . . . sake*: Echoing Matthew 5:6: 'Blessed are they which do hunger and thirst after righteousness: for they shall be filled.'

51. *glass*: Prudence was often depicted looking through a spyglass. *approaching jail*: Debtors' prison that awaits penniless writers.

52–4. *Poetic Justice . . . praise*: Poetic justice normally refers to the distribution of rewards and punishment at the end of a drama, but here it implies a preference for mercenary writing that pays for pudding (54), as against nobler writing that earns 'empty' praise.

55. *Chaos . . . deep*: Recalling the creation of 'waters dark and deep', and Chaos as 'the womb of Nature, and perhaps her grave' (*Paradise Lost*, I, 11; II, 911).

57. *genial Jacob*: The publisher Jacob Tonson; 'genial' implies

'generative' powers. *third day*: Playwrights received the box office take from a play's third performance only.

59. *quick*: Alive.

61. *Maggots*: 'maggot: whim; caprice; odd fancy' (*Dictionary*), with a pun on scavenging larvae; 'feet' (62) likewise puns on the metrical units, known as feet, into which poetic lines were scanned.

63. *clenches*: Puns.

64. *ductile*: Malleable.

74. *Zembla*: In the icy Arctic. *Barca*: In the Libyan desert.

77. *chaplets*: 'chaplet: a garland or wreath to be worn about the head' (*Dictionary*).

85. * *: Originally 'Thorold', the Lord Mayor in Theobald's day (see headnote), but no longer appropriate for Cibber.

86. *Cimon*: Athenian who won victories in battle and at sea; the Lord Mayor's celebration took place both in the streets and on the river.

90. *Settle*: Elkanah Settle, who had served as official poet of the City earlier in the century; 'one day more' implies that poems like his were extremely short-lived.

91. *Shrieves*: Sheriffs.

96. *City swans*: The City poets, whose position died out after Settle's time. *the walls*: Of the City of London.

97. *revolves*: 'revolve: to consider; to meditate on' (*Dictionary*).

98. *Heywood*: Thomas Heywood, seventeenth-century playwright and author of pageants for the City.

100. *imprest*: 'impress: to print by pressure; to stamp' (*Dictionary*). His image is stamped or 'impressed' on his offspring.

101. *Bruin . . . care*: According to an old belief, bear cubs were born shapeless and had to be licked into form. *plastic*: 'having the power to give form' (*Dictionary*).

103. *Prynne*: William Prynne, seventeenth-century Puritan controversialist. *Daniel*: The novelist Daniel Defoe, who as a Presbyterian was a Dissenter from the Church of England. Both were punished in the pillory for writings that offended the government. For Defoe, see also II, 147n.

104. *Blackmore's endless line*: See 'Essay on Criticism', 463n.; 'endless line' puns also on the line of inheritance in which Eusden is Blackmore's successor.

105. *Tate*: Nahum Tate: see 'Arbuthnot', 190n.; also 258 below.

106. *mighty mad in Dennis*: John Dennis championed poetic inspiration, which Pope interprets as actual insanity; see also 'Essay on Criticism', 270n.

108. BAYS: Ever since Buckingham's *Rehearsal* (see Argument note),

traditional name for a bad poet; here, Cibber. *monster-breeding*: Creating deformed literary works.

109. *stage and Town*: As a successful stage actor, Cibber pleased the fashionable 'Town'; by implication, it was a mistake for him to turn author.

110. *coxcomb*: See 'Essay on Criticism', 27n.

111. *transport*: 'rapture; ecstasy' (*Dictionary*).

112. *pertness*: 'brisk folly; sauciness; petulance' (*Dictionary*, citing this line).

113. *ill run at play*: Bad luck with dice.

114. *Blanked his bold visage*: Erased his usually confident expression.

115. *Swearing*: Cibber was known for constant swearing. *sate*: Sat.

118. *a vast profound*: Milton calls the chaos that preceded Creation 'the vast profundity' (*Paradise Lost*, VII, 229).

122. *future . . . Play*: Struggling to compose the odes required of the Laureate, Cibber abandoned unfinished plays.

126. *sooterkins*: 'sooterkin: a kind of false birth fabled to be produced by the Dutch women from sitting over their stoves' (*Dictionary*); thus, Cibber's 'dull heat' produces literary abortions.

128. *stole*: Cibber frequently adapted material from old plays.

131. *Fletcher's half-eat scenes*: Plays by the Jacobean dramatist John Fletcher, left in tatters by Cibber's borrowings.

132. *frippery*: 'old clothes; tattered rags' (*Dictionary*). *crucified Molière*: In *The Non-Juror*, Cibber's adaptation of *Tartuffe*.

133. *of Tibbald sore*: Theobald called his book *Shakespeare Restored*, claiming to recover correct readings, but Pope implies that Shakespeare suffered injury.

134. *blotted*: Erased, rewrote; see 'Preface to *Shakespeare*', note 13.

138. *red and gold*: In expensive bindings, just as parents might dress their children in finery.

140. *Quarles*: Francis Quarles, whose aphoristic *Emblems* were illustrated with allegorical pictures.

141. *Ogilby*: Scottish cartographer John Ogilby, poet and translator; by calling him 'the great', Pope may be remembering his own boyhood fascination with an illustrated edition of Ogilby's Homer; he also translated Aesop's Fables (327–8).

142. *Newcastle*: Margaret Cavendish, Duchess of Newcastle, prolific seventeenth-century author and pioneer feminist; her coat of arms was stamped on the covers of her books.

144. *jakes and fire*: Pages from unwanted books could be used in privies ('jakes') or to light fires.

145. *Gothic*: Medieval (with pejorative connotations); as Johnson

observed, it was incongruous for the pedantic Tibbald's old-fashioned books to be reassigned to Cibber.

146. *Well purged . . . Banks, and Broome Well purged*: i.e. empty of books by classical authors. John Banks and Richard Brome, seventeenth-century playwrights. Pope may have altered the spelling of Brome's name to rhyme with 'Rome', often pronounced 'Room' at the time, but there may also be a covert dig at William Broome, who translated part of the *Odyssey* for Pope and was offended to find himself included in an earlier version of the 'Dunciad'.

149. *Caxton*: William Caxton, the first printer of books in England. *Wynkyn*: Wynkyn de Worde, his colleague and successor.

150. *wood . . . cow-hide*: Bookbinding materials (wood was used for heavy medieval books).

151. *saved by spice*: Like embalmed mummies, valuable books were protected from bookworms by aromatic spices.

152. *Divinity*: Theological writings; Pope has in mind the *Complete Body of Divinity* by Thomas Stackhouse, who had attacked Bishop Francis Atterbury (see 'Arbuthnot', 135–41n.).

153. *De Lyra*: Nicholas de Lyra, fourteenth-century writer (though Pope was actually thinking of a sixteenth-century writer, Nicholas Harpsfield). *front*: 'the face, in a sense of censure or dislike' (*Dictionary*).

154. *Philemon*: Philemon Holland, seventeenth-century physician who translated so many books that the shelves groan under their weight.

156. *tapers . . . pies*: Books whose pages could have been used to light candles or line pie-plates.

158. *hecatomb*: Sacrifice of a hundred animals (Greek). *unsullied lays*: Poems never 'sullied' by being bought.

159. *folio Commonplace*: Large-format anthology of quotations, the 'base' of Bays's writings since he has no ideas of his own.

161. *Quartos, octavos*: Books of decreasing size at the top of the pyre.

162. *birthday ode*: See 'Arbuthnot', 222n.

163. *Great Tamer*: Dullness suppresses energy and imagination.

165. *good old cause*: Puritan term for their crusade to overturn the monarchy, thus associating bad writing with political disloyalty.

167. *Sir Fopling's periwig*: For Sir Fopling, see 'Rape of the Lock', V, 63n. Cibber had been applauded for a spectacular wig.

168. *butt*: Cask or 'butt', of wine that was a perquisite of the Laureate; see also 293 and note. *bays*: The laurels symbolic of his position.

170. *bias . . . bowl*: In bowls (lawn bowling), 'the weight lodged on one side of a bowl, which turns it from the straight line' (*Dictionary*).

181. *wind-guns*: Guns using compressed air rather than gunpowder.

184. *the load below*: Large clocks were driven by heavy hanging weights.

187. *Daemon*: Guardian spirit.

191–2. *on the stage . . . ampler lessons*: i.e. if the characterization of fops in Cibber's plays seems limited, his personal life furnishes a fine example of foppishness.

195. *had Heav'n*: If Heaven had. *save the State*: Echoing Aeneas' hope to save the 'state' of Troy.

198. *grey-goose weapon*: Quill pen.

199. *my Fletcher*: His copy of Fletcher's plays, from which he has freely borrowed.

200. *once my better guide*: Cibber once thought of entering the Church.

202. *box*: In which dice were shaken.

203. *White's*: Gambling club to which Cibber belonged; also 321. *amidst the doctors*: Learned men, recalling the child Jesus 'in the temple, sitting in the midst of the doctors' (Luke 2:46); but 'doctors' was also a slang word for loaded dice.

205. *Party*: Political faction, a reliable source of income for hack writers.

208. *Ridpath . . . Mist*: George Ridpath and Nathaniel Mist, editors, respectively, of a Whig and Tory newspaper, with a pun on foggy 'mist' as well. On Ridpath, see also II, 149n.

209. *Curtius*: Heroic Roman who threw himself into a chasm in the Roman forum because an oracle said Rome would be saved if its greatest strength were thrown into it.

210. *Commonweal*: The Puritans' term for England when they ruled.

211–12. *geese . . . Tories*: The cackling of geese warned Rome of an attack by the Gauls. Bays/Cibber considers going over to the Tories, with their loyalty to monarchy, if they should pay better than the Whigs.

213–14. *the Minister . . . Queen*: The prime minister Walpole, who had a close working relationship with Queen Caroline.

215. *Gazetteers give o'er*: When Walpole resigned in 1742 after two decades in office, his propaganda organ, the *Daily Gazetteer*, adopted a more moderate policy.

216. *Ralph . . . Henley*: James Ralph and John ('Orator') Henley, who had both ceased to write for the Whig ministry. For Ralph, see III, 165n., and for Henley, see 'Donne', 51n.

219. *squire*: Unsophisticated country squires (as contrasted with peers (220)) appreciate Cibber's brisk liveliness.

222. *Hockley Hole*: See Horace, Satire, II, i, 49n.; also 326 below.

224. *bear and fiddle*: Bear-baiting was preceded by fiddle music.

225-6. *born in sin ... Works damned*: Audiences 'damned' unsuccessful plays (and books), as the human race was guilty of the original sin of Adam and Eve.

227. *purified by flames*: Cibber burns his writings, as if in a religious sacrifice.

228. *more Christian progeny*: i.e. his literary offspring can ascend to salvation after being purified; see 225-6n. above.

229-30. *maiden sheets ... smutty sisters*: Unsold and thus virginal writings are being sacrificed, contrasted with their streetwalker sisters who do find customers.

231. *Bland*: Henry Bland, headmaster of Eton and friend of Walpole, wrote pro-government news-sheets that were permitted to circulate free of postal charges; he is imagined here as a beggar given special permission to beg beyond the limits of his own parish.

233. *Ward*: Edward Ward, journalist who kept a tavern; his scurrilous *London Spy* is imagined as popular among expatriates in distant colonies ('ape-and-monkey climes').

234. *mundungus*: Cheap tobacco from Jamaica. *trucks*: 'truck: to traffic by exchange; to give one commodity for another' (*Dictionary*).

236. *wrap ... sire*: Oranges were sold in theatres; wrapped in the pages of their 'sire' Bays, they could be used to pelt him.

240. *Shadwell*: One of Cibber's predecessors as Laureate; see also Horace, Epistle, II, i, 85n.

244. *sev'nfold face*: i.e. an actor's repertoire of expressions, with an allusion to the Greek hero Ajax's 'sevenfold shield'.

245. *Birthday brand*: Firebrand, evidently one of Cibber's odes for a royal birthday.

248. *involve*: Envelop.

250-53. *the Cid ... Nonjuror*: All plays by Cibber: *Ximena, or, The Heroic Daughter* (adapted from Pierre Corneille's *Le Cid*), *Perolla and Izadora*, *Caesar in Egypt*, *Papal Tyranny in the Reign of King John*, and *The Nonjuror*.

255. *Priam*: King of Troy who watches his city ('Ilion' (256)) burn at the end of the Trojan War.

258. *a sheet of Thulè*: 'It is an usual method of putting out a fire to cast wet sheets upon it. Some critics have been of the opinion that this sheet was of the nature of the asbestos, which cannot be

consumed by fire; but I rather think it an allegorical allusion to the coldness and heaviness of the writing' (Pope's note).

265. *wait*: 'to attend; to accompany with submission or respect' (*Dictionary*).

266. *confessed*: Acknowledged.

269. *Great Mother*: The mother-goddess Cybele of Asia Minor was known as Magna Mater.

270. *quidnuncs*: What now? – a question constantly asked by gossipy members of political clubs. *Guildhall*: See Horace, Epistle, II, ii, 104n.

271. *opium*: Legally available, and used as a painkiller or to alleviate hunger.

280. *science*: Knowledge in general. *by the tail*: A book's index enables the user to locate information, a comparison borrowed from Swift's satire *A Tale of a Tub*, VII: 'the index by which the whole book is governed and turned, like fishes by the tail'.

281. *makes felons scape*: In the Middle Ages felons could escape hanging by pleading 'benefit of clergy', proving that they could read.

283. *Small thanks ... Greece*: i.e. with only casual knowledge of recent French literature, and none at all of the classics.

284. *vamped*: 'vamp: to piece an old thing with some new part' (*Dictionary*).

286. *Ozell*: John Ozell, translator of foreign plays.

290. *Heideggre*: John James Heidegger, Swiss theatrical promoter, widely considered the ugliest man in London; in bird form here he represents the Holy Spirit in a parodic Trinity, with Dullness as God the Mother and Cibber as the Son.

292. *the promised land*: The Israelites' destination when Moses led them out of Egypt.

293. *sack*: White wine, a perquisite of the Laureate (see 168 and note), and especially welcome to the alcoholic Eusden.

295. *duns*: Bill collectors.

296. *Withers ... Gildon*: George Withers and Charles Gildon, minor writers.

297. *high-born Howard*: Edward Howard, son of the Earl of Berkshire, derided as a hopelessly bad poet by numerous seventeenth-century satirists.

298. *Fool of Quality*: Lord John Hervey (see 'Arbuthnot', 'Advertisement' note), seen here as a royal jester or 'fool', but one of 'quality': 'rank; superiority of birth or station' (*Dictionary*).

299. *his*: Eusden's.

301. *Lift up your gates*: Recalling Psalm 24:7: 'Lift up your heads, O ye gates ... and the king of glory shall come in', with Bays/ Cibber as a parodic Messiah.

302. *viols*: Violins in theatre orchestras. *cat-call*: Shrill whistle used by dissatisfied patrons.

303–4. *bay ... ivy*: The bay (or laurel) of poetry is 'madding' with demented inspiration; the wine-producing vine is 'drunken' with Bacchic excess; and the ivy is 'creeping' (or crawling) with syco-phancy at court.

305. *his aide de camp*: Hervey.

306. *points*: 'point: a sting of an epigram; a sentence terminated with some remarkable turn of words or thought' (*Dictionary*). *antith-eses*: i.e. used as laboured poetic devices; Pope called Hervey 'one vile antithesis' in 'Arbuthnot', 325.

307. *billingsgate*: 'a cant word, borrowed from Billingsgate in Lon-don, a place where there is always a crowd of low people, and frequent brawls and foul language' (*Dictionary*).

309. *Archer*: Thomas Archer, a royal groom who took advantage of his position's privileges to keep a gambling den.

312. *nursing-mother*: Cf. 'queens shall be thy nursing mothers' (Isaiah 43:23).

314. *Shade ... law*: Dullness prefers a king who is shielded from his people's needs, and is told that he is above the law.

315. *learnèd band*: Scholars, who get no support from the regime.

316. *suckle armies*: Support standing armies, which Tories resented as enabling the monarchy's foreign wars. *dry-nurse*: A wet-nurse would give milk; the dry-nurse Dullness has none.

317. *senates*: Parliament. *lullabies divine*: Soothing sermons by court preachers.

318. *an Ode of thine*: One of Cibber's soporific official odes.

319. *Chapel Royal*: The chapel of the court at St James's Palace, whose musicians played at the performance of the Laureate's official odes.

321. *Familiar*: Because Cibber was a member.

322. *Drury Lane*: Site of brothels and theatres (including the Drury Lane Theatre, managed by Cibber).

323. *Needham*: The notorious madam 'Mother' Needham. *dropped the name of God*: i.e. used it in a blasphemous oath.

325. *the Devil*: 'the Devil Tavern in Fleet Street, where these odes are usually rehearsed before they are performed at court' (Pope's note).

327. *Jove's block*: In Aesop's fable, frogs asked for a king, were given instead a log, and failed at first to notice its inertness.

Book the Second

Argument: *Pythia, Isthmia*: Sites of games in ancient Greece; Pope's mock-epic games imitate those in *Iliad*, XXIII and *Aeneid*, V. *Thetis*: Achilles' mother, who presided over funeral games held in his honour. *booksellers*: Publishers (who also owned bookshops). *fustian*: See 'Arbuthnot', 187n. *Party-writers*: Political propagandists. *their parts*: Abilities.

1.   *High . . . outshone*: Echoing *Paradise Lost*, II, 1–2, 5: 'High on a throne of royal state, that far / Outshone the wealth of Ormus and of Ind . . . Satan exalted sat.'

2.   *Henley*: John Henley: see 'Donne', 51n.; also 370n. below. *tub*: Contemptuous term for a pulpit. *Fleckno's Irish throne*: Dryden's satire presents Richard Flecknoe 'high on a throne of his own labours reared' ('Mac Flecknoe', 106), i.e. on a pile of his own books; he was not in fact Irish, though his detractors claimed that his father was an Irish priest.

3.   *Or that*: The pillory. *her curls*: A dig at Edmund Curll, who had once been placed in the pillory; see also I, 40n.

4.   *fragrant grains and golden show'rs*: Rank barley fermented during brewing, and eggs.

5.   *Parnassian*: See 'Arbuthnot', 96n.

9.   *His peers*: The rest of the Dunces, and also an allusion to Cibber's popularity among the nobility.

10.   *new-bronze*: Suggesting Cibber's brazen impudence.

12.   *sparks*: With a pun on 'spark': see 'Rape of the Lock', I, 73n. *horns*: The sign of cuckoldry.

14.   *scarlet hats*: Worn by cardinals.

15.   *Capitol*: The Capitoline Hill in Rome. *Querno*: Camillo Querno, sixteenth-century buffoonish poetic improvisor whom Pope Leo X jokingly appointed Poet Laureate of Rome.

16.   *sev'n hills*: The Book of Revelation associates the Antichrist with the seven hills of Rome.

18.   *hawkers*: Pedlars.

21–2.   *long wigs . . . garters*: A truly 'motley' assemblage: long wigs were favoured by older gentlemen, bag wigs (with the hair drawn into a pouch at the back) by the young, silks by the wealthy, crapes (woollen cloth) by the lower clergy, and garters by the highly distinguished members of the Order of the Garter.

24. *hacks*: Hired hackney carriages. *chariots*: The carriages of the rich.

27. *that area wide*: The square in front of the church of St Mary le Strand, built on the order of Queen Anne, at which time a festive maypole was taken down (28).

30. *saints of Drury Lane*: i.e. prostitutes.

31. *Stationers*: Booksellers, who also functioned as publishers.

35. *A poet's form*: Recalling the phantom of Aeneas created by Juno to mislead his enemy Turnus (*Aeneid*, X, 636–40).

37. *adust*: Dried out and gloomy.

38. *nightgown*: Loose gown for casual dress at home.

45. *sounding strain*: Resounding lines of verse.

48. *just*: Exact.

50. *More*: James Moore-Smyth, notorious for plagiarism; hence, the 'phantom' of an author, not a real one; see also 'Arbuthnot', 23n.

52. *sword-knot*: Ornament on the hilt of a sword.

53. *lofty Lintot*: The publisher Bernard Lintot was a tall man; see 82n. below and see also 'Arbuthnot', 62n.

54. *tempt*: Attempt.

63. *dabchick*: A waterbird, clumsy on land.

64–5. *On feet ... and head*: As Satan, struggling through Chaos to reach the newly created Earth, 'With head, hands, wings, or feet pursues his way, / And swims or sinks, or wades, or creeps, or flies' (*Paradise Lost*, II, 949–50).

67–8. *Bernard ... Jacob*: Lintot and Tonson (see I, 57n).

70. *Corinna*: A classical name affected by Curll's mistress.

71–2. *Such ... shop*: 'Cates' are delicacies; i.e. it is her custom ('wont') to empty her chamber pot in the street, but not in front of Curll's bookshop.

73. *Here fortuned*: Curll's bad luck resembles that of runners in the *Iliad* and *Aeneid*, who slip on blood and entrails from the sacrifices that preceded the games.

74. *Strand*: Then as today, major London thoroughfare.

75. *bewrayed*: Exposed, visible.

76. *plash*: 'a small lake of water or puddle' (*Dictionary*, citing this line). *his wickedness*: In having spent the night with Corinna.

78. *caitiff vaticide*: Despicable poet-murderer (*vates* is Latin for poet).

80. *as any god's*: i.e. Curll and the writers he publishes are as likely to worship a Greek god as the Christian one.

82. *Down with ... Arms*: Lintot had taken down his shop sign that

featured a Bible, replacing it with the Pope's Head (evidently a dig at Alexander Pope).

84. *ambrosia*: Food of the Olympian gods. *ease*: A privy was euphemistically called a 'house of ease'.

87. *fond*: 'foolish; silly' (*Dictionary*).

91. *bills*: The petitions.

92. *ichor*: The ethereal blood of the gods; here, evidently, divine excrement.

93. *office*: Privy; see 84n. *Cloacina*: Minor Roman deity, named from *cloaca*, 'sewer'.

95. *vot'ry*: i.e Votary, worshipper.

98. *black grottos*: Coal wharves on the Thames, near the legal centre known as the Temple.

100. *link-boys*: Boys hired to carry torches for pedestrians in unlit streets. *watermen*: Boatmen who rowed passengers on the Thames.

101. *fished her nether realms*: Searched the privy for manuscripts that had been used there.

103. *sympathetic*: Having an affinity with; i.e. Curll finds excrement congenial.

104. *magic juices*: 'alluding to the opinion that there are ointments used by witches to enable them to fly in the air' (Pope's note).

106. *scours*: 'scour: to pass swiftly over' (*Dictionary*).

107. *vindicates*: Claims victory.

114. *fly diverse*: Fly in different directions (borrowed from *Paradise Lost*, X, 284).

116. *Evans, Young, and Swift*: Abel Evans, Edward Young, and Jonathan Swift, writers from whom the 'papers' had been plagiarized.

118. *unpaid tailor snatched away*: Not having been paid, the tailor has repossessed the suit.

123. *imps*: 'imp: offspring; progeny' (*Dictionary*).

124. *decked ... Prior*: Publishers could boost sales of hack writing by claiming it was the work of a famous writer; all three of these had died relatively recently.

125-6. *Mears ... Besaleel*: William Mears, Thomas Warner, etc., publishers, none very prominent; also 238. *varlets*: Rascals.

128. *Joseph ... John*: Curll attributed a number of pamphlets to a fictional 'Joseph Gay', to deceive buyers into thinking it was the popular John Gay (a 'joseph' was also a kind of cloak).

130. *puppy*: 'a name of contemptuous reproach to a man' (*Dictionary*). *ape*: i.e. facile imitator.

132. *turn ... the town*: Persuade the whole town that the spurious pieces were by important writers.

133–4. *the sage dame ... jade*: The madam of a brothel claims that her prostitutes ('jades') are beauties toasted by fashionable admirers.

135–6. *Monsieur ... Lady Mary's*: Alluding to old gossip involving Lady Mary Wortley Montagu and a Frenchman.

138. *Cook ... Concanen*: Thomas Cooke and Matthew Concanen; when they complained, after an earlier edition appeared, that Pope had maligned them unjustly, he claimed in a disingenuous note that he had inserted their names 'merely to fill up the verse, and give ease to the ear of the reader'.

140. *Garth*: Samuel Garth: see 'Essay on Criticism', 619n.

142. *length of face*: A 'long face' expressed discouragement.

144. *Codrus*: In Juvenal (Satire, III, 202), a bad poet too poor to afford a full-size bed. *Dunton*: John Dunton, writer of libellous satires.

145. *wry-mouthed*: Grimacing in pain.

146. *confessors*: 'confessor: one who makes profession of his faith in the face of danger' (*Dictionary*); accented on the first syllable.

147. *Earless ... De Foe*: The novelist Defoe spent time in the pillory for a satire that was considered libellous, but his ears were not in fact clipped; he was 'unabashed' inasmuch as he believed the punishment was undeserved.

148. *Tutchin*: John Tutchin, a satirist who was publicly flogged with a 'scourge', which Pope imagines as leaving his posterior red and 'flagrant'.

149. *Ridpath, Roper*: George Ridpath (see I, 208n.) and Abel Roper, Whig and Tory propagandist respectively, authors of libels 'for which they equally and alternately deserved to be cudgeled, and were so' (Pope's note).

150. *worsted*: 'from Worsted, a town in Norfolk famous for the woollen manufacture: woolen yarn; wool spun' (*Dictionary*, citing this line).

151. *Himself*: Curll.

152. *the blanket*: Curll was indeed tossed in a blanket by Westminster School students, as revenge for his unauthorized publication of writing by one of their number.

154. *pumpings*: Drenching an offender under a pump.

155. *In ev'ry loom*: As a theme for tapestry-weavers.

157. *Eliza*: The novelist Eliza Haywood.

158. *babes of love*: Illegitimate children.

159. *confessed*: Exposed.

160. *Kirkall*: Elisha Kirkall, an engraver whom Pope imagines as supplying Haywood's portrait as frontispiece to her works.

162. *salient*: 'springing or shooting with a quick motion' (*Dictionary*, citing this line).

164. *ox-like eyes*: Homeric epithet for Juno (but not, of course, the 'cow-like udders').

165. *jordan*: Chamber pot, imitating the majestic kettles offered as prizes in Homer.

167. *Osborne*: Thomas Osborne, bookseller. 'Osborne was a man entirely destitute of shame, without sense of any disgrace but that of poverty. He told me, when he was doing that which raised Pope's resentment, that he should be put into *The Dunciad*' (Johnson, *Life of Pope*, p. 187).

168. *this*: Curll. *that*: Osborne.

169. *One*: Osborne.

171. *lettered post*: Advertisements for books were fastened to posts.

172. *a curve at most*: i.e. his stream is weak.

173-4. *Jove's bright bow ... drowned*: Like the rainbow that signalled the end of Noah's Flood.

176. *meander ... face*: Osborne splashes his own face.

178. *cock*: Tap, with a pun on Osborne's genitals.

179. *impetuous*: 'violent; forcible' (*Dictionary*).

181. *horns*: Worn by river gods, but also by cuckolds.

182. *Eridanus ... scorns*: The river Eridanus (see 'Windsor Forest', 227n.) hastens to depart from its source.

183. *urn*: As in the constellation Aquarius.

184. *burn*: Hinting that Curll suffers from venereal disease.

191. *But now for Authors*: As contrasted with the booksellers. *palms*: Prizes.

193. *chair*: Sedan chair.

196. *tickle*: Flatter.

198. *quills*: Quill pens, useful for tickling as well as writing. *Dedicators*: Authors who dedicate their works to wealthy patrons in hope of financial reward.

200. *th' imputed sense*: Mental abilities attributed to the noble patron by the flatterers.

202. *struts Adonis*: Struts with vanity because the dedicators have told him he is as handsome as Adonis.

203. *Rolli*: Paolo Antonio Rolli, who taught Italian to the nobility and directed operas.

205. *Bentley*: Richard Bentley (see Horace, Epistle, II, i, 104n.), who flattered George II.

206. *puffed*: 'puff: to swell or blow up with praise' (*Dictionary*). *tropes*: Figures of speech.

207. *Welsted*: Leonard Welsted: see 'Arbuthnot', 375n. *healing balm*: i.e. money.

210. *gripes*: Grips.

213. *unknown to Phoebus*: The god of poetry is unaware of his existence.

215. *Queen of Love*: Venus.

217. *As taught by Venus*: The Trojan prince Paris chose Venus (Greek Aphrodite) as the most beautiful of three goddesses; his arrow mortally wounded Achilles by striking his heel, the 'only tender part' that remained dry when his mother dipped him as an infant in the water of immortality.

221. *the Goddess*: Dullness.

226. *the . . . bowl*: In the theatre, pounding on a wooden bowl to simulate thunder.

230. *sense is at a stand*: Meaning is at a standstill.

231. *cat-calls*: See I, 302n.

238. *Norton*: Benjamin Norton Defoe, son of Daniel Defoe; also 415n. *Brangling*: noisy quarrelling.

239. *captious*: Carping.

240. *Snip-snap*: 'tart dialogue' (*Dictionary*, citing this line).

241. *Demonstration . . . Theses*: Terms from disputations in logic.

242. *Major, Minor, and Conclusion*: The three elements of a syllogism.

246. *welkin*: The sky (archaic).

247. *milky mothers*: Asses whose milk ('defrauded' from their own offspring (249)) was used for medicinal purposes.

250. *guild*: Association of artisans or merchants; here, the herd of asses.

251. *Sir Gilbert*: Sir Gilbert Heathcote: see 'III Bathurst', 101n.

252. *three groats*: Equivalent to a shilling, a trivial sum for a rich man to worry about. For groat, see Horace, Epistle, II, ii, 51n.

254. *leather*: Of bagpipes.

255–6. *Enthusiast . . . nose*: 'Enthusiastic' evangelical preachers intoned through their noses; see also III, Argument note.

257. *deep Divine*: Profound clergyman.

258. *Webster*: William Webster, clergyman and political journalist. *Whitfield*: George Whitefield, celebrated open-air Methodist evangelist.

261. *Tot'nam Fields*: The Tottenham area in upper Westminster was

open country in Pope's day. *brethren*: Common term for Dissenting congregations; here, actual asses.

263. *Chanc'ry Lane retentive*: The Court of Chancery, which handled cases of equity, was notorious for protracting cases indefinitely (and long remained so, as in Dickens's *Bleak House*).

265. *Rufus' roaring hall*: Westminster Hall, built by William II, known as 'Rufus'; the site of noisy trials.

266. *Hungerford*: Market.

269. *Bridewell*: Prison in which prostitutes were incarcerated.

270. *flagellation*: Whipping of prisoners, parodying Homer's indications of the time of day by reference to familiar occupations.

271. *disemboguing*: 'disembogue: to pour out at the mouth of a river' (*Dictionary*).

273. *dikes*: Ditches; Fleet Ditch was a filthy river that still flows through London and gave its name to Fleet Street; it was covered over in the nineteenth century.

274. *sable*: Black.

281. *pig*: 'an oblong mass of lead or unforged iron' (*Dictionary*, citing this line).

282. *peck of coals*: Not a very generous amount, suggesting that the writers are normally too poor to heat their garrets at all.

283. *Oldmixon*: John Oldmixon: 'he was all his life a virulent party-writer for hire' (Pope's note); see 289n and see also 'Donne', 61n.

284. *Milo-like*: Similar to a Greek wrestling champion who in old age lamented his shrunken muscles.

287. *stranded lighter*: Barge, grounded by low tide.

288. *downright*: Straight down.

289. *senior's*: Oldmixon was 70 when the final version of the 'Dunciad' was published.

291. *Smedley*: Jonathan Smedley, clergyman and 'author and publisher of many scurrilous pieces' (Pope's note).

295. ***: Replaces the name of [Aaron] Hill, who persuaded Pope to remove it; he is described as surfacing after only a brief immersion with the dunces.

298. *swans of Thames*: As Shakespeare was sometimes called the 'swan of Avon'.

306. *brother at his back*: 'These were daily papers, a number of which, to lessen the expense, were printed one on the back of another' (Pope's note).

310. *blind puppies*: Unwanted puppies – blind because newborn – were drowned in Fleet Ditch.

311. *Niobe . . . gone*: Mother who boastfully claimed that her four-teen children excelled Apollo and Diana, the children of the goddess Latona, who punished her by turning them to stone.

312. *Mother Osborne*: James Pitt, a Whig journalist, used the pseudo-nym Francis Osborne; he was nicknamed Mother Osborne for his ponderous style.

315. *Arnall*: William Arnall, political writer.

317. *invest*: Enclose, encompass.

323. *plunging Prelate*: Thomas Sherlock, Bishop of London, as a boy used to dive into icy water. *his pond'rous Grace*: Possibly John Potter, Archbishop of Canterbury (addressed as 'your Grace'), whose person and writings were both heavy.

326. *Slow rose a form*: Presumably Smedley is finally resurfacing.

330. *the wonders of the deep*: Adapted from Psalm 107:24.

332. *Smit with his mien*: Smitten with his features and demeanour.

333. *Lutetia*: The Roman name for ancient Paris, muddy at the time (*luteus* is mud). *down*: Feathers.

334. *Nigrina*: Black (from *nigra*). *Merdamante*: Lover of excrement (from *merda* and *amans*); Fleet Ditch was used as an open sewer.

335. *jetty*: Jet-black ('jet' is black coal).

336. *Hylas*: Greek youth pulled down by water nymphs while drinking.

338. *Styx*: Chief river of the underworld ('the shades').

339. *Lethe*: Underworld river of forgetfulness.

340. *Land of Dreams*: A place spirits pass through when they die (*Odyssey*, XXIV); 'Lethe and the Land of Dreams allegorically represent the *stupefaction* and *visionary madness* of poets, equally dull and extravagant' (Pope's note).

341-2. *Alphaeus . . . Arethuse*: The river Alphaeus was believed to flow unaltered beneath the sea from the Greek (not the Italian) town of Pisa to the fountain of Arethusa in Sicily, carrying objects ('off'rings') that had been thrown into it at Pisa.

345. *brisker . . . the Temple*: The young lawyers, although dunces, are 'brisk' ones.

346. *Paul's to Aldgate*: The central City of London, from St Paul's Cathedral to Aldgate.

347. *rev'rend Bards*: Numerous poets who were also clergymen.

349. *Milbourne*: The Reverend Luke Milbourn, poet and critic.

350. *cassock, surcingle, and vest*: Ecclesiastical gown, belt, and other vestments.

352. *Dullness is sacred*: Lay persons are cautious about attacking the clergy. *sound divine*: Theologically correct clergyman.

354. *Flamen*: Roman priest. *lengthened dress*: Long cassock reaching to the ground.

355. *sable army*: Priests dressed in black (and eager to cultivate political favours).

357. *or . . . or*: Either . . . or.

358. *Swiss*: Swiss guards, employed all over Europe.

359. *Lud . . . Fleet*: Fleet Street passed through the wall of the City at Ludgate, named for a legendary King Lud.

361. *Characters*: Literary sketches of character types.

364. *volumes*: Rolling clouds, but also books ('so called because books were anciently rolled upon a staff', *Dictionary*), with dark covers that shed snowy white pages when torn apart.

370. *Henley's periods*: Long sentences by either Bishop Benjamin Hoadley or John ('Orator') Henley (on Hoadley, see 'Donne', 73n.; also 400n. below); in manuscript Pope tried out both names.

372. *wake*: Stay awake.

374. *Ulysses' ear*: Odysseus (Ulysses) had himself tied to the mast in order to resist the seductive song of the sirens. *Argus' eye*: Monster covered with a hundred eyes, only two of which slept at any time; see also IV, 637n.

375. *To him*: Whoever can manage not to fall asleep.

379. *Sophs*: Sophomores, second-year university students (from *sophistes*, sophist). *Templars*: Lawyers and law students at the Temple.

382. *Prate*: 'tattle; slight talk; unmeaning loquacity' (*Dictionary*); the line recalls *Paradise Lost*, III, 29: 'smit with the love of sacred song'.

384. *vulgar*: Common people.

385. *mum*: 'ale brewed with wheat' (*Dictionary*, citing this line).

387. *Clerks*: The undergraduates.

396. *the drowsy god*: Morpheus, god of sleep.

397. *Budgell*: Eustace Budgell: see 'Donne', 51n., and Horoce, Satire, II, i, 100n.

398. *Arthur*: Blackmore (see I, 104n.) wrote two epics about King Arthur.

399. *Toland and Tindal*: John Toland and Matthew Tindal, freethinkers whose deistical books scandalized the orthodox.

400. *Christ's No Kingdom*: Sermon preached by Bishop Hoadley, paraphrasing 'My kingdom is not of this world' (John 18:36), and denying the existence of a visible church of Christ.

408. *Like*: Similar.

409. *nutation*: Nodding.

411. *Centlivre*: Susanna Centlivre, playwright, poet, and critic of Pope.

412. *Motteux*: See 'Donne', 50n.

413. *Boyer*: Abel Boyer, prolific political writer. *Law*: William Law, clergyman who denounced the theatre.

414. *Morgan*: Thomas Morgan, writer against religion. *Mandeville*: Bernard Mandeville, whose *Fable of the Bees* claimed that immorality works to the advantage of society.

415. *Ostroea*: John Gay's invented word for an oyster-seller; Norton's mother was said to have been an oyster-wench, noted for coarse language ('mother's tongue' (416)).

416. *front*: Effrontery.

420. *bulks*: Stalls in front of shops, 'as usual' because they cannot afford lodgings.

422. *Did slumb'ring visit*: As the Muse visited Milton's 'slumbers nightly' (*Paradise Lost*, VII, 29). *stews*: Brothels.

424. *roundhouse*: 'the constable's prison, in which disorderly persons found in the street are confined' (*Dictionary*, citing this line).

425. *sink*: Sewer.

427. *Fleet*: Debtors' prison close to Fleet Ditch.

Book the Third

Argument: *enthusiasts*: Ecstatic or fanatical religious people. *projectors*: Entrepreneurs promoting 'projects'. *inamoratos*: People sick with love. *castle-builders*: People fantasizing about castles in the air. *chemists*: Alchemists, hoping to turn base metals into gold. *and poets*: i.e. as crazy as the rest. *Sybil*: Priestess of Apollo, who leads Aeneas into the underworld ('Elysian shade') to learn his future. *Bavius*: A bad poet in Virgil (*Eclogue*, III, 90), invoked here as initiating souls into duncehood; also 24, 317. *Settle*: Elkanah Settle: see I, 90n. *Science*: Knowledge in general. *the King himself*: Bays/Cibber. *types*: Prefigurations of things to come. *Pisgah-sight*: As Moses, who died before reaching the Promised Land, was granted a sight of it from Mount Pisgah.

2. *anointed*: Consecrated, chosen.

4. *Cimmerian dew*: Fog like that of the mythical realm of Cimmeria, perpetually dark.

6. *refined from reason*: Purged of reason, i.e. mad.

7. *Bedlam's*: Bethlehem hospital for the insane. *nods*: Dozes.

9–12. *fool's paradise . . . fame*: Repeating the various forms of madness and folly listed in the Argument.

13. *Fancy*: Imagination, fantasy.

15. *slipshod*: 'having the shoes not pulled up at the heels, but barely slipped on' (*Dictionary*).

17. *staring*: Standing on end.

18. *Castalia's streams*: Water from the spring sacred to the Muses; i.e. she never washes her hair with actual water.

19. *Taylor*: John Taylor, a boatman who became known as the Water Poet, and thus an appropriate equivalent for Charon, who ferried the dead across the River Styx.

20. *swan of Thames*: See II, 298n.

21. *Benlowes*: Edward Benlowes, a country gentleman 'famous for his own bad poetry and for patronizing bad poets' (Pope's note).

22. *poppy*: Source of opium, conducive to sleep; Shadwell was in fact a heavy user and died of an overdose; see also Horace, Epistle, II, i, 85n.

28. *Brown and Mears*: 'printers for anybody; the allegory of the souls of the dull coming forth in the form of books, dressed in calf's leather, and being let abroad in vast numbers by the booksellers, is sufficiently intelligible' (Pope's note).

34. *Ward*: John Ward: see 'III Bathurst', 20n.

36. *length of ears*: i.e. he is an ass.

37. *band*: Collar.

44. *th' oblivious Lake*: Formed by Lethe (see II, 339n.).

50. *Baeotian*: See I, 25n.

51. *Dutchmen*: Conventionally thought of as heavy and dull. *thrid*: 'to slide through a narrow passage' (*Dictionary*).

52. *rid*: Rode, by stages, at each of which tired horses are exchanged for fresh ones.

57. *whirligigs*: Toys that spin on a string. *swain*: Rural youth.

66. *let the past and future*: 'First, those places in the globe are shown where Science *never* rose; then those where she was destroyed by *tyranny*; [then] by inundations of *barbarians*; [then] by *superstition*' (Pope's note).

70. *Line*: The equator.

74. *orient Science*: Learning, which began in the East.

75. *monarch*: 'Chi Ho-am-ti [Ch'in Shi Huangdi], Emperor of China, the same who built the Great Wall between China and Tartary, destroyed all the books and learned men of that empire' (Pope's note).

80–82. *rival flames . . . physic of the soul*: Destroyed the great Alexandrian Library in Egypt; 'the Caliph Omar I, having conquered Egypt, caused his general to burn the Ptolemaean library, on the gates of which was this inscription, The Physic of the Soul' (Pope's note).

81. *Vulcan*: God of fire.

83. *ball*: The earth.

84. *Science*: Learning.

85. *hyperborean*: Northern, beyond the source of the cold north wind Boreas.

86–90. *Vandals ... Goths ... Huns*: Nomadic tribes from the eastern steppes which invaded Europe in successive waves.

87–8. *Lo ... snows*: The river Tanais (the Don) in Russia flows into Maeotis (the Sea of Azov); this couplet was said to have been Pope's favourite in all his works.

91. *Alaric's stern port*: The demeanour of Alaric the Goth, who conquered Rome in 410.

92. *Genseric*: King of the Vandals, who sacked Rome in 455.

93. *Ostrogoths*: East Goths. *Latium*: Italy.

94. *Visigoths*: West Goths.

96. *The soil*: 'Phoenicia, Syria, etc., where letters are said to have been invented' (Pope's note).

97. *th' Arabian prophet*: Muhammad.

98. *saving Ignorance enthrones by laws*: Religious laws, promising salvation, promoted ignorance rather than learning.

99. *one heavy sabbath*: i.e. every day of the week was an anti-intellectual day of rest.

101. *Rome*: The Papacy.

103. *synods*: Ecclesiastical councils, where 'grey-haired' theologians decided which books were to be prohibited.

104. *Bacon*: The medieval friar and philosopher Roger Bacon, who supposedly made a bronze head that could speak, was accused of magic, and was forced to give up writing.

105. *Livy*: Ancient historian, born at Padua, which grieves because most of his voluminous writings are lost.

106. *th' Antipodes Vigilius mourn*: Eighth-century saint and Bishop of Salzburg, who was denounced by the Church (which believed the earth was flat) for asserting that there were people in the Antipodes, on the opposite side of the earth.

107. *Cirque*: Circus, the Roman Colosseum.

108. *Streets paved ... gods*: Pagan statues were broken up or thrown into the river.

109. *Peter's keys ... christened Jove*: The Pope, heir to the keys of St Peter, sometimes authorized the conversion of temples into churches.

110. *Pan . . . horn*: Moses was thought to have had horns (a misreading of a passage in the Vulgate Bible that refers to rays of light); i.e. they were borrowed from the similarly horned nature-god Pan.

111. *graceless Venus*: The goddess of love, lacking divine grace, is transformed by the Church into the Virgin Mary.

112. *Phidias . . . Apelles*: The greatest sculptor and painter of antiquity.

113. *palmers*: Pilgrims who brought back palm branches from the Holy Land.

114. *cowled*: Wearing the hoods of monks.

115. *linsey-woolsey*: 'made of linen and wool mixed; vile; mean; of different and unsuitable parts' (*Dictionary*, citing this line).

116. *mummers*: 'mummer: a masker; one who performs frolics in a personated dress' (*Dictionary*, citing this line).

118. *had Easter never been*: In the seventh century there was bitter controversy over the correct date of Easter between the Celtic church of Britain and the Church of Rome; the latter used this issue to assert its authority.

121. *visit*: 'to send good or evil' (*Dictionary*).

127. *scene she draws*: Pulls back the curtain to reveal the stage (scenery).

131. *Berecynthia*: Cybele, the Great Mother of the Mediterranean, who had a hundred offspring.

139. *that youth*: Cibber's son Theophilus, also an actor.

144. *modest*: i.e. discreetly drinking in secret.

145. *drams*: 'spirits; distilled liquor' (*Dictionary*, citing this line).

146. *Durfey*: Thomas Durfey, author of popular drinking songs. *Ward*: Edward Ward: see I, 232n.

147. *gill house*: Tavern where liquor was served in small quantities (*gill*: quarter of a pint).

149. *Jacob*: Giles Jacob, a critic of Pope, but not in fact guilty of bad grammar.

150. *blunderbuss*: 'a gun that is charged with many bullets, so that, without any exact aim, there is a chance of hitting the mark' (*Dictionary*); Jacob had been trained in the law.

151. *Popple*: William Popple, lawyer and playwright; just how he was 'tremendous' is unclear.

152−3. *Horneck's . . . Roome's . . . Goode*: Writers who had all satirized Pope; Roome's family were morticians.

155. *cygnet*: Immature swan; Pope acknowledges that the writers in the next several lines are too obscure even to be named.

158. *damned to Fame*: i.e. damned by disappointed readers.

160. *jacks*: Noisy device, driven by clockwork, to keep a roast turning on a spit.

162. *Priscian*: Roman grammarian. *Pegasus*: The winged horse of poetic inspiration.

163. *larum*: Cry of alarm; thus, battle cries.

165. *Ralph*: James Ralph, who got into the 'Dunciad' after writing an abusive attack on Pope called *Sawney* (a diminutive for 'Alexander'). *Cynthia*: The moon; also 243.

166. *makes Night hideous*: Pope cleverly invokes the Shakespearean phrase 'making night hideous' (*Hamlet*, I, iv, 54) to apply to an ambitious poem by Ralph called *Night*.

168. *Morris*: Besaleel Morris: see II, 126n.

169–72. *Flow . . . not full*: These lines parody John Denham's *Cooper's Hill*, the principal inspiration of 'Windsor Forest' (see its headnote).

169. *Welsted*: Leonard Welsted: see II, 207n.

173. *Gildon*: Charles Gildon; Pope apparently alludes to some forgotten quarrel between Gildon and Welsted.

175. *wits*: Persons of intelligence.

179. *in strict embraces*: Embracing tightly. Although Pope unconvincingly denied it, this passage was believed to suggest a homosexual relationship between George Duckett and Thomas Burnet, authors of *Pasquin* and *The Grumbler* respectively; also 184n.

184. *consul . . . commissioner*: Burnet served as British Consul in Lisbon, and Duckett as Commissioner of Excise.

185–8. *close y-pent . . . hight*: Parodic Spenserian language, satirizing the antiquarian scholar Thomas Hearne. *y-pent*: Penned up, confined. *besprent*: Bestrewed. *arede*: Perceive. *myster wight*: Uncouth person. *Wormius hight*: 'named Wormius', implying fondness for worm-eaten old manuscripts, but also the name of a Danish antiquarian scholar.

191. *scholiasts*: Textual commentators.

193. *lumberhouse*: Junk room.

195. *lifts its modern type*: Holds up an allegorical representation of itself.

196. *pot*: Of ale.

197. *repines*: Frets, feels discontented.

198. *Dishonest*: Disgraceful.

199. *Henley*: John Henley (see 'Donne', 51n.); 'he preached on the Sundays upon theological matters, and on the Wednesdays upon all other sciences' (Pope's note).

200. *balancing his hands*: Henley was fond of eccentric gestures.

203. *break the benches . . . thy strain*: Bring down the house with your eloquence.

204. *Sherlock, Hare, and Gibson*: Pro-Walpole bishops, by implication less successful at attracting congregations than the ludicrous Henley.

206. *zany*: 'one employed to raise laughter by his gestures, actions, and speeches' (*Dictionary*, citing this line).

209. *butchers . . . stall*: Henley preached near Newport Market; Pope implies that he kept a 'priestly stall' equivalent to the butchers' stalls.

212. *Toland, Tindal*: See II, 399n. *Woolston*: Thomas Woolston, 'an impious madman, who wrote in a most insolent style against the miracles of the Gospel' (Pope's note).

214. *preserve the ears you lend*: Lest their ears be cut off for blasphemy, with an allusion to 'lend me your ears' in Shakespeare's *Julius Caesar*.

215. *Bacon*: Francis Bacon, statesman and philosopher of science under Elizabeth and James I. *Locke*: John Locke: see Horace, Epistle, I, i, 26n.

216. *flame*: Inspiration.

217. *One*: God, whom the Dunces are advised not to offend.

218. *sense*: 'perception of intellect; apprehension of mind' (*Dictionary*).

219. *Content*: i.e. be content to attack everything God has created, but not God himself.

231. *His never-blushing head*: Apparently Cibber's, who doesn't blush because he is shameless.

232. *Goodman prophesied*: Veteran actor Cardell Goodman heard Cibber in one of his first rehearsals and predicted that he would be highly successful.

233. *sorc'rer*: Dr Faustus, in a farcical *Harlequin Doctor Faustus*, played by John Rich (see 261 and note).

234. *wingèd volume flies*: A special stage effect in the farce.

235. *gorgons*: Mythical sisters with snakes for hair.

246. *dolphins in the skies*: Echoing Horace on incongruous poetic images, *Ars Poetica*, 30.

248. *egg*: In a farce, 'Harlequin is hatched upon the stage, out of a large egg' (Pope's note).

249. *his soul*: Cibber's.

254. *sarsenet*: Or sarcenet, 'fine thin woven silk' (*Dictionary*); here, as used onstage to suggest clouds.

258. *unclassic ground*: Echoing Addison's poem 'A Letter from Italy': 'I seem to tread on classic ground.' See also 'Arbuthnot', 150n.

261. *Rich*: John Rich, manager of the Covent Garden theatre and noted for these spectacular effects; he also produced Gay's *Beggar's Opera*, which was said to have 'made Gay rich, and Rich gay', i.e. merry.

262. *paper . . . peas*: Dissatisfied audiences would throw crumpled paper at the stage or blow dried peas through peashooters.

263–4. *And proud . . . directs the storm*: Adapting Addison's *Campaign*, I, 291–2: 'And pleased th' Almighty's orders to perform / Rides in the whirlwind, and directs the storm'. *his Mistress*: Dullness.

267. *Booth*: Barton Booth: see Horace, Epistle, II, i, 123.

277. *Lud*: London: see II, 359n.

278. *Bow*: See 'Rape of the Lock', IV, 118n.

282. *annual . . . wars*: '*annual trophies*, on the Lord Mayor's Day, and *monthly wars* [militia exercises] in the Artillery Ground' (Pope's note).

283. *my party*: The Whigs.

284. *roasting Popes*: Settle organized a symbolic Pope burning.

286. *dragon*: Settle 'acted in his old age in a dragon of green leather of his own invention' (Pope's note).

288. *Smithfield Fair*: Entertainment at the Smithfield meat market.

291. *Coached*: Provided with a gentleman's coach. *carted*: Carried through the streets in a cart as a punishment.

292. *in some dog's tail*: Apparently suggesting that he is reduced to the dirt of the street.

297. *Patriot*: See 'III Bathurst', 139n.; hence, the opposite of a 'courtier'.

299. *booths*: Stalls at a fair.

301. *Opera*: Italian opera, still something of a novelty, was criticized as a mindless spectacle in a language that few in the audience could understand.

302. *sway*: 'power; rule; dominion' (*Dictionary*).

303. *drabs*: Whores.

304. *doting*: Senile.

305. *Polypheme*: The one-eyed giant Polyphemus of the *Odyssey*, in an Italian opera called *Polifemo* that Cibber adapted (where it would be incongruous for a giant to warble).

308–10. *Faustus . . . Pluto . . . Proserpine*: 'miserable farces which it was the custom to act at the end of the best tragedies' (Pope's note), e.g. Addison's *Cato* and Congreve's *The Mourning Bride*.

312. *fire*: Spectacular fires were incorporated in stage productions.

313. *Another Aeschylus*: 'It is reported of Aeschylus that when his tragedy of the Furies [the *Eumenides*] was acted, the audience were so terrified that the children fell into fits and the big-bellied women miscarried' (Pope's note).

315. *Semele*: Mortal woman who asked Jupiter to come to her bed in his full glory, whereupon his lightning burned her up.

316. *wildfire*: 'a composition of inflammable materials, easy to take fire, and hard to be extinguished' (*Dictionary*, citing this line).

320. *Augustus ... Saturnian times*: Aeneas had a vision of the Emperor Augustus in Rome's future, and was told that he would found a golden age in fields that were once ruled by Saturn (*Aeneid*, VI), but Saturn is associated not with gold but with lead.

323. *Phoebus*: Apollo, god of poetry.

324. *Midas*: King who unwisely judged Pan a better musician than Apollo, and was punished with ass's ears. *Lord Chancellor*: Official who granted or refused permission for every new play; Cibber is a sort of unofficial Lord Chancellor.

325. *Benson's titles*: William Benson erected a monument to Milton, incorporating his own 'titles', in Westminster Abbey; see also 329n.

326. *Ambrose Philips*: See I, Argument note. *preferred*: Given a preferment, 'a place of honour or profit' (*Dictionary*), not for 'wit' but for political support.

327. *Ripley*: Thomas Ripley, a former carpenter who designed unimpressive new buildings for the Admiralty, contrasted ironically here with the noble Whitehall edifice that burned down in the Great Fire of 1666.

328. *Jones*: Inigo Jones: See 'IV Burlington', 46n. *Boyle*: Richard Boyle: see 'IV Burlington', Dedication note.

329. *Wren*: Christopher Wren, architect of St Paul's Cathedral and many London churches built after the Fire, who was replaced by the inept Benson as Surveyor-General of Works.

330. *Gay dies unpensioned*: John Gay hoped in vain for a government pension, such as inferior writers with political connections often received. See also 'Epistle to T. Blount', 47n.

331. *Hibernian*: Irish; Swift's expectation of a bishopric in England was dashed at the death of Queen Anne, and he spent the rest of his life in his native Ireland.

332. *Pope's ... translate*: Much of Pope's time from 1713 to 1726

was devoted to his translation of Homer and his edition of Shakespeare.

334. *birch shall blush*: i.e. whips of birch twigs reddened with the blood of thrashed schoolboys.

335–6. *Eton . . . Westminster*: Two of the most distinguished schools in England, on the Thames close to Pope's boyhood home near Windsor, and adjoining Westminster Abbey, respectively.

337. *Isis*: The river at Oxford University. *elders reel*: The tutors reel in consequence of heavy drinking.

338. *dissolved in port*: Incapacitated after imbibing their favourite drink, port wine, with a pun on ships becalmed 'in port'.

339. *Monarch*: Bays/Cibber.

340. *iv'ry gate*: Dreams that pass through the gate of horn bring true visions, while those through the gate of ivory are false (*Odyssey*, XIX; *Aeneid*, VI).

Book the Fourth

Argument: *Virtuosos*: 'virtuoso: a man skilled in antique or natural curiosities; a man studious of painting, statuary, or architecture' (*Dictionary*).

3. *darkness visible*: Milton's phrase describing Hell, 'no light, but rather darkness visible' (*Paradise Lost*, I, 63).

7. *force inertly strong*: 'alluding to the *vis inertiae* of matter, which, though it really be no power, is yet the foundation of all the qualities and attributes of that sluggish substance' (Pope's note).

9. *Dog-star*: See 'Arbuthnot', 3n.

10. *bay*: The laurel of poetic achievement.

13. *seed*: Offspring (of Dullness).

15. *new world*: 'in allusion to the Epicurean opinion that from the dissolution of the natural world into night and chaos, a new one should arise' (Pope's note).

16. *Saturnian*: Not only reversing the Virgilian prophecy in which the Saturnian age of lead will be superseded by gold (as in III, 320 and note), but including gold as well, since money is the chief object of the Dunces.

18. *below revealed*: In a mock-Scriblerian footnote, Pope quoted an 'old adage: the higher you climb, the more you show your arse'.

21. *Science*: Learning in general.

22. *Wit*: Intelligence. *exile, penalties and pains*: As experienced in 1723 by Pope's friend Francis Atterbury, Bishop of Rochester, who was condemned under the Act of Pains and Penalties for

conspiring to bring back the Stuart monarchy; also 246 and note.

26. *Billingsgate*: Vulgar and abusive language; see also I, 307n.

28. *Chicane in furs*: Legal trickery by judges, dressed in ermine robes. *Casuistry in lawn*: Sophistry by bishops, wearing sleeves of lawn (see 'I Cobham', 136n.).

29. *straiten*: 'to make tight' (*Dictionary*), thus strangling Morality.

30. *Page*: Serving as the Goddess's court 'page' is Sir Francis Page, 'always ready to hang any man, of which he was suffered to give a hundred miserable examples during a long life' (Pope's note). See also Horace, Satire, II, i, 82n.

31. *Mathesis*: Mathematics ('mad', with reference to arcane theories).

33. *ecstatic*: 'ravished; rapturous; elevated to ecstasy' (*Dictionary*).

34. *circle ... square*: The famously insoluble problem of ancient geometry: to construct a square whose area equals that of a given circle.

37. *addressed*: Aimed.

38. *wont*: Wonted, accustomed.

41. *Thalia*: The muse of comedy; accented on the second syllable.

42. *Satyr*: See 'Essay on Criticism', 592n.

43. CHESTERFIELD: Philip Stanhope, fourth Earl of Chesterfield, unsuccessfully opposed passage of the Licensing Act that required every play to be approved in advance by the Lord Chamberlain.

45. *harlot form*: Italian opera, with 'its affected airs, its effeminate sounds, and the practice of patching up these operas with favourite songs incoherently put together' (Pope's note).

51. *Nine*: The Muses.

52. *recitativo*: Musical declamation, midway between singing and speaking.

53. *cara*: Dear (Italian). *that train*: The Muses and their followers.

54. *Division*: Series of notes sung to a single syllable of text.

57. *One trill shall harmonize*: i.e. the music takes no account of emotional contexts.

64. *Music ... Sense*: The music in Handel's oratorios was closely allied to the meaning of the words.

66. *Briareus*: Giant, son of the earth-mother Gaia, with a hundred hands.

70. *Hibernian*: Irish; the *Messiah* had recently received its first performance in Dublin. Handel had lived in England since 1712, but Pope implies that his music had lost favour with London

audiences, in part because of the loud 'thunder' and 'drums' (68).

75–6.   *attraction . . . gravity*: As in Newtonian physics.

77.   *want a place*: Fail to get a place.

84.   *vortex*: A whirlpool sucking in its victims (Descartes thought the planets were whirled around in invisible cosmic 'vortices').

85.   *own*: Acknowledge.

87.   *Town*: London.

88.   *toupee*: Or toupet, 'a curl; an artificial lock of hair' (*Dictionary*). *gown*: Of college scholars.

89.   *mungril*: Mongrel, 'generated between different natures; base-born; degenerate' (*Dictionary*).

92.   *the Great*: The aristocracy: see I, 3n.

93.   *bow the knee to Baal*: St Paul preached to those who had not 'bowed the knee to the image of Baal' (Romans 11:4), i.e. to false gods.

94.   *without a call*: Enter holy orders for career advancement, rather than in response to a calling.

96.   *Withhold . . . head*: Commission a bust of a poet who received no pension during his lifetime.

97.   *vest . . . gown*: Reward a flatterer with a rich church benefice.

98.   *from fool . . . crown*: The succession of contemptible Poets Laureate.

100. *Muse's Hypocrite*: 'he who thinks the only end of poetry is to amuse, and the only business of the poet to be witty; and consequently who cultivates only such trifling talents in himself, and encourages only such in others' (Pope's note).

103–4.   *Narcissus . . . show'r*: Lord John Hervey, with his lily-white face (as in 'Arbuthnot', 306), was 'showered' with flattery by the clergyman Conyers Middleton.

105. *Montalto*: High mountain, referring to Sir Thomas Hanmer, speaker of the House of Commons and editor of an edition of Shakespeare (the 'Volume fair' (106)); see also 113–18 and note.

109. *awful*: 'that which strikes with awe, or fills with reverence' (*Dictionary*).

110–12.   *Benson . . . Johnston's name*: William Benson erected a monument to Milton (see III, 325 and note), but also sought to make his reputation by publishing a poetic version of the Psalms by a Scottish physician, Arthur Johnston.

113–18.   *decent knight . . . off in state*: Hanmer was furious when it appeared that there would be insufficient purchasers for his Shakespeare edition, but it was afterward subsidized by the Clarendon Press at Oxford. In so doing the Vice-Chancellor and the heads of Oxford Houses have demeaned themselves as 'Apollo's may'r and aldermen'; the 'gold-capped youths' are wealthy gentlemen commoners, with gold tassels on their caps.

122. *Aeson*: The father of Jason, whom Medea restored to youthful vigour by draining his blood and replacing it with a magic brew.

123. *standard-Authors*: Standard in the sense of canonical texts, but also flying the battle flag so known.

125. *the chequered shade*: From Milton, *L'Allegro*, 96.

133. *triumphal car*: In ancient Rome, a chariot in a procession celebrating a military 'triumph'.

134. *slave*: A general being honoured with a triumph would be accompanied by captives in chains.

136. *Address*: Petition.

138. *complaisance*: 'civility; desire of pleasing; act of adulation' (*Dictionary*).

139–40. *Spectre . . . dreadful wand*: The ghost of Dr Richard Busby, seventeenth-century headmaster of Westminster School, famous for thrashing his students; the 'index-hand' is his right hand.

141. *beavered brow*: Busby wore a beaver hat; also, a play on the 'beaver' or visor on a medieval helmet.

144–5. *Eton . . . Westminster*: See III, 335–6. *Winton*: Nickname for Winchester School in Hampshire.

146. *Genius of the place*: Guardian spirit.

147. *boy-senator*: Youthful Member of Parliament, clutching his breeches because he still fears Busby's birch rod.

151. *Samian letter*: 'the letter Y, used by Pythagoras as an emblem of the different roads of virtue and vice' (Pope's note).

156. *Sense*: The understanding.

159. *exercise the breath*: 'by obliging them to get the classic poets by heart, which furnishes them with endless matter for conversation, and verbal amusement for their whole lives' (Pope's note).

160. *pale*: Enclosure.

161. *howe'er designed*: Whatever career they may be in training for.

162. *jingling*: In rhyme and metre.

163. *A poet the first day*: Schoolboys were required from the beginning to compose Latin verse.

166. *House or Hall*: Westminster Hall, site of law courts, and the House of Commons.

167–70. *WYNDHAM . . . TALBOT . . . MURRAY . . . PULT'NEY*: Sir William Wyndham; Charles Talbot, Earl of Shrewsbury; William Murray (see Horace, Ode, IV, i, 9–10n.); and William Pulteney, Earl of Bath; all politicians whom Pope admired, 'lost' to

Dullness because they devoted their writing talents to important causes rather than to mere verbal exercises.

174. *that Masterpiece*: 'viz. an epigram. The famous Dr [Robert] South declared a perfect epigram to be as difficult a performance as an epic poem' (Pope's note).

176. *JAMES*: James I was proud of his Latin scholarship.

177. *Doctor*: Learned teacher.

180. *Council*: The Privy Council, the king's closest advisers.

181. *grateful*: 'pleasing; acceptable; delightful' (*Dictionary*).

187. *Cam, and Isis*: The rivers flowing through Cambridge and Oxford, respectively.

188. *RIGHT DIVINE*: Though a Tory, Pope was not sympathetic to the old doctrine of the divine right of kings, fiercely asserted by James I.

190. *shoal*: 'a crowd; a great multitude; a throng' (*Dictionary*, citing this line).

192. *Aristotle*: His philosophy dominated medieval scholarship and by Pope's time was widely considered discredited, but there were still Aristotelians at Oxford.

194. *Christ Church*: Distinguished Oxford college, appreciated by Pope for attacking Richard Bentley (see II, 205 and note); the brackets parody Bentley's custom of indicating passages that he considered spurious.

195. *Polemic*: Controversialist.

196. *expelling Locke*: 'In the year 1703 there was a meeting of the heads of the University of Oxford to censure Mr Locke's *Essay on Human Understanding*, and to forbid the reading it' (Pope's note).

198. *Crouzas*: Jean-Pierre de Crousaz (Swiss, not German), who had attacked Pope's 'Essay on Man' on religious grounds. *Burgersdyck*: Francis Burgersdijk, Dutch professor of philosophy whose old-fashioned treatises were still studied at Oxford.

200. *Marg'ret and Clare Hall*: Colleges at Cambridge; St John's College is also known by the name of its founder, Lady Margaret Beaufort, and Clare College was known as Clare Hall in Pope's day.

202. *troubled waters*: Bentley was a ferocious controversialist. *sleeps in port*: Like a ship safely in harbour, with punning reference to Bentley's fondness for port wine.

203. *Aristarch*: A severe critic, from a Greek grammarian of that name.

204. *Remark*: Bentley published numerous *Remarks* on classical subjects.

205. *vailed*: 'vail: to let fall in token of respect' (*Dictionary*).

206. *Walker*: Richard Walker, Vice-Master of Trinity College, Cambridge, of which Bentley was Master; he was said to have sedulously looked after Bentley's hat.

208. *upright Quakers*: As an affirmation of spiritual equality, Quakers would take off their hats to God but not to social superiors.

211. *Scholiast*: Textual commentator.

212. *humbled Milton's strains*: See Horace, Epistle, II, i, 104n.

216–18. *something yet more great ... o'er-tops them all*: Bentley plumed himself on restoring the digamma – a double Greek letter gamma, larger than other letters and thus 'something yet more great' – in the text of Homer. *Saul*: Taller than other Israelites (1 Samuel 9:2).

220–22. *Disputes ... or K*: Controversies about Latin pronunciation and spelling, including whether Cicero's name should be pronounced with hard or soft Cs.

223–4. *Freind ... Alsop*: 'Dr Robert Freind, master of Westminster School and a canon of Christ Church; Dr Anthony Alsop, a happy imitator of the Horatian style' (Pope's note).

225–6. *Virgil ... Solinus*: 'Some critics having had it in their choice to comment either on Virgil or Manilius, Pliny or Solinus, have chosen the worse author, the more freely to display their critical capacity' (Pope's note). Bentley had published an edition of Manilius' treatise on astronomy; Solinus wrote an unremarkable compendium of historical information.

227. *Attic*: See 'Epilogue to the Satires', II, 85n.

228–31. *Suidas ... Gellius ... Stobaeus*: Ancient grammarians whom Pope considered inferior.

237. *Kuster, Burman, Wasse*: Foreign classical scholars admired by Bentley.

243. *House*: An Oxford or Cambridge college.

244. Νοῦς: Mind (Greek), pronounced to rhyme with 'house', used by Plato to refer to the rational and immortal part of the soul; 'a word much affected by the learned Aristarchus [i.e. Bentley] in common conversation, to signify *genius* or natural *acumen*' (Pope's note).

245. BARROW: Isaac Barrow, a master before Bentley of Trinity College, Cambridge, and the teacher of Isaac Newton. *block*: Blockhead.

246. ATTERBURY: Exiled from England and thus, in Dullness' opinion, unable to 'spoil' the faithful.

247. *Canon*: Deliberately spelled with a single *n* to emphasize the pun on a clergyman attached to a cathedral or college.

248. *involve the pole*: Cloud the sky.

260. *Dispute*: Logical disputation.

262. *what he must divorce*: Because most students will have to give up poetry after graduation.

266. *Show all his paces*: Like a horse at a riding school, 'going through its paces' without actually advancing.

267. *cement*: Accented on the first syllable.

270. *hew . . . the Man*: 'a notion of Aristotle that there was originally in every block of marble a statue, which would appear on the removal of the superfluous parts' (Pope's note); actually it was Plato.

272. *governor*: Travelling tutor on the Grand Tour of the Continent, taken to complete a young gentleman's education.

274. *Ajax*: His ghost turns bitterly away when his fellow warrior Odysseus encounters him in the underworld (*Odyssey*, XI).

278. *op'ning*: Barking, giving tongue.

281. *th' attendant Orator*: The governor of 272.

283. *sacred from the rod*: Protected from being beaten, and therefore, by implication, overindulged.

286. *begged the blessing*: His mother hopes he will turn into a play-boy 'rake'.

290. *Safe and unseen*: Aeneas enters Carthage hidden by Venus in a cloud of invisibility (*Aeneid*, I).

291. *let down*: Set down in London (having left the university behind).

297. *obsequious*: The Seine in Paris is as obsequious to the absolute monarchy as the population is understood to be.

298. *great Bourbon*: Louis XV, King of France at the time.

299. *no longer Roman*: The modern inhabitants of Rome, where the Tiber flows, have abandoned their own classical culture.

301. *bosomed deep in vines*: French monasteries (or 'convents') often produced excellent wine, much of which the abbot and monks would keep for their own enjoyment.

305. *dancing slaves*: Not literally slaves, but servile subjects of the monarchy who are content to spend their time in pleasure-seeking.

307–10. *her shrine . . . swain*: Venice on the Adriatic, with the winged lion of St Mark as its emblem, had once been a mighty naval and commercial power, but by Pope's time it attracted visitors mainly for its carnival, opera (where eunuchs starred), and prostitutes. *keeps*: Dwells.

314. *His royal sense*: Young Englishmen were supposedly gaining understanding of foreign political systems, but conversation at court centred on operas and beautiful women.

315. *stews*: Brothels.

316. *Intrigued*: Carried on sexual intrigues.

317. *hors-d'oeuvres ... liqueurs*: Still regarded as pretentious foreign expressions.

318. *greatly-daring*: A frequent epithet for Homeric heroes.

319. *Latin store*: Storehouse of classical learning.

320. *acquired no more*: Failed to learn any foreign languages, another professed goal of the Grand Tour.

322. *turned Air*: The young man's knowledge is now reduced to operatic arias (literally 'airs').

323. *half-cured*: Like meat cured by smoking or salting.

324. *solo*: Regarded as an affected foreign word.

326. *Jansen, Fleetwood, Cibber*: Extravagant gamblers, who plunder his 'Estate' (325) when he returns home.

327. *followed by a nun*: He brings back a nun as his mistress ('one Venus more' (330)).

328. *not undone*: Immune from prosecution for debt if elected a Member of Parliament.

335. *Hero ... Dame*: The young man and his foreign mistress.

338. *senate*: The House of Commons, playfully using the Roman term.

341. *Paridel*: Spenserian name for a young wandering squire, noted for seductions.

347. *Annius*: Fifteenth-century Italian forger of manuscripts. *ebon*: Ebony.

348. *dissembled*: Simulated.

349. *cankered*: Tarnished or corroded.

350. *capon*: Rooster castrated so it can be fattened for the table. *Pollio*: Any rich patron of the arts.

360–63. *other Caesars ... Cecrops*: Heads of emperors and other figures on the forged coins.

361. *th' Athenian fowl*: Athena's emblematic bird, the owl of wisdom, appeared on Athenian coins.

364. *the pigeon*: In anti-Islamic tradition, Muhammad trained a pigeon to take a grain from his ear, persuading believers that it was a visitation of the Holy Spirit.

366. *Lares*: Roman household gods, who remain after his house is sold to pay his debts.

367. *headless ... postpone*: Instead of spending time with his bride, he prefers a headless statue of Phoebe, goddess of chastity.

369–70. *Otho ... Niger*: Rare coins issued by emperors whose reigns were very short.

371. *Mummius*: A collector of Egyptian mummies.

372. *Cheops stinks*: A fake mummy, supposedly of the emperor Cheops, decomposing disgustingly.

374. *sistrum*: Rattle used in Egyptian religious rites.

376. *hornèd race*: The successors of Alexander the Great had themselves depicted on coins with the rams' horns associated with Jupiter Ammon; see also 'Essay on Criticism', 376n.

380. *Sallee rovers*: North African pirates.

381. *Hermes*: God of thieves and travellers.

382. *Down his own throat*: In a long note Pope tells the story of a collector who concealed valuable coins from pirates this way.

383. *demigod*: As the ancient emperors claimed to be.

391. *clear of all design*: Not plotting in any way.

394. *Douglas*: James Douglas, well-known obstetrician and also collector of rare books.

407. *leaves*: Petals.

409. *CAROLINE*: George II's queen, for whom a superb new hybrid might be named; she had died in 1737.

411. *pencil*: Paintbrush; i.e. the hybrid flower has colours that Nature would never produce.

415. *the wretch*: A rival in horticulture. *insect lust*: Destroying the flower as an insect would.

417. *Elysian*: The Elysian Fields in the underworld, where it is forever springtime and flowers do not fade.

421. *enamelled race*: Butterflies.

422. *zephyrs*: Gentle breezes.

425. *vernal*: In springtime.

430. *bird*: Any flying creature; here, a butterfly.

435. *paper*: On which the butterfly is mounted.

440. *our sleeping friends*: The lolling loiterers whom Dullness put to sleep (337–46).

444. *what's o'clock*: The night watchman would call out the hours.

448. *Congenial ... cockle-kind*: The collector feels a personal affinity with the tightly closed shellfish.

451. *superlunar things*: Unchangeable and eternal verities, playing on the old terminology in which 'sublunary' things were mutable.

452. *Poised*: Balanced. *Wilkins' wings*: Bishop John Wilkins, first secretary of the Royal Society and author of *The Discovery of a World in the Moon*, suggested that it might be possible some day to fly there.

459. *Clerk*: Pronounced 'clark': cleric, clergyman; with a pun on the name of the Rev. Samuel Clarke, regarded as a freethinker whose books promoted deistic 'natural religion'.

460. *Myst'ry*: The mysteries of Christian revelation; Pope is defending himself from the criticism that 'Essay on Man' ignored revelation and faith. *divinely dark*: i.e. the arguments of the rationalist 'divine' are unintelligible.

463. *implicit faith*: Doctrines accepted on faith, even if not fully understood.

464. *impose . . . dogmatize*: Though attacking orthodox dogma, freethinkers are quick to impose their own views and dogmas.

471. *high priori*: Pun on 'a priori'; having reasoned 'downward' (472) from preconceived assumptions, such as that a just God could not permit the existence of evil, the thinker ends by doubting God's existence altogether.

475-6. *mechanic cause . . . diffuse in space*: 'The first of these follies is that of Descartes, the second of Hobbes, the third of some succeeding philosophers' (Pope's note).

477. *at one bound*: Recalling Satan invading Paradise 'at one slight bound' (*Paradise Lost*, IV, 181).

478. *Make God Man's image*: Reversing the biblical statement that man was made in God's image (Genesis 1:26). *final Cause*: The ultimate end or purpose of the creation.

479. *Virtue local*: i.e. not universal. *all Relation scorn*: Scorn relationships with other human beings and with God.

482. *Soul and Will*: 'two things the most self-evident, the existence of our soul, and the freedom of our will' (Pope's note).

484. *Lucretius drew*: In *De Rerum Naturae*, the Roman poet Lucretius imagined the gods as indifferent to humanity.

487. *bright Image*: 'the title given by the later Platonists to that idea of Nature which they had formed in their fancy' (Pope's note).

488. *Theocles*: The speaker in the Earl of Shaftesbury's *The Moralists*, who extols a 'Nature' that seems virtually divine.

489. *Genius*: Guardian spirit.

492. *Tindal*: See II, 399n. *Silenus*: Drunken tutor to the wine god Dionysus (thus, 'the boozy sire' (493)); Pope seems to have had in mind the corpulent Thomas Gordon, a freethinker and Commissioner for Wine Licences under Walpole.

494. *seeds of fire*: A Virgilian phrase, *semina ignis* (*Eclogue*, VI, 33) and *semina flammae* (*Aeneid*, VI, 6).

495. *snapped his box*: Snapped shut his tobacco box.

496. *gown*: As worn by the clergy.

498. *the Youth*: Understood as a plural, 'the Youths'.

499. *priestcraft*: A term of contempt used by critics of the established Church.

501. *vassal to a name*: Giving unquestioning obedience to some authority, such as Aristotle.

502. *child and man the same*: He never grows into independent adulthood.

504. *A trifling ... heart*: Echoing the portrait of Sporus in 'Arbuthnot', 327.

506. *a Queen*: Another dig at the late Queen Caroline, who patronized freethinking clergymen.

510. *in pension, or in punk*: Corrupted by government pay or by prostitutes.

511. *Kent ... Berkeley*: Henry de Grey, Duke of Kent, and James, third Earl of Berkeley, accused (somewhat obscurely here) of corruption.

513. *Warwick*: The Earl of Warwick, a dissipated nobleman who died young.

516. *Magus*: Magician, wizard (517).

517. *his Cup*: 'the cup of self-love, which causes a total oblivion of the obligations of friendship or honour, and of the service of God or our country, all sacrificed to vainglory, court-worship, or yet meaner considerations of lucre and brutal pleasures' (Pope's note).

520. *Star*: Emblem of a knightly order. *Endymion*: Mortal who loved Selene, the moon, and died of longing (or, in other versions, fell into perpetual sleep); the implication is that desire for a knighthood causes one's principles to die.

521. *Feather*: In the cap of the Order of the Garter.

528. *human shape*: 'the effects of the Magus's cup are just contrary to that of Circe: hers took away the shape, and left the human mind; this takes away the mind, and leaves the human shape' (Pope's note). The enchantress Circe used a magical potion to turn Odysseus' sailors into swine (*Odyssey*, X).

531. *strait*: Straightway, immediately.

532. *Cimmerian gloom*: See III, 4n.

538. *Int'rest*: Political allegiance. *parti-coloured*: 'having diversity of colours' (*Dictionary*), with a pun on political 'party'.

541. *syren sisters*: Opera singers (likened to the seductive sirens in *Odyssey*, IV).

545. *Cowper ... King*: Peers who rose to distinction by their own efforts, and whose sons were undistinguished.

549. *priest succinct in amice white*: i.e. a French chef in tightly belted ('succinct') white linen; *amice*: 'the first or undermost part of a priest's habit' (*Dictionary*, citing this line).

550. *all flesh is nothing*: Alluding to John 6:63: 'It is the spirit that quickeneth; the flesh profiteth nothing'; invoked ironically to describe an elaborate process of reducing meat.

551. *Beeves*: Plural of 'beef'.

553. *board*: Table. *specious*: Plausible.

554. *hares . . . toads*: There was a fashion for altering the appearance of a dish to simulate something else.

556. *sève and verdeur*: The wine's qualities of strength and tartness (French).

558. *Perigord*: French province. *Bayonne*: French town.

559. *French libation*: Wine. *Italian strain*: Opera (musical 'strains').

560–61. *Bladen . . . Knight*: Well-known gamblers. *crowds undone*: By the collapse of the South Sea Bubble investment scheme, itself a kind of gambling, in which these individuals were apparently involved.

562. *three essential partridges in one*: 'two dissolved into quintessence to make sauce for the third' (Pope's note), with an ironic allusion to the Holy Trinity.

568. *Inns of Court*: The complex of buildings belonging to the legal societies, whose members neglect their profession in favour of literary dabbling.

569. *Vertù*: connoisseurship (Gallic form of Italian *virtù*).

570. *F. R. S.*: Fellow of the Royal Society, a distinguished honour which Pope nevertheless disparages.

571–2. *Freemasons . . . Pythagoras*: i.e. for members of the secret society of Freemasons, as for ancient followers of Pythagoras, 'taciturnity is the only essential qualification' (Pope's note).

573. *Florists at the least*: i.e. merely producing flowers for show, hence inferior to botanists who seek scientific knowledge.

574. *annual feast*: Of any civic or professional organization.

576. *Gregorian . . . Gormogon*: Societies founded to make fun of the Freemasons.

578. *Isis and Cam*: Rivers at Oxford and Cambridge.

585. *cap and switch*: Of a jockey. *his Grace*: A duke.

586. *staff and pumps*: Stick and shoes used by 'running footmen' who trotted alongside their master's coach; here, the young Marquis amuses himself by dressing as a footman.

587. *licensed Earl*: He has obtained a licence permitting him to drive a stagecoach, an occupation obviously beneath him.

588. *the Sun*: In Greek mythology, Helios, who drives his chariot daily from east to west.

589. *design*: Sketch, draw.

590. *Arachne*: The spider; the baron seeks a way to make silk from spiderwebs.

591. *sergeant*: Or serjeant: a barrister in the common law, who would address his fellow lawyers as 'brother'; the 'dance' refers to ceremonial revels at the Inns of Court.

593. *The Bishop*: William Talbot, Bishop of Durham, who would have a hundred turkeys reduced by cooking until they filled a single pie.

602. *First Ministers*: Prime ministers; Walpole (the 'daring son' (599)), who had recently fallen from power, was thought by the opposition to have had excessive influence over George II.

603. *three Estates*: The Lords Spiritual (bishops), Lords Temporal (peers), and Commons.

608. *St James's*: The chapel royal. *Gilbert*: John Gilbert, Archbishop of York, who is 'leaden' in helping to bring in the Age of Lead.

609. *Hall*: The law courts at Westminster Hall.

610. *Convocation*: Assembly of clergy.

611. *Nation's Sense*: A majority decision by the House of Commons was sometimes called 'the sense of the nation'.

614. *Palinurus*: The pilot of Aeneas' ship, who went to sleep and fell into the sea; thus, Walpole losing office.

618. *navies yawned for orders*: The opposition denounced Walpole for resisting going to war to avenge Spanish attacks on English shipping. *the main*: The sea.

627. *In vain*: The asterisks indicate a break to set off the eloquent conclusion.

633. *Wit*: Intelligence.

635. *Medea*: In Seneca's *Medea*, the sorceress calls upon the monsters of the celestial constellations as she prepares to murder her children.

637. *Argus' eyes*: Hermes, messenger of the gods, used his caduceus 'wand' (the herald's staff with wings and entwined snakes) to put the hundred-eyed monster Argus to sleep, and then slew him.

642. *Casuistry*: Specious reasoning.

644. *second cause*: God being the 'first cause', a 'second cause' acts in reaction to something else; the reference appears to be the scientific theorists who stop at material causes and ignore the ultimate power of God.

645. *Physic*: Science, also medicine.

647. *Mystery to Mathematics fly*: i.e. deists claim that the laws of physics, rather than the 'mysteries' of faith, can confirm the existence and goodness of God.

650. *unawares Morality expires*: Since morality has been dependent on religion, it unexpectedly expires.

654. *uncreating word*: Reversing the Word of divine creation: 'In the beginning was the Word, and the Word was with God, and the Word was God' (John 1:1), and 'God said, Let there be light, and there was light' (Genesis 1:3).

655. *Anarch*: Monarch of anarchy, a term Milton uses for Chaos (*Paradise Lost*, II, 988).

PROSE WRITINGS

FROM THE PREFACE TO THE *ILIAD*

Pope's preface appeared in 1715 in the first instalment of his *Iliad* translation; approximately half of it is given here. With allusions to theorists of epic and to previous translators, he describes his attempt to achieve a poetic style that will make the archaic poem fresh and alive for his contemporaries, with equivalents for expressions that they would find obscure or peculiar. Invoking a traditional contrast between Homer and Virgil, Pope insists that Homer's greatness lies in creative 'invention', and in the poetic energy that he calls 'spirit and fire'.

1. *invention*: Creative power (literally 'finding out' the possibilities of a work).
2. *'They pour . . . it'*: *Iliad*, II, 780.
3. *numbers*: Metre, versification.
4. *vivida vis animi*: 'active power of mind' (Lucretius, *De Rerum Naturae*).
5. *Lucan*: Author of *Pharsalia*, an epic poem about the civil war between Julius Caesar and Pompey. *Statius*: Author of the *Thebaid*, an epic poem about the legendary conflict between the sons of Oedipus in the Greek city Thebes.
6. *fable*: 'the series or contexture of events which constitute a poem epic or dramatic' (*Dictionary*).
7. *'soul of poetry'*: Aristotle, *Poetics*, ch. 6.
8. *Aristotle expresses it*: *Poetics*, ch. 24. Manners are 'general way of life; morals; habits' (*Dictionary*).
9. *sentiments*: 'sentiment: thought; notion; opinion' (*Dictionary*).

10. *Longinus*: Greek rhetorician, supposed author of a treatise *On the Sublime*.

11. *Gnomologia Homerica*: By James Duport, Cambridge classicist, whose book (1660) compares aphorisms from Homer to sayings from the Bible.

12. *an excellent modern writer*: Joseph Addison, in *Spectator*, 279.

13. *living words*: Aristotle, *Rhetoric*, III, 11.

14. *machines*: Supernatural beings or 'Machinery' intervene in human affairs.

15. *Ancient*: Ever since the previous century, there had been an ongoing controversy between 'ancients', who championed the superiority of classical literature, and 'moderns'.

16. *fustian*: 'a high swelling kind of writing made up of heterogeneous parts, or of words and ideas ill associated; bombast' (*Dictionary*).

17. *tricked up*: Adorned in a showy manner.

18. *'junto'*: 'a cabal; a kind of men combined in any secret design' (*Dictionary*).

19. *hemistich*: Half-line of verse.

20. *very few*: Ever since 'Essay on Criticism', Pope had been admired for his remarkable skill in making sound echo sense.

21. *Chapman, Hobbes, and Ogilby*: George Chapman's Elizabethan translation would be rediscovered in the next century and admired for its muscular energy (as in Keats's sonnet 'On First Looking into Chapman's Homer'). In the seventeenth century the political theorist Thomas Hobbes made a prose translation, and John Ogilby (see 'Dunciad', I, 141n.) a poetic one, neither of which had much success.

22. *Bussy D'Ambois*: Jacobean tragedy by Chapman.

23. *figures*: Figures of speech.

24. *periods*: 'period: a complete sentence from one full stop to another' (*Dictionary*).

FROM THE PREFACE TO
THE WORKS OF SHAKESPEARE

Capitalizing on Pope's poetic fame, the publisher Jacob Tonson recruited him to serve as editor of an expensive six-volume edition of Shakespeare that came out in 1725. In his preface, approximately half of which is given here, Pope praises Shakespeare's genius and seeks to defend him from accusations of carelessness and 'faults' by arguing that he should not be held to the rules of neoclassical drama. Pope does take it for granted, however, that Shakespeare had no education, pandered to a popular audience, and wrote from spontaneous inspiration by 'Nature' rather than as a conscientious artist. The final analogy with Gothic architecture is double-edged, since it concedes a certain grandeur to the Gothic, but assumes as well the superiority of the classical style of Pope's own time. Pope's edition was vulnerable to scholarly attacks that soon appeared, since although he and his helpers had diligently compared early versions of the plays, he trusted too confidently in his own judgement to select particular readings, and to alter the text whenever he thought it was called for.

1. *beauties and faults*: It was customary for editors to single out specific passages either as especially fine, or as offending against good taste and theoretical 'rules'.
2. *passions*: Strong emotions such as love and anger, which were considered involuntary; a skilful playwright would know how to 'raise' them in his audience.
3. *spleen*: Depression or 'melancholy', thought to originate in disorders of the spleen.
4. *sentiments*: See 'Preface to *Iliad*', n. 9.
5. *accidents*: Non-essential elements.
6. *subsistence*: Adequate income.
7. *mechanics*: Manual labourers.
8. *vulgar*: 'plebeian; practised among the common people' (*Dictionary*).
9. *extraction*: 'derivation of an original; lineage; descent' (*Dictionary*).
10. *Grex*: Troop or group, a pair of characters who act as commentators in Jonson's *Every Man Out of His Humour*.
11. *prince*: Monarch (Elizabeth I, followed by James I).
12. *player*: Actor.
13. *blotted*: Erased; Ben Jonson wrote in *Timber, or Discoveries* (1641): 'I remember the players have often mentioned it as an honour to Shakespeare that in his writing, whatsoever he penned, he never blotted out a line. My answer hath been, "Would he had blotted a thousand."'
14. *folio*: The large-format First Folio edition of Shakespeare's plays was published in 1623, seven years after his death, by his colleagues John Heminges and Henry Condell.
15. *most wit and fancy*: Lively intelligence and imagination.
16. *glaring*: Striking.

FROM *PERI BATHOUS, OR: OF THE ART OF SINKING IN POETRY*

By 1714 Pope and a group of friends – Swift, Arbuthnot, Gay, and the then-popular Irish poet Thomas Parnell – had formed a group that called itself the Scriblerians, meeting weekly in London to compose the mock biography of an absurd pedant they called Martinus Scriblerus. Over the ensuing years Pope never lost sight of the project, and eventually published the *Memoirs of Scriblerus* in 1741. Meanwhile, he conceived the idea of a parodic treatise ironically praising bad poetry of all kinds, and in 1728 – the same year that Gay's *Beggar's Opera* had a triumphant success on stage, and a couple of months before the first version of the 'Dunciad' – he and Swift brought out a volume of *Miscellanies* that included *Peri Bathous*. The title of Longinus' much-admired Greek treatise *On the Sublime* is *Peri Houpsos* in Greek; since *bathous* (or 'bathos') can mean 'depth', the suggestion was that the Ancients had soared up to the sublime but had neglected to descend to the ridiculous. Swift and Arbuthnot both contributed to *Peri Bathous*, of which approximately one-fifth is given here, but the bulk of the work was Pope's.

1. *morbid secretion*: Discharge of diseased fluid; as in Swift's satire *The Mechanical Operation of the Spirit*, aberrant mental behaviour is ascribed to physiological disturbance.
2. *issue*: Discharge (of mucus).
3. *evacuation*: A medical term: 'the practice of emptying the body by physic' (*Dictionary*).
4. *nascimur poetae*: We are born poets.
5. *pruritus*: Itching.
6. *conceive*: Punning on the double meaning of 'have an idea' and 'get pregnant'.
7. *peccant humour*: Diseased bodily fluid.
8. *purulent metre*: 'purulent: consisting of pus or the running of wounds' (*Dictionary*); puns on the medical term 'purulent matter'.
9. *the Ministry*: The cabinet of the prime minister and his colleagues.
10. *Horace*: In *Ars Poetica*, 373–4, Horace says that neither gods nor men can tolerate mediocrity in poets.
11. *vivacité de pesanteur*: Quickness in sinking (French).
12. *an English author . . . sinking*: Shakespeare, *The Merry Wives of*

484 NOTES – PROSE WRITINGS

Windsor III, v, 12, spoken by Falstaff after being thrown into a river.

13. *lessen the book*: i.e. make it shorter, and hence less profitable to the author.

14. *his feet in butter*: 'When I washed my steps with butter, and the rock poured me out rivers of oil' (Job 29:6 in the King James Version; the Roman Catholic Douay Bible, which Pope may sometimes have used, has 'washed my feet').

15. *With teats . . . feet*: Richard Blackmore, *Job* (a poetic adaptation of the biblical book). On Blackmore, see 'Essay on Criticism', 463n.

16. *In flaming . . . blue*: Blackmore, *Prince Arthur*.

17. *His eye-balls . . . mane*: Labelled 'anonymous' by Pope, and probably written by himself.

18. *They brandish . . . end*: Blackmore, *Prince Arthur*. *staves*: Staffs or sticks. *osier*: Willow branches used to make baskets.

19. *Periphrase*: 'circumlocution; use of many words to express the sense of one' (*Dictionary*).

20. *A waving . . . fed*: Blackmore, *Job*.

21. *'No light . . . visible'*: *Paradise Lost*, I, 63.

22. *He roared . . . him*: *Vetus autor* (Pope's note), old author, i.e. probably by himself.

23. *The silver . . . black*: Likewise probably by Pope.

24. *The obscureness . . . light*: Lewis Theobald, *The Double False-hood*. On Theobald, see 'Arbuthnot', 164n.

25. *Up to . . . sky*: Blackmore, *Prince Arthur*.

26. *Behold . . . eyes*: 'anonymous' (Pope's note), so probably by himself.

27. *Ye gods . . . happy*: Probably by Pope.

28. *circumbendibus*: A made-up Latin word (by Dryden) meaning a roundabout method.

29. *prospect*: View.

30. *I'd call . . . high*: 'anonymous' (Pope's note), so probably by himself.

31. *Under . . . yoke*: Edmund Waller, *Upon the Late Storm*.

32. *And thou . . . Mar*: 'anonymous' (Pope's note), so probably by himself.

33. *Finical*: 'foppish; pretending to superfluous elegance' (*Dictionary*).

34. *Won by . . . away*: Blackmore, *Job*.

35. *When watchful . . . granary*: Ibid.

36. *Oaks . . . by*: John Dennis, *Upon Our Victory at Sea*.

37. *The sparkling . . . while*: From an anonymous poem in a miscellany published by Jacob Tonson. *liquor*: Liquid.

38. *BUSKIN*: Shoe worn by Greek tragic actors in order to appear taller.

39. *engine*: 'any means used to bring to pass, or to effect' (*Dictionary*).
40. *breech*: Buttocks.
41. *For whom . . . enter*: Probably by Pope, as are all the remaining quotations with the exception of the two noted below.
42. *Advance . . . yonder*: Shakespeare, *The Tempest*, I, ii, 409–10.
43. *Wax . . . trust*: Theobald, *The Double Falsehood* (referring to sealing wax).
44. *Bacchus . . . Ceres*: The god of wine and the goddess of the harvest, hence of grain.
45. *Receipt*: Recipe. This chapter is a revised version of an essay in the *Guardian*, no. 78, which Pope had published in 1713.
46. *undertakers*: Persons who undertake a task.
47. *Molière . . . dinner*: In *The Miser*, III, i.
48. *Fable*: Story, plot.
49. *Geoffrey of Monmouth*: Twelfth-century chronicler of British traditions, including the Arthurian legends.
50. *Don Belianis*: Hero of a Spanish chivalric romance.
51. *an honest man*: A number of theorists claimed that an epic hero had to be morally upright.
52. *Machines*: See 'Preface to the *Iliad*', note 14.
53. *volatile Mercury*: Mercury, the brisk messenger of the gods, gave his name to the unstable or 'volatile' metal mercury.
54. *Tasso*: Torquato Tasso, sixteenth-century Italian poet, author of *Gerusalemme Liberata*.
55. *Nec . . . inciderit*: 'And let no god intervene, unless the knot is worthy of such a deliverer' (*Ars Poetica*, 191–2).
56. *Eurus . . . Boreas*: The east, west, south, and north winds.
57. *quantum sufficit*: As much as is sufficient, phrase commonly used in medical prescriptions.
58. *Theory of the Conflagration*: Thomas Burnet's *Sacred Theory of the Earth* (1681) predicted a 'general conflagration' that would occur at the end of the world.
59. *succedaneum*: Substitute; often used of food, and thus appropriate for the epic 'recipe'.
60. *Bookseller*: Publisher (who would also keep a bookshop).

SELECTED LETTERS

Pope's letters were artfully composed, carefully varied in style to suit the various recipients, and in many cases clearly intended for publication. Since it would have seemed unpardonable vanity for a living person to publish his own letters, in 1735 he successfully schemed to get some of his early correspondence into the hands of the unscrupulous publisher Edmund Curll, who believed he was outwitting Pope by bringing out an unauthorized collection. Pope was then, of course, free to bring out an 'authentic' edition of his own, in which he occasionally revised letters and even assigned them to different recipients than the original ones. The examples here (of which the first is the only one abridged) give insight into some of the relationships that were so important to him throughout his life.

1. *Lady Mary Wortley Montagu*: Pope was indulging in a somewhat artificial flirtation with Lady Mary, who had recently departed for Constantinople where her husband would be ambassador. This letter exhibits the elegantly amorous style that Pope picked up from older friends whose taste had been formed during the Restoration. In later years he and Lady Mary became implacable enemies.

2. *accidents*: Unexpected occurrences (not mishaps); nothing is known of the news that 'afflicted' Pope.

3. *period*: Final word or phrase in a sentence.

4. *spleenatic enthusiasts*: Persons afflicted by the spleen, i.e. melancholics and those subject to 'enthusiasm', religious fervour.

5. *Teresa and Martha Blount*: The sisters were Catholic neighbours whom Pope met when all three were still in their teens. He was at first most attracted to the charming but self-centred and fickle Teresa, to whom 'Epistle to Mrs Teresa Blount' is addressed, and afterwards formed a lifelong friendship with Martha, known as 'Patty', to whom Epistle II 'To a Lady' is dedicated.

6. *my unhappiness*: Probably referring to the death of Pope's father that year.

7. *wait upon you*: Pay you a visit.

8. *men of my make*: Pope had heard of a queen who had a fondness for a deformed dwarf in her court.

9. *Mr Caryll*: John Caryll, Pope's lifelong friend: see 'Rape of the Lock', I, 3 and note.

10. *bower*: A pretty glade in Pope's garden at Twickenham.

11. *Downs*: Rolling, grassy hills nearby.

12. *Lord B.*: Pope's close friend Henry St John, Lord Bolingbroke, dedicatee of 'Essay on Man' and source of some of its ideas.

13. *Commerce . . . play pretty high*: A card game, which they play for high stakes.

14. *valley of Jehosaphat*: According to the prophet Joel, the site of the Last Judgement.

15. *Edward Blount*: A distant relative of Martha and Teresa, whose Devonshire estate Pope had visited.

16. *wilderness*: Another part of Pope's garden, made to appear uncultivated and wild.

17. *perspective glass*: Telescope, which would make objects seem smaller if viewed in reverse.

18. *camera obscura*: Literally, 'dark room'; a lens would throw images from outside on a wall in the way Pope describes.

19. *Hujus ... tace*: Verses by the Renaissance scholar-poet Cardinal Pietro Bembo, followed by Pope's translation of them.

20. *lave*: Wash.

21. *John Gay*: Poet and playwright for whom Pope felt deep affection; he had scored an immense success with *The Beggar's Opera* two years previously, and was now living comfortably with his patrons, the Duke and Duchess of Queensberry. See also 'Epistle to T. Blount', 47n.

22. *old man of Verona*: Probably alluding to the poem *De Sene Veronensi* by the Roman poet Claudian.

23. *loss of poor Mr Gay*: Gay had died four months previously, at the age of 47.

24. *whatever Is, is Right*: The final words of 'Essay on Man', I.

25. *Epitaph*: See 'Arbuthnot', 258n.

26. *coming over hither*: From Ireland to England; it never happened, and apart from two short visits in 1726 and 1727, Pope never saw Swift at all after he took up his position as Dean of St Patrick's Cathedral in Dublin in 1714.

27. *characters*: (Satiric) character sketches.

28. *performance*: The *Verses*, savagely abusive of Pope, mentioned in the Advertisement to 'Arbuthnot'.

29. *that poem*: 'Essay on Man'.

30. *the system*: The ambitious *Opus Magnum* which Pope still hoped to create.

31. *exercitandi gratia*: For the sake of keeping in practice.

32. *another of Horace's*: Pope's imitation of Satire, II, ii (in this volume).

33. *our poor Lady*: A mutual friend, Lady Suffolk.

34. *in folio*: On large sheets of paper.

35. *a few years before us*: Swift was 28 years older than Pope.

36. *your memory*: Swift was experiencing the first symptoms of the dementia that would devastate his final years; as it turned out he outlived Pope by a year, dying in 1745.

37. *carcase ... hinder me*: Pope had just emerged from a long bedridden episode at Lord Oxford's house in London.

38. *Dawley . . . this place*: Dawley Farm, Bolingbroke's manor in Middlesex, and Pope's villa at Twickenham, respectively.

39. *paper . . . Arbuthnot*: 'Arbuthnot', which would be published in a few weeks' time.

40. *broke*: Broken in health; he would die less than three months later.

41. *three Treatises*: the first three Epistles of the 'Essay on Man'.

42. *that work printed*: Bolingbroke's writings on various subjects were not printed until after he and Pope were dead.

43. *I had written . . . Bath*: i.e. I would have sent you a letter in care of that gentleman from Bath.

44. *William Warburton*: Clergyman whom Pope had not yet met, who won his gratitude by defending 'Essay on Man' in a series of *Letters* against Jean-Pierre de Crousaz (see 'Dunciad', IV, 198n.); Warburton later became Bishop of Gloucester and Pope's literary executor and editor.

PENGUIN CLASSICS

THE LIFE OF SAMUEL JOHNSON
JAMES BOSWELL

> 'Johnson, to be sure, has a roughness in his manner,
> but no man alive has a more tender heart'

In Boswell's *Life of Samuel Johnson*, one of the towering figures of English literature is revealed with unparalleled immediacy and originality, in a biography to which we owe much of our knowledge of the man himself. Through a series of richly detailed anecdotes, Johnson emerges as a sociable figure, vigorously engaging and fencing with great contemporaries such as Garrick, Goldsmith, Burney and Burke, and of course with Boswell himself. Yet anxieties and obsessions also darkened Johnson's private hours, and Boswell's attentiveness to every facet of Johnson's character makes this biography as moving as it is entertaining.

In this entirely new and unabridged edition, David Womersley's introduction examines the motives behind Boswell's work, and the differences between the two men that drew them to each other. It also contains chronologies of Boswell and Johnson, appendices and comprehensive indexes, including biographical details.

Edited with notes and an introduction by David Womersley

PENGUIN CLASSICS

THE STORM
DANIEL DEFOE

'Horror and Confusion seiz'd upon all ... No Pen can describe it, no Tongue can express it, no Thought conceive it'

On the evening of 26 November 1703, a hurricane from the north Atlantic hammered into Britain: it remains the worst storm the nation has ever experienced. Eyewitnesses saw cows thrown into trees and windmills ablaze from the friction of their whirling sails – and some 8,000 people lost their lives. For Defoe, bankrupt and just released from prison for his 'seditious' writings, the storm struck during one of his bleakest moments. But it also furnished him with material for his first book, and in this powerful depiction of suffering and survival played out against a backdrop of natural devastation, we can trace the outlines of Defoe's later masterpieces, *A Journal of the Plague Year* and *Robinson Crusoe*.

This new Penguin Classics edition marks the 300th anniversary of the first publication of The Storm. It also includes two other pieces by Defoe inspired by that momentous night, an introduction, chronology, further reading, notes and maps.

'Astonishing ... a masterpiece of reportage' Sunday Telegraph

Edited with an introduction by Richard Hamblyn

PENGUIN CLASSICS

THE DIARIES OF SAMUEL PEPYS: A SELECTION
SAMUEL PEPYS

> 'But Lord, what a sad sight it was by moonlight
> to see the whole City almost on fire'

The 1660s represent a turning point in English history, and for the main events
– the Restoration, the Dutch War, the Great Plague and the Fire of London
– Pepys provides a definitive eyewitness account. As well as recording public
and historical events, Pepys paints a vivid picture of his personal life, from his
socializing and amorous entanglements, to theatre going and his work at the Navy
Board. Unequalled for its frankness, high spirits and sharp observations, the diary
is both a literary masterpiece and a marvellous portrait of seventeenth-century life.

'This prince of Diarists, this most amiable and admirable of men, has at last been
worthily served' Paul Johnson, *Spectator*

PREVIOUSLY PUBLISHED AS *THE SHORTER PEPYS*

Selected and edited by Robert Latham

---

www.penguin.com

PENGUIN CLASSICS

THE COMPLETE POEMS
JOHN MILTON

> 'I may assert Eternal Providence
> And justify the ways of God to men'

John Milton was a master of almost every type of verse, from the classical to the religious and from the lyrical to the epic. His early poems include the devotional 'On the Morning of Christ's Nativity', 'Comus', a masque, and the pastoral elegy 'Lycidas'. After Cromwell's death and the dashing of Milton's political hopes, he began composing *Paradise Lost*, which reflects his profound understanding of politics and power. Written when Milton was at the height of his abilities, this great masterpiece fuses the Christian with the classical in its description of the Fall of Man. In *Samson Agonistes*, Milton's last work, the poet draws a parallel with his own life in the hero's struggle to renew his faith in God.

In this edition of the *Complete Poems*, John Leonard draws attention to words coined by Milton and those that have changed their meaning since his time. He also provides full notes to elucidate biblical, classical and historical allusions and has modernized spelling, capitalization and punctuation.

Edited with a preface and notes by John Leonard